The Ministers Manual for 1976

American Bicentennial Edition

By the same editor

Holy Holy Land
The Treasure Chest
Words of Life
Our American Heritage
1010 Sermon Illustrations from the Bible
Worship Resources for the Christian Year
Stories on Stone: A Book of American Epitaphs
American Epitaphs: Grave and Humorous
The Funeral Encyclopedia
A Treasury of Story-Sermons for Children
Treasury of Sermon Illustrations
Selected Poems of John Oxenham
Poems of Edwin Markham
Notable Sermons from Protestant Pulpits
Treasury of Poems for Worship and Devotion
88 Evangelistic Sermons
Speaker's Resources from Contemporary Literature
Christmas in Our Hearts (with Charles L. Allen)
Candle, Star, and Christmas Tree (with Charles L. Allen)
When Christmas Came to Bethlehem (with Charles L. Allen)
The Charles L. Allen Treasury
Lenten-Easter Sourcebook
365 Table Graces for the Christian Home
Speaker's Illustrations for Special Days
Table of the Lord
The Eternal Light
Twentieth Century Bible Commentary (co-editor)
Prayers for Public Worship (co-editor)

FIFTY-FIRST ANNUAL ISSUE

The

MINISTERS
MANUAL

(Doran's)

1976 EDITION

Edited by
CHARLES L. WALLIS

HARPER & ROW, PUBLISHERS

New York, Evanston, San Francisco, London

Editors of THE MINISTERS MANUAL

G. B. F. HALLOCK, D.D., 1926–1958
M. K. W. HEICHER, PH.D., 1943–1968
CHARLES L. WALLIS, M.DIV., 1969–

THE MINISTERS MANUAL FOR 1976

Copyright © 1975 by Charles L. Wallis. Printed in the United States of America. All rights reserved. For information address Harper & Row, Publishers, Inc., 10 East 53rd Street, New York, N. Y. 10022.

FIRST EDITION

STANDARD BOOK NUMBER: 0-06-069021-6

LIBRARY OF CONGRESS CATALOG CARD NUMBER: 25-21658

PREFACE

This fifty-first annual publication of *The Ministers Manual,* like the preceding volumes, is a many-faceted homiletic and worship resource book containing materials emphasizing the affirmations, commitments, and witness that Christians hold in common regarding the redemptive life, ministry, death, and resurrection of the Lord Jesus.

Section X provides a variety of resources appropriate for the American Bicentennial. An index covering this topic identifies useful materials found elsewhere in this book.

Three new indexes have been added. The first cross-indexes sermonic materials according to the lectionary followed by many Episcopalian, Lutheran, Presbyterian, Roman Catholic, and United Church of Christ clergymen.

The second is an index of materials useful for small groups and includes topics and ideas not found in Section V.

The third index lists stories and illustrations not included in Section IX that may be adapted for use as children's sermons or for Sunday school teaching.

Five other indexes, featured in previous issues of *The Ministers Manual,* are also found in this year's publication.

The Christian calendar has been expanded to include the special days, festivals, and seasons of the traditional Christian year and also the American and Canadian holidays. The designated days and emphases of the various denominations have been listed insofar as these were available when *The Ministers Manual* was published.

Also considerably enlarged is "The Idea Box" containing activities and ideas of individual churches which may be adapted to the needs of other churches.

The "Daily Bible Reading Guide for 1976," prepared by the American Bible Society, gives biblical references according to topical subheadings.

The editor acknowledges with appreciation the permission of contributors to reprint, adapt, and abbreviate their writings.

Rev. Charles L. Wallis
Keuka College
Keuka Park, N. Y. 14478

v

CONTENTS

CONTENTS

SECTION I. General Aids and Resources

Civil Year Calendars

1976

JANUARY	FEBRUARY	MARCH	APRIL
S M T W T F S	S M T W T F S	S M T W T F S	S M T W T F S
1 2 3	1 2 3 4 5 6 7	1 2 3 4 5 6	1 2 3
4 5 6 7 8 9 10	8 9 10 11 12 13 14	7 8 9 10 11 12 13	4 5 6 7 8 9 10
11 12 13 14 15 16 17	15 16 17 18 19 20 21	14 15 16 17 18 19 20	11 12 13 14 15 16 17
18 19 20 21 22 23 24	22 23 24 25 26 27 28	21 22 23 24 25 26 27	18 19 20 21 22 23 24
25 26 27 28 29 30 31	29	28 29 30 31	25 26 27 28 29 30

MAY	JUNE	JULY	AUGUST
S M T W T F S	S M T W T F S	S M T W T F S	S M T W T F S
1	1 2 3 4 5	1 2 3	1 2 3 4 5 6 7
2 3 4 5 6 7 8	6 7 8 9 10 11 12	4 5 6 7 8 9 10	8 9 10 11 12 13 14
9 10 11 12 13 14 15	13 14 15 16 17 18 19	11 12 13 14 15 16 17	15 16 17 18 19 20 21
16 17 18 19 20 21 22	20 21 22 23 24 25 26	18 19 20 21 22 23 24	22 23 24 25 26 27 28
23 24 25 26 27 28 29	27 28 29 30	25 26 27 28 29 30 31	29 30 31
30 31			

SEPTEMBER	OCTOBER	NOVEMBER	DECEMBER
S M T W T F S	S M T W T F S	S M T W T F S	S M T W T F S
1 2 3 4	1 2	1 2 3 4 5 6	1 2 3 4
5 6 7 8 9 10 11	3 4 5 6 7 8 9	7 8 9 10 11 12 13	5 6 7 8 9 10 11
12 13 14 15 16 17 18	10 11 12 13 14 15 16	14 15 16 17 18 19 20	12 13 14 15 16 17 18
19 20 21 22 23 24 25	17 18 19 20 21 22 23	21 22 23 24 25 26 27	19 20 21 22 23 24 25
26 27 28 29 30	24 25 26 27 28 29 30	28 29 30	26 27 28 29 30 31
	31		

1977

JANUARY	FEBRUARY	MARCH	APRIL
S M T W T F S	S M T W T F S	S M T W T F S	S M T W T F S
1	1 2 3 4 5	1 2 3 4 5	1 2
2 3 4 5 6 7 8	6 7 8 9 10 11 12	6 7 8 9 10 11 12	3 4 5 6 7 8 9
9 10 11 12 13 14 15	13 14 15 16 17 18 19	13 14 15 16 17 18 19	10 11 12 13 14 15 16
16 17 18 19 20 21 22	20 21 22 23 24 25 26	20 21 22 23 24 25 26	17 18 19 20 21 22 23
23 24 25 26 27 28 29	27 28	27 28 29 30 31	24 25 26 27 28 29 30
30 31			

MAY	JUNE	JULY	AUGUST
S M T W T F S	S M T W T F S	S M T W T F S	S M T W T F S
1 2 3 4 5 6 7	1 2 3 4	1 2	1 2 3 4 5 6
8 9 10 11 12 13 14	5 6 7 8 9 10 11	3 4 5 6 7 8 9	7 8 9 10 11 12 13
15 16 17 18 19 20 21	12 13 14 15 16 17 18	10 11 12 13 14 15 16	14 15 16 17 18 19 20
22 23 24 25 26 27 28	19 20 21 22 23 24 25	17 18 19 20 21 22 23	21 22 23 24 25 26 27
29 30 31	26 27 28 29 30	24 25 26 27 28 29 30	28 29 30 31
		31	

SEPTEMBER	OCTOBER	NOVEMBER	DECEMBER
S M T W T F S	S M T W T F S	S M T W T F S	S M T W T F S
1 2 3	1	1 2 3 4 5	1 2 3
4 5 6 7 8 9 10	2 3 4 5 6 7 8	6 7 8 9 10 11 12	4 5 6 7 8 9 10
11 12 13 14 15 16 17	9 10 11 12 13 14 15	13 14 15 16 17 18 19	11 12 13 14 15 16 17
18 19 20 21 22 23 24	16 17 18 19 20 21 22	20 21 22 23 24 25 26	18 19 20 21 22 23 24
25 26 27 28 29 30	23 24 25 26 27 28 29	27 28 29 30	25 26 27 28 29 30 31
	30 31		

Christian Calendar for 1976

JANUARY

1	New Year's Day
	Festival of the Christening
4	*Covenant Sunday (UM)*
5	Twelfth Night
5–9	*Bible Study Week (SBC)*
6	Epiphany
11	The Baptism of our Lord
	Soul-Winning Commitment Day (SBC)
	World Mission Sunday (ABC)
15	*Martin Luther King, Jr. Birthday (ABC, CC, UCC)*
18	Confession of St. Peter
	Missionary Day
18–25	Week of Prayer for Christian Unity
25	Conversion of St. Paul
	Baptist Men's Day (SBC)
	Human Relations Day (UM)
25–31	*Week of the Laity (CC)*
	Youth Week (Lu, RCA)

FEBRUARY

1	*Church Vocations Sunday (UCC)*
	Baptist World Alliance Sunday (ABC, SBC)
2	Presentation of Jesus in the Temple
8	Boy Scout Sunday
	Race Relations Sunday
	Outreach Day (AG)
12	Lincoln's Birthday
14	St. Valentine's Day
15	*Seminaries, Colleges, and Schools Day (SBC)*
15–22	Brotherhood Week
16	Washington's Birthday
22–29	*Week of Compassion (CC)*
24	St. Matthias, Apostle
29	The Transfiguration

MARCH

3	Ash Wednesday
5	World Day of Prayer
	Day of Prayer for Crops and Industry (RCA)

7	First Sunday in Lent
	Girl Scout Sunday
	America for Christ Sunday (ABC)
14	Second Sunday in Lent
14–21	*Youth Week (SBC)*
21	Third Sunday in Lent
	Camp Fire Girl Sunday
	Child Care Day (AG)
	Earth Day (UCC)
23	*Good News Crusade Day (AG)*
25	The Annunciation
28	Fourth Sunday in Lent
	One Great Hour of Sharing
30	*National Shut-in Day (AG)*

APRIL

4	Passion Sunday
11	Palm Sunday
	Sunday of the Passion (Lu)
	Youth Day (AG)
11–17	Holy Week
	Easter Week of Prayer (CC)
12–18	*Jewish Fellowship Week (SBC)*
15	Maundy Thursday
16	Good Friday
18	Easter
19–23	*Doctrinal Emphasis Week (SBC)*
25	Easter (Orthodox)
	St. Mark, Evangelist
	Christian College Day (RCA)
	College Sunday (Lu)
	Life Commitment Sunday (SBC)
	Women's Sunday (ABC)

MAY

1	St. Philip and St. James, Apostles
2	*Children's Day (UM)*
	Consultation on Church Union Sunday (UCC)
	Golden Cross Sunday (UM)
	Light-for-the-Lost Day (AG)
	Rural Life Sunday (CC)
2–9	National Family Week
7	May Fellowship Day
9	Mother's Day
	Festival of the Christian Home

9–15 *Family Week (Lu)*
16 *High School Day (AG)*
World Action Sunday (Lu)
19 Victoria Day (Canada)
23 Rogation Sunday
Rural Life Sunday
Heritage Sunday (UM)
24 *Aldersgate Day (UM)*
27 Ascension Day
30 *Church Music Sunday (Lu)*
31 Memorial Day
The Visitation

JUNE

6 Pentecost (Whitsunday)
13 Children's Sunday
Trinity Sunday
Religious Liberty Sunday (SBC)
Student Day (UM)
14 Flag Day
20 Father's Day
Men's Day (AG)
24 Nativity of St. John the
Baptizer
25 *Presentation of the Augsburg
Confession (Lu)*
27 *Achievement Day (CC)*
29 St. Peter and St. John, Apostles

JULY

1 Dominion Day (Canada)
4 Independence Day
Christian Citizenship Day (SBC)
*Day of Prayer for Those in the
Military Service (Lu)*
*Freedom and Democracy Sunday
(CC)*
Servicemen's Day (AG)
11 *Bethany Day (AG)*
Christian Literature Day (SBC)
22 St. Mary Magdalene
25 St. James the Elder, Apostle

AUGUST

6 The Transfiguration (alternate)
8 *Language Missions Day (SBC)*
15 Mary, Mother of Our Lord
24 St. Bartholomew, Apostle
29 Festival of Christ the King

SEPTEMBER

5 Labor Sunday
6 Labor Day
14 Holy Cross Day
19 *Ministry Sunday (UM)*
21 St. Matthew, Evangelist and
Apostle
23 World Life Day
26 *Christian Education Sunday
(ABC, UM)*
26–3 *Christian Education Week
(UCC, UM)*
*Reconciliation Emphasis Week
(CC)*

OCTOBER

3 World Communion Sunday
*World Fellowship Sunday
(ABC)*
10 Laity Sunday
Men's Sunday (ABC)
10–16 *Week of the Ministry (CC)*
11 Columbus Day
Thanksgiving Day (Canada)
17 World Order Day
Speed-the-Light Day (AG)
18 St. Luke, Evangelist
24 United Nations Day
25 Veterans' Day
26 *Link of Love (Day's Wage for
Christ) (RCA)*
28 St. Simon and St. Jude, Apostles
31 Reformation Day
UNICEF Day
Youth Sunday (UCC)
31–7 *Youth Week (CC)*

NOVEMBER

1 All Saints' Day
All Souls' Day
Election Day
5 World Community Day
7 All Saints' Sunday
World Temperance Day
*Communion Fellowship Sunday
(ABC)*
7–13 *Royal Ambassador Week (SBC)*
11 Remembrance Day (Canada)
Veterans' Day (alternate)

14 *American Bible Society Day*
     (SBC)
     College Sunday (ABC)
     Drug and Alcohol Concerns
        Day (UM)
     Prison Sunday (AG)
     Stewardship Sunday (UCC)
21 Bible Sunday
     Stewardship Day
     Thanksgiving Sunday
     Child Care Day (SBC)
     Heritage Sunday (UCC)
21–28 National Bible Week
25 Thanksgiving Day
28 First Sunday in Advent
28–5 *Week of Prayer for Foreign*
        Missions (SBC)
30 St. Andrew, Apostle

DECEMBER

 5 Second Sunday in Advent
     Health and Welfare Sunday
        (UCC)
     Pensions Sunday (RCA)
10 Human Rights Day
12 Third Sunday in Advent
15 Bill of Rights Day
19 Fourth Sunday in Advent
21 St. Thomas, Apostle
25 Christmas
26 St. Stephen, Deacon and Martyr
     Student Recognition Sunday
        (ABC, Lu, UM)
27 St. John, Apostle and Evangelist
28 The Holy Innocents
31 Watch Night

ABC—American Baptist Churches; AG—Assemblies of God; CC—Christian Church (Disciples of Christ); Lu—Lutheran bodies; RCA—Reformed Church in America; SBC—Southern Baptist Convention; UCC—United Church of Christ; UM—United Methodist Church.

Four-Year Church Calendar

	1976	1977	1978	1979
Ash Wednesday	March 3	February 23	February 8	February 28
Palm Sunday	April 11	April 3	March 19	April 8
Good Friday	April 16	April 8	March 24	April 13
Easter	April 18	April 10	March 26	April 15
Ascension Day	May 27	May 19	May 4	May 24
Pentecost	June 6	May 29	May 14	June 3
Trinity Sunday	June 13	June 5	May 21	June 10
Thanksgiving	November 25	November 24	November 23	November 22
Advent Sunday	November 28	November 27	December 3	December 2

Forty-Year Easter Calendar

1976	April 18	1986	March 30	1996	April 7	2006	April 16
1977	April 10	1987	April 19	1997	March 30	2007	April 8
1978	March 26	1988	April 3	1998	April 12	2008	March 23
1979	April 15	1989	March 26	1999	April 4	2009	April 12
1980	April 6	1990	April 15	2000	April 23	2010	April 4
1981	April 19	1991	March 31	2001	April 14	2011	April 24
1982	April 11	1992	April 19	2002	March 31	2012	April 8
1983	April 3	1993	April 11	2003	April 20	2013	March 31
1984	April 22	1994	April 3	2004	April 11	2014	April 20
1985	April 7	1995	April 16	2005	March 27	2015	April 5

Four-Year Jewish Calendar

	1976	1977	1978	1979
Purim	March 16	March 4	March 23	March 13
Passover	April 15	April 3	April 22	April 12
Shabuoth (Revelation of the Law)	June 4	May 23	June 11	June 1
Rosh Hashanah (New Year)	September 25	September 13	October 2	September 22
Yom Kippur (Day of Atonement)	October 4	September 22	October 11	October 1
Sukkoth (Thanksgiving)	October 9	September 27	October 16	October 6
Simhath Torah (Rejoicing in the Law)	October 17	October 5	October 24	October 14
Hanukkah	December 17	December 5	December 25	December 15

Holidays begin at sunset on the evening before the date given.

Traditional Wedding Anniversary Identifications

1	Paper	7	Wool	13	Lace	35	Coral
2	Cotton	8	Bronze	14	Ivory	40	Ruby
3	Leather	9	Pottery	15	Crystal	45	Sapphire
4	Linen	10	Tin	20	China	50	Gold
5	Wood	11	Steel	25	Silver	55	Emerald
6	Iron	12	Silk	30	Pearl	60	Diamond

Colors Appropriate for Days and Seasons

White. Symbolizes purity, perfection, and joy and identifies festivals marking events, except Good Friday, in the life of Jesus: Christmas, Easter, Eastertide, Ascension Day, Trinity Sunday, All Saints' Day, weddings, funerals.

Red. Symbolizes the Holy Spirit, martyrdom, and the love of God: Pentecost and Sundays following.

Violet. Symbolizes penitence: Advent, Lent.

Green. Symbolizes mission to the world, hope, regeneration, nurture, and growth: Epiphany season, Kingdomtide, Rural Life Sunday, Labor Sunday, Thanksgiving Sunday.

Black. Symbolizes mourning: Good Friday.

Historical, Cultural, and Religious Anniversaries in 1976

5 years (1971). *January 30:* Apollo 14 in thirty-three-hour lunar exploration. *April 10:* nine American Ping Pong players compete in China. *April 20:* Supreme Court rules on busing to achieve racial desegregation in public schools. *April 24:* 200,000 join antiwar protest in Washington, D. C. *September 9:* Attica prison riot. *October 25:* Communist China granted UN membership.

10 years (1966). *January 12:* Robert C. Weaver first black cabinet member. *February 3:* USSR Luna 9 in first landing on moon. *March 15:* black teenagers riot in Watts. *April 21:* first artificial heart implant. *July 1:* Medicare begun. *November 8:* Edward Brooke first black elected to Senate in eighty-five years.

20 years (1956). *May 21:* first aerial H-bomb tested. *September 25:* first transatlantic telephone cable system. *October 23:* Hungarian revolt begun. *November 6:* Eisenhower elected president.

25 years (1951). *September 4:* first transcontinental television broadcast. *September 8:* Japanese Peace Treaty signed.

30 years (1946). *January 10:* first General Assembly of the UN. *March 5:* Churchill "iron curtain" speech at Fulton, Missouri. *July 4:* Philippine independence granted. *August 1:* Atomic Energy Commission founded. *September 30:* twenty-two Nazi leaders convicted at Nuremberg. *December 31:* Truman proclaims cessation of World War II hostilities.

50 years (1926). *May 9:* Byrd and Bennett in first flight over North Pole. *November 15:* NBC in first network radio operation.

75 years (1901). *January 1:* Commonwealth of Australia formed. *January 22:* Queen Victoria died after sixty-four-year reign. *September 6:* McKinley assassinated by anarchist. *December 12:* Marconi in first transatlantic radio communication.

100 years (1876). *February 2:* National Baseball League founded. *March 7:* Bell patented telephone. *June 25:* Custer's "last stand" in the Battle of Little Big Horn. *August 1:* Colorado became thirty-eighth state.

150 years (1826). Bolivar convened first Pan-American Congress. *July 4:* deaths of John Adams and Thomas Jefferson on fiftieth anniversary of the Declaration of Independence they signed.

200 years (1776). Edward Gibbon began writing *The Decline and Fall of the Roman Empire.* Adam Smith published *The Wealth of Nations. May 15:* Virginia voted independence. *June 7:* Richard Henry Lee in the Continental Congress moved "that these united colonies are, and of right ought to be, free and independent states." *July 2:* Lee resolution adopted. *July 4:* Declaration of Independence adopted. *September 22:* Nathan Hale executed as a spy by the British. *December 25–26:* Washington crossed the Delaware River and defeated 1,400 Hessians at Trenton, New Jersey.

350 years (1626). *May 6:* Peter Minuit bought Manhattan from Indians for trinkets worth $24.

400 years (1576): Frobisher began search for the Northwest Passage. *August 27:* Titian died.

450 years (1526). In Cologne Tyndale produced first printed version of the New Testament in English.

500 years (1476). Caxton established his printing press at Westminster.

750 years (1226). *October 3:* death of Francis of Assisi.

1700 years (276). Great wall around Rome erected.

Anniversaries of Hymns, Hymn Writers, and Composers in 1976

20 years (1956). Death of J. Edgar Park (b. 1879), American Congregationalist and educator, author of "We would see Jesus."

25 years (1951). Death of Marion Franklin Ham (b. 1867), American Unitarian, author of "O church of God, divided" and "O who shall roll away the stone."

40 years (1936). Writing of hymn-tune HOLMES ("God of the nations, near and far") by Edward S. Barnes (b. 1887), American organist; "What doth the Lord require of thee" by Allen Eastman Cross (1864–1943), American Congregationalist. Death of Felix Adler (b. 1851), American educator, author of "Hail, the glorious golden city"; Peter P. Bilhorn (b. 1861), author and composer of "Sweet peace, the gift of God's love" and composer of "I will sing the wondrous story"; Gilbert Keith Chesterton (b. 1874), British poet and writer, author of "O God of earth and altar"; Percy Dearmer (b. 1867), British Anglican, author of "Book of books, our people's strength" and other hymns; James H. Fillmore (b. 1849), composer of "I know that my Redeemer liveth"; Frank Fletcher (b. 1870), British Anglican, author of "O Son of man, our hero strong and tender"; Lewis E. Jones (b. 1865), author and composer of "There is power in the blood"; Rudyard Kipling (b. 1865), British poet and writer, author of "God of our fathers, known of old"; Jay Thomas Stocking (b. 1870), American Congregationalist, author of "O Master Workman of the race."

50 years (1926). Writing of "O Son of man, our hero strong and tender" by Frank Fletcher (1870–1936), British Anglican; "O gracious Father of mankind" by Harry Hallam Tweedy (1868–1953), American Congregationalist. Death of Arthur Henry Brown (b. 1830), British composer of more than 800 hymn-tunes including SAFFRON WALDEN ("Just as I am") and ST. ANATOLIUS ("The day is past and over"); Johnson Oatman, Jr. (b. 1856), author of "Count your blessings."

75 years (1901). Publication of "Be strong! We are not here to play" and "This is my Father's world" by Maltbie D. Babcock (1858–1901), American Pres-

byterian. Birth of Albert Frederick Bayly, British Congregationalist, author of many hymns including "Lord, whose love through humble service"; Jan Struther (d. 1953), British poet and novelist, author of "High o'er the lonely hills," "Lord of all hopefulness," and "We thank you, Lord of heaven"; John Wesley Work III (d. 1967), American composer, adapter and arranger of "Go, tell it on the mountains." Death of William Bright (b. 1824), British Anglican, author of "And now, O Father, needful of thy love" and "One, only one, and once for all"; Edward J. Hopkins (b. 1818), British organist, composer of hymn-tune ELLERS ("Savior, again to thy dear name we raise"); William McDonald (b. 1820), American Methodist, author of "I am coming to the cross"; Frederic William Henry Myers (b. 1843), British poet and essayist, author of "Hark, what a sound"; Richard Redhead (b. 1820), British organist, composer of hymn-tune GETHSEMANE, also called PETRA, ("Go to dark Gethsemane"); John Stainer (b. 1840), British organist, composer of MAGDALEN ("My hope is built on nothing less"), SEBASTE ("Hail, gladdening light"), and "The sevenfold amen"; James Walch (b. 1837), British organist, composer of hymn-tunes SAWLEY ("Jesus, the very thought of thee") and TIDINGS ("Hark, hark, my soul" and "O Zion, haste"); Daniel Webster Whittle (b. 1840), author of "Moment by moment" and "There shall be showers of blessing."

100 years (1876). Writing of "O thou, in all thy might so far" by Frederick L. Hosmer (1840–1929), American Unitarian; hymn-tune WENTWORTH ("My God, I thank thee") by Frederick C. Maker (1844–1927), British organist; "God of our fathers" by Daniel C. Roberts (1841–1907), American Episcopalian. Birth of Sybil F. Partridge (Sister Mary Xavier), British nun, author of "Lord, for tomorrow and its needs"; Howard Chandler Robbins (d. 1952), American Episcopalian, author of "And have the bright immensities" and "Put forth, O God, thy

Spirit's might." Death of Philip Paul Bliss (b. 1838), American singing evangelist, author and composer of "Brightly beams our Father's mercy" and "Sing them over again to me," composer of hymn-tunes for "I gave my life for thee" and other gospel songs; John B. Dykes (b. 1823), British Anglican, composer of 100 hymn-tunes including BLAIRGOWRIE ("O young and fearless prophet"), DOMINUS REGIT ME ("The king of love my shepherd is"), KEBLE ("Forth in thy name, O Lord, I go" and "Sun of my soul"), LUX BENIGNA ("Lead, kindly light"), MELITA ("O Master of the waking world" and "Eternal Father, strong to save"), NICAEA ("Holy, holy, holy! Lord God Almighty"), ST. AGNES ("Jesus, the very thought of thee"), and VOX DILECTI ("I heard the voice of Jesus say"); Edward Francis Rimbault (b. 1816), British musicologist, composer of hymn-tune HAPPY DAY ("O happy day, that fixed my choice"); Edmund Hamilton Sears (b. 1810), American Unitarian, author of "It came upon the midnight clear"; Samuel Sebastian Wesley (b. 1810), British organist and grandson of Charles Wesley, composer of more than 130 hymn-tunes including ALLELUIA ("Joyful, joyful, we adore thee") and AURELIA ("The church's one foundation" and "Jerusalem the golden").

150 years (1826). Birth of John Ellerton (d. 1893), British Anglican, author of 68 hymns including "Behold us, Lord, a little space," "The day thou gavest, Lord, is ended," and "Savior, again to thy dear name we raise"; Henry Hiles (d. 1904), British musicologist, composer of hymn-tune ST. LEONARD ("O Spirit of the living God"); Erastus Johnson (d. 1909), American writer, author of "O sometimes the shadows are deep"; Lucy Larcom (d. 1893), American poet, author of "Draw thou my soul, O Christ"; Robert Lowry (d. 1899), American Baptist, author of "Low in the grave he lay," composer of hymn-tunes ALL THE WAY ("All the way my Savior leads me"), NEED ("I need thee every hour"), and SOMETHING FOR JESUS ("Savior, thy dying love"); Timothy Richard Mat-

thews (d. 1910), British Anglican, composer of more than 100 hymn-tunes including MARGARET ("Thou didst leave thy throne"); William Fiske Sherwin (d. 1888), American musical director, composer of hymn-tunes BREAD OF LIFE ("Break thou the bread of life") and CHAUTAUQUA ("Day is dying in the west"); Henry Percy Smith (d. 1898), British Anglican, composer of hymn-tune MARYTON ("O Master, let me walk with thee" and "Sun of my soul"). Death of Reginald Heber (b. 1783), British Anglican, author of "Bread of the world, in mercy broken," "Brightest and best of the sons of the morning," "From Greenland's icy mountains," "God, that madest earth and heaven," "Holy, holy, holy! Lord God Almighty," and "The Son of God goes forth to war"; Siegfried August Mahlmann (b. 1771), German poet, author of "God bless our native land."

200 years (1776). Writing of "Rock of ages, cleft for me" by Augustus M. Toplady (1740–1778), British Calvinist. Death of Aaron Williams (b. 1731), composer of hymn-tune ST. THOMAS ("Come, ye that love the Lord" and "I love thy kingdom, Lord").

250 years (1726). Birth of William Jones (d. 1800), British Anglican, composer of hymn-tune ST. STEPHEN ("Break forth, O living light of God" and "One holy church of God appears"); Edward Perronet (d. 1792), British Methodist, author of "All hail the power of Jesus' name."

300 years (1676). Birth of Charles Coffin (d. 1749), French Latinist, author of 100 hymns including "On Jordan's banks the Baptist's cry" and "What star is this, with beams so bright." Death of Johann Georg Eberling (b. 1637), German musician, composer of 120 hymn-tunes and settings for hymns by Paul Gerhardt including EBERLING ("All my heart this night rejoices"); Paul Gerhardt (b. 1607), German Lutheran, author of 132 hymns including "Give to the winds thy fears," "Jesus, thy boundless love to me," and "O sacred head, now wounded."

350 years (1626). Publication of "We gather together to ask the Lord's blessing" written by an unknown Dutch author.

750 years (1226). Death of St. Francis of Assisi (b. 1182), Italian friar and preacher, author of "All creatures of our God and king."

1200 years (776). Birth of Rhabanus Maurus (d. 856), German abbot, credited with writing of "Come, Holy Spirit, our souls inspire."

Quotable Quotations

JANUARY

1. No clever arrangement of bad eggs ever made a good omelet. C. S. Lewis.

2. Next to God, respect time. John R. Mott.

3. Hope is believing in the future and faith is dancing to it. Edward B. Lindaman.

4. Faith is the sunlight on the skyline of tomorrow.

5. To believe in God is to know all the rules will be fair and that there will be many surprises. Sister Corita.

6. We must carry our share of the misery which lies about the world. Albert Schweitzer.

7. I sought after God until he found me. Blaise Pascal.

8. All truth is God's truth. Frank E. Gaebelein.

9. Do not wish to be anything but what you are and try to be that perfectly. St. Francis de Sales.

FEBRUARY

10. Heaven must be full of answers to prayers for which no one even bothered to ask. Cameron Thompson.

11. No two leaves of a tree are identical in shape. Why should we expect two people to be identical? Havelock Ellis.

12. Folks who have no vices have very few virtues. Abraham Lincoln.

13. We cannot always trace God's hand, but we can always trust his heart. Vance Havner.

14. The real test of love is the amount of tension it can stand. Krister Stendahl.

15. Make love obvious. Quaker saying.

16. The scorn with which a man shakes his fist at the empty sky shows that the sky is not really empty. Edmund P. Clowney.

17. The difference between a conviction and a prejudice is that you can explain a conviction without getting angry.

MARCH

18. Early Christianity succeeded by the contagion of an enthusiasm. Kirsopp Lake.

19. Christianity is not subscription to a creed; it is loving attachment to a person, Jesus Christ. Robert J. McCracken.

20. Lent is a way of growing into Easter, a way of making the truth of Easter part of our lives. Eugene R. Fairweather.

21. An act of love may tip the balance.

22. The darkest hour is only sixty minutes long.

23. There is no better way to observe Lent than to be Christlike at heart. Bert Van Soest.

24. Belief in God gives elasticity of mind. Herbert Butterfield.

25. There is no lost good. George A. Buttrick.

26. The presence of mystery is the footprint of the divine.

27. We are, all of us, from birth to death guests at a table we did not spread. Rebecca Harding Davis.

APRIL

28. The world is about to starve to death for a little love. John Owen Smith.

29. Any crisis may be the hour when God gives birth to new dimensions in our lives. C. Neil Strait.

30. When Christ calls a man, he bids him to come and die. Dietrich Bonhoeffer.

31. Let a disciple live as Christ lived, and he will easily believe in living again as Christ does. William Mountford.

32. It is only through the mystery of self-sacrifice that a man may find himself anew. Carl G. Jung.

33. Easter is not a passport to another world; it is a quality of perception for this one. W. P. Lemmon.

34. Every church is, at least potentially, a resurrection center. Theodore P. Ferris.

35. Each time a man stands up for an ideal he sends forth a tiny ripple of hope.

36. The Christian does not go home in the dark; he is home before dark. W. Kenneth Goodson.

MAY

37. The abdication of belief makes our behavior small. Emily Dickinson.

38. Worship is man's response to God's revelation of himself. Andrew W. Blackwood.

39. Our first duty to society is to be somebody, that is, ourselves. Abbe Dimnet.

40. To be human is to be in danger. Ashley Montagu.

41. When it comes to repentance every hour is the eleventh hour. Søren Kierkegaard.

42. The greatest influence on a child begins with the birth of his parents. Les Crane.

43. Unless a tree has borne blossoms in spring you will vainly look for fruit on it in the fall. J. C. Hare.

44. By sharing with others we divide the care and multiply the joy.

45. Among God's gifts to us are the people who love us.

JUNE

46. The function of Christianity is to keep men in their proper spiritual orbit.

47. Issues in which God has a stake can never be ultimately defeated. Joseph R. Sizoo.

48. We cannot be sure that we have something worth living for unless we are ready to die for it. Eric Hoffer.

49. Civilization is movement, not a condition; a voyage, not a harbor. Arnold J. Toynbee.

50. The sun does not rise by natural law. It rises because God says, "Get up and do it again." Gilbert K. Chesterton.

51. He who clasps the hand of the poor may be sure God will take him by the other hand. Abbe Pierre.

52. To teach religion the first thing needful, and the last, and indeed the only thing, is to find a man who has religion. Thomas Carlyle.

53. If you do not raise your eyes, you will think that you are the highest point. Antonio Porchia.

JULY

54. Freedom has never relied on uniformity of opinion. John F. Kennedy.

55. Whatever America hopes to bring to pass in the world must first come to pass in the heart of America. Dwight D. Eisenhower.

56. Compassion is a main ingredient of leadership. Charles G. Griffo.

57. Only a mediocre person is always at his best. W. Somerset Maugham.

58. Democracy is more than liberty; it is responsibility.

59. The ideal life is in our blood and will never be still. Phillips Brooks.

60. The great Architect of the universe never built a stairway that leads to nowhere. Robert A. Millikan.

61. Truth always originates in a minority of one. Will Durant.

AUGUST

62. We must care what is happening to mankind. Carl Sandburg.

63. I believe in Christianity as I believe in the sun: not only because I see

it but because by it I see everything else. C. S. Lewis.

64. Make the most of all that comes and the least of all that goes.

65. A man who has once lived under the smile of God finds agony when that smile has turned to a frown. C. M. Ward.

66. Character is the result of the things we care for. John Holland.

67. When we pray for rain and do not bother to repair our roof our petition is full of holes. William A. Ward.

68. Peace is not needing to know what will happen next.

SEPTEMBER

69. Prayer is an acknowledgment of faith; worry is a denial of faith. Lovett Barnes.

70. You don't live in a world all your own. Albert Schweitzer.

71. No life is full unless it is linked to something that goes on after we are dead. Ralph W. Sockman.

72. You can loaf your way to hell, but the kingdom of heaven can only be seized by force. Helmut Thielicke.

73. Nothing is more dangerous for a man than unlimited success. Paul Tournier.

74. There are too many people who expect God to work by miracle what God expects man to work by muscle. W. Galloway Tyson.

75. The worst blasphemy is not profanity but lip service. Elton Trueblood.

76. On God's farm there are no fences. Barbara Lemmond.

OCTOBER

77. Life is a circle whose center is God. Forbes Robertson.

78. A man's life is useless if it is not useful to others. Louis Pasteur.

79. The sight of a good man is like the moon and the stars to one on a journey. John Bunyan.

80. The greatest power that a person

possesses is the power to choose. J. Martin Kohe.

81. Do not let the good things of life rob you of the best things. Buster Rothman.

82. Live your life so that a deaf man can understand what you say. Tommy Scott Gilmore.

83. Religion is the result of what man does with his ultimate wonder, with moments of awe, with the sense of mystery. Abraham Heschel.

84. The recognition of a need and the ability to meet that need constitutes a call. John R. Mott.

NOVEMBER

85. The only true gift is a portion of yourself. Ralph Waldo Emerson.

86. If things are ever to move forward, someone must be willing to take the first step. Jane Addams.

87. Men can be provincial in time as well as in place. Alfred North Whitehead.

88. We are self-possessed only when we are possessed by Christ. Charles G. Trumbull.

89. Belief is a truth held in the mind; faith is a fire in the heart. Joseph Fort Newton.

90. Gratitude is the dominant emotion in the heart of a right-minded man. John Baillie.

91. We Americans are in danger of becoming prisoners of our own price tags. John F. Kennedy.

DECEMBER

92. God rejoices to see the light shining from the candle of our honesty. Leonard Griffith.

93. Oaks grow strong in contrary winds. Peter Marshall.

94. Every man is a divine incarnation brought up to date. Charles H. Parkhurst.

95. Only by the keeping of a true Advent can we know the meaning of a true Christmas. Raymond Calkins.

96. The best of gifts around a Christ-

mas tree is the presence of a happy family all wrapped up in each other. Burton Hillis.

97. Christmas was and is a gift: God giving himself in Jesus. Wilson O. Weldon.

98. One act of obedience is better than one hundred sermons. Dietrich Bonhoeffer.

99. We are never hurt by anything we did not say.

100. Truth exists for the individual only as he himself produces it in action. Søren Kierkegaard.

Questions of Religion and Life

These questions may be useful to prime homiletic pumps, as discussion starters, or for study groups.

1. How can I know I am accepted by God?

2. What was the Baal worship that Elijah contested on Mount Carmel?

3. In what ways can our political system be improved?

4. Is baptism distinctly Christian?

5. Does the Bible teach the equality of men and women?

6. What is the message of Christian evangelism?

7. Does the world birth rate threaten the world's natural resources?

8. What permanent values have come from the vast expenditures for space exploration?

9. Why are the first five books in the Bible attributed to Moses?

10. For what reasons do X-rated movies appeal to so many persons?

11. What are the seven cardinal sins of the twentieth century?

12. Why do some churches resist the ordination of women?

13. What progress is Christianity making in the Third World?

14. How have minority groups enriched our common life?

15. Explain the last judgment.

16. Is there a Christian doctrine of humor?

17. Are Christian missions expanding or declining?

18. Is the computer a threat to personality?

19. Why is there an increase in the number of divorces?

20. Are we living in a post-Christian age?

21. Is modesty a lost virtue?

22. How can we curb the spread of obscene literature?

23. What is our national purpose?

24. Should teen-agers serve on the official boards in local churches?

25. Is creedal conformity desirable?

26. Should the Supreme Court determine the standards of public morality?

27. Is there a code of clerical ethics?

28. Relate grace to salvation.

29. Are there biblical teachings relating to ecology?

30. What is a successful church?

31. Which Old Testament books are most important to our understanding of the New Testament?

32. What is meant by identity crisis?

33. What is the average age of church members?

34. How may grief be overcome?

35. How complete is the forgiveness of God?

36. Can a Christian realistically aspire to be Christlike?

37. Is historical Christianity sexist?

38. Comment on the practice of cremation.

39. Interpret the ascension.

40. Can there be salvation without the cross?

41. What are the important differences among the various denominations?

42. Tell me about the second coming of Christ.

43. Is the pursuit of excellence a Christian teaching?

44. What is the nature of the future life?

45. Are there any Christian martyrs today?

46. What are the different interpretations of Holy Communion.

47. What will be the hallmarks of Christianity in the year 2976?

48. Is the increasing popularity of Sunday sports an indication of a growing spirit of godlessness?

49. What liturgical changes have been introduced in recent years?

50. Are there limitations in faith healings?

51. How can we Christianize our funerals?

52. Who are our contemporary heroes?

53. What is Christian holiness?

54. Explain God's role in history.

55. Are my doubts indications of weak faith?

56. What are the distinguishing characteristics of the Christian home?

57. Is there an active Christian witness to organized labor?

58. Has the age of miracles passed?

59. How did St. Paul permanently influence historical Christianity?

60. Why doesn't prayer seem real to me?

61. How may the church serve as a reconciling agent?

62. Why are there so many interpretations of the Bible?

63. What is the role of the sermon in worship?

64. Does the church talk too much about money?

65. Is there a close relationship between suffering and faith?

66. How can I learn to be content?

67. Is personal ambition antagonistic to Christian faith?

68. What does the church believe about Jesus Christ?

69. Are there any outstanding Christian poets today?

70. What do young people want the church to do?

71. Why are my prayers not answered?

72. How can I know I'm in love?

73. Is there less prejudice today than in former years?

74. Why don't our churches grow faster?

75. What forces are working for Christian cooperation?

76. Is the Golden Rule an adequate Christian guideline?

77. What is the future of the United Nations?

78. Why is there so much violence on television?

79. Does an individual have a Christian responsibility to vote?

80. How should I observe Lent?

81. Explain the uniqueness of Jesus.

82. Do interfaith marriages contribute to interfaith harmony?

83. Were the good old days really that good?

84. Are there dangers in teaching sex education in public schools?

85. How does the new evangelism differ from the old?

86. How can I be secure in my faith?

87. Why does Christian faith center in the cross rather than in the open tomb?

88. Why don't Christians act more like Christians?

89. If you could live your life over what changes would you make?

90. How can I help an alcoholic friend?

91. What are the responsibilities of Christian parents?

92. What beliefs do Christians and Jews hold in common?

93. Who are the outstanding black leaders in the church today?

94. Is the belief in immortality more than wish projection?

95. What makes a sin sinful?

96. Are there meaningful alternatives to Christian creeds?

97. Does ritual hamper spontaneity in worship?

98. Is the world food problem a matter of shortage or distribution?

99. How have our churches changed during the past fifty years?

100. Does television help or hinder family life?

The Idea Box

FAMILY AFFAIR.   Smiles across the aisles is one way couples reflect the joy of giving when husbands and wives serve as usher teams in our worship services. The offering also involves an element of surprise because the people in the pews do not know who will be receiving the collection on a given Sunday. When the children are old enough they are invited to join their parents in serving. —Lawrence MacColl Horton, Noroton Presbyterian Church, Noroton, Connecticut.

HONORING COMMUNITY SERVANTS.   Each month our congregation offers special prayers of thanksgiving for the contributions of a community service group. These groups include the volunteer fire department, elected political officials at the various levels of government, emergency ambulance volunteers, school board members, Red Cross Gray Ladies, school bus drivers, police officers, service club members, and Scout and 4-H leaders. Members of each group are invited to a designated thanksgiving service, a bulletin insert provides a list of the organization's members and the history and service of the organization, and church and group members join for an informal coffee hour following the worship service.—John R. Lepke, Congregational United Church of Christ, Coloma, Michigan.

YOKEFELLOWS.   Our baptismal candidates and new members from other parishes are asked to choose any member of the congregation as a partner in Christian living. Both parties sign a three-year agreement indicating a willingness to look for each other at worship each week, to remember one another on birthdays and holidays, to visit their respective homes, to share intimate experiences relating to Christian growth, and to be available in times of need and sickness.—John Y. Elliott, Genesee Baptist Church, Rochester, New York.

AWARENESS DAY.   In order to acquaint parishioners with the diverse functions and services of the church, members are invited to "Awareness Day," a weekday program which begins with Holy Communion at 9:30 a.m. and continues through the lunch hour. Members of the clerical and musical staffs interpret their individual roles within the total structure of the parish life and speak informally and answer questions.—Herbert M. Barrall, St. John's Cathedral, Denver, Colorado.

A PERSONAL BULLETIN BOARD.   Most churches have an exterior bulletin board. Instead of announcing next Sunday's sermon title, put snapshots of church members on the bulletin board under this heading: "We'll be here on Sunday. Come join us!" Then watch passersby stop and return for a second and third look.—A.D.

THANK YOU BOARD.   A special bulletin board in the foyer of our church provides a place where thank you notes may be posted. This saves space in the printed bulletin and stimulates appreciation and fellowship among the members.—William E. Truitt, Brilliant Christian Church, Brilliant, Ohio.

QUESTION BOX.   Our members are encouraged to put questions on any topic in a question box in the church foyer. Individuals requesting private answers must sign their names. Unsigned questions are answered at public services. Occasionally a midweek prayer meeting is given to these questions. Acknowledgment is made for questions that cannot be readily answered.—W. D. Johnson, Church of the Nazarene, Churubusco, Indiana.

HELPER CLINICS.   Our evangelism training program includes "Helper" clinics (How to Equip Lay People to Evangelism Regularly) having five goals: (1) to develop a teamwork involving pastors and members, (2) to offer several approaches and styles to evangelism, (3) to emphasize a follow-up to meet the total needs of persons (4) to encourage clinics to develop their own models of evangelism, and (5) to provide specific ideas for programs in growth and renewal for active and inactive members and for new members.—Ronald R. Rand, College Hill Presbyterian Church, Cincinnati, Ohio.

LIGHT OF EVANGELISM. For 464 consecutive weeks first-time visitors have been in attendance at the evening worship service of the First Christian Church, Longmont, Colorado, where Dale McCann is minister. A Light of Evangelism is used to indicate the presence of first-time visitors. Each week a family is designated as the Guardian of the Light.—*The Lookout.*

FAMILY SUPPORT. Our concern that the family as a traditional institution is threatened and possibly disintegrating prompted us to develop a New Family Centre designed to be an agent of enrichment for the healthy or normal family not in crisis and providing counseling, group work, classes in meditation and exercise as growth experiences, and consultant services to other churches.—Raymond P. Jennings, First Baptist Church, Berkeley, California.

SUNDAY SCHOOL RECOGNITION. Older members and workers are honored at our "Golden Age Sunday" observance when certificates or awards are given to the oldest member, the member who has attended for the longest period of time, the oldest active teacher, and the teacher having the longest period of service.—Terry Kemp, Central Christian Church, Toledo, Ohio.

DIAL-A-MISSIONARY DAY. Our congregation listens in during a worship service to a two-way conversation between the pulpit and our missionaries and their families via satellite transmission and a special conference phone connected to our public address system.—Alf H. Skognes, Scotsdale Baptist Church, El Paso, Texas.

NOEL OASIS. A different kind of church outreach is offered by members of the Calvary Baptist Church, Jackson, Mississippi, who during the Christmas shopping period sponsor a "Noel Oasis" in the massive Jackson Mall Shopping Center and offer weary shoppers coffee, spiced tea, a place to sit, friendly conversation, and Christian literature. More than 200 laypersons volunteer for two to four-hour shifts.

TURNABOUT SUNDAY. Children and young people remain in church and parents and other adults attend church school classes on "Turnabout Sunday," an effort to better acquaint the congregation with the church school staff and the goals and methods of the Christian education program.—David L. Tucker, Second Congregational Church, Ashtabula, Ohio.

"SUPPER EIGHT." The "Supper Eight" program helps college and career-age members get better acquainted. Couples wishing to participate put their names "in the hat" from which names are drawn at random for groups of four couples each. Once a month for four months the couples have a potluck dinner together. Then names are shuffled and new groups formed.—Rich Marshall, Knott Avenue Christian Church, Anaheim, California.

CHRISTIAN INVOLVEMENT. As a part of its mission to the community and in response to the need for Christian social action, the First United Methodist Church, Adrian, Michigan, has on its staff a director of Christian involvement whose responsibilities include the following: (1) to be in direct conversation with poor people and community leaders to determine the needs of people not now being met, (2) to discover the significant issues in the community and ask how a Christian witness may be expressed, (3) to determine the resources and skills of the members of the church and to relate these to the people in need through volunteer service and vocational outreach, and (4) to be sensitive to the larger issues in the nation and the world and enable the church to address these issues with courage and wisdom.—*Michigan Christian Advocate.*

A LITTLE HONEY.   Taking a clue from the words of Jacob in Gen. 43:11, "A Little Honey" is a part of our Sunday morning service. A church leader or an unsung worker is asked to stand and he or she is recognized and a plaque of appreciation is presented. This is followed by a prayer of thanksgiving to God for time and talent dedicated to his work. Any member may suggest nominees for this special recognition by putting names and pertinent data in "the silent secretary," a slot in the church office door.—Max R. Hickerson, Clovernook Christian Church, Cincinnati, Ohio.

CHURCH BIRTHDAY.   On Pentecost our people celebrate the birthday of the church at an outdoor service on a large grassy lot near the church. Informally dressed children and adults bring flowers, collected by a "flower squad" of church school children. These are placed as an offering at the front of the worship area. Some people bring homemade banners. The service, which includes an outline of the original Pentecost story, reception of new members, and communion, is followed by a congregational picnic.—Roger Lambert, First Community Church, Columbus, Ohio.

Daily Bible Reading Guide for 1976

JANUARY.   (a) **Christ the source of life.** *1:* John 10:22–29; *2:* John 14:1–14; *3:* John 17:1–26. (b) **Life vs. death.** *4 (Sunday):* Deut. 30:11–20; *5:* Ps. 1:1–6; *6:* Matt. 7:13–20; *7:* Mark 8:34–38; *8:* Luke 13:22–35; *9:* Luke 16:19–31; *10:* Mark 12:1–12. (c) **Life through God's grace.** *11: (Sunday):* Exod. 12:1–14; *12:* Ps. 51:1–17; *13:* Ps. 130:1–8; *14:* Isa. 40: 1–11; *15:* Eph. 2:1–10; *16:* Titus 2:7–14; *17:* Heb. 4:16. (d) **Life based on forgiveness.** *18 (Sunday):* Exod. 34:1–10; *19:* Mark 2:1–12; *20:* Luke 7:36–50; *21:* Matt. 18:21–35; *22:* Luke 18:9–14; *23:* Luke 19:1–10; *24:* Eph. 4:25–32. (e) **A life of peace.** *25 (Sunday):* Num. 6:22–27; *26:* Prov. 3:13–26; *27:* Isa. 26:1–9; *28:* Matt. 8:23–34; *29:* Matt. 11:20–30; *30:* Rom. 5:1–11; *31:* Rom. 8:1–17.

FEBRUARY.   (a) **A life of high privilege.** *1 (Sunday):* Ps. 8:1–9; *2:* Isa. 41: 8–14; *3:* John 10:1–11; *4:* I Cor. 1:18–31; *5:* Eph. 1:1–14; *6:* I Pet. 2:1–10; *7:* I John 3:1–10. (b) **Living the spirit of Christ.** *8 (Sunday):* Luke 4:14–21; *9:* Mark 9:30–37; *10:* Mark 10:35–45; *11:* I Cor. 9:19–27; *12:* II Cor. 5:11–21; *13:* Phil. 2:1–16; *14:* II Tim. 3:14–4:8. (c) **Life in dependence of God.** *15 (Sunday):* Deut. 8:11–20; *16:* Deut. 31:1–8; *17:* Ps. 25:1–14; *18:* Ps. 28:1–9; *19:* I Pet. 5:1–11; *20:* I John; *21:* Jas. 4:13–17. (d) **Righteous life.** *22 (Sunday):* Exod. 20:1–17; *23:*

Deut. 6:1–9; *24:* Prov. 16:1–11; *25:* Isa. 58:1–12; *26:* Amos 5:11–24; *27:* Mic. 6: 1–8; *28:* Matt. 5:13–20. (e) **Sacrificial life.** *29 (Sunday):* Esther 4:9–16.

MARCH.   *1:* Matt. 16:13–26; *2:* Luke 14:25–35; *3:* Mark 10:17–31; *4:* Acts 20: 17–35; *5:* Rom. 12:1–8; *6:* II Tim. 2: 1–15. (a) **Strength for life's adversities.** *7 (Sunday):* Job 23:1–10; *8:* Ps. 37:1–11; *9:* Ps. 37:18–31; *10:* Ps. 63:1–11; *11:* Ps. 119:46–72; *12:* John 16:16–24; *13:* Heb. 13:1–8. (b) **A witness-bearing life.** *14 (Sunday):* John 1:43–51; *15:* Matt. 9: 35–10:8; *16:* Luke 5:1–11; *17:* Mark 4: 1–20; *18:* Acts 8:26–40; *19:* John 9:13–25; *20:* Acts 7:59–8:8. (c) **Life through the Savior's death.** *21 (Sunday):* Mark 11: 1–11; *22:* Mark 14:1–9; *23:* Matt. 26: 14–25; *24:* Matt. 26:36–46; *25:* Matt. 27: 11–31; *26:* Mark 15:25–41; *27:* Heb. 9:11– 28. (d) **Life with the Risen Lord.** *28 (Sunday):* Matt. 28:1:10; *29:* John 20:1– 18; *30:* Luke 24:13–35; *31:* Luke 24:36–49.

APRIL.   *1:* John 20:19–23; *2:* John 20: 24–31; *3:* John 21:1–19. (a) **A life of faithfulness.** *4 (Sunday):* Matt. 24:42–51; *5:* Ps. 119:25–40; *6:* II Tim. 1:1–14; *7:* Heb. 10:11–25; *8:* Heb. 12:1–13; *9:* Jude 17–25; *10:* Rev. 2:1–11. (b) **The word of life.** *11 (Sunday):* Ps. 19:7–14; *12:* Ps. 119:1–16; *13:* Ps. 119:33–48; *14:* Ps. 119: 129–144; *15:* Prov. 3:13–26; *16:* Matt.

4:1–11; *17:* II Tim. 3:10–17. (c) **A life of trust in God.** *18 (Sunday):* Ps. 3:1–8; *19:* Ps. 4:1–8; *20:* Ps. 27:1–4; *21:* Ps. 91: 1–16; *22:* Isa. 30:15–21; *23:* Hab. 3:13–19; *24:* Matt. 6:24–34. (d) **A courageous life.** *25 (Sunday):* I Sam. 17:41–50; *26:* Dan. 1:1–17; *27:* Dan. 3:13–28; *28:* Dan. 6:10–23; *29:* Acts 4:5–21; *30:* Acts 4:23–31.

MAY. *1:* Acts 6:8–15. (a) **A life of love.** *2 (Sunday):* II Sam. 9:1–13; *3:* Luke 10:25–37; *4:* John 13:1–17; *5:* Rom. 12:9–21; *6:* I Cor. 13:1–13; *7:* Gal. 6:1–10; *8:* I John 3:13–24. (b) **Life through the Holy Spirit.** *9 (Sunday):* Joel 2:21–32; *10:* John 14:16–27; *11:* John 15:26–16:15; *12:* Acts 1:1–14; *13:* Acts 2:1–12; *14:* Acts 2:29–41; *15:* Gal. 5:18–26. (c) **Life for all people.** *16 (Sunday):* Isa. 49: 5–13; *17:* Acts 10:30–48; *18:* Acts 14:21–27; *19:* Acts 16:6–15; *20:* Acts 16:16–34; *21:* Rom. 10:1–13; *22:* Eph. 3:1–13. (d) **A transformed life.** *23 (Sunday):* Gen. 32:24–30; *24:* Jer. 18:1–6; *25:* Jer. 31: 27–34; *26:* John 1:29–42; *27:* John 3:1–16; *28:* Acts 9:1–22; *29:* II Cor. 3:17–4:6. (e) **A satisfying life.** *30 (Sunday):* Ps. 147:1–11; *31:* Prov. 4:10–19.

JUNE. *1:* Ezek. 34:22–31; *2:* John 4: 27–38; *3:* John 6:27–40; *4:* Rom. 8:26–39; *5:* II Cor. 1:3–11. (a) **A life of praise.** *6 (Sunday):* Ps. 30:1–12; *7:* Ps. 40:1–10; *8:* Ps. 48:1–14; *9:* Ps. 61:1–8; *10:* Ps. 107:1–9; *11:* Ps. 126:1–6; *12:* Ps. 146:1–10. (b) **A life of watchfulness.** *13 (Sunday):* Ezek. 3:16–21; *14:* Luke 12:35–48; *15:* Mark 13:33–37; *16:* Matt. 25:1–13; *17:* Luke 22:54–62; *18:* Eph. 6: 10–20; *19:* I Thess. 5:1–11. (c) **The life of prayer.** *20 (Sunday):* Gen. 18:22–33; *21:* I Sam. 1:9–18; *22:* I Kings 3:3–14; *23:* II Kings 19:14–20; *24:* Mark 1:29–39; *25:* Luke 11:1–13; *26:* Luke 18:1–8. (d) **Life in personal relations.** *27 (Sunday):* Gen. 26:17–25; *28:* Gen. 50:15–21; *29:* Luke 6:27–36; *30:* John 15:9–17.

JULY. *1:* Matt. 25:31–46; *2:* Eph. 5: 21–6:9; *3:* Jas. 2:1–17. (a) **Life with the master teacher.** *4 (Sunday):* Matt. 5:1–12; *5:* Matt. 6:1–8; *6:* Luke 6:37–42; *7:*

Matt. 13:1–9; *8:* Matt. 13:31–52; *9:* Luke 12:13–21; *10:* Mark 12:28–34. (b) **Life through repentance.** *11 (Sunday):* Neh. 9:5–20; *12:* Isa. 1:10–20; *13:* Isa. 55:1–13; *14:* Jer. 3:12–22; *15:* Hos. 14:1–9; *16:* Luke 3:1–18; *17:* Luke 23:33–43. (c) **Life through faith.** *18 (Sunday):* Num. 21:4–9; *19:* John 3:14–21; *20:* Matt. 9:18–31; *21:* Mark 9:14–29; *22:* Heb. 11:1–10; *23:* Heb. 11:17–26; *24:* Jas. 2:14–26. (d) **A life of obedience.** *25 (Sunday):* Gen. 12:1–8; *26:* Num. 20: 2–13; *27:* Deut. 4:5–14; *28:* Josh. 1:1–9; *29:* Josh. 24:1–15; *30:* Isa. 50:4–10; *31:* Matt. 7:21–27.

AUGUST. (a) **Life in God's world of nature.** *1 (Sunday):* Gen. 1:1–25; *2:* Gen. 1:26–31; *3:* Job 38:1–18; *4:* Ps. 19: 1–6; *5:* Ps. 65:1–13; *6:* Ps. 104:1–35; *7:* Isa. 40:12–24. (b) **A worshipful life.** *8 (Sunday):* Ps. 24:1–10; *9:* Ps. 42:1–11; *10:* Ps. 139:1–24; *11:* Ps. 145: 1–21; *12:* Isa. 6:1–8; *13:* Rev. 4:1–11; *14:* Rev. 5: 9–14. (c) **A life of adequate resources.** *15 (Sunday):* Ps. 46:1–11; *16:* Ps. 121:1–8; *17:* Isa. 40:21–31; *18:* Lam. 3:25–33; *19:* I Cor. 10:1–13; *20:* II Cor. 12:1–10; *21:* Phil. 4:4–19. (d) **The immortal life.** *22 (Sunday):* Job 19:13–27; *23:* John 11: 20–27; *24:* II Cor. 5:1–10; *25:* I Thess. 4:13–18; *26:* Rev. 7:9–17; *27:* Rev. 21:1–8; *28:* Rev. 22:1–7. (e) **The joyous life.** *29 (Sunday):* Neh. 8:1–12; *30:* Ps. 32:1–11; *31:* Ps. 92:1–15.

SEPTEMBER. *1:* Isa. 12:1–6; *2:* Isa. 35: 1–10; *3:* Luke 15:1–10; *4:* Luke 15:11–32. (a) **The responsible life.** *5 (Sunday):* II Sam. 12:1–14; *6:* II Kings 7:3–11; *7:* II Chron. 7:12–22; *8:* II Chron. 36:11–21; *9:* Isa. 5:1–7; *10:* Mal. 3:6–12; *11:* Matt. 25:14–30. (b) **Life under God's sovereignty and care.** *12 (Sunday):* Ps. 47:1–9; *13:* Ps. 67:1–7; *14:* Isa. 42:1–9; *15:* Isa. 43:1–13; *16:* Isa. 51:1–11; *17:* Ezek. 34:6–16; *18:* Hos. 11:1–12. (c) **A separated life.** *19 (Sunday):* Josh. 23:1–11; *20:* I Sam. 12:13–25; *21:* Matt. 6:19–24; *22:* Luke 14:15–24; *23:* John 6:53–69; *24:* Phil. 3:1–16; *25:* II Cor. 6:14–7: 1. (d) **A divinely-guided life.** *26 (Sunday):* Gen. 28:10–22; *27:* Exod. 3:1–15;

28: Exod. 13:17–22; *29:* Deut. 32:1–12; *30:* Ps. 119:105–112.

OCTOBER.   *1:* Prov. 3:1–12; *2:* John 8:12–15. (a) **Life from Jesus Christ.** *3 (Sunday):* John 4:7–26; *4:* John 4:43–54; *5:* Mark 10:46–52; *6:* Luke 7:11–23; *7:* John 9:1–11; *8:* John 11:32–45; *9:* Acts 3:1–10. (b) **Resurrection life.** *10 (Sunday):* Acts 13:28–39; *11:* I Cor. 15:1–11; *12:* I Cor. 15:12–28; *13:* I Cor. 15:50–58; *14:* II Cor. 4:7–16; *15:* Eph. 4:17–24; *16:* Col. 3:1–19. (c) **Life in fellowship with God.** *17 (Sunday):* Gen. 5:21–24; *18:* Ps. 16:1–11; *19:* Ps. 23:1–6; *20:* John 15:1–8; *21:* Rom. 6:1–14; *22:* Phil. 1:12–30; *23:* I John 1:1–10. (d) **Life in the church.** *24 (Sunday):* Matt. 18:15–20; *25:* Acts 2:42–47; *26:* Acts 4:32–37; *27:* I Thess. 1:1–10; *28:* I Cor. 12:4–13; *29:* Col. 1:1–29; *30:* Rev. 1:1–20. (e) **A life of spiritual insight.** *31 (Sunday):* II Kings 6:8–17.

NOVEMBER.   *1:* Ps. 73:13–28; *2:* Ps. 119:89–104; *3:* Prov. 4:1–9; *4:* I Cor. 2:6–16; *5:* Eph. 1:15–23; *6:* Eph. 3:14–21. (a) **An evergrowing life.** *7 (Sunday):* Luke 2:40–52; *8:* Matt. 5:38–48; *9:* I Cor. 3:1–15; *10:* Eph. 4:1–16; *11:* Phil. 1:1–11; *12:* II Pet. 1:1–8; *13:* II Pet. 3:9–

18. (b) **A life of true freedom.** *14 (Sunday):* John 8:31–36; *15:* Rom. 6:15–23; *16:* I Cor. 9:1–18; *17:* I Cor. 9:19–27; *18:* Gal. 5:1–6; *19:* Eph. 6:1–9; *20:* I Pet. 2:11–25. (c) **A life of gratitude.** *21 (Sunday):* Ps: 9:1–11; *22:* Ps. 34:1–22; *23:* Ps. 103:1–22; *24:* Ps. 116:1–19; *25:* Ps. 118:1–29; *26:* Isa. 25:1–9; *27:* I Pet. 1: 1–9. (d) **A life of wisdom.** *28 (Sunday):* Ps. 90:1–17; *29:* Ps. 111:1–10; *30:* Prov. 2:1–9.

DECEMBER.   *1:* Prov. 8:1–11; *2:* Prov. 8:32–36; *3:* Prov. 16:1–9; *4:* Jas. 3:13–18. (a) **Life dedicated to God.** *5 (Sunday):* Gen. 22:1–18; *6:* Gen. 35:1–15; *7:* Deut. 4:32–40; *8:* I Kings 18:20–39; *9:* Isa. 53: 1–12; *10:* Matt. 3:1–17; *11:* John 12:20–36. (b) **Life in fulfillment of promise.** *12 (Sunday):* Isa. 9:1–7; *13:* Isa. 11:1–10; *14:* Isa. 61:1–11; *15:* Mic. 4:1–7; *16:* Mic. 5:2–4; *17:* Jer. 33:14–21; *18:* Mal. 3:1–5. (c) **Life through the incarnation.** *19 (Sunday):* John 1:1–14; *20:* Luke 1:26–38; *21:* Luke 1:46–55; *22:* Luke 1:67–79; *23:* Luke 2:1–20; *24:* Matt. 1:18–25; *25:* Matt. 2:1–12. (d) **A life of hope.** *26 (Sunday):* Ps. 71:16–24; *27:* Ps. 43:1–5; *28:* Rom. 12:9–21; *29:* Rom. 15:1–13; *30:* Rev. 22:6–13; *31:* Rom. 8:18–25.— American Bible Society.

SECTION II. Vital Themes for Vital Preaching

January 4. A Church on the Go (New Year)
SCRIPTURE: Gen. 12:1-9; Matt. 28:16-20.

I. God calls us as a church to go into the new year in a spirit of adventure—expecting new experiences and doing new things. (See Gen. 12:1-2.)

II. God calls us as a church to help him let his enslaved and oppressed people go. (See Exod. 7:16.)

III. God calls us as a church to go out to disciple the world. Our church has an evangelistic task to accomplish in the coming year. Jesus gave us this imperative. (See Matt. 28:19-20.)—Colbert S. Cartwright.

January 11. James: The Balanced Life
SCRIPTURE: Acts 15:13-21.

I. James promoted a positive mentality. He expected answer to prayer. He spoke of joy, but it is joy even in the midst of adversity. (See Jas. 1:2-3.)

II. James was a leader, a man of stature, head of the church in Jerusalem. Though a man of influence and half brother of Jesus, he was also humble, a servant of God and friend of the poor. (See Jas. 4:6.)

III. James knew how to listen, a tremendous quality for any Christian. At the great council of Jerusalem he first let others have their say. (See Jas. 1:19.)

IV. James knew how to talk as a Christian. When he finally did speak up at Jerusalem, everyone listened. He spoke with wisdom and authority, the kind that could come only of the Holy Spirit. The people recognized it. They accepted his counsel. Later he wrote forcefully about a Christian's control of his tongue. (See Jas. 3:2-6.)

V. James demonstrated the real meaning of faith. His Jerusalem edict left no room for mixing law and grace in man's justification before God. Only faith could save. Yet he was a doer. Unless Christians put their faith into action, he said, nonbelievers would not believe it genuine. (See Jas. 2:14-26.)

VI. James was a peacemaker, yet without compromise. He demonstrated this gift at the Jerusalem council. In his epistle he applauds the role of the peacemaker whose source of wisdom truly is "from above" (Jas. 1:17).

VII. James saw clearly the source of evil and the source of good, and unlike some critics today he did not confuse the two. Temptation, lust, lies, envy, and war ultimately originate with Satan. Sin is a reality. He describes God as the author of all good "with whom is no variableness, neither shadow of turning" (Jas. 1:17).

VIII. James unmasks Satan for who he is, yet he is not overwhelmed by his power. God's power is far greater. (See Jas. 4:7.)

IX. James understood the shortness of life, the folly of preoccupation with financial gain in this world, and the eventual return of the Lord. Yet a

19

strong Christian social conscience would not allow him to neglect the here and now—the poor, the orphans, the afflicted, the oppressed. (See Jas. 1:27.)

X. James urged involvement with the world around, yet warned the believer to keep himself unspotted from it. (See Jas. 1:27.)—*The Moody Monthly.*

January 18. The Salty Tang
TEXT: Matt. 5:13.

I. Is not salt a figure of what our *service* should be—making the lives of others happier and more meaningful, yet unobtrusive as the salt in a well-cooked meal?

II. Does not salt tell us how our *leadership* should be—helping a group to realize its possibilities, yet causing the group to feel in the end, "We have done it ourselves"?

III. Is not salt a figure of Christian *humility* since when it becomes noticeable by its overabundance it also becomes objectionable? Salt does its best work when it is entirely unnoticed.—D. A. Reily.

January 25. Making Frustrations Fruitful
SCRIPTURE: Luke 4:16–30.

I. Frustrations are common to everyone. They are par for the course of life. Even Jesus, according to the scripture lesson, suffered frustration.

II. Resentment of frustration is fruitless. Resentment against the inevitable makes sour grumps.

III. Let us cultivate resiliency of soul and roll with the blows rather than permit them to knock us off our feet. Let us win a few and lose a few.

IV. Let frustrations stimulate us to grow in patience and not stymie us.

V. In times of frustration ask, "What is God trying to tell me?" We need to look for the divine hand shaping our lives, to watch God working frustrations into good ends, and to give him thanks for his providence—Robert W. Rae.

February 1. Living by the Golden Rule
TEXT: Matt. 7:12.

I. Accept others as you find them.

II. Help others to make of their life a useful experience.

III. Inspire others to help themselves.

IV. Encourage another to "do his best."—Roy Felder.

February 8. Measuring Maturity
TEXT. Eph. 4:13.

I. Maturity is dependability.

II. Maturity is humility.

III. Maturity is patience.

IV. Maturity is perseverance.

V. Maturity is unselfishness.

VI. Maturity is decisiveness.

VII. Maturity is the ability to control anger and settle differences without violence or destruction, the ability to face unpleasantness and discomfort, frustration and defeat without complaint, without giving up, and the achievement of living in peace with that which cannot be changed.

February 15. Overcoming Indifference (Brotherhood Week)
SCRIPTURE: I Cor. 5:1–8.

If indifference to moral wrong is a sin can Christians become concerned?

I. We can determine to know right from wrong, and we have the entire history of the Christian faith to guide us. There is something called *right* and another something called *wrong*. We can make distinctions; we must make them.

II. We can believe that discipline is necessary to right living. The words "discipline" and "disciple" are closely related. To be a disciple is to be teachable in the school of Christ. Without discipline we become like unbroken horses.

III. We are members of the human race; we must help others to be men and women under God.—Earl F. Zeigler.

February 22. The Golden Text of the Deeper Life
SCRIPTURE: Rom. 12:1–13.

I. *An exclusive relevance to Christians, to "brethren," who have been born again.* They have experienced the mercy of God in forgiveness of sins. Now they also have the mercies of God through intelligent ministering to God. How many sinners are intelligently ministering to God?

II. *A demanding relationship to your total being.* "I beseech you"—here Paul appeals to the will. "By the mercies of God"—here to the emotions. "That ye present your bodies"—put them at the disposal of God to be used according to his discretion. Here Paul refers to every part of the human person. In response to such total dedication of the self the Holy Spirit enters and becomes our Christian possession.

III. *A personal rendition in daily living.* In the Greek "a living sacrifice" is that which gives continuing evidence of being alive. Being filled with the Spirit is an inner experience; it is also a growing, developing life with evidences of the Spirit's continuing presence. (a) A dedication that is continuing. (b) A transformation that is inward. (c) A revelation that is practical. (d) An evaluation that is realistic. (e) A cooperation that is binding.—Frank B. Stanger.

February 29. Maintaining Spiritual Freshness

SCRIPTURE: II Cor. 5:1–21.

I. *Awareness of the divine presence.* (See v. 18.) The God who has provided a means of reconciliation between the sinner and himself continues to share his grace with the one he has redeemed.

II. *A sense of man's spirituality.* (See v. 16.) Paul no longer bases his knowledge of a man on his outward life but evaluates him according to his inner worth as a child of God with capacity to exist forever.

III. *A balance of spiritual motives.* (See v. 14.) When the love of Christ controls a man there is no limit to his endurance. To him the Spirit imparts greater stability and spiritual vitality for daily needs. In order through Christ to have vitality for each opportunity of life, he feels that he must go beyond himself.

IV. *Active partnership with God.* (See vv. 18–20.) By committing to his partner the ministry of reconciliation God shows how completely he trusts the apostle. This trust gives him a new sense of his worth and a new zeal in the ministry of reconciliation. What an unfailing source of vitality for God's work!

V. *Assurance of hope for the future.* (See v. 1.) Being "in Christ" means a fellowship not to be broken by death. Then the believer enters the place the Lord has gone before to make ready and receives the reward for his faithfulness. In every conflict of earth this assurance strengthens Paul and makes him more than conqueror.—Lewis T. Corlett.

March 7. Lenten Living (Lent)

Consider some positive things you can do that are truly worthy of the spiritual dimensions of Lent.

I. Forgive someone who has hurt you, and if it is possible at all find a way to offer that person your forgiveness.

II. Write to someone who would be happy to hear from you and you have had on your mind from time to time and just never seemed to have found the time to write.

III. Do something thoughtful for a lonely person—a personal visit, a phone call, a small remembrance.

IV. Smile at the "butcher, baker, and candlestick maker" for smiles are all too seldom seen these days.

V. Offer a word of encouragement to another person or a sincere compliment.

VI. If you find yourself wallowing in negativism—it is so easy to do this these days—find something hopeful to say or something positive to do.

VII. Judge others, if at all, with kindness. Be gentle toward them. Guard your tongue when you would speak of them.

VIII. Set aside some time for those closest to you who are longing to share more of your life with you and to whom you always seem so very busy.

IX. Seek God's help, asking for his guidance at the beginning of a day, putting yourself in his care at the day's end.

X. Think on the things in your life that are reasons for thanksgiving, and remembering them, cultivate a grateful heart.—Charles L. Copenhaver.

March 14. A Spiritual Lift (Lent)

TEXT: Heb. 12:12–13.

I. As Christians we need to lift up our spirits (attitude). This is what the writer is saying: Lift up your limp hands, strengthen your weak knees, and keep on walking a straight path so that your lame foot be not disabled.

II. As Christians we need to lift up our fellowman. In Eccles. 4:9–12 the writer stresses the importance of friendship and cooperation.

III. As Christians we need to lift up our hearts in worship. (a) In dependence. (See Ps. 121:1.) (b) In obedience. (See Ps. 123:1–2.) (c) In repentance. (See Judg. 2:4.) (d) In praise. (See Ps. 134:2.)

IV. As Christians we need to lift up our vision of the work. In John 4:35, Jesus says in essence: "Stop procrastinating, take a good look at the field for the crops are ready. You will be paid for your work, and there will be joy in serving."

V. As Christians we should lift up our heads for the return of the Lord. (See Luke 21:28.)—Leon Emery.

March 21. Listen to Him! (Lent)

TEXT: Matt. 17:5 (RSV).

I. Listen to his words of judgment upon our pride, our greed, our unbelief. This judgment descends on the whole of sinful mankind. From this sentence none dare claim to be exempt. For "all have sinned and come short of the glory of God" (Rom. 3:23).

II. Listen to his words of forgiveness of our sin. His grace abounds to cover every sin, no matter how grievously we have erred, no matter how far we have strayed. His pardon is ours through repentance and faith. For "the Son of man is come to seek and to save that which was lost" (Luke 19:10).

III. Listen to his words of comfort in our sadness and bereavement, our anxiety and despair. He is the source of true and lasting comfort, for "he has borne our griefs and carried our sorrows" (Isa. 53:4).

IV. Listen to his words of a life of freedom in his gospel, a life of power through his spirit, a life of service in his love.

March 28. This Happened at Calvary (Lent)

TEXT: Luke 23:33.

I. God's nature was revealed to the world. Look at the cross and see revelation.

II. God redeemed a lost world. Look at the cross and see redemption.

III. God restored men to the kingdom. Look at the cross and see reconciliation. —John R. Brokhoff.

April 4. The Inevitable Cross (Passion Sunday)

TEXT: John 12:27.

I. *A unique event in history.* The cross has changed the course of history and may change the course of your life today. The Bible says that the preaching of the cross becomes to the believer both the wisdom and the power of God. So on Passion Sunday we begin with the cross, and we stay with the cross.

II. *The unique word of Jesus Christ.* As we see from the hymns, creeds, and prayers of the universal church, authentic Christianity has always known that the cross speaks the unique word of Christ, the climax of his teaching.

III. *The inevitability of God's love.* (a) "For this cause." With these words his destiny is clear. He came to die. The cross that was now almost within sight would be freely chosen. Why?

(1) Because there was no other way in which he could reach to the depth of the human agony he came to endure, so as to "bear our griefs and carry our sorrows."

(2) Because there was no other way he could draw upon himself the hopeless weight of our sins and absorb the evil that blocks us from the holiness of God.

(b) "The Lord hath laid on him the iniquity of us all." The only way the

God of peace and joy can reach his suffering family is in this amazing fashion to share that suffering. The only way the God of perfect purity and goodness can reach his disobedient people is himself to offer the sacrifice for sin. "For this cause came I into the world."—David H. C. Read.

April 11. Palm Sunday Revolution (Palm Sunday)

TEXT: Matt. 5:21–22.

I. Jesus came not to destroy but to fulfill. (See Matt. 5:17, 10:52.) Jesus never lost sight of the goal: the coming of the kingdom of God into the lives of men. He was positive, not negative; constructive, not destructive.

II. Jesus placed man and his welfare at the center of all his mission. Not the institution, not even a rigid set of laws, but man. (See Mark 2:27.) Our modern revolutionaries should weigh their teachings and programs against the simple rule: what will this do for people from the least to the greatest?

III. The revolution of Jesus was seen within the framework of the will of God and not as a scheme to laugh God out of existence and put a crown on man, that he might rule instead. Man at his best is a poor substitute for God. Granted that we need an ever-larger understanding of God, it is our concept of God, not God, that needs to be changed. The Palm Sunday revolution was actually led by God himself. That is what makes it so authentic.

IV. When Jesus upset his world it was because he deeply loved the people he was trying to upset. So with Paul. So with every genuine Christian revolutionary. We have no right to tamper with the status quo unless we have genuine love for capitalist and Communist, integrationist and segregationist, liberal and conservative. For only love can creatively and constructively turn revolution to serve the purposes of God. Only in this light can we understand the cross in either its original or its contemporary setting.—Ivan B. Bell.

April 18. Eternal Living (Easter)

TEXT: John 17:3.

Easter speaks to us about eternal life. For the Christian, immortality, which means endless existence, is not enough. We believe in eternal life which has to do with the *quality* of experience rather than the *quantity* of experience.

I. Eternal life means life survives because it is structured on eternal principals.

II. Eternal life means growing in our understanding of the nature and purposes of God. It frees us from enslavement to things and time and enables us to see life in its broader setting.

III. Eternal life means growing more and more into the likeness of the divine character as we live the Christ-centered life.

IV. Eternal life means building our lives into the lives of other persons as we witness and serve. Someone said: "Some people remember themselves into oblivion, while others forget themselves into immortality." The self-centered life gets smaller and smaller as the years pass. The other-centered life grows larger and larger, for it is linked with the eternal, creative life of God.

V. Eternal life means growing in our appreciation of goodness, truth, beauty, love, creativity, and material blessings.

VI. Eternal life means meeting disappointment, sorrow, suffering, tragedy, and frustration in the light of the larger purposes and perspective of God and creating meaning out of them.

VII. Eternal life means growing in faith, hope, and love. Death becomes a turn in the road of life, the means whereby we are freed for "life that shall endless be."—Eugene E. Golay.

April 25. The Greatest Verse in the Bible

TEXT: John 3:16.

I. *A definition of God* in terms of *love:* "God so loved the world." To the Greeks God was beauty; to the Romans, powers; to the Hebrews, law; to the scientist, the unknowable; to the Christian, love.

II. *A definition of love* in terms of *service:* "God so loved the world that he gave." Love is not sentiment but is service. It is not mere emotion. It is energy. God's love gives.

III. *A definition of service* in terms of *personality:* "God so loved the world that he gave his only begotten Son." He gave himself. God was in Christ. He was the last of a long series of gifts.

IV. *A definition of faith* in terms of *trust:* "That whosoever believeth on him." Faith has to do with its object. We do not need a great faith. We need a great God.

V. *A definition of salvation* in terms of *life:* "That whosoever believeth on him should not perish, but have everlasting life." Jesus comes to give life and to give it more abundantly. Life must be defined, not in terms of faith, but in terms of breadth and depth and height.—Hugh T. Kerr.

May 2. Living with Jesus

TEXT: Matt. 16:16

I. Live with this Jesus and God ceases to be a phantasy, a theory, a glorified "Perhaps." He becomes an ever-present companion whose loving presence we feel, whose redeeming power we know. In the face of Jesus we see God. In his words we hear God. Through him we experience and know God most vividly, completely, redemptively.

II. Live with Jesus and crippling sins lose their grip. We see them clearly enough to hate them and seek God's pardon and cleansing. The love of righteousness grows in us. Sunrise ends our night. We are born again.

III. Live with Jesus and the heart-throb of brotherhood makes music in the soul. It is music of the "New World Symphony," the world which is meant to be, the world he summons us to usher in.

IV. Live with Jesus the man and soon he becomes more than man. He stands before us as all of God whom we can see, know, feel, love—Everett W. Palmer.

May 9. Hannah: An Exemplary Mother (Mother's Day)

TEXT: 1 Sam. 1:11.

The first two chapters of I Samuel focus on two families: Elkanah, a Levite and Eli, a priest. Elkanah had two wives: Peninnah, who had many children, and Hannah, who had none.

I. *Hannah's aggravation.* The deep humiliation that childlessness meant to a Hebrew wife is not understandable to us, but Hannah's lot was made unbearable by Peninnah's constant taunts about her barrenness.

II. *Hannah's supplication.* Instead of going to pieces, Hannah went to prayer, but not ordinary prayer. In anguish of soul Hannah poured out her plight before the Lord with supplication and weeping. Hers was not a single petition but a persistent, tenacious prayer, multiplied again and again in desperation.

III. *Hannah's consecration.* (a) God granted Hannah's wish by giving her a son. Note first that Hannah gave Samuel to the service of God. Of course, we cannot call our children into the ministry—only God can do that. But we can tell and show them that full-time service to the Lord is the greatest privilege of the child of God.

(b) Hannah proved her sincerity by fulfilling her vow as quickly as possible. As soon as she had weaned Samuel she took him to the temple.

(c) She put upon her son a Nazarite vow, which meant he would always be separated unto God and would never defile himself. Hannah's approach was not, "Samuel, you can do these things and still be a believer." But in effect she said, "Samuel, there are some things you cannot do because you are a believer."

(d) Samuel knew that God came first; his mother had taught him this before anyone else. By dedicating Samuel to God as a child and never trying to repossess him for her own, Hannah showed her boy that his body was a temple of God; his talents and abilities, his service and time were God's.

IV. *Hannah's exaltation.* Although Hannah and Samuel have long ago walked off the stage of life to receive their eternal rewards, the influence of their lives are blessing multitudes every day. Samuel dedicated himself to God but not until his mother had dedicated him to God—after she had dedicated herself to the Lord. Hannah was a mother of prayer, praise, and purpose. —Robert G. Graham in *Church of God Evangel.*

May 16. Christian Hospitality in Church
TEXT: Rom. 15:7.

I. Speak to people.
II. Smile at people.
III. Call people by name.
IV. Be friendly and helpful.
V. Be cordial.
VI. Be genuinely interested in people.
VII. Be considerate.
VIII. Be thoughtful.
IX. Be alert and give service.
X. Be generous with praise and cautious with criticism.—P. A. Willis.

May 23. Man and God's Good Earth (Rural Life Sunday)
TEXT: Num. 35.34.

I. We have been mistreating God's beautiful earth. We have filled the air with 142 million tons of smoke and fumes. The countryside is cluttered with seven million junk cars. Pollution endangers the health of all living things.

II. We have not been good stewards of the earth's resources. We have been treating nature as if it were ours to use in any way. We have not been thinking of the generations yet to come.

III. We need to see the interrelatedness of all God's creation. What happens to God's natural creation affects God's human creation. Human life is possible only when we properly protect the world of nature.

IV. We need to keep some of God's world as it is. One does not have to oppose all change to recognize that there must be a stopping point. There is a need within man for nature and wilderness areas.—Lovett Hayes Weems, Jr.

May 30. How to Help Other People

I. Learn to listen.
II. Learn to communicate.
III. Learn to share.
IV. Learn to love.
V. Learn to lift.
VI. Learn to believe.
VII. Learn to pray.
VIII. Learn to follow.

June 6. The Holy Spirit in the Book of Acts (Pentecost)

I. The baptism of the Holy Spirit is more meaningful than baptism with water (1:5).

II. The Holy Spirit gives power to be witness of Jesus Christ "in Jerusalem, throughout Judea, in Samaria, and to the ends of the earth" (1:8).

III. The Holy Spirit is given to those persons who obey God (5:32).

IV. The Holy Spirit gives strength to suffer martyrdom for Christ if necessary, as Stephen did (7:55).

V. The Holy Spirit cannot be bought with money, as Simon tried to do (8:17–24).

VI. The Holy Spirit heals, as it restored Paul's sight (9:17).

VII. The Holy Spirit gives the church the power to grow (9:31).

VIII. The Holy Spirit is for all people, Jews and Gentiles (10:45).

IX. The Holy Spirit calls missionaries (13:2–4).

X. The Holy Spirit gives power to speak in tongues and to prophesy (10:1–7).

XI. The Holy Spirit gives warning of what to expect, as it told Paul that jail and suffering awaited him (20:23).

XII. The Holy Spirit holds the leaders of the church responsible for feeding and shepherding God's flock, the church (20:28).—Walter A. Whitehurst.

June 13. Interim Living
SCRIPTURE: Exod. 16:1–3; Rev. 21:1–4.
Every moment we are given is an interim.

I. We live between what we have been and what we will become.

II. The present holds all of the exciting possibilities of love, learning, and beauty which our past has told us can be.

III. The future holds unquenchable hope, not because we can create it but because we know that by truly caring we can be creative in it.—James W. Stewart.

June 20. A Faithful Father's Benediction (Father's Day)

TEXT: Num. 6:24–26.

I. "The Father bless you." "Bless" means to grant divine favor, to consecrate, to pronounce holy, to guard and protect for the sake of God.

II. "The Father keep you." "Keep" means custody, care, and charge—all of which are certainly a father's responsibility.

III. "The Father make his face to shine upon you." The shining face of God the Father should shine on the face of a human father's conscience, spirit, soul, and demeanor.

IV. "The Father be gracious to you." When a father demonstrates in thought, word, and deed the fatherly goodness of God, he leaves a legacy to his children that time will not tarnish.

V. "The Father lift up his countenance upon you." How does your father look? If he looks the part of a parental tyrant or a parental tramp or a parental Frankenstein, then the comment may not be so complimentary.

VI. "The Father give you peace." The central meaning of biblical peace is "harmony within the total community." And such harmony is impossible without God. In the Old and New Testaments, God is both the source and the center of all peace.—Leslie Conrad, Jr.

June 27. I Will Be a Good Samaritan

SCRIPTURE: Luke 10:25–37.

I. I will be sensitive to the needs of my fellow man and actively look for ways to befriend him.

II. I will become aware of man's suffering, get involved in his struggle, and comfort him in his sorrow.

III. I will withhold judgment of my brother and attempt to understand his thinking, his attitudes, and his behavior.

IV. I will forgive those who have injured me; I will forgive even those who hurt those I love.

V. I will not close my eyes or pass by on the other side wherever there is need of my service, my friendship, or my presence.

VI. I will lift someone's spirits by giving the most needed gift of all—a word of hope and encouragement.

VII. I will remember to be grateful to those who have been good Samaritans to me and who keep me from falling into the ditches of discouragement, depression, and defeat.

VIII. I will be a good Samaritan for the inner joy of serving, because helping others is what the Golden Rule is about.

IX. I will recognize that my neighbor is anyone and that my brother is everyone.

X. I will feel so much joy, experience so much growth, and receive such a blessing as a good Samaritan today that I will be a good Samaritan again tomorrow.—William Arthur Ward.

July 4. Rebels for Freedom (Independence Day)

TEXT: I Pet. 2:15–16.

I. The fundamental proposition undergirding a free society is that it is God's will to do right no matter how anyone in power may feel about it. The emperor and his governors are under God's judgment, and they are to be defied if necessary on the altars of integrity. The doctrine, of course, was and is an explosive one.

II. "It is God's will that by doing right you should put to silence the ignorance of foolish men," Peter insists. Right, he seemed to think, is its own validation. Truth carries its own lamp and the darkness of ignorance or folly cannot put it out.

III. Peter added an invitation to his contemporaries to "live as free men," using their powers as "servants of God." If the Christians were to be "the light of the world," they were constrained to know the truth and yield voluntarily to its discipline. Peter knew that free men are disciplined "as servants of God." As Paul noted, we are free only when we are "bond slaves of Christ," disciplined by our devotion to the truth in him that makes us free.

IV. We do not deserve to be free unless we live "as servants of God," thinking and serving in obedience to Jesus Christ. It is suggestive to notice that the word "free" comes to us from the old English word "freon," meaning "to love." Free has the same root as "friend," and it suggests one who is especially dear. The words of Jesus to his disciples in John 15:15 are therefore particularly significant. They are no longer servants; they are free men.—Harold Blake Walker.

July 11. Can a Good Man Be Saved?
TEXT: Matt. 19:24.

I. A "good" man is lost because he is blind to his true condition. (See Rom. 3:23.)

II. A "good" man is lost because he relies on an insufficient remedy. (See Isa. 64:6.)

III. A "good" man is lost because he does not repent. (See Mark 2:17; Luke 13:3.)

IV. A "good" man is lost because he rejects his only hope. (See Heb. 2:3.)

V. There is hope for a "good" man because God loves him despite his condition. (See John 3:16.)

(a) God's first act of grace will be to lend a mirror which will portray the "good" man in his true condition, the way God sees him. Then the "good" man can be saved just like any other sinner. (See Eph. 2:8–9.)

(b) Jesus was talking about the difficulty of saving "good" men when he said, "With men this is impossible; but with God all things are possible" (Matt. 19:26).—Horace Ward.

July 18. Emulating Christ
TEXT: Phil. 1:27–28.

Paul outlines what it means for the Philippians to emulate Christ.

I. They are to be consistent. Paul's faith is reckoning on the possibility of release from prison. But, he says, whether I am with you or not should make no difference in your way of living.

II. Paul expects the Philippians to be steadfast. They are not to be retreating Christians who, when the going gets rough, conceal or at least play down their Christianity. They are to stand fast and unashamed in any company.

III. The Philippian church is to be unified. Let the world fight, quarrel, and hate—Christians must be one.

IV. Paul desires for the believers to be unconquerable. These are days when it is evident that Satan is working overtime. Paul tells us not to be afraid but to trust, hope, and fight.—Mrs. Norman S. Marshall.

July 25. On Seeing Art in an Artichoke
SCRIPTURE: Mark 14:3–9.

French artist Henri Matisse was asked by a visitor to his studio where he got his inspiration for his painting. "I grow artichokes" was the puzzling reply. "Every morning," Matisse went on to explain, "I go into my garden and watch these plants. I see the play of light and shade on the leaves, and I discover new combinations of colors and fantastic patterns. I study them. They inspire me. Then I go back into the studio and paint." So one of this century's great painters literally saw art in an artichoke!

(1) Jesus knew this secret of effective living. He was forever seeing things that others overlooked. He saw the kingdom of God in the faces of children who to others were only a nuisance; he noted the sacrificial spirit of a widow who dropped only a couple of coppers into the offering; he sensed Zaccheus' inner dissatisfaction with himself; he saw possibilities in Peter and called him a rock when to most other people he looked more like shifting sand, unstable as water, thick-skulled, and impulsive. But Jesus saw art in an artichoke like that.

(2) Let's look at the cultivation of this

ability to see the unseen in the seen, art in an artichoke.

I. We can enlarge and enhance the elusive ability to see the unusual in the ordinary if we *cultivate the passive as well as the active mood in life*. There is a time to perceive as well as to achieve, a time to receive as well as get, a time to accept as well as to acquire.

II. It will help to see the art in the artichoke if we will *cultivate the appreciative as well as the critical mood*. We actually help to create good just by recognizing it and expressing appreciation of it.

III. It will help us to see the possibilities in the ordinary if we *cultivate the redemptive more than the destructive mood*. One sees more in a person he is trying to help than in one he is determined to cut down to size.—Raymond E. Balcomb.

August 1. Christian Inventory

TEXT: Rom. 10:10.

I. Do you look for something to criticize, or do you look for something to praise? For instance, if in your church the choir puts on an anthem or a cantata or an oratorio, do you jump on the mistakes and the inadequacies that are bound to be there, or do you comment on the parts which were well sung, stressing that a very creditable attempt has been made to sing a piece of great music, even if did not reach professional standards?

II. Do you encourage or discourage? When some course of action is suggested do you promptly see all the difficulties which make it impossible, or do you see the possibilities which make it well worth trying? Are you one of the people who sit and consider or one of the people who rise and march?

III. Do you count your blessings, or do you count your misfortunes? Do you thank God for what you have, or do you curse God for what you have lost?

IV. Do you look on a difficult situation as a disaster or as an opportunity? Do you regard a crisis as a time to sit down and wail or a time to rise up and act?—William Barclay.

August 8. Living Sacrifices

TEXT: Rom. 12:1–2.

I. *The total body, a living sacrifice*. God does not want martyrs; he wants witnesses. He wants man so completely that man will be willing to sacrifice, give without reservation, every aspect of his life.

II. *Holy*. A holy body is one that is clean, without spot or blemish, not serving two masters, subservient to his will. The body, sin marred and scarred, must be washed by the blood of Christ before it is presented.

III. *Acceptable*. God can refuse a gift. He will not accept that which is hypocritical, halfhearted, and in love with the world.

IV. *A reasonable service*. The more correct rendition would be "spiritual service or an act of worship." Worship is a form of service and service is a form of worship.

V. *Not conformed to this world*. The gift to God should not be molded by the things of the world to conform to the world but fashioned by the hand of God to conform to his pattern. And this is done by the Spirit renewing man's mind. As a man thinketh, so is he. His thoughts mold his face. When man thinks upon those things which are pure, lovely, just, honest, and of good report, then the transformation occurs and he changes into the transfigured life. His gift then is appropriate.—Herbert C. Gabhart.

August 15. Institutionalized Religion

TEXT: Rev. 3:17–18.

I. A church becomes institutionalized when its members are related primarily to it as an institution rather than to Christ.

II. A church becomes institutionalized when its primary concern is turned inward and its chief concern is with its existence, not with the reason for its existence.

III. A church becomes institutionalized when means becomes ends and ends become means or, to put it bluntly, when we get the cart before the horse.

IV. A church becomes institutionalized when it becomes more concerned with the correctness of belief than with the quality of living.

V. A church becomes institutionalized when form replaces the Spirit, when the Spirit is lost and only form remains. Form is acceptable, but not having the Spirit is unacceptable. The body of Christ is either alive by the Spirit, or it is dead.—Adapted from Finley B. Edge.

August 22. Pulled in Three Directions

There are three facts which every person must face—the fact of God, the fact of man, and the fact of sin. In these days we feel the tug of all three, and we feel them simultaneously.

I. *The upward pull.* God is seeking to take hold of us and lift us to higher ground. We resist him to the hurt of our souls. When we become contented with our achievements, complacent, smug, possessed with a sense of "having arrived," we are headed for trouble. When one ceases to feel and respond to the upward pull, deterioration has already begun. Paul had the Christian view when he said: "I count not myself to have apprehended. . . . I press on." He was keenly sensitive to the upward pull.

II. *The downward pull.* Whether it be called an impersonal influence or a personal force, there is that with which we must contend in life. One is seeking our spiritual downfall. The adversary like a roaring lion is seeking whom he may devour.

III. *The outward pull.* To feel it is to believe that we are our brother's keeper. It reminds us that what happens to our fellowman is of tremendous importance and a matter of personal concern. We are admonished in the Word to love our neighbor as ourselves. (See Matt. 25:40.)—Marie W. Deusner.

August 29. More Power to You

SCRIPTURE: I Cor. 12:3–11.

I. Power is a basic need of persons.

Our power base as Christians comes from our baptism wherein we receive our identity as children of God. This is our identity.

II. We are created in God's image (a) We are creative, as God is creative. We have the power to create, to shape, to style, to bring into being. When a person is creating he is in touch with power.

(b) God is love; therefore we have the capacity to give and receive love.

(c) We have the capacity for decision, choice. Man has a will; he is not a robot. Man is in touch with power as he exercises his freedom in choosing and making decisions.

(d) When man is creative, loving, exercising choices, he receives satisfaction, completeness, and fulfillment. This is power.

III. The Holy Spirit is associated with power. (a) You have the Holy Spirit if you are able to confess Christ as Lord.

(b) The Spirit gives every person a gift (a charisma); thus every person is vital to the group and unique to the group.

(c) The gift is to be exercised for the sake of the group.

IV. Power comes to us as we see our worth, discover our gift, and exercise that gift. Then we experience true power that comes from God, and we develop our human potential.—Dennis J. Johnson.

September 5. The Church Not Blessed

SCRIPTURE: Rev. 3:14–22.

In the district around Laodicea are mineral springs. As long as the water is boiling you can somehow drink it, but if tepid it is of all things most nauseating. Our Lord uses these springs as a background for the only one of the seven churches for which he has no word of commendation or encouragement.

I. *Indifferent to God.* There is about some churches a "goodishness" that passes for Christianity. A sort of civic betterment program, with "pay your debts, love your mother, and don't kill anybody," a maudlin sentimentality supposed to be Christianity. You don't have religion without zeal. Christianity is a fire in the bones, a moving in the soul, a stirring of the heart, a vast illimitable commitment of life to God.

II. *Deceived about self.* They said: "We are rich. We have need of nothing." Christ said, "You are poor, naked, blind." In proportion to their lukewarmness they were filled with self-satisfaction. "We don't need God. We don't need to pray, or repent." That is humanism.

III. *Exclusive of Christ.* Outside the Laodicean church is Christ, knocking. He has been gone a long time. The centuries have watched the progress and the regress of his church. Now he comes back. Is the door open to receive him? This is the end of the age. What a tragedy when the Lord came the first time and his own received him not! How infinitely more sad when our Lord shall come back to earth and knock at the door, wishing to come in and eat the last supper! Will there be anybody watching in true devotion, waiting for the appearing of Christ Jesus?—W. A. Criswell.

September 12. God's Wisdom for Man's Folly

TEXT: I Cor. 1:22–24.

What are the needs God's wisdom in Christ meets?

I. It meets our need to realize that this is a friendly universe. The world is not hostile. Its Creator is for us. Jesus is "sent" to us with that good news.

II. It meets our need to realize that who I am is more important than my skills or my IQ. I don't have to be super-talented or brilliant to be good in the sight of God.

III. It meets our need to have conviction about what life is for and how I fit into a vast world. It gives a sense of mission and purpose; without these ingredients life is boredom.

IV. It meets our need to feel that someone is in control. The world is not a colossal accident, though beautiful; it is a beautiful design, though colossal!

The end is in the process, like an oak is "in" an acorn.—David H. Smith.

September 19. How Do You Know You're in Love?

TEXT: Gen. 2:24 (NASB).

Two can say they are in love and have a good marriage when each:

I. Unconditionally places Jesus Christ first in everything.

II. Desires to stay and not to run.

III. Desires to express approval as quickly as disapproval.

IV. Desires a person and not a body.

V. Desires to complement and not to compete.

VI. Thinks in the plural and not in the singular.

VII. Has a sense of security and not apprehension.

VIII. Accepts the other for what he or she is—not as a project.

IX. Finds fulfillment in giving rather than in getting.

X. Centers attention on one person only, not on a third person or thing.

XI. Realizes that one does not fall in love but grows in love—A. W. Jackson.

September 26. The Power of Music

TEXT: Eph. 5:19.

I. In the hour of rest, music will uplift your spirit and carry refreshment to every faculty of your being.

II. In the hour of work, you will rejoice in the strength and energies which music has given you.

III. In the hour of jubilee, music will bring you thrills of delight that compensate for all that is dull and commonplace.

IV. In the hour of prayer, music will quicken the aspirations of your soul and perfume your life with the breath of evening.

V. In the hour of fellowship, music will join your spirit with others in unity and understanding.

VI. In the hour of love, music will enrich your heart with feelings that magnify the meaning of existence.

VII. In the hour of memory, music will unseal the treasures of the past and bring the sacred glory to the present.

VIII. In the hour of death, music will speak to you of a life filled with an eternity of joy and song.

IX. In the hour of vision, music will give power and scope to your imagination and bring into reality the things that were not.

X. In the hour of high purpose, music will summon the potentialities of your soul and urge them forward to great and glorious achievement.

October 3. Keeping the Family Together (World Communion Sunday)

TEXT: John 17:11.

I. *We are a family born of belief.* There is a single question, What do you believe? It is the only door by which you enter, and it is open to all who will come. Yet it is not so easy as it seems. It cannot be forced by any man, no matter how powerful. From the very beginning this has been the one requirement if you are to become a part of this family of Christ. His family is open to all who profess Christ as Lord and Savior and, believing in him, are ready to accept the privileges and responsibilities.

II. *We are a family nurtured by concern.* We care what happens to everyone else in the family of Christ. The New Testament is clear that that has been true from the very beginning. We find Paul writing of the urgency of taking a collection for the church in Jerusalem. Struggling though they were to keep a foothold in the ancient world, they were thinking always of one another. So the churches of Asia Minor took an offering for the relief of the church in Jerusalem.

III. *We are enriched by our differences.* It is one of the ways God blesses us all. Here is one of the great differences between people: some are afraid of difference and resist it; others welcome differences and are enriched by them. "All things are yours," wrote Paul and set the tone for the Christian church. We are not afraid of difference; we are enriched by it. It is a part of the freedom which God, who has come to us in Christ, has given that we should not withdraw but should welcome our differing gifts, knowing that all of them together are not enough to express our love of God.

IV. *We are united by a mission.* "Go ye into all parts of the world and preach the gospel." From our earliest beginnings it has been our mission. It doesn't set some point at which we are free from our obligation. The mission remains until the end of time. We are still under orders. We cannot come to Christ and say, "Mission accomplished." The family has work to do, and it makes us one in purpose as we come to this table today. —Gene E. Bartlett.

October 10. How My Church Looks to Me (Laity Sunday)

TEXT: Matt. 16:18.

I. It is a poor, worldly thing, often concerned with petty matters, yet it is the doorway to the great church.

II. It is often helplessly behind the times, yet it is the gateway to the future.

III. It is often torn by controversy, yet it holds the key to eternal harmony.

IV. Its minister is only human and often makes mistakes, yet he is the type and substance of the Great High Priest.

V. Its altar is humble and plain, yet from it is dispensed the bread of life.

VI. Its choir sings but indifferently, yet through it sing the choirs of angels and archangels.

VII. Its organizations are petty and often seem to have little to do with religion, yet through them the organism that is Christ's holy body may function.

VIII. Its preaching is often pedestrian, even dull, yet through its pulpit the Word of God speaks to his children.

IX. Its church school is noisy and the teachers are not well trained, yet through them a new generation is learning to carry on the faith.

X. It seems to have little influence on the community, yet within it is to be found the great treasure.

XI. Its missionary flame burns low, yet through it men are sent forth to preach the gospel to all nations.

XII. It is full of sinners like me, yet it is the mother of saints.

XIII. In the eyes of the world it is a poor and perhaps a pitiful thing, one that can be easily overlooked or ignored, yet in the eyes of God it is his holy church, the manifestation of his presence in that particular corner of his world.

XIV. My parish may seem weak, inefficient, inadequate, and worldly, yet it is my link with the great reality; it is the very means whereby God comes down to earth and dwells among his people.—Clifford Morehouse.

October 17. How's Your Courage?
TEXT: Acts 27:23–24.

I. *Physical courage.* Wherever you point in the records of the struggles which have made possible the civilization of our time, you will find the names of men and women who have had the physical courage to risk their all.

II. *Emotional courage.* To become courageous demands that we develop the quality of character known as fortitude. This is like courage in the sense that it means the strength of mind to endure unfalteringly any form of anguish, adversity, or pain.

III. *Social courage.* The Old Testament prophets were men who believed themselves to be commissioned of God to speak out when it would have been easier and safer to have remained silent. Standing up against the multitude with the conviction that one with God makes a majority is true social courage.

IV. *Spiritual courage.* The man of courage knows that in order to handle this great powerhouse of physical energy in a courageous manner, to find stamina for facing up to the many demands for emotional courage, and most of all in order to channel his social courage into creative purposes, he must keep close to the great source of all life and courage—to the very life of God. By reading the Bible, worshiping, praying, having companionship with people of like mind, one gains those convictions which produce courage.—Homer J. R. Elford.

October 24. Growth: An Index to Church Life
TEXT: II Pet. 3:18.

Growth is an index of life. The most viable members and the most vital churches are the ones that are growing.

I. May the *direction* of our growth be away from prideful parochialism toward our objective of helping persons to help themselves to accept Jesus Christ as Lord and Savior.

II. May the *motivation* for our growth be not a thinly veiled obsession with size but a magnificent obsession with souls.

III. May the *means* of our growth be not in reliance upon techniques but in the radiant and relevant ministries we render in the spirit of our Master.

IV. May the *goal* of our growth be a redemptive community of Christians who, while recognizing and appreciating differences among them, will take their place together as members of the body of Christ, ministering to one another and to the world with every means that God has placed at our disposal.

October 31. Prodigals Who Do Not Return
TEXT: Luke 15:18.

Why do so few prodigals return?

I. Partly because not all are in some far country of riotous living. They are not feeding swine; they simply are sleeping in indifference, or they are so caught up in competing interests that they do not know how far from home they have wandered.

II. Some prodigals are loath to return because they are reluctant to face the Father and give an account of their stewardship. We begin life with the heritage of opportunity. Who is there who has not wasted something of time and talent? We are afraid to face condemnation. God is prepared to meet us on the way with mercy.

III. The self-righteous, like the elder brother, stay outside the door. They were the most difficult group with whom Jesus dealt. Their sins were not obvious, and their needs were unfelt. Some of us stand among the self-righteous. It is self-righteousness which makes worship unreal, fellowship difficult, and brotherhood impossible.—Roy L. Minich.

November 7. To Live Is Christ

TEXT: Phil. 1:21.

Paul lived in Christ. It is Christ who lived in him. It is Christ through whom he could do all things. It is Christ with whom he longed to dwell forever.

I. Christ is his purpose.

II. Christ is his pattern.

III. Christ is his power.

IV. Christ is his prize.—William R. Seaman.

November 14. What the Bible Teaches Concerning Stewardship (Stewardship Day)

I. Nothing is my own; all I have belongs to God. (See Gen. 1:1; Ps. 24:1; Hag. 2:8.)

II. I must give an accounting to God for my use of everything. (See Luke 16:2; Rom. 14:12; I Cor. 4:2.)

III. The tithe is the Lord's and is to be returned to him. (See Lev. 27:30, 32; Mal. 3:8, 10.)

IV. My life and my income are a trust from God to be used as he directs. (See Matt. 25:15, 19–21; Rom. 12:1.)

V. The Christian ought to do more because he is under grace. (See Matt. 5:47–48; 23:23; Luke 12:48; Rom. 6:15.)

VI. I am to give (a) through my church (Mal. 3:10), (b) liberally (Luke 6:38), (c) sacrificially (II Cor. 8:1–4), (d) cheerfully (II Cor. 9:7), and (e) regularly (I Cor. 16:2).

VII. I am to conquer covetousness and to lay up eternal treasures. (See Matt. 6:19–20; Luke 12:15.)

VIII. God will reward the faithful steward. (See Prov. 3:9–10; Mal. 3:10; II Cor. 9:6.)

IX. Self-surrender is the basis of stewardship. (See Rom. 12:1; II Cor. 8:5.)

X. Love is the motive in all my giving. (See John 14:15; Rom. 13:10; II Cor. 5:14.)—Merrill D. Moore.

November 21. The Depth of Thankfulness

SCRIPTURE: Luke 17:11–19.

The story of Jesus' healing of the ten lepers and how only one, a Samaritan, returned to pour out praise and thanksgiving to the Lord remains fascinating and intriguing. We begin to discover here a two-edged exercise in realism.

I. We see ourselves in the nine lepers. They did nothing wrong. The fact is they did exactly what Jesus told them to. Yet somehow we are left with an uncomfortable feeling. Maybe as God's chosen people they had the feeling that healing was their rightful due. It is hard to get carried away with thankfulness if you honestly believe that the good things that come your way are deserved.

II. The Samaritan transcended mere obedience. Joy and thankfulness became his spontaneous language. Perhaps he like the publican and the woman who wept on Jesus' feet didn't feel any sense of deserving God's blessings. Chances are he was even thankful for a few things *in* his leprosy. Profound thanksgiving never exists in spurts. It underlies everything.

III. How does one get that way? (a) Penitence—the admission that we are more like the nine and less like the Samaritan. There is need for depth! (b) Celebrate the possibilities for thankfulness all around us. (c) Practice expressing thanks every day, especially in the little things.—Roger Bourland.

November 28. St. Andrew Speaks to Our Day (St. Andrew's Day)

SCRIPTURE: John 1:41; 6:5–13; 12:20–22.

I. Andrew was a man of decision. He did not hesitate or procrastinate. He saw clearly the choices before him, and he acted immediately to follow Christ without delay and then to communicate and share his enthusiasm with his brother and bring him also to Christ.

II. Andrew was a resourceful man. When the multitude had no food Andrew saw the "lad here who has three loaves and two small fishes." Andrew brought this to the attention of Jesus, and the miracle followed. He helped to bring plenty out of scarcity.

III. Andrew was a hospitable man. When the Greek visitors appeared at the Jewish celebration and inquired how they might see Jesus, Andrew arranged it quickly and quietly. Andrew may have been a vital link between early Christianity and the Greek people because he was cordial, interested, and alert.

IV. Tradition tells us that at the end of his apostleship, Andrew was confronted by those who were determined to crucify him. To this Andrew consented, asking only that he not be crucified in the same manner as his Master but upside down. Hence the Cross of St. Andrew is the symbol X.—Herbert M. Barrall.

December 5. Born of a Virgin

TEXT: The Apostles' Creed.

I. In this space age we are in danger of becoming so earthbound that we evade the possibility of miracles, forgetting the power of God and ignoring the reality of the supernatural. The virgin birth forcibly proclaims that the supernatural came to this world with Christ. As we are challenged by the otherworldly life of Christ, so are we challenged initially by his otherworldly birth.

II. The virgin birth is a unique attestation of the person of the Savior. The redemptive work of Christ depends upon his supernatural birth to the Virgin Mary. When we are asked, "Is the virgin birth historically necessary for salvation?" we must reply affirmatively. This miracle tells us not what we have to do to gain our salvation but what Christ had to become in order to gain our redemption. It tells us that God has intervened on our behalf by a man, bone of our bone, flesh of our flesh. The man dying on Calvary for our sins was no angel sent from heaven but a person born as every other child is born, to a woman.

III. The virgin birth guarantees for us that this man, born to a woman but not by the will of man, is the God-Man. Conceived by the Holy Spirit, this child of Mary's womb does not stand in the fallen sequence of Adam, sharing mankind's guilt and sin. He is man without man's sin. That this is so is demonstrated by the life he lived in relation to his Father during his sojourn in the flesh upon earth. His sinless life, born from Mary, is revealed in his perfect obedience to his Father's will.

IV. The virgin birth is the sovereign God's perfect answer to the problem of how to find a suitable sacrifice for man's sin. The sacrifice must be man yet must be free from man's foul taint. Only in the sinless Son of God, born as a man in this world by the sovereign act of the Spirit in Mary's womb, could such a sacrifice be found.—James Taylor.

December 12. Mary Belongs to Christmas

SCRIPTURE: Luke 1:46–55.

What do her human qualities, reported in scripture and dwelt upon so lovingly in Christian tradition, have to tell us about God's intention for his world?

I. *Mary's humility.* Mary's song, the Magnificat, has been made the church's own, in part because it conveys so simply yet profoundly the true lowliness of faith—eager, expectant, sure of God but not of its own virtue or religiousness.

II. *Mary's obedience.* Mary's obedience has the character of eager fidelity rather than of mere submission. Resignation to God's will for her has already been transcended in a spirit of joyous gravity and resolve: "Let it be to me according to your word."

III. *Mary's relationship to Jesus.* The place of Mary in our faith must always be determined by her relationship to Jesus Christ. That this is a unique and exalted relationship we cannot doubt. It is unlike that of any other human being in both kind and degree. In kind, because of all women God chose this one to bring his Son into the world. And in degree as well, because Mary's maternity is the perfection of human lowliness and obedience before God, hence the inspiration and example for our own.—Roger Hazelton.

December 19. Christmas Contrasts (Christmas)

TEXT: Col. 3:11.

I. Contrasts found in the biblical story of Christ's birth include God and man, divine majesty and human simplicity, the riches of heaven and the poverty of earth, angels and sheep, wise men and simple shepherds, the silence of night and the marvelous music of the angel chorus, the shining splendor of the star and the dim light inside the manger, a great multitude of the heavenly host praising God and a little newborn baby's cry.

II. The wise men had studied the stars, so they were led to Christ. The shepherds were simple unlettered men, but they had a firm belief in the doctrine of angelic ministry. So by means of angels they received the thrilling tidings of the birth of Jesus.

III. The lesson for us all is that, while God speaks differently to different men, his voice and messages are carefully fitted to meet the need and nature of each individual, reaching the right person, in the right way, at the right time, with the right message.—W. J. Thompson.

December 26. The Valley of Decision (Watch Night)

TEXT: Joel 3:4.

I. *We must choose.* Life is full of choices that have to be faced. No one else can choose for us. All our life long we are in the valley of decision.

II. *We can choose.* It is wonderful that we can. We are not robots or marionettes or the plaything of chance. God has given us free will.

III. *We do choose.* That is why we are where we are in this our day. What we choose is reflected in our life and walk. What we choose shapes our future. On the fields of destiny we reap what we have sown. Our decisions judge us, and by them we pass sentence on ourselves. The valley of decision is also the valley of judgment; it is the valley of the verdict.—Ernest Edward Smith.

SECTION III. *Resources for Communion Services*

SERMON SUGGESTIONS

Topic: The Shared Meal
SCRIPTURE: I Cor. 11:17–34.

The shared meal is referred to in three ways in the New Testament, and each has a special significance.

I. Although Protestants do not often use *eucharist*, it is so used in the New Testament of the observance (I Cor. 10:16) of *blessing the cup* and (I Cor. 11:24) *giving thanks* for the bread. The meal is a thanksgiving to God for the *bread of life*, even as at ordinary meals we thank God for material bread.

II. Many groups use the designation *Lord's Supper* for the meal, but it is only called that in I Cor. 11:20. This designation is a reminder of the *memorial* aspect of our Lord's life and sacrifice on our behalf.

III. A third name for the meal is *communion*, which designates the marvelous unity of fellowship between God and man and man and his brothers. The KJV translates I Cor. 10:16 as: "The cup of blessing which we bless, is it not the communion of the blood of Christ? The bread we break, is it not the communion of the body of Christ?" The word for communion is *koinonia* or fellowship. The phrase "the breaking of bread" (Acts 2:42) connotes the same unity.—Ralph H. Elliott in *Christian Herald*.

Topic: Four-Dimensional Living

TEXT: I Cor. 11:24.

In the service of Holy Communion we are led into four directions of great religious experience. We are led backward, outward, upward, and forward.

I. We hear the invitation of Jesus, "Do this in remembrance of me," and at once we are led back through the corridors of time and are reminded of the foundation of our faith.

II. Gathering at Christ's table we are invited to look outward. There is no single act which brings before us our bond of unity with all men quite so readily as the act of Christian worship.

III. As we kneel in humility at this service of Holy Communion we are led upward. It is as we lift our thoughts upward, as we "set our affection on things above," we are having high fellowship with God.

IV. The Lord's Supper can help us to look forward to the experience of the kingdom of God. When we have been led upward into the presence of the Most High God we begin to see challenging opportunities, and our hearts are so filled with enthusiasm for Christ that we feel impelled to give our best energy toward realizing his ideals in the world.—Homer J. R. Elford.

Topic: The Choice of Bread and Wine
TEXT: I Cor. 10:16.

Why did our Lord use bread and wine as the elements of this memorial?

I. No two substances in nature better

36

symbolize unity than bread and wine. As bread is made from a multiplicity of grains of wheat and wine is made from a multiplicity of grapes, so we who are many are one in Christ.

II. No two substances in nature have to suffer more to become what they are than bread and wine. Wheat has to pass through the rigors of winter, be ground beneath the Calvary of a mill, and then be subjected to urging fire before it can become bread. Grapes in their turn must be subjected to the Gethsemane of a wine press and have their life squeezed from them to become wine. Thus do they symbolize the passion and sufferings of our own salvation, for unless we die to ourselves we cannot live in Christ.

III. There are no two substances in nature which have more traditionally nourished men than bread and wine. In bringing these elements we are equivalently bringing ourselves. When we take bread and wine into ourselves they are changed into our body and blood. But he changes them into his body and blood.—Fulton J. Sheen.

Topic: Prodigals at the Table
SCRIPTURE: Luke 15:11–32.

In the parable of the prodigal son Jesus tells how we must be prepared to get the good of forgiveness and oneness with the Father.

I. *The prodigal came to his senses.* He realized what he had done and what a mess he made of his life. He felt the shame of having slipped so low that he was then feeding pigs. This means that we must realize how far we have missed the mark of God's calling.

II. *The prodigal repented.* He decided he would return to his father. He would leave the far country and his present employment. He would go home. That is the meaning of repentance. We will receive no good from the Lord's Supper if we wish to continue living the same after communion as before it. We cannot come to the Lord's table with hatred, spite, and resentment. We cannot expect to return to the old way of living. To be repentant means to

give up and forsake old sinful thoughts, attitudes, and ways of life.

III. *The prodigal had a sense of unworthiness.* He did not ask to be taken back as a son but as a servant. He wanted to be permitted only to work with the other servants as they waited on the father's table or cared for his cattle. He did not feel worthy to be a son again. We must not come to the Lord's table saying to ourselves: "I lived a good life. If anyone has a right to come forward I have." The true Christian who receives forgiveness comes with utmost humility. He knows he is not at all worthy to take the crumbs that fall from the Master's table.

IV. *The prodigal had faith.* It was an act of faith when the prodigal decided to go home. He believed his father was good and merciful enough not to turn him away. The father had every right to say to the wayward boy: "Be gone, you scallawag! You wasted half my savings. You have come to the end of your road. Now you have the nerve to come back and live on me." The prodigal's faith was justified. His father ran to meet him, called for clean clothes, ordered a ring, had water brought for his son's bath, and commanded that a fatted calf be killed. He was overjoyed at his son's return. As he hugged and kissed his boy, the father exclaimed, "This my son which was lost is found again." To get this love and forgiveness from the heavenly Father, we must have the faith to believe Christ is present in the Lord's Supper, ready to receive and to forgive us.—John R. Brokhoff.

Topic: Lessons from Luke
SCRIPTURE: Luke 22:7–27.

I. Jesus wanted and needed the close presence of his comrades in his hour of deepest need and most desperate stress and strain.

(a) And so, under like circumstances, do we! A "solitary" Christian, someone has said, is a contradiction in terms. The pilgrimage of faith was never meant to be a lonely journey for any of us. Like Peter, we also have a ministry to one another. Of this we are reminded every time we approach the communion table. Our religion was not meant to be locked up inside us but to be shared.

(b) Not only the *word* of faith that brings insight and new courage to others but also the *action* that comforts, strengthens, and encourages are part of our ministry to one another in the Christian community.

II. Jesus prepared for his own suffering and death by celebrating a divine victory—the Exodus from Egypt, the event in which for the Hebrews the hand of the living God was more conspicuously and surely evident than anywhere else in human history. He found himself sustained not only by the presence of his friends but also by the traditions and memories of his religious community.

III. Jesus apparently wished to equip his disciples not only for the impending crisis but also for the long range future.

(a) He gave them the cup and the bread in order that they might become for them a sacrament or symbol of a new covenant. As they repeated his actions it was to become an occasion for remembrance and dedication that would remind his followers of their identity as his people in future days.

(b) As the Hebrews celebrated the release of their people from bondage at the Passover supper, so our Lord's disciples were to celebrate his living and dying in age after age. Every time the bread is broken and the cup is shared, it is to be for them a renewal of the covenant of love and loyalty that would continue to exist between him and his people, just as the Passover involved a renewal of their covenant of loyalty and obedience to Jehovah for the Jews of his time as well as today.

IV. Jesus found on this occasion an opportunity to leave the memory of an acted parable with his disciples that sums up more adequately than anything except the cross the mood and thrust of his entire life and ministry. In the act of washing the feet of his disciples he underscored unforgettably the centrality of self-giving and servanthood in his scheme of things.

(a) Something like that ought to be said of you and of me. We too come from God and go to God, and while we are here we are to serve others, making this our primary aim. What we give to life is more important than what we receive. This above all else is the Christian way.

(b) Everyone in need was part of his community of concern. It should be that way with the Christians of our day. We are fully Christian only to the extent that we join him in his ministry of service, however much knowledge, religious insight, or power and prestige it may be our lot to achieve.—Edward C. Dahl.

Meditation: The Peace of God

TEXT: Phil. 4:7.

The peace of God is not to be found in those escape avenues which most of us are exploring. They are deceiving cul-de-sacs. This peace is not discovered by wrestling for it, arguing about it, fighting for it, or chasing every shadow which may hint of its presence.

It dawns on us; it never takes us by storm. It comes, as does a beautiful sunset, a glorious view unfolded in the bend of a road, or an act of love which overwhelms us by its surprise and joy.

God's peace is an unexpected thing because its arrival is always prepared by our own unself-consciousness. It is upon us in those moments when we look beyond ourselves and our desires to the contemplation of the true and the good and the beautiful.

When I forget myself, always an undeliberate action, I come nearest to God. Is that not possible at the conclusion of the Holy Communion service? My heart is full of gratitude to God for his love to me, a sinful man. Through his Son Jesus Christ I have known forgiveness and tasted of the bread of life. Around me are my brothers and sisters, united as one family, helping me by their worship and reverence and sharing in this common joy. Suddenly I look up and there is the Lord's table and standing before it, one of his representatives, assuring all of us of the peace of God. In that moment I can indeed become aware of it and possess it as it possesses me.—Mark Sullivan.

Topic: Communion at Year's End

I. One theme of communion is death and resurrection. The theme is appropriate as one year is dying and another year is beginning. Let this be a time in our lives when the old and dying order is made new in Christ.

II. Let this be a new year in our personal lives—in our worship, study, prayer, stewardship, witness, personal morality, and social responsibility.

III. Let this be a new year in our church—in our outreach, worship vitality, inclusiveness, mutual love, spiritual growth, ministry of reconciliation, and search for truth.

IV. As we come to communion let us examine our personal lives and the life of our church. And let us pray that today will be a time of resurrection and new life for each of us and for our church—Lovett Hayes Weems, Jr.

ILLUSTRATIONS

RECONCILING IMAGE. We need a reconciling image—huge enough to hold all things, compassionate enough to leave nothing in man outside its mercy or insights, holy enough to bring God's blessing, hopeful enough to restore man's trust in life, honest enough to reach the lowest level of earth, touched with shame enough not to equivocate, and faithful enough to labor tirelessly at the endless shaping of the world to fit God's dream.—Samuel H. Miller.

LITURGY. The word "liturgy" comes to us from the Greek. The ancient Greek city-states were surrounded by walls as a bulwark and protection from the assaults of enemies from without. Every male citizen was assigned responsibility for a portion of the city wall. It was his solemn obligation to keep his assigned section of the wall strong and in a state of good repair. The peace and safety of the inhabitants depended upon faithful performance of the liturgy, "the work of the people." We Christians have absorbed the word "liturgy" into our language as one of the more popular names for the Holy Eucharist. Holy work for God's holy people begins in the Eucharist. We *do* the Eucharist. Together, we construct the Eucharist to the praise and glory of God and to the salvation of our souls.—Ferdinand D. Saunders.

A PROPER PREPARATION. One of the most satisfying of all human experiences is participation in the Lord's Supper after proper preparation and in the right spirit. Center your mind upon the joyous possibilities of this act. Before the emblems of broken body and shed blood, memory brings a surge of thanksgiving, gratitude to God for Jesus, for his life, teaching, and living presence. Then comes self-examination when gratitude prompts confession. Unworthiness, failure, and sin are acknowledged, and the soul reaches out for forgiveness and new power. The bread and wine are taken in thankfulness, contrition, and commitment. God becomes more real, communion with the living Lord is more vital, and fellowship with other members of the holy family throbs with a warm sense of solidarity.—Kirby Page.

IDENTITY. On a cold wintry day in 1945 an old missionary was marching with a company of miserable prisoners from one Japanese concentration camp to another. His long life of loving service among these people seemed now to be nearing its end, a bitter end. His strength was ebbing fast. He had not eaten since noon of the day before. His weakened condition made walking difficult. His remaining strength was being quickly sapped by the rapid pace enforced by the guards in the bitter cold. He begged the young guard nearby to let him fall out of line and die in peace.

There was only a curt reply, "Walk on!" He did. But as he got weaker he asked for permission to drop out and die in the ditch. Once again the only reply, "Walk on!" When he asked a third time the guard gave the same cold reply, loud and clear, "Walk on!" But this time he came closer to the old man and whispered, "For we are coming to my grandmother's house." The missionary stumbled on wondering what that could mean. Soon his section of the procession was halted by this young guard, who hurried into a little house by the roadside. He returned quickly, holding something between his hands. He approached the old missionary and ordered him to hold out his hands. Then slipping his hands inside the hands of the old man, he left there—a hot potato. Bending close to the missionary's ear, the young soldier uttered two familiar words from the communion ritual, "Take, eat." Then stepping back, he raised his voice in the familiar gruff command, "Walk on!"

The old man understood. The gruff commands came because the soldier feared his officers. But the soldier's heart was full of sympathy and his use of the words of the ritual, "Take, eat," could mean only one thing: the youth was a Christian.—Hoover Rupert.

THE GOOD NEWS. There are times at the Lord's table when we are forced to think of what we are, of what kind of a place we have made our world, of the reception we have given to our God when in his love he has come to help us and to call us more wholly into his service. Do we not then feel that we have no right at all to his love and his help? All we deserve is that God should cast us off and give us up. This would be justice, but this is not what God has given us. God has not forsaken us as he could have forsaken us. This is the glad news that we can rejoice in as we receive the bread and wine, pledges of his forgiving love, and know that he trusts us to continue to be his servants. —Ronald Wallace.

FIRST EDITION. If we see the fellowship of the disciples with Jesus in the upper room that night as a tiny first edition of the church, we can recognize some of the complexities that are involved in our own congregations. There are streaks of Judas in all of us. The will and intentions of our Lord are not clear to us either. And however faithful we may be —as faithful as Peter even—we are all potential deserters. Clearly the strength in that upper room and the strength in the church is Jesus Christ. He who presided at the table, washed the feet, broke the bread; he who is the head, the life, the power of the church—he is our strength and our peace.—Rudolph W. Raber.

SECTION IV. *Resources for Funeral Services*

SERMON SUGGESTIONS

Topic: How Shall We Think of Our Christian Dead?

TEXT: Rev. 14:13.

I. Our Christian dead are radiantly alive with the life that Christ shares.

II. Our Christian dead are endowed with bodies adapted to that life.

III. Our Christian dead are intimately and indissolubly related to God.

(a) They live in his fellowship constantly. (See Rev. 21:3.)

(b) Their status and security are assured. (See Rev. 7:14.)

(c) They are in God's service. (See Rev. 7:15.)

(d) All of their needs are satisfied. (See Rev. 7:16.)

(e) God throws his protection over them.

(f) God shall heal them of all sorrow. (See Rev. 21:4.)

IV. Our Christian dead live active, interesting, developing lives. (See Rev. 7:17.)—Wallace McPherson Alston.

Topic: The Comfort of Christ

TEXT: Matt. 5:4.

Ours can be a happy grief because it is followed by lasting comfort. (1) Jesus' promise of comfort was more than a passing word of cheer. It was more than a line on a greeting card. It was the assurance of strength and encouragement, of courage and hope.

(2) Jesus' promise of comfort was not just a handshake at the funeral, a thoughtful note at the hospital. It was a declaration of good news, a commitment of everlasting care.

(3) The new age that Jesus heralded with its God-given pattern for happiness brought comfort in ways that men and women had never known before. In Jesus Christ, God came with personal words and deeds of comfort. The God of all comfort was present in the person of Jesus of Nazareth, who called himself the comforter, the counselor, and the one who brought all needed help and strength. When Jesus called the Holy Spirit "another comforter" or "another counselor," what did he mean but that he himself—Jesus—was also a comforter and counselor (John 14:16–17).

I. Jesus' comfort lasts because it is *the comfort of sins forgiven*. It is a comfort that really deals with our problems. Forgiveness is not like a superficial massage that loosens a few muscles but does not reach the real ache. It is deep therapy. It treats not just the symptoms of our mourning but its cause.

II. Jesus' comfort lasts because it is *the comfort of a life renewed*.

(a) The verb "comfort" in the clause "for they shall be comforted" is directly related to the name "comforter" or "counselor" given to the Holy Spirit in John's gospel. Part of the comfort that Jesus promised is the renewing ministry of the Spirit who "dwells with you, and will be in you" (John 14:17). Only to the penitent, to "those who mourn" over their sins, does he come, but when he does he makes all things new.

(b) Forgiveness of sin is followed by a renewed life, committed to God's purposes and blessed by his power. Christ's comfort is not just an initial act of consolation; it is a life-changing relationship. His Spirit is in us if we have become true mourners, and day by day he turns our mourning into happiness.

III. Jesus' comfort lasts because it is *the comfort of a destiny assured.*

(a) The comfort of the new age, the comfort of the good news that Jesus offered so dramatically on the mountain, is a comfort that continues to the end of history—and beyond. Death cannot defeat it; hell cannot conquer it. It is the comfort of God's eternal commitment to the welfare of those who mourn.

(b) One of the last scenes of the Bible describes it beautifully: "He will wipe away every tear from their eyes, and death shall be no more, neither shall there be mourning nor crying nor pain any more, for the former things have passed away" (Rev. 21:4). Then and only then will we know the full happiness that comes to those who mourn. But in the meantime we gladly acknowledge our sin, we gratefully confess our utter need of God, and we begin to mourn our way to happiness.—David Allan Hubbard.

Meditation: The Forerunner

In olden times in harbors of inland waters there was often found what was called an "anchoria." It was a massive rock embedded in the shore.

At times vessels could not make port under their own sail because of storm or calm. At such times a sailor, called a "forerunner," would embark in a small boat. Carrying to shore a stout rope, he would secure one end of it to the anchoria. The crew aboard ship would fasten the other end to a winch. Little by little they would then tighten the rope, and the vessel would be slowly drawn into the harbor.

The writer of Hebrews says, "Jesus has gone as a forerunner on our behalf" (Heb. 6:20, rsv). He has entered the harbor of heaven to secure our souls to the eternal God, our rock. We are attached to him by love's strong cord. Day by day the Holy Spirit draws us closer and will one day bring us to the end of life's voyage to be with God in heaven's harbor.—Duane E. Spencer in *The Upper Room.*

Meditation: Death Is Not Final

As time unfolds the events of our temporal existence, the doings of God accumulate to reveal his purposes. As in any pattern the individual pieces seem valueless and unrelated. Man has yet to see the whole pattern, the whole creation of God—"creature and all." He can but faintly see the sketch and hear the music afar. Not because it is incomplete or sketchy but only because he is listening to the noise of the events and is watching only the movement of now. The symphony of God's creative action is in full orchestration. The movements are complete but continuous and growing.

The cross by its empty self is an experience of pain, but set in the context of the resurrection it comes into full harmony. It is beauty that washes sin away. The cross on a lonely hill is as useless as it is barren until it is set in the experience of the resurrection. The cross unifies. It brings all history into focus. It is always difficult to die. Death is painful, but when you can live again death is not final. When you can live again there is no need for the desperate graspings for meanings, no fear of growing old and the attending need to indulge oneself in the pleasures of this world.—Norman W. Klump.

Topic: The Bright Side of Death

Text: I Cor. 15:55.

There is a bright side since Christ died for our sins and rose again on the third day and lives today, interceding for us before the Father.

I. The bright side of death is eternal

life through Jesus Christ our Lord. (See John 6:40; Rev. 1:18.)

II. The bright side of death because it is God's will and plan that these mortal bodies shall not live forever. (II Cor. 5:1.)

III. The bright side of death in the promise that we do not approach death alone but with the certain assurance that God is there. (See Ps. 23:4.)

IV. The bright side of death in the Christian's understanding of what follows it. (See Luke 23:43; Rom. 8:18; II Cor. 4:17; Rev. 21:4.)

V. The bright side of death to be with Christ. (See John 17:24.)—James McGraw in *The Preacher's Magazine*.

Topic: What the Bible Tells Us about Death

I. The Bible refers to death in four specific ways.

(a) Death is a change of dwelling place. (See II Cor. 5:1.)

(b) Death is a change of locality. (See II Cor. 5:8; John 14:2.)

(c) Death is known in terms of expendability in the service of the Lord. (See Acts 7:54-60.)

(d) Death is likened unto sleep. (See I Thess. 4:13-14.)

II. The Bible tells us four facts about death.

(a) You will be resurrected from the dead. (See I Cor. 15:21-22.)

(b) You will have a resurrected body free from the blemishes of the present. (See I Cor. 15:35-49.)

(c) You will be reunited with your loved ones. (See Matt. 17:1-13.)

(d) You will experience the immediate presence of Christ. (See Luke 23:43.)
—John A. Huffman, Jr.

Topic: How to Deal with Grief

TEXT: Rom. 8:28.

What is the Christian attitude toward grief?

I. *We must learn to look heavenward.* Jesus said that not one sparrow falls but God knows of its falling. God cares. God is interested. This is the first thing to learn. God is not indifferent to our pain.

The lilies bloom and are clothed in all their beauty by a loving God. Nothing on this earth is left to chance. Under the direction of our heavenly Father, man is directed in his steps toward one who cares and loves. In tears or in rejoicing, it is God's care and direction of our lives that is important.

II. *We must learn to lean on others.* Friends care. They may not be able to express in words the deep feelings of their concern but remember that friends care. A man I know had suffered greatly. His life had been swept up in the terrible caldron of sudden tragedy. Many had tried to communicate their concern and Christian love. One man came and was found sitting in a quiet place, shining his friend's shoes. A simple example? But he cared. It is good to lean on friends, for they wish to share in the sorrow.

III. *We must learn to look outward.* Oftentimes sorrow experienced makes our sympathies quicken toward others. In some degree, sorrow makes a man a true representative of our Lord in all his sympathy. There are many others who may have such problems as you have experienced, and you may be the only friend that can truly understand.
—Paul E. Blake.

Topic: The Future Resurrection

TEXT: John 11:25.

I. *The prospect of future resurrection.* (a) Assurance of personal immortality is established early in the annals of patriarchal history. (See Job 19:25-27.)

(b) The action of Abraham attested an abiding conviction in the power and discretion of God thus to perform. (See Heb. 11:17-19.)

(c) David in a later period related his own prospect of eternal life to that of his Messiah. (See Ps. 16:9-11; 17:15.)

(d) The New Testament affirms and amplifies that ancient faith, identifying the resurrection of Jesus Christ, victor over death, hell, and the grave, as both the rationale and the power of that prospect. (See I Cor. 15:12-28; 54-57.)

(e) The believer will be delivered not only from the power and penalty of sin but also from its very presence. (See Heb. 9:28.) That joyous event is designated as the first resurrection. (See Rev. 20:5–6.)

II. *The pattern of future resurrection.* (a) Scripture discusses more the prospect of glorification than the pattern. Paul has asserted that God predestinated the believer "to be conformed to the image of his Son" (Rom. 8:29); John has promised that "we shall be like him" (I John 3:2); but what is the nature of Jesus' glorified body we cannot know certainly.

(b) The nature of that new body remains a mystery. Now we can but "see through a glass, darkly," as it were, in any attempt to discern a pattern. But the scriptures do suggest at least this much: it will be a spiritual body (I Cor. 15:35–50); it will be a substantial body (Luke 24:36–43); it will be a permanent body (John 20:19–29); and it will be a recognizable body (I Cor. 13:12).

(c) Transformation to that higher estate, Paul tells us, will be effected "in a moment, in the twinkling of an eye" (I Cor. 15:52). (See Phil. 3:21.)

(d) In our new bodies we shall be like our risen Lord. And the present indwelling of the Holy Spirit, who has resurrected us from deadness in sins, is the "earnest" of that eternal quality of new life. (See Rom. 8:9, 11; II Cor. 1:22; Eph. 1:13–14; 2:1, 5.) God does all things well, and we have but to trust his discretion.

III. *The pursuit of future resurrection.* (a) The challenge of the gospel is found in I John 3:2–3.

(b) The anticipation of the first resurrection compels one to live circumspectly. Those who would eventually participate in his spiritual body must presently identify with his purity. Hope in Christ motivates us to the pursuit of a holy life.

(c) Glorification will render the order of salvation complete. (See Rom. 8:30.)—

Donald N. Bowdle in *Church of God Evangel.*

ILLUSTRATIONS

THE WORD OF JESUS. Philosopher may come up with a dozen argument for life after death. They tell us our lives are incomplete and unfinished there must be a continuation; there must be a reward or retribution in the next world by which the injustices and unfairness of life can be adjusted, it wrongs righted, its losses compensated its sins atoned. But all of this argumen of philosophy is not enough for me I have the word of Jesus, given with certainty, conviction, and truth. He said, "Because I live, you will live also." As far as I am concerned the issue i closed.—Billy Graham.

THE SAME VOICE. When I shall enter the invisible world I do not expect to find things different from what the Word of God represented them to me here. The voice I shall then hear will be the same I now hear upon the earth and I shall say, "This is indeed wha God said to me; and how thankful am that I did not wait till I had seer in order to believe."—Adolph Monod

THE GLORY OF THAT DAY. How di vinely full of glory and pleasure shal that hour be when all the millions o mankind that have been redeemed b the blood of the Lamb shall meet to gether and stand around him with every tongue and every heart full o joy and praise. How astonishing will be the glory and the joy of that day when all the saints shall join together in one common song of gratitude and of love and of everlasting thankfulness to the Redeemer! With what unknown delight and inexpressible satisfaction shall all that are saved from the ruins of sin and hell address the Lamb that wa slain and rejoice in his presence.—Isaac Watts.

FINEST FLOWERING. There are obviou

incompletions in this life that seem almost to require a period beyond if our strivings are really to matter. To deny this would be to deny that God in whom we profess to believe is a purposing deity who cares what we do. There are obvious injustices in this life which equally seem almost to require a hereafter with its chance for righting wrongs if the God we worship is indeed righteous. Spiritual qualities and attainments come to their finest flowering in those who have most fully lived the life of God in Christ. If these mountaintops of human living are of no lasting significance, belief in a God of goodness and power is itself hardly significant.—G. Gardner Monks.

TRIANGLE OF LOVE. In the triangle of love between ourselves, God, and other people is found the secret of existence and the best foretaste, I suspect, that we can have on earth of what heaven will probably be like.—Samuel M. Shoemaker.

THINKING OF REST. Let us think much of rest, the rest which is not in indolence but of powers in perfect equilibrium. The rest which is as deep as summer midnight yet full of life and force as summer sunshine, the sabbath of eternity. Let us think of the love of God which we shall feel in its full tide upon our souls. Let us think of that marvelous career of sublime occupation which shall belong to the spirits of just men made perfect, when we shall fill a higher place in God's universe and more consciously, and with more distinct insight cooperate with God in the rule over his creation.—Frederick W. Robertson.

OCCUPIED WITH HEAVEN. If you read history you'll find that the Christians who did the most for the present world were just those who thought most of the next. The apostles themselves, who set on foot the conversion of the Roman Empire, the great men who built up the Middle Ages, the English evangelicals who abolished the slave trade, all left their mark on earth precisely because their minds were occupied with heaven.—C. S. Lewis.

ETERNAL LIFE NOW. In so far as I am willing to be made an instrument of God's peace, in that far have I already entered into eternal life. Heaven to me is here, and whatever else it may be, I can know it now in so far as I am the instrument of that peace. What happens to me after I die, I do not know, nor do I really want to know. I have no evidence on which to deny that there is life after death, but what kind of life it would be, I have no idea. So let us think and reflect more on the proposition that we are even now in eternal life, and whatever happens after the physical death, we do so continue, for we are in God's will, and God's will continues.—Alan Paton in *Instrument of Thy Peace.*

A SPECIAL FEELING. Our attitude toward all men would be Christian if we regarded them as though they were dying and determined our relation to them in the light of death, both of their death and our own. A person who is dying calls forth a special kind of feeling. Our attitude to him is at once softened and lifted on to a higher plane. We then can feel compassion for people whom we did not love. But every man is dying. I too am dying and must never forget about death.—Nicolas Berdyaev.

UNSATISFIED DESIRES. If I find in myself a desire which no experience in this world can satisfy, the most probable explanation is that I was made for another world.—C. S. Lewis.

COURAGEOUS WITNESS. Daniel T. Niles told of some missionaries who had labored long and hard among the members of an African tribe until finally one family became Christians. Now the future of their ministry to that tribe seemed to depend on the future of that family. What should happen but the child in that home contracted a terrible sickness. The parents prayed for his recovery. The missionaries prayed as seldom before that God would hold back this enemy death and thereby show these superstitious folk the power of Christian faith. But, lo, the child died. The missionaries went on with their work, but the prospects did not seem too bright. Three months later the leaders of the tribe came to the missionary hut and said, "We too want to become Christians." The missionaries were startled and wanted to know why. The answer was simple. "We want to have a God who makes us strong to face death. We have never seen death faced the way you and the parents of the boy faced it."— H. Louis Patrick.

AUTHORITATIVE WORDS. Sometimes in dark caves men have gone to the edge of unspeaking precipices and, wondering what was the depth, have cast down fragments of rock and listened for the report of their fall that they might judge how deep that blackness was; and listening, still listening—no sound returns, no sudden splash, no clinking stroke as of rock against rock—nothing but silence, utter silence! And so I stand upon the precipice of life. I sound the depths of the other world with curious inquiries. But from it comes no echo and no answer to my questions. No analogies can grapple and bring up from the depths of darkness of the lost world the probable truths. No philosophy has line and plummet long enough to sound the depths. There remains for us only the few authoritative and solemn words of God.—Henry Ward Beecher.

A CARING GOD. There is the peace which passes knowledge and strength made perfect in weakness. There is the daily bread broken by the pierced hands of the Most High God. For fellowship we have the glorious company of the church visible and invisible.

However great the suffering, there is for our enabling the grace of the Lord Jesus Christ and the love of God and the fellowship of the Holy Spirit.— Maldwyn Edwards.

CONVICTION. We cannot resist the conviction that this world is for us only the porch of another and more magnificent temple of the Creator's majesty.— Frederick William Faber.

PRAYERS

THE ASSURANCE OF FAITH. Our Father and our God, thou knowest the loneliness of hearts that are broken because of the vacant chair in the home, the absence of our loved one. And because thou art able to fathom the depths of all sorrow and assuage all grief we put our trust in thee.

Thy love does not end at the grave. We know it follows us into every experience of life that is eternal. May we feel thy nearness to us as we realize that our "life is but a moment of eternity lived in time." Bless us with the assurances of faith that crosses every chasm and bids us follow the gleam of life that conquers death, that travels on beyond the cycles of the years.

May those memories which linger in our benighted souls remind us of thy love and so become the tie which binds us closer in the bonds of life eternal. Make us brave and grateful for those who have walked this path beside us. More particularly do we ask thy blessing upon those near and dear to one "whom we have loved long since, and lost awhile."

Our fellowship was so beautiful, and now we know that thou art able to unite our lives through the assurance of faith in Christ. May our faith be so strengthened that all who share thy blessing may have thy eternal presence. —John Lewis Sandlin.

ACQUAINTED WITH GRIEF. O Man of sorrows and acquainted with grief, who knowest the depth of human pain, grant us grace to read our tragedies in the context of eternal love. Help us to know, even when we cannot understand, that in all things the Father worketh for good with those who love him; and teach us to do our part. Help us to realize that though the price of human love is the risk of loss, only through the love of those we have seen may we understand how to love him whom we have not seen. Grant that through our sorrow we may see more deeply into the hearts of all who suffer; and strengthen our hands to help. O Lord, open our eyes to behold the reality of the world unseen, where live the blessed dead in thy companionship.—Charles T. Webb.

THY EVERLASTING ARMS. Eternal God, thou who art from everlasting to everlasting, we draw near to thee with the confidence that thou art already turned toward us in the eternity of thy love. We thank thee that as we walk through the valley of the shadow of death we can know the strength of thy everlasting arms. For thy Word, which is as a lamp unto our feet and as a light unto our pathway in the shadows of this hour, we are grateful. That in the presence of death we can celebrate a life that is kept in thy livingness, we thank thee. For the fellowship of thy church, where we can bare our souls to one another and not be misunderstood, where we can be natural and not be censored, where we can weep and not be chagrined, and where we can laugh in the presence of death and not be thought frivolous, we are grateful.

In our weakness may we know thy strength; in our sorrow may we know thy comfort; in our perplexity may we know thy light. Through him who is our life.—John Thompson.

SECTION V. Resources for Small Groups

BACKGROUND MATERIALS

WHAT ARE SMALL GROUPS. They are relatively small, ranging from eight to eighteen members. They meet as a self-conscious unit over a long enough period of time to develop a fairly intense sense of groupness, usually fifteen to twenty hours minimum. They meet in a relatively unstructured, agendaless way with a goal of greater awareness of self in relationship to others. Often some content is introduced, but the subject matter develops naturally rather than being formally introduced. The role of the leader is characteristically more of a catalyst than it is that of an authority. He strives to create a climate conducive to growth rather than to become the answer man. The focus is more on feeling than it is on rational thought, although a good deal of cognitive learning actually takes place. —Robert C. Leslie in *Sharing Groups in the Church* (Nashville: Abingdon Press, 1971).

SMALL GROUP STRUCTURES. There are many kinds of groups that can be developed within the churches. The following, while not intended to be a complete summary, is indicative of some of the major directions groups may take.

Person-centered groups. — Sometimes called "spiritual growth" groups or "encounter" groups or "listening" groups, this type of group places a premium on a person's feelings, responses, and reactions. The interaction of persons is uppermost. Sharing and listening are the two principal directives. Discovery and acceptance of the other are the results. One possible disadvantage in this kind of group is that a highly skilled resource person is usually required. A person who understands group dynamics should be present to interpret and to evaluate interaction to the group. Otherwise, hurt feelings, unresolved conflicts, and personal frustrations can easily result.

Mission-centered groups. — Some groups meet to prepare themselves for service in the community. Their principal purpose is not so much personal sharing as personal ministry outside the group. This approach is more program centered than person-centered.

Bible study groups.—The Greek word *koinonia* is used to describe these groups. This New Testament word is an especially rich one. It means fellowship, participation, communion, and sharing. *Koinonia* rather than "Bible study" better describes the pervasive variety of dynamics that occurs in the group. Bible study is important, and it is one of the activities. But self discovery, personal sharing, prayer, and supportive ministry also take place.

Bible study is an effective means of structuring the group for several reasons. The Bible is the beginning of the group's focus. Some persons may

48

be too threatened to come into a "self-discovery" group, a "personal sharing" group, or a "prayer" group. These terms are too subjective for some. Self-discovery may well happen, sharing will no doubt occur, and prayer will be meaningful; but Bible study supplies a more positive, nonthreatening approach. The Bible provides objective, authoritative material that guards against the group's becoming a psychiatrically oriented "group therapy" unit. Bible study also supplies theological rootage for facing the social issues of the day.—Thomas Conley in *On Becoming a Group* (Nashville: Broadman Press, 1974).

ESSENTIAL ELEMENTS. Essential elements for small groups in a church seem to be: (1) *a definable membership* meeting on a regular basis in a face-to-face relationship—this means that persons cannot just drop in to "sample" whenever they feel like it, nor can persons visit from time to time without making a commitment to the other group members; (2) there develops a sense of *common identity* which says that the group achieves a group consciousness of itself; (3) at the same time the group develops a *common purpose* which holds it on a definite direction; (4) a binding sense of *interdependence* emerges which can be labeled as "community" for all are participants (there are no spectators) and such elements as acceptance, mutual accountability, trust, honesty, risking, caring, sharing, and commitment are present; and (5) there grows out of the group a *self-administered discipline* (some would call this the "group contract," but it usually involves those things that hold persons accountable for personal growth and mutual support).—William Clemmons and Harvey Hester in *Growth through Groups* (Nashville: Broadman Press, 1974).

CHANNELS. Groups can and should be a mission extension of every local church. When church members are the nuclei around which groups form, many neighborhoods can be penetrated. The home can be neutral ground for weekly meetings at which people from any tradition could feel free to gather. Church members would be using the channels of relationship already established to deepen those relationships and to communicate the meaning of their life in Christ to others in the group.—Keith Harris in *On Becoming a Group* (Nashville: Broadman Press, 1974).

BIBLIOGRAPHY. John L. Casteel, editor, *The Creative Role of Interpersonal Groups in the Church,* New York: Association Press, 1968. William Clemmons and Harvey Hester, *Growth through Groups,* Nashville: Broadman Press, 1974. Howard J. Clinebell, Jr., *The People Dynamic,* New York: Harper & Row, 1972. John Hendrix, editor, *On Becoming a Group,* Nashville: Broadman Press, 1974. Robert C. Leslie, *Sharing Groups in the Church,* Nashville: Abingdon Press, 1971. Clyde Reid, *Groups Alive— Church Alive,* New York: Harper & Row, 1969. Carl Rogers, *On Encounter Groups,* New York: Harper & Row, 1970.

DISCUSSION SUGGESTIONS

Topic: Christian Horizons
  I. Transforming our ideas.
  II. Developing our characters.
  III. Forgiving our sins.
  IV. Solving our problems.
  V. Expanding our sympathies.
  VI. Enlarging our influence.
  VII. Stimulating our ambitions.
  VIII. Energizing our wills.
  IX. Answering our prayers.
  X. Loving our enemies.
  XI. Sanctifying our homes.
  XII. Dedicating our lives.
  XIII. Determining our destinies.

Topic: What in the World Is God Doing?
  I. God active in society as father and creator.
  II. God active as revealer and teacher.

III. God active as revealer of righteousness.

IV. God active as ruler in righteousness.

V. God active in society in the worth of all persons.

VI. God active in society as redeemer.

VII. God active in Jesus Christ.

Topic: We Shall Overcome

I. Overcoming pretenses (Matt. 6:1–15).

II. Overcoming anxiety (Matt. 6:24–34).

III. Overcoming the urge to be critical (Matt. 7:1–6).

IV. Overcoming error (Matt. 7:15–23).

V. Overcoming the tempest (Matt. 7:24–27).

VI. Overcoming the lust for wealth (Luke 12:13–21).

VII. Overcoming lust (I Thess. 4:1–7).

VIII. Overcoming selfishness (I Cor. 10:23–33).

IX. Overcoming our divisions (I Cor. 11:17–22).

X. Overcoming racial individualism (I Cor. 12:1–27).

XI. Overcoming confusion (I Cor. 14:20–33).

XII. Overcoming externals (Matt. 15:1–20).

XIII. Overcoming divided loyalties (Matt. 18:7–14).

XIV. Overcoming bitterness (Matt. 18:21–35).

XV. Overcoming our possessions (Matt. 19:16–22).

XVI. Overcoming our aggressiveness (Matt. 20:20–28).

XVII. Overcoming sanctified evil (Matt. 21:12–17).—*Today*.

Topic: Involved Christians

I. What *in the world* are you doing? (John 4:35.)

II. What *in the secular world* are you doing? (I Cor. 9:22–23, NEB.)

III. What *in the religious world* are you doing? (II Chron. 7:14.)

IV. What *in your personal world* are you doing? (Luke 10:33–34.)—William Fisher.

Topic: If I Be His Disciple

I. I will grow into his likeness (Eph. 4:14–17). (a) The need for growth. (b) Elements of growth. (c) Evidences of growth. (d) The goal of our growth.

II. I will grow in reflecting his spirit every day (John 15:1–11; Jas. 2:14–24).

III. I will grow in meeting life's crises (John 15:4–5; Rom. 8:28; Phil. 4:8, 11, 13, 19; Eph. 6:10–13).

IV. I will grow more sensitive to human needs (Matt. 9:10–13, 11:2–5; Mark 6:35–43; Luke 18:15–17; John 4:6–30, 8:3–7).

V. I will grow in using my life for him. (a) Why should we serve? Because we love. (See Lev. 19:18; I John 4:20.) (b) Why should we serve? Because we know. (See John 13:17.) (c) How can we serve? By seeing and answering need. (See Matt. 14:15–24.)

Topic: Where Jesus Walked

I. Nazareth: Growth of Jesus (Luke 2:40–52).

II. The Jordan: Baptism of Jesus (Matt. 3:13–17).

III. The wilderness of Judea: The Temptation (Matt. 4:1–11).

IV. Jacob's well: The woman of Sychar (John 4:1–26).

V. The synagogue: Jesus at worship (Luke 4:16–30).

VI. Sea of Galilee: Calling disciples (Luke 5:1–11).

VII. Sea of Galilee: Feeding the hungry (John 6:1–15).

VIII. Mt. Hermon: The transfiguration. (Matt. 17:1–8).

IX. Tyre and Sidon: A pleading mother (Matt. 15:21–28).

X. Perea: Hiring the laborers (Matt. 20:1–16).

XI. Jericho: Jesus and Zacchaeus (Luke 19:1–10).

XII. Bethany: The anointing of Jesus (Matt. 26:6–13).

XIII. The upper room: The last supper (Matt. 26:17–29).

XIV. Gethsemane: The agony of Jesus (Matt. 26:36–46).

XV. The courtyard: The trials of Jesus (Matt. 26:57–68).

XVI. Calvary: The death of Jesus (Matt. 27:32–50).

XVII. Joseph's garden: The resurrection (Matt. 28:1–10).

XVIII. The upper room: The benediction (John 20:19–29).

Theme: Jesus, Pray for Us

I. Pray that we may have eternal life (John 17:3).

II. Pray that we may be kept secure (John 17:11).

III. Pray for our sanctification (John 17:17).

IV. Pray for our unity (John 17:21).

V. Pray that we may go to heaven (John 17:24).—Harold J. Ockenga.

Theme: Ephesians: The Beginnings of the Christian Life

I. Redemption from sin (Eph. 1:5, 7).

II. Rescue from darkness (Eph. 5:8).

III. Resurrection from death (Eph. 2:1).

IV. Release from captivity (Eph. 2:2, 6).

V. Return from exile (Eph. 2:12–13).

VI. Reconciliation from enmity (Eph. 2:14, 16).—John Macbeath.

Theme: The Great Physician

I. The Great Physician's character. (See Luke 6:17–19.) (a) His wisdom was peerless, and his insights and judgments were perfect. (b) He felt deep compassion for every needy person. (c) He possessed an overflowing, compelling love.

II. The Great Physician's diagnostic skill. (See Luke 5:27–31.) (a) Jesus was so sensitive to physical, mental, and ethical abnormalities that he never failed to detect them and never made an error in identifying them. (b) In his examination Jesus went to the focus of the infection. He never mistook symptoms for the disease itself. (c) He took into consideration the whole person and all the factors contributing to his condition.

III. The Great Physician's treatment. (See Luke 6:7–10.) (a) Our Lord insisted upon a clean operation and prescribed complete removal of the evil virus or the baleful malignancy. (b) He inspired confidence. (c) He required personal initiative, personal effort, and the use of available resources. (d) He gave the patient a sense of personal worth and endowed life with meaningfulness. (e) He encouraged appreciation of personal excellence. (f) He developed high self-respect in people by revealing that a person is a child of a loving and divine father and has a spiritual mission.—A. C. Reid.

SECTION VI. Resources for Lenten and Easter Preaching

SERMON SUGGESTIONS

Topic: Once and for All for Sins

TEXT: I Pet. 3:18.

I. *Sin and the settlement of the cross.* "Christ . . . died once and for all." (a) The singularity of this settlement lies in the uniqueness of Christ, and Christ alone is able to make settlement.

(b) The sufficiency of the settlement should be noted. Unlike the Old Testament sacrifices, our Lord's sacrifice is adequate for all sins, for all men, and for all time.

II. *Sin and the sacrifice of the cross.* "Christ . . . died . . . for sins." (a) A relinquishment. Christ laid down his life.

(b) A redemption. We were bought for a price.

(c) A reconciliation. Christ laid down his life in order that we might have access to the Father.

III. *Sin and the substitution of the cross.* "Christ . . . died . . . the just for the unjust." The efficacy of Christ's work on the cross depended on his innocence.

(a) That he was innocent is the testimony of his birth.

(b) That he was innocent is the testimony of his life.

(c) That he was innocent is the testimony of his death.

IV. *Sin and the solution of the cross.* "Christ . . . died . . . that he might bring us back to God." The word translated "bring" has, as Barclay points out, a twofold background.

(a) It is of Jewish lineage, meaning the bringing of those who were to be priests to God. But as Barclay puts it, "Jesus brings *us* to God!"

(b) It is of Greek lineage, meaning "access." Thus we are enabled to enter into the very presence of God.—Arthur G. McPhee.

Topic: Experiencing Calvary

TEXT: I Cor. 2:2.

I. The cross is the way of salvation. It is the only way to come to God, the only means of salvation, the only bridge from sinful man to holy God. Thus it is emphasized in the law, the psalms, the prophets, the gospels, and the epistles. It is the essence of the gospel which is presented throughout the Bible.

II. The second way of experiencing the cross is for sanctification or victory of Christian life. The believer accepts the cross as the means of his dying to the old man. He takes his position with Christ as crucified to the old nature and the motions of sin. By faith he reckons himself to be dead. Once the believer so accepts the cross, he may then be united with Christ in resurrection life. By the Spirit he is quickened and seated with Christ in heavenly places. Thus the resurrected, glorified, reigning Christ may release the Spirit in the life of the crucified and resurrected believer, producing all the fruit of the Spirit which makes the believer like unto Christ.

III. The third meaning of the cross in Christian experience is as a way of service or of living. The principle was set down by the Lord Jesus when he said, "Except a corn of wheat fall to the ground and die, it abideth alone, but if it die it bringeth forth much fruit." The cross must become a constant way of life. The believer must voluntarily accept his position of self-denial, sacrifice, and service for Christ's sake. In so far as he does this, he shall bear fruit, for "he that loses his life for my sake shall find it." Only as the believer voluntarily follows the pattern laid down by Christ in his acceptance of crucifixion is he able to effectively serve the Lord.—Harold John Ockenga.

Topic: Looking Toward the Cross
TEXT: John 8:28.

I. Jesus went to the cross with determination. Satan tried to deter him from his divine purpose at the beginning of his ministry. Later Peter said protestingly, "No, Lord, this must not happen to thee." Then when he was crucified those who witnessed the event challenged Jesus to come down from the cross.

II. Jesus went to the cross obediently, knowing well that this was the path his heavenly Father had marked out for him. The cross marks the supreme hour of self-surrender in the life of Christ.

III. Jesus went to the cross in actuality. There was reality about his death on Calvary. There was reality when the awful burden of the cross was laid on him. There was reality when he fainted under its weight. There was reality when the nails were driven through his hands and feet. There was reality when the fever burned his body and he said, "I thirst." There was reality when he yielded up his spirit and cried, "It is finished."

Topic: On Getting Involved
TEXT: Matt. 12:27.

I. To choose to be involved in behalf of the highest is never easy, and even for Jesus Christ it was a struggle. To see him coming into Jerusalem riding upon a colt and then moving past the crowd to cleanse the temple is to see the acts of a man with his mind made up. But when one acts with such determination and delicate precision it is evidence that somewhere he has had a period of struggle and hard decision. We are impressed by great figures in history who act with their minds made up and their resolutions firm. But before we see them in public, even these pass through hesitations, doubts, and mental struggles. Decision for the highest is never easy.

II. For Jesus the personal struggle was intensified, for his was a twofold choice.

(a) To give his life in the pursuit of God's purpose he would seek first God's kingdom, and God's kingdom includes the greatest good for all. This much of Jesus' decision could be termed a popular choice. People of his day, as men of our day, wanted the best for all.

(b) Having made God's purpose his goal, Jesus believed that it could only be attained through the use of God's methods. Here he found himself constantly in the arena of conflict. He believed that means determine the ends, that you do not destroy one man or one nation to achieve good for another. If the kingdom of love was the goal, then love was the only way by which it could be obtained.

III. To involve oneself in God's purpose and God's method and to live only by broad sympathy and high ideals is to experience conflict. When he declared himself wholly and only on the side of good, those not ready to be good turned against him. Many whom Jesus would like to have had for friends became his enemies. Some who had earlier shouted "Blessed be he" now were yelling "Crucify him!"

IV. To choose the highest is to be willing to let some things go. We cannot have everything; some things must be put down so other things can be picked up. Whoever begins the journey to the kingdom of love had better be prepared to leave some things to the wolves. Choice is made because we cannot have everything.

V. In commitment there is a sense of

mission. With Jesus Christ we too can be involved in the very work of God. We do not need to be spectators in the bleachers; we are meant for action in the game.

VI. To be involved on the side of Jesus Christ is to be so concerned that the will of God be done on earth that one strives to make his own life Godlike. Now one prays not only "Thy will be done" but also "Thy will be done beginning with me." The unsolved problems in our world are not the result of the scenery; they are centered instead in the actors. Because so much is at stake we who are the players need the help of Christian commitment.—Wesley P. Ford.

Topic: What Palm Sunday Says to Us
TEXT: Luke 9:51.

I. Go into the city. (a) Go where the people are. Go into the hospitals, into the slums, into the prisons, into the depressed areas. Don't hang back in the safety of the shadows. Don't be afraid of getting involved in life at the point of its greatest confusion and despair. Aim at the trouble spots—war and peace, human rights and responsibilities, law and order, juvenile delinquency, and the care of the aged. You cannot hit them all. You can avoid them only at your own peril.

(b) Go into the city the way Jesus went. He didn't have to. He could have stayed in Galilee, safe and sound in the shadows of obscurity, teaching and preaching by the lakeside till the end of his days.

II. Go to the temple, as Jesus went to the temple the next day and in his own way cleaned it. He cleared out the people who were doing business in the place where the Gentiles were supposed to be free to worship.

(a) Go to the church; make it a house of prayer; make it a powerhouse of the spirit, not a religious gymnasium where people simply go through their exercises day by day, not really knowing what they mean or why they do them.

(b) Make it a place where men and women can find God. They do not talk

much about God now, but don't think that they don't need him. Their hearts thirst for God just as truly as they thirsted for him when the psalmist wrote, "My soul is athirst for God."

III. Go unarmed; go without a weapon, the way Jesus went into Jerusalem.

(a) Men will never live without any weapons at all. So long as one man forces his way into another man's house and attacks him or his wife or his child, that other man will do the best he can to force him out; and if he needs a weapon to do it he will use a weapon.

(b) There are some things that you cannot do by force. You cannot force a child to grow up, no matter how strong the force may be. You cannot possibly force two people to love each other. You cannot force a person to be good.

(c) Faith means believing what you know but cannot see and cannot prove beyond the shadow of a doubt. Faith is loving what you cannot force. Faith is daring what you cannot do. Faith is acting in the present and leaving the future with God.

IV. Go simply, the way Jesus went, just as he was, without any pretense or any outward show of power or prestige.

(a) It is amazing how that young man dared to ride into the hostile city of Jerusalem without any protection, without any security whatever, just as he was, depending only upon himself and his Father. He had always been like that. He came from simple people, but he had a large following in Galilee. Popularity goes to a man's head more quickly than almost anything else. But it did not go to his. He was as simple when he rode into Jerusalem as he was in his own hometown.

(b) We are always tempted to put on airs. When we do well we are tempted to let everyone know it; and when we do not do well we try to cover it up with the uniform of our position and exercise more vigorously than ever our authority. We try to exert our authority by relying on things that are not in ourselves but outside ourselves.—Theodore P. Ferris.

Topic: Five Gardens

I. Eden is the garden of infancy. We all begin life here, and unless we are sheltered, cared for, loved, and our every essential need met, we perish. Humanity must always begin in Eden; the tragedy ensues when man tries to stay there.

II. The garden of Solomon is the garden of youth, yet youth is an essential and joyous part of life. It is in youth when the burgeoning of human love with all its tumultuous and strange experiences transforms permanently the whole meaning of living.

III. Gethsemane is the garden of tragedy, sorrow, suffering. This is the garden of moral conflict. This is the garden where a man must face the awful challenge: "If it be thy will let this cup pass from me; yet thy will, not mine, be done." The garden of Gethsemane is the place of spiritual maturity.

IV. In the Resurrection garden man achieves his union with immortality and the assurance of his rightful destiny. As the garden of Gethsemane is the place of moral decision, so the garden of the Resurrection is the place of moral victory.

V. The garden of the New Jerusalem is a garden with streets of gold and gates of precious jewels. Here flows the river of the water of life, and the tree of life is there—the tree whose leaves are given for the healing of the nations.

Topic: As It Began to Dawn

TEXT: Matt. 28:1.

Our Easter faith stresses life not death, dawn not darkness, hope not despair, faith not doubt, and love not hate.

I. It is grounded in the love of God.
II. It is centered in the integrity of the universe itself.
III. It is a way of eternal life revealed through Christ that we may experience here and now.

IV. It makes a difference in our attitude toward others.
V. It is an affirmation that those deathless values we know in Christ may become our own.
VI. It is the assurance that life's great adventure is always on ahead.—Frank A. Court.

ILLUSTRATIONS

PATTERN OF PRIVATION. The forty week-days of Lent reflect a pattern of privation in scripture—the people of God forty years in the wilderness, our Lord's forty days of temptation, and the forty black hours in the tomb before Easter. If life is to be affirmed at a higher level it must be deprived at a lower level. Those who followed Moses deprived themselves of the fleshpots of Egypt; our Lord conquered megalomaniacal dreams; and God himself gave up his one incarnate life. In each instance the self or some aspect of it was considered disposable. This then is the nub of Lent, that its celebrants do without something in memory of him who did without everything, in penitence for betraying him who betrayed no one, and in prayer that we shall have the courage to take his yoke upon us.—Willis E. Elliott.

EVERY WEEK IS HOLY. There is danger that the emphasis upon Holy Week will develop the idea that only one week in the year is holy. Anyone who lives according to this idea might be considered only one fifty-second of a Christian. To the genuine Christian every week is a holy week. The need for God is not a matter of the calendar. The value of the Christ-spirit in our lives is as great every week as it is during the period which we call Holy Week. The need for strength, understanding, courage, comfort, and peace is constant. The idea of the hymn, "I Need Thee Every Hour," is far more than a matter of poetry. It is a necessity of life.—L. Wendell Fifield.

BONHOEFFER ON FASTING. In The Cost of Discipleship, Dietrich Bonhoeffer suggested that "strict exercise of self-control is an essential feature of the Christian's life." These religious customs have but one purpose—to make Christians eager to accomplish those things which God would have done. Fasting, according to Bonhoeffer, disciplines the self-indulgent and slothful will that is so reluctant to serve God. "If there is no element of asceticism in our lives, if we give free rein to the desires of the flesh . . . we shall find it hard to train for the service of Christ." It is hard, he continued, to devote oneself to a life of service when the flesh is satisfied.

Bonhoeffer suggested further that when the Christian has lost his joy in God and has grown weary of prayer, it is time to prepare for better service by fasting and praying. We should never let prayer and Bible study grow stale because sleep, food, and sensuality have deprived us of the joy of communion with God.— W. M. Carmichael.

THE PERSPECTIVE OF GOD. Salvador Dali, the surrealist painter, has a breath-taking view of the crucifixion. In his "Christ of St. John of the Cross" you seem to look down from above with the perspective of God. It tears your heart out. Can you understand the cross except from the perspective of God? You are involved here. You are challenged to decide, to respond. Here God is making his last-ditch attempt to bring you to your senses and to himself. Here he is hammering out our eternal well-being.— George W. Eberhard.

CROSS AND CROWN. When the body of King George V was being taken through the streets of London, his crown was placed on his coffin. A part of the symbolism of the crown is the cross, and as the gun carriage rumbled along that cross was shaken loose and fell to the street. Immediately one of the sailors picked it up and said to his commanding officer, "This cross, sir, must be replaced." The officer did not wish to hold up the procession and he asked, "Must it be replaced now?" "Yes, sir," replied the sailor, "the crown is never complete without the cross."—Howard C. Scharfe.

WHY THE CROSS? Citizens of Boulder, Colorado, erected a huge cross on the side of Flagstaff Mountain, which overlooks the city. Every year during Holy Week this cross is lighted and is visible for many miles around. It is a source of inspiration. One day a small boy asked his father why this cross had been put there. The father tried to explain what it meant in terms of Christ's suffering and atonement but felt that his explanation was not adequate to the child's understanding. Then suddenly a light dawned on the boy's face. He cried: "Oh, I see. The cross means God is looking after us."—Edith L. Gibson.

TILL HE COME. The table of the Lord stands between those two marvelous epochs, the cross and the advent—the death and the glory. The believer can look up from the table and see the beams of the glory gilding the horizon. It is our privilege as we gather around the Lord's table to show forth the Lord's death till he come and to be able to say: "This may be the last occasion of celebrating this precious feast. Ere another Lord's day dawn upon us, he himself may come."—Charles H. Morris.

THE GIVING OF SELF. The heart of Christianity is a cross. Not a balance sheet nor a prudential calculation about how much to give or keep but a cross. The cross is the furthest thing in the world from neutrality. It is not a symbol to be pulled or twisted in any way one likes. Though we sing about it in our hymns, paint it with gold in our churches, and emblazon it on our flags it is in fact something quite removed from any of these. The cross is the actual sacrifice of all that one has for the kingdom of God. It is the literal giving of oneself in the most absolute fashion imaginable, reserving nothing for oneself, not even life.—Robert J. Arnott.

CHASM BRIDGED. The effect of the resurrection upon the modes of human thought, upon the hopes and aspirations of the human heart, upon the ways and means of human endeavor, transcends the abilities of the human mind. It has bridged the chasm between the known and the unknown, scourged the trembling fears from the temple of the heart, and poured into the dark recesses of the tomb the radiance of undying light and glory.—Henry S. Lobinger.

THE SERMON ON EASTER DAY. Easter is a day on which the best Christians are hardly in a mood for sermons. Their hearts are full of joy, and they come to church as they would come to a wedding, to make their congratulations and to utter their hymns of joy and praise to the King of kings on the anniversary of his great victory. Their hearts say more to them than any fellow man can possibly say, and much of what their hearts tell them cannot well be rendered into human language. They wish to be left alone with their joy. Sermons, they say, are very well in seasons and on days of penitence, but when the heart is bursting with triumphant emotion sermons either lag behind our feelings or are out of harmony with them. And for this reason it has been said that a sermon on Easter requires an apology.—H. P. Liddon.

TWO DAYS. The little company of women who were last at the cross came first to the tomb. But they were not the first. Life was there first; hope broke out of the tomb before they came. Life and hope and immortality and love shook that tomb with an earthquake, and angels sped to earth to tell the news to men. The women came and found a broken tomb and the angels there before them. They came to the tomb to find death and found life. They came sorrowing; they left rejoicing. Last Friday they had left an empty cross; today they find an empty tomb. Two days before they had known the saddest day of their lives; today they know the gladdest, for Easter is the gladdest day of all the world. Mary's tears were changed to laughter; Peter had a chance to say, "Thou knowest that I love thee," and Thomas to say, "My Lord and my God." They were all able to say, "We have seen the Lord."—Leroy M. Whitney.

SECTION VII. Resources for Advent and Christmas Preaching

SERMON SUGGESTIONS

Topic: The Messiah's Character

TEXT: Mal. 3:3.

Malachi indicates three qualities of the Messiah's character: dedication, discipline, and determination.

I. His dedication centered in the knowledge that God had anointed him to save sinful men. So he would devote his concern to leading men in paths which God has prepared for their feet.

II. For the fulfillment of this holy purpose he carefully disciplined himself. Never would he forget his divine responsibility. However often men might fail, he would return again and again with infinite patience to the task of relating them to the eternal grace of God.

III. Nor would he become discouraged. Dedicated as he was to the divine cause, he knew that evil carries within itself the seeds of its own destruction. He knew also that truth ultimately prevails. Possessed of that truth, he would reveal it by word and deed to the sons of men everywhere.—Gordon Pratt Baker.

Topic: A Word is Born

TEXT: John 1:14.

Is there a word that would sum up adequately the significance of Christ's birth, one word that would add up all that Christ means? "Love" might be the word, but here in the manger we see a new kind of love that the world had never seen before. This new love demanded a new word. When Christ was born, a new word also had to be born.

I. This love is a personalized love. Christmas is not a love in general but a love in particular. It is true "God so loved the world" in the sense that his love is generally for all. On Christmas we find God's love becoming specific, personal, individual. Here in this manger-child is God's love.

II. This love of God's in Christ is a free love. God loves us of his own accord. A man cannot buy it. He cannot secure a token of it, not even for all the money in the world. God's love is beyond price. God loves us because he is love. It is his nature, his very being, his character to love. At Christmas one of the most fundamental questions of life is answered, "How does God feel toward us?" The answer is "love."

III. This love of God is an undeserved love. How could we as sinners ever deserve this pure, free love of God? He knows us better than we know ourselves. He knows all our sins and shortcomings. In spite of them, in spite of us, God still loves us with an undeserved love. Because of this, St. Paul shouts, "Thanks be to God for his inexpressible gift!" The unspeakable gift became articulate on Christmas in terms of love.

IV. Our gratitude for God's love is expressed in our love to our fellow men.

We cannot love God except through men. We love God when we love men. The second commandment is "love thy neighbor as thyself." It is a follow-up of the first command.—John R. Brokhoff.

Topic: Why Shepherds?
SCRIPTURE: Luke 2:8–20.

I. The shepherds were humble enough to be teachable. So they could give hospitality to the truth of Christmas. So also they could be the first of men to hear what God was trying to say to mankind of love and hope in the birth of Jesus Christ.

II. The shepherds were lowly enough to be unafraid of change. They most probably were merely servants of the high priest and kept watch over sheep to be used as sacrifices in the temple at Jerusalem. They had little at stake in the status quo. They were not hampered unduly by self-interest.

III. The shepherds were convinced enough to tell others of their discovery. They made it "known abroad." They became the first bearers of the "good news," the first evangels, "evangelists." This was their way of saying thank you to God for his gift.—Everett W. Palmer.

Topic: The Meanings of Christmas

I. Christmas is the birthday of the man who changed the world and split all time in two, so that all events are dated either before or after his coming.

II. Christmas is the day that children love because it is their day and has done more for their happiness and welfare than any other day in the year.

III. Christmas is a spirit. You don't catch the Christmas spirit; it catches you. The first thing you know, if you don't watch out, you'll be happy and childlike and generous all over again. It is so strong that you almost forget yourself and believe this world is a pretty good place and can be made much better.

IV. Christmas is light. Its happy symbolism is light, telling us of one who has been rightly called the Light of the world. And after two thousand years the darkness has not been able to put the light out.

V. Christmas is kindness, not just the word but the thing itself. Hardly a heart is so frosty that it does not thaw out a little on hearing "Merry Christmas!"

VI. Christmas is generosity, the living, annual proof that it is more blessed to give than to receive.

VII. Christmas is believing the best about our fellow men and hopeful expectancy that the best will win out.

VIII. Christmas is a dream that the fine things that come to the fore at this season will be as strong all the year as now they are for a few days.

IX. Christmas is sober reality. Its words about peace and good will are seen as no longer visionary but as the basic principles of a decent and secure world.

X. Christmas is a golden cord that binds the years and the centuries together in beauty and meaning.—Bertram L. Davies.

Topic: Kneel Before the Radiant Boy
TEXT: Matt. 2:11 (PHILLIPS).

I. *Kneeling is recognition of divinity.* He is virgin-born Lord and God-appointed king. All the titles of Isa. 9:6 apply to him: "Wonderful, Counselor, the almighty God, the everlasting Father, the Prince of peace." In the presence of royalty the bent knee is the symbol of acceptance and honor. This is the Lord, God's only begotten Son.

II. *Kneeling is submission.* This is the position of surrender, and it is one which God wants from all of those who are his own. Rom. 10:3 reminds us that after we have established our righteousness through faith, we must submit ourselves. "The bent knee is as much a part of saving faith as the open hand."

III. *Kneeling is the position of a person ready to receive God's gift.* This spiritual kneeling has a thrilling side to it. This means not only yielding.

With the submission come also receiving.—Jackson Wilcox.

Topic: Crossing Christ Out of Christmas

Are you annoyed by the practice of writing the unsightly abbreviation "Xmas" for the beautiful word "Christmas"? It really means "the mass of Christ" and deserves spelling out in its full, sacred significance. Somebody has even said that those who use the "X" are "crossing Christ out of Christmas." Annoyed as I am, I doubt this, for "X" does not stand for the unknown quantity in an algebraic equation or for the wide range of heat and light waves in the Xray but for the Greek letter "Chi," which is an abbreviation for "Christos."

There are, however, certain ways in which we do cross Christ out of his day.

I. We cross Christ out of Christmas when we bury its blessed meaning under the tinseled trappings of a mere festival.

II. We cross Christ out of Christmas when we permit our fears and our hates to put us in the camp of the darkness that has always tried to snuff out the light of love and good will kindling the hope of the world.

III. We cross Christ out of Christmas when we try to suppress its immortal music.

IV. We cross Christ out of Christmas when we allow selfishness or sensitiveness to curtail our giving. The stories of Caspar, Melchior, and Balthazzar (and let us never forget that Christ glorifies these accounts far more than they glorify him) are an indispensable part of the tradition of Christmas. It would not be Christmas without the giving of gifts, not only to each other but to the Christ of Christmas.—T. Otto Nall.

Topic: Take Him Out of the Cattleshed

TEXT: Luke 2:40.

Far too many folk in the church have a Christmas religion. It is full of music and poetry; it is a fine emotional thing, but it never gets Christ out of the cowbarn.

I. Despite all our sentimental singing during the Yuletide, the fact remains that Jesus couldn't have done very much for the world if he had stayed a baby. Babies are wonderful, they bring us happiness; but they aren't very helpful in building things or in tilling soil or in running hospitals.

II. Jesus as a baby couldn't have given us the Sermon on the Mount. He couldn't have lived his mighty life before the eyes of mankind. He couldn't have taken his death-beam to Calvary. He had to quit the stable and become a man before he could perform his mission for God and to man.

III. A stable-faith is not enough. We must have a cross-faith, a resurrection-faith. We must do better than that. We must have a Pentecost-faith. We must have a faith that fulfills the words of the apostle Paul: "Christ in you, the hope of glory."—Lon Woodrum.

ILLUSTRATIONS

TWO REMINDERS. It is the church's intention to remind us of two things during Advent. One is the proximate coming of Christ as child and savior and his incarnation at Christmas. The other is the final coming of Christ as king and judge in the last day. Advent is a joyous time of expectation as touching Christmas. Advent is a very solemn time as touching the last judgment. Being more or less like children, we love the former. But if we are to be true to the gospel we must also heed the latter.—Samuel M. Shoemaker.

THE LITTLE LENT. Advent is sometimes spoken of as the Little Lent. There are similarities between Advent and Lent. The liturgical color for both seasons is purple—symbolic of waiting, watching, repentance. Both are seasons of preparation for festivals of celebration. Advent prepares us for celebrating Christ's birth; Lent for celebrating his glorious resurrection.

Traditionally the church has placed more emphasis on Lent than Advent. Lent is a longer season—forty days excluding Sundays before Easter Day. Advent is a little over half the length. Hence the reference to it as the Little Lent.

We need to recover Advent before Christmas can mean very much to us. Preparation is essential for celebration. In a sense we all prepare for Christmas during Advent. We make our Christmas lists and rush to get our shopping done. We haul out the lights to decorate the tree. We attend parties and visit friends.

But Advent calls for us to prepare ourselves on a deeper level of existence —to ready our hearts for the coming of a king. How can this be done? Through the corporate worship of the church, family worship, Bible reading, prayer, involvement in person's needs, and renewed dedication to the high calling of Jesus Christ.—Michael Daves.

LIKE THE DAWN.   Since Jesus is never pushy, we may miss his advent. He won't be as gaudy as our baubles, bangles, and beads, nor as conspicuous as our colored lights, decorated windows, and Christmas spectaculars. Well-meaning souls suggest that we put Christ back into Christmas. We couldn't if we tried. But we can try to discern his presence, hidden by the spotlighted facades we find so impressive. Like the dawn, he has come into our world. But also like the dawn, he won't force himself into the shuttered lives of those who prefer artificial light.—H. Louis Patrick.

MOMENT OF INSIGHT.   The first Christmas night the shepherds, burdened by problems and fears and misgivings about life itself, were suddenly aware they could trust the love of God. God had not left them alone to make the best of a bad situation. He was the living comrade of life who cared enough to seek them out in the darkness of the night, even though they were unimportant people in an insignificant province of the Roman Empire. In one flashing moment of insight they knew God had invaded their lives with love that could be trusted, and henceforth would never be the same again.— Harold Blake Walker.

THE FIRST CHRISTMAS BELLS.   When Jesus was born in Bethlehem there were no churches or towers from which bells could be rung. When I visited Bethlehem there were other bells which I heard that were like those ringing at the time of the advent.

There was the sheep bell, the bell that told of the shepherd's faith. There was also the camel bell, the bell that told of the wise men's hope. And there was the donkey bell, the bell that told of Mary's and Joseph's love.

These were the first Christmas bells, which attuned to the saviorhood of Christ have from the beginning been ringing out their message to all mankind—the message of faith, of hope, and of love. May their notes be heard in all our hearts and be expressed in all our lives as we keep Christmas continuously.—*Today*.

MESSAGE OF THE STARS.   The dome of heaven, studded with stars, is a priceless gift to sight; stars, in their crisp and distant beauty, twinkling, yet static; pointed yet pouring out lucid light. For untold years the stars stood sentinel over a sleeping world. They were the decorations of the darkness, the brooches that fastened the evening securely about the shoulders of earth. They were always lovely, always remote. And then one night he who had formed them ordained for them a vaster task. They were to reflect a new depth of meaning and transport a message to all who would but lift their eyes. God chose the birth night of his Son for this great commission. From the throne rooms of his holy heaven he bade angels fly to earth, singing that there was born, in the splendor of God and in the simplicity of straw, a savior who is Christ the Lord. And when the angels returned the stars were to take up the word.—Philip Rodgers Magee.

ROAD OF THE MAGI. Near Bethlehem is the oldest highway in the world. This is the pathway worn between the first civilizations, that of the Nile and the Euphrates valleys. Along this road pass merchants from Egypt, caravans to Damascus, pilgrims, Roman princes with their litters, the legions behind their shining eagles, chariots and camels, and the patient donkey, which has been the burden bearer for man since the dawn of civilization. Here the children of Israel fought the Philistines, seeing from the burning desert this green land of milk and honey. Here David gathered the tribes together and made himself king and moved on to Jerusalem. Alexander the Great and Nebuchadnezzar and all the conquering hordes of the heathen came this way like the sands of the sea. Down this road came the wise men bearing the first Christmas gifts, gold, frankincense, and myrrh.

SHARED FESTIVAL. Christmas would mean nothing if it were not shared with someone. It is a festival which cannot be indulged in alone. The gaudy red ribbon about the simplest gift causes that gift to take on a merit which it did not possess before; and just as a single rose may light up a room, so one word on a card, written in sincerity, may brighten the dimmest winter day.—Charles Hanson Towne.

A GIFT FOR EACH. There was a gift for each of us left under the tree of life two thousand years ago by him whose birthday we celebrate today. The gift was withheld from no man. Some have left the packages unclaimed. Some have accepted the gift and carry it around but have failed to remove the wrappings and look inside to discover the hidden splendor. The packages are all alike: in each is a scroll on which is written, "All that the Father hath is thine."—Augusta E. Rundel.

EMMANUEL. Men seek God in the colors of the sunset, in the rush of waters, in the passage of the wind. They seek him in the destinies of nations, the rise and fall of empires. But they find him in the person of Jesus the Christ, find him there because of the great Christmas event. No longer so distant as to be indefinite, no longer so great as to be unapproachable, no longer so awesome as to be fear-inspiring, in the Master he has come to be with us. Born into human life, he becomes one with us in our problems, one with us in our needs, one with us in our joys and in our triumphs.—Frederick W. Brink.

THE MASTER. I heard a magnificent performance of The Messiah conducted by Sir Malcolm Sargent. In his program notes the conductor made this observation, "I have known, loved, rehearsed and performed The Messiah for nearly forty years—a photographic facsimile of the original manuscript has been my musical Bible for fifty years—I am still very conscious that the best of me is not worthy of this masterpiece."

Sir Malcolm approaches The Messiah with a sense of reverence and awe. He does this because it is universally acknowledged as a masterpiece. However, as the conductor's notes explain, there is another compelling reason for this approach to The Messiah. The fact is that the composer did not leave "detailed instructions to the interpretive artist." This being so, Sir Malcolm makes this observation, "Given the original score of The Messiah, a conductor must make a personal decision at almost every bar."

I find here a striking analogy for the Christian. Anyone who takes Jesus Christ seriously looks upon his life as a masterpiece. Remember he was called "Master." Those who walked the earth with him felt they were not worthy of him. Who does? And yet the challenge continues. Even as the distinguished conductor who has studied Handel's Messiah for fifty years confesses, "I am still very conscious that the best of me is not worthy of this masterpiece." So do you and I feel as we contemplate Christ.—Charles L. Copenhaver.

CHRISTMAS QUESTIONS.   The great Christmas question is not so much what we may think about the little baby asleep in Bethlehem's manger but rather what that strange and noble figure outside Jerusalem might think about us. Do we really want him standing by our side, raising questions about the way in which we treat our family and friends whom we know, about the way in which we make and spend our money, about the way in which we handle our resentments and hurts, about the way in which the church conducts its business, about the way in which the community faces its problems, about the way in which a nation establishes its foreign policy?— Clark Hunt.

THE BOY GREW UP.   At Christmas time we pay homage to the Christ child. The divine comes very close to us when we take a little child in our arms. But the Christ child grew up, and the meaning of the truth we call "incarnation" is that the divine is just as close to us when we walk through the years with the growing Jesus as when we welcome the Christ child into our hearts. The lad who felt that he "must be in my Father's house" reveals to us the divine significance of youthful idealism. The joys and sorrows, the struggles and disappointments and final agony of the savior Christ make our own mixed-up experiences easier to bear. Life takes on new meaning as we walk through the vicissitudes of our days with the growing, ministering, suffering Son of Man.—Carl M. Gates.

SECTION VIII. Evangelism and World Missions

SERMON SUGGESTIONS

Topic: Motives for Evangelism

I. The first motive is to be found in the words of Jesus in the great commission when he said, "Go make disciples." In these three words is to be found the timeless mandate of our Lord. Here is his divine imperative for every Christian and the marching orders for every church. The Lord of the church calls us to a crusade for the evangelization of men and nations.

II. The need of America is another strong motive. Our nation needs God these days as never before. All over our country, from ocean to ocean and from the lakes to the gulf, there are crime, gambling, alcoholism, juvenile delinquency, dishonesty, and other forms of lawlessness. Many are living like pagans. Everywhere there are urgent needs.

III. The need of the churches is a driving motive in the work of evangelism. The churches need evangelism to save them from the sterility of a merely cultural religion. Without evangelism at its heart as a compelling motive, a local congregation can degenerate into a club. There is no question but that every local congregation is in grave danger of becoming a complacent, chummy, clubbing collection of nice folk—a sort of closed shop for the edification of the saints. Evangelism, that is the New Testament kind, will keep the churches of America growing spiritually and numerically. If and when churches neglect evangelism they do so at their peril.

IV. The love of people is another motive to keep Christians at the job of evangelism. The writer is not thinking of a shallow, sentimental kind of love but rather a love of people that is of the nature of Christ's love for others. When he saw the multitudes he was moved with compassion. The measure of his love for men is to be found in the cross of Calvary.

V. The phrase of St. Paul, "I am debtor," is an evangelistic motive that urges Christians on in this work. What put the apostle in debt? Just this— Christ did something for him. After his conversion he went about trying to pay his debt. In this twentieth century anyone who has come to know Jesus Christ is in debt. He is in debt to everyone who does not know Christ, anywhere in America or in the world.— Jesse M. Bader.

Topic: The Three Rs of Evangelism

I. *Repentance.* (a) Turning from self to God.

(b) Genuine sorrow for breaking the heart of God rather than sorrow for being caught.

(c) Calls for confession of need and purposing to be his obedient child.

II. *Reconciliation.* (a) Result of repentance and faith.

(b) Restoration of our intended relationship with God.

(c) Fulfillment of ministry to which all Christians are called.

(d) Strengthening lines of communication with bonds of love.

(e) Right relationship among all God's children.

III. *Renewal.* (a) A complete overhaul rather than a polish job.

(b) No longer controlled by self-centeredness but by the spirit of Jesus.

(c) Finding purpose for living and loving.

(d) Happens to church when Christ becomes chairman of the board.

IV. *Revival* follows these three Rs. (a) Experience before expression and worship before witness.

(b) Paying the price in honest-to-goodness renewal before sharing the joys of meaningful evangelism.—General Board of Evangelism, United Methodist Church.

Topic: Why Witness?

I. *In our call witness is foremost.* (See Matt. 4:17–25.) We become Christians by faith in Jesus Christ. Faith is following Jesus with the mind, feet, and attitude. Faith is following and following is fishing. This three-link chain cannot be broken at any point. Is there any way to reduce an axiom to an option?

II. *In our world witness is needed.* (See Luke 14:15–23.) As God chose a nation to reach other nations, his Son has formed a church to reach people. We will never meet anyone who does not need Jesus more than he needs anything else. All men need Christ, and Christ seeks all men. Are you a part of God's plight or program?

III. *For this witness God gives his utmost.* (See Acts 1:4–8.) There is no greater power on earth than the power of the Holy Spirit. There is no greater task than to witness with the Spirit for Christ. Measure your experience with the Holy Spirit by the quality of your fishing for men. Be filled with the Spirit and fill your net with men.—Neal T. Jones in *The Religious Herald.*

Topic: World Evangelization: God's Command

I. On the evening following Christ's resurrection he met with the frightened band of disciples and gave them the *motive* for their mission. (See John 20:21.)

II. At his command they went north to Galilee, and there he met them and gave them the *method* of their mission. (See Matt. 28:18–20.)

III. The disciples returned then to Jerusalem, and I see the events recorded in the last verses of Luke 24 as taking place at this time rather than before they went to Galilee. Here Christ gave his disciples the *message* of their mission. (See Luke 24:47–48.)

IV. Our Lord then went with the disciples out toward Bethany to the Mount of Olives. They were still thinking of a political mission of restructuring a very unjust society, and they inquired about the timing of Christ's earthly conquest. Our Lord came back to the same theme. (See Acts 1:7–8.)

V. We do not know the occasion of the famous great commission recorded in Mark 16:15. But it may well have been yet a fifth occasion following Christ's resurrection in which world evangelization is expressed as the will of God.

VI. If a person is minded to question that this was the clear statement of the will of God, all he need do is examine the interpretation put on these commands by those who were present and heard him. The disciples who heard these words left us thirty years of action demonstrating how they understood it, and the Holy Spirit considered it important enough to leave a book documenting that interpretation. World evangelization is indeed the expressed will of God.—J. Robertson McQuilkin in *How Biblical Is the Church Growth Movement?* (Moody Press, 1973).

Topic: Power for Witness Bearing

TEXT: Acts 1:8.

Christlike personalities are imperatively required if the Christlike message is to reach a needy world. Nothing can take their place. Words are empty unless the speaker is Christlike. Works are meaningless unless the doer is Christlike. Even the Bible is mere print and paper until its messages of love and forgiveness embody themselves in Christlike individuals. No wonder then at the very beginning of the apostolic age and activity we find this promise of divine power specifically given for witness bearing. How to willing recipients is this power given? The Holy Spirit in giving us personal power for witness bearing uses:

I. *Our experiences*. The memory links us to the past and fills our present with inspiration from God's dealings with ourselves and others.

II. *Our expectations*. The imagination takes the warnings and wooings of God as set forth literally or figuratively in God's word and makes the future with its possible punishment and promised rewards a vital factor in daily living.

III. *Our emotions*. Our hearts gather within themselves our love for the good and our hate for the evil and thus fire us with high purpose and noble resolve.

IV. *Our convictions*. Our judgments summon our convictions concerning the great fundamental truths to our hourly support. The greatest perhaps of all those who bore personal witness to Jesus Christ declared, "I know whom I have believed."

V. *Our impulses*. Our wills marshal our impulses and use them to uplift us from the lower levels of life to a godly walk and conversation and so to effective witness bearing.—Lewis Seymour Mudge.

Topic: The Antioch Way in Missions

SCRIPTURE: Acts 15:22–35.

I. Every missionary should have a home church of which he is an integral part.

(a) Missionaries should cultivate their relationship with all of their supporters but most of all with their home church. Missionaries should have at least one member besides the pastor to communicate with and be honest in their communications. They should inquire pointedly about how things are going in the home church for prayer purposes and let the church know they are praying for them.

(b) When on furlough the majority of time should be spent in the home church. This implies that when such a relationship of involvement is established the church will not only pick up the major part of the missionary's support but also help him in getting support from other nearby churches and groups in the area.

(c) If for reasons of schooling, health, etc., the missionary must spend his furlough in another area, he should find a church where he is, adopt it, and be involved in it as Silas did in Acts 15:32–34.

II. Every missionary should know what his spiritual gift is and be encouraged to use it in his home church and as needed in other supporting churches. Paul and Barnabas didn't just give a report of what God had done in and through him. While in the home church they taught and preached the Word of God along with others so gifted. (See Acts 15:35.)

III. Home churches should be involved in the decision of appointing someone to missionary service, especially if major support is given. They should also be included in solving problems their missionary encounters.

(a) Such involvement would make it far easier to minister to them should the missionary have to return home from the field for some reason. Too often casualties are dropped on the church as an orphan might be left at the door of an orphanage.

(b) Mutual respect must be built between sending church, mission agency, and missionary. We must be careful of the subtle pride and dissension specialization can bring.

IV. Missionaries should be expected to raise a substantial portion of their support from a given area so that the above proposals could be implemented.

(a) At first this might not be easy to do but concerted effort and thorough explanations giving the biblical and logical rationale will help to realize the goal. The home church should try to provide at least 50 percent.

(b) It seems to me young people and missionaries doing deputation in this way will not feel as though they are running into one church after another with their hands out like beggars. Because of the contribution they are making in a church and area they will be earning the respect and support of those they have served. And the security of this relationship would inevitably be greater.—Lud Golz.

Topic: Living Witness
TEXT: Phil. 2:15.
Witnessing is never so much a word spoken as a life lived.

I. To witness to the fact that God is love is to act in such a way that we become channels of God's love.

II. To witness to the fact that God cares is to act in such a way that we become channels of God's care.

III. To witness to the joy of God is to become instruments of joy.

IV. To witness to the encouragement of God is to become instruments of courage.

V. To witness to the suffering of God is to suffer when love requires suffering.

VI. To witness to the forgiving grace of God is graciously to forgive one another.—David Bartlett.

Topic: Total Missions
TEXT: Mark 16:15.

I. Our God is a missionary God. He has eternally hated sin and loved the sinner. From the earliest dawn of human history after our first parents disobeyed their creator, we read in the beautiful words of Genesis that God, walking in the cool of the evening, cried out, "Adam, where art thou?" And from that hour to this hour our God has been the seeking and the saving God.

II. Our Book is a missionary book. Running through the whole narrative is the missionary purpose and plan of its authors. The song of redeeming love for all the children of men sings its way through the pages of Holy Scripture. The house of God is to be the house of prayer for all nations. His kingdom is an everlasting kingdom, and his dominion is to endure throughout all generations.

III. Our Savior is a missionary savior. Was not Jesus in a very real sense the first foreign missionary? Did he not leave his home in heaven, as well as his throne and kingly crown, to come to earth to be the savior of men? I do not know how far it is from heaven to earth, but I do know that the Son of God traversed a thorny way, crossed deep and dark chasms, bridged raging torrents, and conquered immeasurable distances to find the sheep that were lost.

IV. Our church is a missionary church. The Master's word is clear: "As the Father hath sent me, even so I send you. . . . Ye shall be witnesses unto me, both in Jerusalem . . . and unto the uttermost part of the earth. . . . Go ye into all the world and preach the gospel to every creature . . . make disciples of all nations."—Francis Shunk Downs.

ILLUSTRATIONS

GOD-CENTEREDNESS. People have a right to know that when we invite them to become fellow disciples we are not merely offering an emotional jag or intellectual exercise or a sure key to happiness and success. We are asking them rather to permit God to transform them and their entire existence from self-centeredness to God-centeredness, from self-worship to the worship of a crucified and risen Lord.—William Lazareth.

CHRISTIAN PROCLAMATION. No understanding of Christian evangelism is possible without an appreciation of the nature of the Christian proclamation. It is not an affirmation of ideals which men must seek to practice, and it is not an explanation of life and its problems about which men may argue and with which in some form they must agree; it is rather the announcement of an event with which men must reckon. God has made him both Lord and Christ. There is a finality about that pronouncement. It is independent of human opinion and human choice.—Daniel T. Niles.

BEYOND DEFINITION. Evangelism is to the body of Christ what blood is to the human body. Both are inseparable from the organism and upon them depend the life and health of "the body." As Jesus did not try to define "neighbor" but simply gave a description of a neighborly deed in the parable of the good Samaritan, and as Paul did not try to define "love" in I Cor. 13 but simply described its matchless qualities, so evangelism is beyond definition. It can at best only be described.—James H. Glassman in *Monday Morning*.

MISSIONARY CHURCH. As we read the truly exciting story of the early church, persevering as it did in the face of incredible odds, we sense the difference between the task of merely supporting missionaries and of being missionaries. The early church did not have a missionary arm; it was a missionary movement. The church was more than anything else a missionary band.—Elton Trueblood.

TWO WORLDS. One reason why the church is too little "missionary" is that it is established on good terms with its world instead of being a foreign mission from another.—P. T. Forsyth.

THE ONE GIFT. There is only one missionary attitude and action which is appropriate to facing the global realities of today, which like dumb idols are so irresponsible and inhuman. It is love. "Many gifts, one Spirit"—yes. But let us not forget, as Paul reminds us, that however diverse our gifts may be the one gift we must all have if the others are not to become sterile and idolatrous is the gift of love.—Philip A. Potter.

RESOLUTIONS (1) I will endeavor always to observe strictly the golden rule, "To do unto others, as I would have them do to me." (2) I will speak no ill of anyone. If I can say no good concerning persons I will remain silent. (3) I will mind my own business and not interfere with the concerns of others. (4) I will pay particular attention to the rules laid down by my medical adviser with regard to diet and exercise. (5) My children are given to me to train for heaven. They shall have my vigilant attention. (6) My duty to the lost around me shall be strictly observed. (7) I will try to exercise patience and self-denial. (8) I will watch over my temper and endeavor to be amiable. (9) I will love my missionary friends and be merciful and kind to all, especially to the sick and distressed. (10) I will cherish a forgiving spirit and will return good for evil.—Henrietta Hall Shuck (First American woman missionary to China).

COMMON LANGUAGE. Helmut Thielicke made a trip to East Africa. There, out in the bush, he was to speak to a native audience. His interpreter did not arrive. The preacher faced his listeners, and they had no common language. How could they communicate? Thielicke said, "I made the sign of the cross and spoke the name 'Jesus.' Smiles came over their faces, and we were one."

THE SEVENTH DAY. In Puerto Rico I talked with the organist of one of the evangelical churches. As far as I could learn they had some sort of meeting every day except Saturday. Trying to be a little humorous I asked, "And what do you do Saturdays?" I was greatly impressed by her reply: "Saturdays we spend out on the streets inviting people to worship with us at our Sunday services."—Roy L. Minich.

INFORMING OURSELVES. Mission education means we need to inform ourselves in depth about human communities within which we live—local, national, and international—so that we may act differently with and toward our neighbors. Informing ourselves in depth means to look at the hard facts and the hard issues and to risk taking a stand. Education takes place when we see and become involved in an issue or situation in which we can have some influence. Through involvement our actions inform our neighbors, and opportunities for further conversation and contact arise.—Thomas M. Anthony.

IN HIS STEPS. To our century and our civilization belong the curious theories that try to conceive, computerize, and program the missionary enterprise in such a way that suffering will be always avoided and success will be guaranteed. Believe me, there are some social classes, some nations, cultures, and subcultures, some areas of the world that will not hear the gospel unless there are Christians now who are ready to follow in the steps of the suffering Lord.—Samuel Escobar.

EXPRESSION OF EVANGELISM. Evangelism is not a function the church performs so much as a way the church lives and expresses itself. A church is evangelistic when its entire life is a perpetual outreach for God, including the Sunday school, the youth groups, and missionary work. It is involved in the life of each member every day. Evangelism includes the measure of dignity in the worship services, the courtesy of the ushers, the quality of the music, and the grace of the pastor. It includes the keeping of the lawn and the paint on the church. It includes the friendliness of the people on Monday as well as the boast of friendliness in church advertising. It is a way of life.—Doyle Brannon.

SECTION IX. Children's Stories and Sermons

January 4. The Sun and the Son

The sun that shines in the sky is the source of all light and life. Many long years ago the people of Egypt thought so much of the sun that they worshiped it as a god, making sacrifices of animals and even human beings to its greatness and glory. The ancient Greeks thought that their god Helios drove a chariot across the sky bringing the sun and light of each new day with him. Since the sun seemed to sink into the sea in the evening, they imagined that Helios, with his chariot and horses, went there to rest for the night. This caused them to have a religious rite once a year when they would throw a chariot and four horses into the sea for the use of Helios. They thought that after a year's work his old horses and chariot would be worn out, and he would need new ones.

We do not worship the sun today or think of it as being driven across the sky by a man with a chariot and horses, because we know more about it than did the ancient Greeks and Egyptians. We have studied the sun through the telescope, and although we speak about its rising and setting, we know that it does not sink down into the sea. In fact it doesn't move. It stands still, and the earth goes around the sun once every 365 days.

We do not worship the sun, but we worship the God who made the sun, the moon, the stars, and our earth. We believe that God placed the sun in the heavens to shine for us and keep us warm and alive, to melt the ice, and to cause vegetation to grow. As we enjoy the sun, thinking of how it makes the food and flowers grow and gives health to our bodies, we should be thankful to God. We can show our gratitude by doing what his Son Jesus Christ wants us to do. Like the sun in the sky, he is a source of light and life.—Ralph Conover Lankler.

January 11. That You Might Believe

Wouldn't you love to know more about Jesus' boyhood? More about his family—those younger brothers and sisters he must have helped to care for during those "years of silence" before he was free to begin his public ministry?

And the people who flit briefly through the gospel story—what happened to them? The young couple who got married at Cana; the boy who shared his lunch; the tenth leper who said thanks; the rich young ruler; the woman at the well; Zacchaeus—we could go on and on. Truly the world's libraries could be filled with accounts of what Jesus did in a brief lifetime of thirty-three years.

But in Jesus' time books were rare and precious, each handwritten on parchment made from sheepskin, a luxury item. The men who wrote the gospels had to be thrifty with all their resources: parchment, ink, and time. Writing was not their primary job.

Scholars tell us that the oldest gospel, Mark, was not written until at least thirty years after Jesus' death. Until then the gospel was passed on by the spoken word of the eyewitness apostles. It was only as they grew old that the apostles realized that a written record was needed in case Jesus did not return for some generations. So men led of the Holy Spirit wrote down not all we would like to know about Jesus but all that is necessary: that God loved us and sent his Son both to save us from death and to show us how to live.—Charlotte R. Ward.

January 18. The Face of Jesus

An artist in Europe wanted to paint a picture of the Savior on the cross. First he made a sketch of the face of Jesus. He showed it to his landlady's daughter and asked her who she thought it was. She answered, "A good man."

The painter felt that he had failed, and he worked on a second sketch. The little girl told him it looked like a great sufferer. Again he believed that he had failed. He began a third sketch.

After meditation and prayer he completed the head. When the girl saw the portrait she knelt down and said, "It is the Lord!"

Penetrating questions can help us arrive at the true answer about Jesus and his power. Some people might claim that he was only a teacher. Others might accuse him of being a trickster or a revolutionary.

However, when we see what Jesus can do about the sin problem in our lives, we discover that he is the everliving Christ. He has the authority to forgive sins and offer the abundant life. He has the power to promise eternal fellowship with him.—John Warren Steen in *Home Life*. Reprinted by permission.

January 25. The Born Loser

Jeremiah was a born loser. People wanted to hear predictions of peace and prosperity; he foretold destruction and exile.

They wanted to go fight the Baby-

lonians; he told them to lay down their weapons.

They oppressed the poor; he condemned those who exploited "the stranger, the orphan, and the widow."

He was scorned by his own, detested, thrown into jail.

He loved God, prayed, and held on to his faith. At the same time he complained: "I am a daily laughing-stock, everybody's butt. . . . The word of the Lord has meant for me insult, derision, all day long" (Jer. 20:7-8, JER).

Jeremiah had everything going against him. He cursed the day he was born. But he spoke the truth as he was given it to see. And he held on, convinced he had a job to do.—The Christophers.

February 1. A Fearless Feathered Friend

Do you think that most birds fly south for the winter, where it's nice and warm? I used to think so too, until I learned about the chickadee.

Around the winter feeders or underneath the old pine tree, where someone has thrown seeds, chickadees will frequently gather in cheery sociability. The coldest wind will not discourage these symbols of the northern winter, nor will zero temperatures cause them to hide from sight.

Some of the most loved and enjoyed inhabitants of bird land, these songsters are very active, tireless, and inquisitive little creatures. They can be attracted easily to most any spot where food is available. They have even been known to eat seed from a person's hand.

And their numerous acrobatic poses and cheery renditions of "chick-a-dee" entertain many a northern bird watcher all winter long.

As we watch this tiny bird, perhaps we'll become aware that hardships can be overcome. For the chickadee, though small, braves the hardships of the northern winter in its determination to survive.

Indeed the wonders of God's world are many and include this black-capped friend. It just takes the keen observer to learn "how great are his signs, how mighty his wonders" (Dan. 4:3).—Mary E. Allen in *The Church Herald.*

February 8. All Look Alike (Race Relations Sunday)

Several of us were having our vision checked. One of the tests was for color blindness. To check for this we had to look at panels covered with various-colored circles. The circles of one color or another are arranged in patterns to form letters or numbers. A person with normal vision has no trouble discerning the different colored numbers, but one suffering from color blindness will not be able to see the pattern.

As we took turns reading the panels, most of us had no difficulty. But when we came to the red and green panel, one man in the group looked at it carefully and then said: "I can't see any difference. All the circles look alike to me."

We live in a complex society with men of many races and differing social and economic levels. In our relations with those who are different we find it hard to ignore these differences. While physical color blindness may be a serious handicap, yet spiritual color blindness is a great blessing. But we have never achieved this until we can say: "I can't see any difference. They all look alike to me."—John W. Wade.

February 15. Who Will Help Him?

At Eastertime many years ago a special collection of paintings of the events of Holy Week was put on display by a London art gallery. A crowd stood viewing the display in respectful silence until a little girl came in. When she saw the striking picture of Christ standing before Pilate, it is said she could bear the silence no longer. "Will no one come out to help him?" she cried.

The little girl was Evangeline Booth. She spent her long, busy life helping Jesus Christ by serving the needy and unfortunate among her fellow men. As a private, then as an officer, and later as commander-in-chief of the Salvation Army, she was part of a great organiza-

tion which brings lost souls to their Savior in almost every country in the world.—Seth Harmon.

February 22. Held by a Thread

In Whitby Museum there is a magnet in a glass case. Near the top of the case, just below the magnet, is a little steel key which seems to be resting in midair. If you look closer, however, you will see that a very fine black thread is fastened around the key and tied to the bottom of the glass case. The key is trying to get to the magnet and is being drawn to it, but the black thread is holding it back. As you look at it you wish you could cut the thread and let the key fly to the magnet.

Maybe you are like that key. Jesus is like a magnet and he is drawing you to himself, but there is some black thread holding you back. Perhaps it is some sin, some bad habit, some friendship which is bad for you. It may seem to be a very tiny thing that is keeping you from Jesus—just as fine as a piece of thread—but if it is keeping you from coming to Jesus it is evil and needs to be swept away.—Ronald Armstrong.

February 29. The Brains of a Robot

A London professor has developed a robot that can set the table, make beds, dust, sweep, iron clothes, scrub floors, prepare food, and even fold itself up, put itself away, and recharge its own batteries. The professor, a noted engineer and inventor, predicts that within ten years every family will have a robot, priced about the same as the family car, to take the drudgery out of the home. "The robot of the future will have a very good logical brain," he has predicted, "but it can never have an emotional brain. It will never do original or creative work."

Machines, computers, and robots can be nothing more than the extension of the mind and the hands of man. They are neither good nor bad in themselves. Only the one who operates them can be that. The increased power of man in a technological age makes him more accountable to God for the far-reaching results of his actions or omissions. We must seek his aid in matching your responsibility with your potential.—Richard Armstrong in *This Is Your Day*.

March 7. Our Hiding Place (Lent)

In *The Hiding Place*, Corrie ten Boom tells of the tense times in Holland during the German invasion of World War II. One particular night she tossed restlessly in her bed while war planes growled overhead, shattering the blackness with fiery artillery. Finally she heard her sister downstairs in the kitchen, and because sleep would not come she went down for a cup of tea. They talked until the night was still again and the sound of fighters and bombers had died away. Explosions had occurred nearby, but now all was quiet in their vicinity.

Stumbling through the darkness to her room, Corrie reached out to pat her pillow before lying down. Suddenly she felt something sharp cutting her hand. It was a jagged piece of metal ten inches long. She cried out for her sister and raced down the stairs with the shrapnel shard in her hand.

While Betsie bandaged her hand she kept saying, "On your pillow!" Corrie responded, "Betsie, if I hadn't heard you in the kitchen . . ." To this her sister replied: "Don't say it, Corrie! There are no ifs in God's world. The center of his will is our safety."

Later through the trying time in a Nazi prison, Corrie was to prove over and over this marvelous truth, "God's will is our hiding place."—Charles R. Hembree.

March 14. In Him Was Life (Lent)

In 1497 Vasco da Gama's fleet had good fortune, and the sailors were highly successful in reaching India. After spending three rewarding months there, they loaded their ships with spices and jewels and started home to Portugal. They expected a trying journey, but it proved to be terrifying because a dread disease struck them and many died.

When they came to the eastern coast of Africa, they stopped at Malindi. Here the black ruler gave them fruit. Da Gama's men did not know what vitamins were. They did not dream that scurvy could be traced to a shortage of vitamin C. But as a result of eating the fruit for many days, the sick men recovered. They continued their journey around the Cape of Good Hope and arrived safely home.

Vitamin is a word that comes from the Latin *vita,* meaning life. Jesus Christ brought life to a sick humanity.—Woodrow A. Geier in *The Sanctuary*.

March 21. Priceless (Lent)

We attended a session of a numismatic convention. (Numismatists are coin collectors.) There we examined coins of various denominations and dates. Among them were some that are assessed at 10,000 times their face value. An uncirculated Liberty twenty-five-cent piece, with the year 1918 stamped over 1917, was priced at about $2,300. A four-dollar gold coin dated 1880, called a "Stella," sold for about $13,000.

In some way known only to the great heart of God, we worthless sinners are worth limitless multiplications of 10,000 to him. Certainly it is not because we are old or rare, for there are and have been millions upon millions of us of all ages through the centuries. In ourselves we are worthless but not to God. The cost of our redemption was infinitely priceless to him, who gave his only begotten Son that we might live.—*The Pilgrim*.

March 28. A Fable about Three Bulbs (Lent)

A Dutch fable tells about three tulip bulbs named "No," "Maybe," and "Yes" that lived in the bottom of the bin. When autumn came they speculated concerning their destiny. "No" said: "I shall stay in my snug corner of the bin. I don't believe there is any other life for tulip bulbs. Besides, I am satisfied with things as they are." And he rolled over and went to sleep.

"Maybe" said: "I am not satisfied with things as they are. I feel there is a better life than the life I now have. I feel something inside me which I must achieve, and I believe that I can achieve it." So he squeezed and pressed himself until he was utterly frustrated.

Then "Yes" said: "I have been told that we can do nothing of ourselves but that God will fulfill our destiny if we put ourselves in his power."

A hand reached down into the tulip bin feeling for bulbs. "Yes" yielded to the hand and was buried in the ground. "No" and "Maybe" shriveled away untouched in their corners of contentment and frustration. And with the coming of spring, "Yes" burst forth into all the richness and loveliness of new life.—*Scope.*

April 4. The Penitent Thief (Passion Sunday)

There is a legend about the penitent thief who was crucified beside Jesus. When Mary and Joseph were fleeing from Bethlehem to Egypt with the baby Jesus, this legend goes, they were attacked by a band of robbers. One of them was a young boy, son of the leader of the robbers.

When this boy saw what a beautiful baby Jesus was, he could not kill him but said, "O most blessed of children, if ever there come a time for having mercy on me, then remember me and forget not this hour."

Actually the Bible does not tell us whether either of the two thieves between whom Jesus was crucified had ever seen or heard of him until that hour. One was scornful, mocking, and unbelieving, while the other was repentant and believing. The two attitudes made the difference between life and death.

The penitent thief did what every unsaved person must do to be saved: he repented and believed that Jesus could save him.—Evelyn Carter Foote in *Home Life.*

April 11. Bless the Animals in Our Care (Palm Sunday)

Cats for company and birds for music. From Noah's ark to the sparrow which flew through King Edwin's hall in the old English epic, from the animals of Aesop to the world of Disney, animals have occupied a place in the life of mankind.

No good can come to man which does not also come to beast, and no ill can hurt man which does not hurt beast as well. The judgment or survival that awaits our world comes "to both man and beast."

When Jesus Christ rode "to victory" it was upon an unbroken donkey. That little animal recognized its benevolent Master and took him right in. There is a great place for animals in the future when the Lord Jesus Christ reigns in kindness and justice. Until then we are called upon to bless by word and action the animals placed within our earthly care.—Haydn L. Gilmore.

April 18. The Cross That Sprouted (Easter)

There it stood, a rough-hewn cross fashioned from limbs cut from the forest. It was stuck down into the wet sand at the edge of a Florida lake. The teen-aged boy who was showing me around the youth camp said, "We put this cross here to be our worship center."

I noted a strange aspect of this cross. Out of the top edge of it several green shoots were growing, leaves already formed on them, reaching up toward the sun! The cross was sprouting again. It was not dead wood but alive and growing.

Somehow that cross has seemed to me symbolic of the self-renewing power of the church of Jesus Christ throughout the world. New growth is ever emerging. —James R. Webb, Jr.

April 25. Reflection in a Mirror

A six-year-old daughter of Ben Wakes asked her father, "Daddy, where does God really live?" "In the well," he answered absent-mindedly. Then he remembered a scene that had been hidden in memory for thirty years. A band of gypsies had stopped at the well in his courtyard in Poland. One of the group, a giant of a man, leaned over and looked deep into the well. "Curious," says Wakes, "I tried to pull myself up the well's rim to see what he was peering at. He smiled and scooped me up in his arms. 'Do you know who lives down there? God lives there. Look,' and he held me over the edge of the well. There in the still water I saw my own reflection. 'But that's me!' 'Ah,' said the gypsy, 'now you know where God lives.' " —Carl M. Gates.

May 2. Caring Makes the Difference

A nine-year-old girl was found in a city street, begging food for a dog. When the story was put together it was found that she had run away from home because of threatened punishment. In her loneliness she had taken up with a dog that was as forlorn as she was. When she begged food for the dog the story made the papers. The missing persons bureau picked up the clue, and soon the girl was restored to her parents. Caring for the dog made it possible for her to receive the care she herself needed.

We love because God taught us how to love. The love which he gave inspires us to give love. We owe everything to love. It redeems us from selfishness, from aimlessness, from sin. God caring for us makes a difference in our lives and enables us to care for those whom he has created.—Elinor Lennen.

May 9. Holding the Home Together (Mother's Day)

We had a home within our home. We didn't know it because we couldn't see it. It was in the chimney. The way in which we found out about this home within our home was a little frightening. We were sitting in the living room talking, when one, two, three little chimney swift birds came falling through the open fire space into the room. They had no more than landed when their nest came after them. We picked up the little birds and put them outside, and I kept the little nest as a souvenir. It is a very unusual nest, not made

of grass and straw. It is made of little twigs of bushes and trees all fitted together and held in place by some kind of sticky substance. I don't know what we can call this sticky substance unless we call it chimney-swift glue. It is quite strong; it held that little home together and held the nest in its place inside the chimney until the little birds became too big for it. Then they all tumbled down with the nest.

Just as the chimney swift has a glue that will hold her little home together, we have something that holds our homes together. I wonder if you know what it is? It is the spirit of love. It is the love that we have for one another that causes us to stick together through thick or thin, in rain or shine, in fair weather or foul.—Ralph Conover Lankler.

May 16. The Human Touch

A visitor to a telescope factory was fascinated by a workman who was polishing a lens with the palm of his hand. "Why is it necessary to use your hand?" he asked. "There comes a time in the making of a fine lens," the workman replied, "when nothing can be substituted for the human touch." Enthusiasts for automation must never forget that basic fact. The human touch is still essential. The present-day passion for organizing and mechanizing human activities must never be allowed to crowd out the personal touch which gives life and meaning to it all. In the early days the church was strong because of the spirit that bound the group together. It was the human touch that kept their faith alive and growing. So today we find our strength in fellowship with each other and with God.

May 23. What Trees Tell Us

Joyce Kilmer observed that trees look at God all day and lift their leafy arms to pray. The Bible makes many references to trees. It begins with a tree in a garden, and it ends with trees in a city. The psalmist likens a righteous man to a tree, fruitful and prosperous. Jesus was crucified on a tree. We use a tree to commemorate his birth, and an evergreen tree is a symbol of eternal life. A tree is a constant reminder of my Creator's love. Each time you see a tree let it remind you to pray, to reflect upon God's Word, to live fruitfully. Let it remind you of Jesus. Trees are not only a delight to the eye; they have instructive qualities as well.—Roy Heims in *The Secret Place*.

May 30. Beware of Bad Air

Fishermen along certain areas of the Pacific coast have at times found themselves threatened by plankton, that microscopic water life which resembles both plants and animals. When these drifting creatures die they sink and decompose, sending off a poisonous gas which robs the water of its oxygen. When this happens on a large scale, the "red tide" caused by decaying plankton pollutes the water as well as the fish which live in it.

Persons who turn their bad dispositions loose on others likewise have a destructive influence. Sometimes circumstances force us to be where they are, and we suffer from those who choose to poison the atmosphere. Aviators know the danger that lurks in bad air; they take oxygen tests as a precaution.

In the realm of the spirit, the atmosphere is all-important. To guard against the poisonous influences of the world the prayer life must be kept vital so our spirit may be refreshed by his spirit.— Elinor Lennen.

June 6. Stamps and Seeds

A schoolboy in British Guiana, who was a stamp collector, found among some family papers a one-cent stamp which had been produced in 1856 by a local printer because of a shortage of one-cent stamps. The boy sold it to a neighbor for six shillings (about $1.50) so that he could buy other stamps that were more colorful.

The stamp changed hands a number of times, and each time the price increased until recently it was auctioned to a syndicate of eight businessmen for $280,000. How its value increased! The reason for its great value is because it is one of a very few stamps which collectors term unique, meaning it is the only one known of its kind.

This astonishing increase in value reminds us of the parable of the seed which our Lord spoke about in Luke 8. He gave the illustration of a kernel of grain which under favorable conditions can bear fruit one hundredfold. One ordinary cob of corn produced 752 kernels. If they were all planted, what a multiplicity of kernels there would be.

The Lord Jesus compared the seed to the Word of God. If the Word of God is planted in the heart, the fruit—or the blessings—that come through the Word cannot be counted.—*Now*.

June 13. Bluebirds

"Why, it's a little mountain bluebird," my wife said as she reached down to pick up its tiny body from the sidewalk. "And such a shame," she added. "There are so few bluebirds around here anyway." The bluebird apparently died from flying into a glass door.

A day or two later I read about a bird study which William George is making at Southern Illinois University. George, who teaches zoology, is collecting data on why birds kill themselves by flying against windows. Apparently many birds don't realize the glass is there, the same as people who sometimes walk right into a glass door.

But Professor George thinks there may be another reason, and that is an occasional bird which mistakes his own reflection in a window for an enemy. You see, most birds stake off an area as their own private territory. This is particularly true of male birds during mating season. So it is possible that a bird might attack his reflected image.

But is man any smarter than a bluebird? How often do we look into a mirror and mistake something good for something bad? We examine ourselves for faults. Why not an occasional self-search for virtues?—Robert J. Hastings.

June 20. Blue Mussels

Anyone familiar with the coast of Maine knows the common blue mussel. It looks like a clam or an oyster, and it is in fact their first cousin, although it is not usually regarded as a food safe to eat. Either attached to rocks or lying close-packed in beds in astronomical numbers, mussels cover the Maine coast. One takes the mussel as much for granted as seaweed, rock shelf, or tidal flow.

I picked up a mussel shell still wet from the receding tide. I found in my hand a thing of sudden beauty and perfect form. Scribed with a multitude of graceful, curving lines, the outside of the shell, ranging from light to a kind of gun-metal blue, had the misty bleached effect one might expect from a creature half the time washed by the restless tide. And as for the inside of the shell, it was a fantasy of iridescent color—milky white, violet, lavender, purple, and a dozen shades of blue, some roseatehued, some almost black, the whole opalescent as a pearl, exquisite as a work of art.

Because the mussels lie about him in such familiar profusion, a man is likely to ignore them. What a pity for a man to walk a path of pearl and opalescent lavender and see only seaweed and mud flat.—Waldemar Argow.

June 27. Relationships

Baboons must be the best-groomed animals on earth. According to the National Geographic Society, these over-sized monkeys devote several hours a day to grooming themselves and their companions. Females are the chief preeners. When not eating, sleeping, or taken up with their own beautification, baboons run their hands and teeth through each other's hair.

But the grooming is not always mere vanity. It's basic to the survival of the species. It removes dirt and parasites and also strengthens ties between members of what is described as a "remarkably sophisticated society."

People have other ways of building relationships. Some of them are known

as the corporal works of mercy: feeding the hungry, giving drink to the thirsty, clothing the naked, sheltering the homeless, visiting the sick and the imprisoned, burying the dead. Love of neighbor isn't monkey business. It's something only people can do.—The Christophers.

July 4. Independence Bells (Independence Day)

It was July 4, and by common agreement and given signal, the church bells all over our community and throughout our nation began pealing forth. The phrase "Ring out, wild bells" took on a significant meaning. At first it seemed like a confusion of glorious and yet unrelated tones. Then out of the tumult of sounds there came from our own church the irregular ringing of three beautiful but very different bell tones.

One of these, a clear, silver-toned treble, seemed to be urgently, almost nervously calling, "Listen, listen, listen!" Its language was so direct and simple: "Listen to my song. You are free to live in a land where there is a way of life that must be guarded for all generations."

The second bell, a resonant baritone of rich, mellow quality, pealed in strong, compelling tones, "Come, come, come!" Its message was convincing: "Come to realize that you are the rich recipient of rights which protect your dignity and freedom."

As though from another world came the deep-toned voice of the third bell. Its solemn, deliberate stroke spoke the language of eternity. "Be still, be still," it seemed to say. "Be still and know that God's hand is upon us, and he is our creator, judge, and protector."

As I opened the church door I thought how many picnics, family get-togethers, ball games, and such there would be throughout the land. But I found myself in the quiet of the church, having heeded the announcement of the pealing bells to listen, to come, and to be still.—Frank A. Kostyu.

July 11. Handholders

Two-year-old Jimmy went tumbling down the small flight of stairs. Upon hitting the bottom he let out a loud scream. His mother, hearing the commotion, yelled at the top of her voice, "Jimmy, what happened?" Instantly, little Jimmy, who was still in one piece with only his baby's pride being momentarily destroyed, shrieked back tearfully, "I didn't have my handholder."

You see, Jimmy had become accustomed to his mother or father holding his hand while he ventured down those ominous stairs. As little children so often do, this day he felt he was big and brave enough to tackle the task himself. Much to his chagrin he rudely discovered that he still needed his "handholder."

No matter what our position in life we all need a constant and trustworthy handholder. This is where God comes into the picture. He is the great handholder. Through Jesus Christ we at once become acquainted both with the compassion and the firmness of a caring God.—Joseph Viola in *The War Cry*.

July 18. Fairy Rings

Years ago men noticed that mushrooms are sometimes found growing in a circle, inside which grass has died.

Superstitiously, they called these circles "fairy rings" and told stories of fairies dancing in the ring on moonlit nights and trampling down the grass.

What really happens is this: The mushroom, unlike many other plants, does not have chlorophyll and so cannot make any of its own food. It must, therefore, get its entire nourishment from beneath the soil itself. So the "fairy circle" mushroom sends out underground roots which get their food from among the grass roots and crowd out and kill the grass.

Each year the underground roots have to keep moving away from the center of the dead spot and into the outer edge of the original spot to find food. The ring, therefore, grows larger each year, and no grass grows within it.

Men have always been too willing to find some pagan or superstitious explanation for the very understandable system of nature which the Lord created. Everything in nature shouts proof that God is running things.—Max L. Batchelder.

July 25. The Amazing Seed

Of all God's creations one of the most astonishing is the seed. Perhaps we are sowing some of them in our gardens with only a dull awareness of the miracles involved. It is almost incredible that a tiny plant in miniature form can survive inside the hard, dry shell until something signals it and says, "Wake up now, come out, and go through it all again!"

There were some seeds inside a box in the Natural History Museum of London when a fire destroyed part of the buildings in 1940. When the box of seeds, damaged by fire and water, was opened, it was discovered that some of the seeds had germinated and begun to grow, although the seeds had been brought from China to London in 1793 by Sir George Stanton and were 147 years old. In another experiment performed by the same museum some seeds came to life again which were 237 years old.

I have read that "when rain fell once on Death Valley, the desert blossomed as the rose." Seeds long dormant were still vital and sprang into life when the right conditions triggered their growth.

In seeds there is hid a mysterious potential. The same is true of the seed of faith which God plants in the human heart and life. Who can tell what it may some day produce? A young life, especially, is like a seed, with great possibilities latent within it.—James R. Webb, Jr. in *The Wesleyan Christian Advocate*.

August 1. The Mystery of the Thatch

Preacher Peter and his wife found life difficult. In Switzerland in the 1700's Mennonites were persecuted for what they believed.

Peter awoke one night to discover several men removing the thatch from the roof of his house. He heard them whisper: "We will see what kind of man he is. Maybe he isn't all that loving." Peter prayed that God would help him do the right thing. Then he told his wife: "Workmen have come to us. You had better prepare a meal."

She understood. Soon the table was spread. Opening the door, Peter called: "You have worked hard and must be hungry. Come, eat."

The surprised young men came in and stood awkwardly in the friendly candlelit room. When they were seated Peter prayed a kindly prayer for the guests. The plates were filled, but the men could not eat. Suddenly they all pushed back their chairs and bolted out the door. Again sounds could be heard on the roof. But this time it was not the sound of thatch falling. The thatch was being put back on the roof!—Mary Rempel in *Rejoice!*

August 8. Shark Shield

A "shark shield" can now protect fliers and others who find themselves adrift in shark-infested waters. The device, tested successfully both in the Atlantic and Pacific, is a black plastic bag carried in the pocket of a life vest. The survivor can open it to a length of five feet, fill it with sea water, slip inside and orally inflate three rows of air flotation chambers at the bag's top. The strange-looking object tends to frighten sharks and relieve the fears of the man inside. Researchers find it effective even against famished sharks, which avoided the bags although pieces of fish were thrown to them nearby.

Man's resourcefulness against hostile forces is one reason for his continuing survival. Sadly, our most persistent threat comes from other people and the undisciplined forces within our own human nature. The twofold remedy, put at our disposal by a loving Creator, consists in a prudent but generous love of others and growth in self-mastery.—Richard Armstrong in *This Is Your Day.*

August 15. Story of a Favorite Hymn

The hymn "Blest Be the Tie That Binds" was written by the Rev. John Fawcett, who in the latter part of the eighteenth century was the pastor of a poor little church in Lockshire, England. His family and responsibilities were large; his salary was less than $4 a week.

In 1772 he felt himself obliged to accept a call to a London church. His farewell sermon had been preached, six wagons loaded with furniture, and books stood by the door. His congregation, men, women, and children, were in an agony of tears.

Mr. Fawcett and his wife sat down on a packing case and cried with the others. Looking up Mrs. Fawcett said: "Oh, John, John, I cannot bear this! I know not where to go!"

"Nor I either," said he. "Nor will we go. Unload the wagons and put everything back in its old place."

His letter of acceptance to the London church was recalled, and he wrote this hymn to commemorate the episode.

August 22. Showing Our Colors

Paul Gustave Doré, a nineteenth-century painter, once lost his passport while traveling in a foreign country. When the official demanded it, he said: "I am sorry to say that I have lost my passport. I can only tell you I am Doré, the artist."

"Ah!" responded the officer, sneering, "we'll see very quickly whether you are Doré," and, handing him pencil and paper, said, "Prove it if you are."

Taking the pencil, the artist with a few strokes sketched a group of peasants, who happened to be standing by, with such inimitable skill that the official said, "Yes, no doubt of it; you must be Doré."

Can the scrutinizing world say of us, "You must be a Christian?" Do our colors prove it?

August 29. Black Bart

A dropped handkerchief brought a surprising end to the career of California's most colorful stagecoach robber.

"Black Bart" had terrorized stages for six years, committing twenty-eight robberies between 1877 and 1883 in the rugged foothills of the Sierras. Dressed in a long linen duster with a flour sack over his head, he would brandish a shotgun, demanding, "Will you please throw down your treasure box, sir?"

Finally, near Copperopolis, Bart was wounded while escaping a holdup and dropped a handkerchief bearing the laundry mark "FX07." This was traced to San Francisco, where police made one of the most surprising arrests in the city's history. Black Bart, the highwayman, turned out to be Charles E. Bolton, one of San Francisco's leading citizens, with close connections in the police department.

Bolton had a reputation as a nonsmoking, nondrinking, Godfearing man with substantial interest in the gold mines. Amid much publicity he confessed his crime and was sentenced to six years in prison.

Black Bart was neither the first nor the last to live a lie. Millions of others like him have veneers of goodness covering hearts of deceit and despicable evil. Jesus compared such people to "whited sepulchers," attractive on the outside but filled with deadness. Tragically the life of a Black Bart is a tension-filled existence, frustrating not only to the person involved but to all those about him. —Charles R. Hembree.

September 5. The Indian and His Boat

An old Indian was carving his canoe out of a huge log. A man came along and said, "Chief, I think she's too wide for her length." So the Indian narrowed her down.

A little later another man came along who said, "Chief, it looks to me that the stern's too full." So he cut down the stern.

A third man came, watched the Indian chisel awhile, and giving the canoe a close look said, "The bow's too sheer, Chief." So the Indian changed the bow.

When the canoe was finally finished the Indian launched it in the nearby river, but it capsized. He hauled it back on the beach, found another log, and began again. Once more a man came along and offered advice, but this time the Indian answered, "That boat over there—that's everybody's boat," pointing to the monstrosity on the bank. "This one Indian's boat!"—*Sunshine Magazine.*

September 12. Fumbling the Ball

Perhaps no play in football, basketball, or baseball carries with it more disappointment than the fumble. In football it is called a fumble; in basketball a turnover; in a baseball game an error. Fumbles lose ball games. Fumbles kill a team's spirit and disappoint a team's followers.

What causes a fumble? Who knows? It's a combination of several factors. A poor exchange from one to another, a vicious collision with the opponent, carelessness, overambition, lack of concentration are some of the causes.

Fumbles are not just confined to the sports world. All of life can be plagued by fumbles. To fumble is to squander away an opportunity. Day after day we fumble away opportunities for the advancement of God's work in the world.

People who sit in the sanctuary and talk during the sermon or invitation, clip fingernails, play with babies, tease girls, or in other ways distract are fumbling the ball. Fumbling hurts the entire team and so others miss scoring.

Young people fumble away their future with immoral behavior, lack of ambition, failure to apply themselves, and their elders do likewise. Most fumbles can be eliminated by concentration, commitment, hard work, and a greater desire to win.—Jerry Hayner in *Baptist and Reflector.*

September 19. My Best for Him

Out of the past comes the legend of a monk called Anthony and a cobbler named John. Anthony was a devout monk who had gone to the desert to be alone with God. By rites of penance he tried to make his life holy. To him one blazing noonday a voice spoke: "Anthony, thy saintly life rejoices my heart. Yet there in yonder city is one holier than thou, John the cobbler." When Anthony asked what more he could do than he had done, the voice replied, "That you must discover for yourself, my son."

Anthony set out across the desert for the distant city and found the cobbler at his bench. "Tell me, what do you do more than other men that your virtue has been wafted to heaven?"

The modest cobbler replied that he had done nothing, adding: "Unless, it is to me that every shoe I mend is Christ's own. Every shoe is done my very best for him."—*The Secret Place*.

September 26. A Missing Screw

When I was a boy I had a cheap pocket watch. While it didn't keep perfect time it ran accurately enough for my purposes. But I was not satisfied. I wanted my watch to run as accurately as my dad's. And so I proceeded to remove the back from the watch and take out many of the parts. To the amazement of everyone I was able to get all the parts back into place and the works back into the case—except for one small screw. Try as I might I couldn't find any place to put it. However, the watch seemed to perform all right without it, and so I put the back on it and went on my way.

Depending on the watch, I was late for supper that night. It no longer kept even reasonably accurate time. The little screw I had left out had something to do with regulating the hairspring that in turn regulated the watch.

The church is like this. Every member of Christ's body is essential to its healthy function. To ignore or eliminate even one apparently unimportant member is to risk a serious malfunction in the whole body.—John W. Wade.

October 3. Circles (World Communion Sunday)

You and I are constantly drawing circles in life. Circles that include some folk. Circles that shut others out. We cannot help but draw circles around us; life demands that we do. The question is, how large is the circle that we draw with the crayon of the heart upon the page of life?

The Master drew a great circle about his life that included everyone—the sinner, the downcast, and the hopeless, along with the upright and faithful.

How great is the circle of our love? Does it include people of different economic status, different faith, different standards of morality, different race? Or does it exclude some?

We all struggle with the business of drawing circles. The small, egotistical person draws the small circle with himself at the center. The great person draws a large circle with God at the center that includes people of every walk of life. How large is the circle that we are drawing?—Harleigh M. Rosenberger.

October 10. Wrong Goals and Good Intentions

The twelve-and-under church basketball team was behind two points at the half. The parents were excited, the coaches were enthusiastic, and the little players who hadn't won a game through half the season were excited about the chance to win a game.

The second half started. The tip went to Danny and he quickly dribbled and put the ball up and through the basket. But instead of tying the score, he put his team two points farther behind. He had good intentions, but he forgot that the goals changed at the half. He put the ball through the wrong basket. The coach consoled little Danny.

What happened to Danny happens to many of us in the game of life. We get so busy that we forget what our goal is and what it ought to be.—*Home Life*.

October 17. The Golden Rule

All seven of the great religions of the world have "golden rules." A condensation of the various ideologies results in the following:

The Hindu: "The true rule is to

guard and do by the things of others as you do by your own."

The Buddhist: "One should seek for others the happiness one desires for oneself."

The Zoroastrian: "Do as you would be done by."

The Confucian: "What you do not wish done to yourself do not to others."

The Muslim: "Let none of you treat your brother in a way he himself would dislike to be treated."

The Jew: "Whatsoever you do not wish your neighbor to do to you do not unto him."

The Christian: "All things whatsoever ye would that men should do unto you do ye even so to them."—*The Maritime Baptist.*

October 24. We All Make Mistakes

Henry Ford forgot to put a reverse gear on his first automobile. And Thomas Edison once spent two million dollars on an invention that proved to be of very little value. Actually a person who never makes a mistake probably lacks normal boldness and a spirit of adventure so he doesn't try new things and is really a brake on the wheel of progress. And yet if he never makes a mistake, the biggest mistake is that he tries nothing or does nothing. Our greatest inventions have come about through inventors trying over and over, making error after error. But finally they reached perfection. Our Creator expects of us to use all our talents and energies to better others and ourselves. And if we make mistakes along the way, it's only natural and nothing to worry about.—Louise Price Bell in *Family Devotions.*

October 31. Saints (All Saints' Day)

During the early days of his ministry before there were airplanes. Dr. Harry Ironside used to travel many miles by train. On one of these trips, a four-day ride from the west coast to his home in Chicago, the great Bible teacher found himself in the company of a party of nuns. They liked him because of his kind manner and for his interesting

reading and exposition of the Bible. One day Dr. Ironside began a discussion by asking the nuns if any of them had ever seen a saint. They all said that they had never seen one. He then asked if they would like to see one. They all said, yes, they would like to see one. Then he surprised them greatly by saying, "I am a saint; I am saint Harry." And he took them to verses of the Bible such as Phil. 1:1.

So it is with us. Your name may sound funny when you preface it with the title "saint." But you may rest assured that it does not sound funny to God whether you are a Saint George, a Saint Lucy, or a Saint Harriet. God knows us all by name. And it is he who calls us saints in Christ Jesus.—James Montgomery Boice.

November 7. Christian Courage

There never has been a more courageous man than the great preacher Chrysostom. Threatened with banishment by the Roman emperor, his answer was, "Thou canst not, for the world is my Father's house, thou canst not banish me." The emperor threatened to kill him, and he replied, "Thou canst not, for my life is hid with Christ in God." The next threat was to take away his treasure, and his word was "My treasure is in heaven and my heart is there." The last menace was to take away from him all his friends. His triumphant rejoinder was: "That thou canst not, for I have a Friend in heaven from whom thou canst not separate me. I defy thee; there is nothing thou canst do to hurt me." Roman eagles were powerless against such Christian courage.—Howard Wayne Smith.

November 14. For the Gospel's Sake (Stewardship Day)

General Charles G. Gordon was an outstanding man of God. When the English government wanted to reward him for his distinguished service in China, he declined all money and titles. Finally, after much urging, he accepted a gold medal inscribed with his name and a record of his accomplishments. Following his death, however, it could not be found among his belongings. It was learned that on a certain date he had sent it to Manchester during a famine with the request that it be melted and used to buy bread for the poor. In his private diary for that day were written these words: "The only thing I had in this world that I valued I have now given to the Lord Jesus." His love for the Savior had constrained him to relinquish his one treasured possession for the relief of the destitute. He would not cling to earthly honor, but casting its last vestige aside he sought only to serve the Master "for the gospel's sake."— Henry G. Bosch in *Our Daily Bread.*

November 21. When Robinson Crusoe Prayed (Bible Sunday)

Robinson Crusoe was a sailor whose ship was wrecked, and he was cast on a desert island. He was able to save a few things from the wreck of his ship, and one of them was an old medicine chest. It was fortunate that he saved this because one day he became sick. He was sick in body and sick in heart. He went to his medicine chest, and with great effort he managed to lift up the lid. He found medicine to heal his body, but he found something better than that—he found medicine for his soul. He found a Bible. After he had taken his medicine, he opened the Bible, and the first words on which his eyes fell were those from Ps. 50: "Call on me in the day of trouble; and I will deliver thee, and thou shalt glorify my name."

Before he went to bed that night he did something that he had never done before in his life. He knelt down and said his prayers. He asked God to fulfill the promise of the verse which he had just read. After he prayed he felt so much better that he fell into a sound sleep. The medicine healed his body and the Bible healed his soul, and God answered his prayer by sending him a companion, the man Friday.—Ralph Conover Lankler.

November 28. The Light of the Face (Advent)

There are many different faces— young, kind, weary, and beautiful. Our very habits and thoughts seem reflected in our facial lines. Sad as well as the smiling faces reveal the inner mind and heart.

Because we have a great deal to do with how we appear to others, we need to think constantly on *whatsoever things are beautiful,* that we may reflect only the good things. We may say, "I can't help how I look." But is that true?

There were Daniel and his friends, who showed by their healthy "glow" the reward of temperate living as well as their confidence in God. Their strength of character and depth of purpose could not be hidden.

Stephen's face shone with light, trust in God, and forgiveness. His face reflected the love of Jesus, which could not fail to impress those that saw him. —Alicia Bishop.

December 5. Bethlehem in Song (Advent)

One Christmas Eve one hundred and seventeen years ago an American minister rode horseback into the hills of the Holy Land and stopped his horse in the very fields where the shepherds watched their flocks by night so long ago. He looked about him in reverent silence.

Below him he saw the dark streets of a little town called Bethlehem. Above him he saw the same stars shining in the dark blue sky that shone there the night the baby Jesus was born. Though the air was cold, Phillips Brooks found it hard to leave. He was deeply moved.

The scene Dr. Brooks had observed in Palestine could not be erased from his mind. He returned to the United States and transposed the vision into a haunting poem.

Lewis Redner, organist in Dr. Brooks's church, was inspired by the poem to set the words to music.

Many others have stood on Palestinian soil and observed the sacred scene, but only Dr. Brooks resolved to give the scene to the world. "O Little Town of Bethlehem" has become one of the best-loved Christmas carols. — Mabel-Ruth Jackson.

December 12. The Friendly Stars (Advent)

A child looks uncounted millions of miles upward into the night sky and asks, "Which is the Christmas star?" All stars are Christmas stars.

The silent stars that look down on us tonight are the identical stars that blended their golden beams with the star of Bethlehem into a brilliant symphony of light on the night of the Master's birth. They are the identical stars that shone on the Magi as they followed the guiding light of the star in the east that led them to Bethlehem. They are the identical stars that have stirred the hearts and minds of men through the ages, impelling them to reach out beyond the confines of the known world, seeking what lies above and beyond.

They shine in the heavens as eternal reminders that the Prince of peace is the Light of the world. They are the Christmas stars.—*Sunshine Magazine*.

December 19. The Gift Giver (Christmas)

Bishop Nicholas stopped for a moment, shifted the heavy pack to a more comfortable position on his frail back, and with a glance at the twinkling stars overhead continued happily through the night. His footsteps never faltered as he crossed the deserted market square and entered a narrow, foul-smelling lane in Myra's worst slum. Shortly the old man halted and tapped on the entrance to one of the solid rows of mud hovels which pressed in from either side. The door of the hovel swung open and three children, dirty faces tensely expectant, appeared.

Noting the rags barely covering the children's skinny bodies, Bishop Nicholas lowered his pack to the rough stone and fumbled inside. Withdrawing three warm robes, he blessed the children and spread a robe across each of their eagerly out-stretched arms. Joyful eyes watched the kindly old man shoulder his pack and disappear in the dank darkness of the cobbled lane.

Thus it was that Saint Nicholas, the patron saint of children, honored the anniversary of the birth of Jesus Christ during the fourth century in the city of Myra, Asia Minor. And this giving of gifts on the eve of the birth of our Lord has been handed down through the ages by the people who loved the old bishop.—Hardy B. Arrendale.

December 26. The Days of Our Years

An old-timer was sitting on a city park bench. "How old are you?" a little boy asked.

"Well, son," the old-timer answered, "I don't know exactly."

"You don't know your own age?" the little boy said in disbelief.

"No, son, I've never counted the years. I've always thought of the days of my life as months in a year."

This confused the little boy. "I don't understand."

"Well," said the old-timer, "for instance, take the day I was born. That was like New Year's Day." He stopped and looked at the little boy carefully. "I'd say you were enjoying the Valentine's Day of your life now."

"I'm seven years old," the little boy boasted, "if that's what you mean."

"That's what I mean," the old-timer smiled. "When I celebrated my twenty-first birthday it was like the first of May. The fourth of July was the day I got married."

"What month are you now?" the little boy asked.

"I'm about December 29th in my life."

"That's sad," the little boy said. "That's almost the end of the year."

"Yes," said the old-timer, "December 31st is creeping up on me. But it's not sad. When you've lived all the months of your life as I have, you'll come to realize—and have faith—that after the days of December, a whole new year begins!"—Dan Valentine, Jr.

SECTION X. Resources for the American Bicentennial

SERMON SUGGESTIONS

Topic: Founding Fathers' Idea of Liberty

TEXT: II Cor. 3:17.

I. In the thinking of our Founding Fathers, liberty was a natural right that came from God and permitted each person to gain or lose health, knowledge, understanding, influence, friends, happiness and wealth without individually or collectively using fraud or aggression or initiating force or the threat of force.

II. Liberty might be defined as respect for the right of the individual to initiate and achieve in his own way physical, intellectual, spiritual, and financial improvement. In other words liberty means no more and no less than the right to be sovereign over one's life.

III. Liberty is the right to do with respect to others as one hopes others will do to him. In this sense liberty means the right to attempt to supply one's desires without the use of coercion and in ways that are not harmful to others.

IV. Liberty or freedom can exist only in the absence of aggression or the threat of aggression individually or collectively. Under liberty, as understood by the Founding Fathers, a man will accept only that to which all have access on the same terms. As used by the Founding Fathers and by the libertarians, freedom and liberty permit force or the threat of force to be used collectively or individually only to restrain fraud or predation and to require the aggressor to indemnify his victim.

V. Liberty gives every person an equal right to help establish values. It gives every man a monopoly of his own life and property, no more, no less.—R. C. Hoiles.

Topic: This Nation under God

TEXT: Heb. 11:16.

When we who at one and the same time are concerned about being serious Christians and conscientious American citizens think of what it may mean to say, "This nation under God," we are given insight to see our responsibilities here and now in the light of God's eternal purpose and to see how our faith in God's evaluation of personhood must be reflected in practical political and economic decisions. This is always true. It is particularly significant whenever the nation passes a major milestone in its march through history.

I. There is the here and now with what it seems to demand. Regardless of our faith the immediacies of life cry out for attention and have to be dealt with in practical terms. The larger perspective may have a lot to do with providing those entrusted with national leadership with a philosophical background for strategy, but this is only one side of the picture. There is always wood to be hewn and water to be drawn wherever people are engaged in the enterprise of living. Abraham of old had to plan for food and water, shelter and pasture, and how to get along with the peoples through whose land he passed. Even though he might be inspired by the vision of the holy people of God reflecting the eternal purpose on earth, he had at the same time to take care of the immediate service functions, and this provides a moral balance wheel in the divine scheme of things.

II. The kind of faith that frames our lives in the Christian scheme of things is more than a moral reminder. It provides in one sense the larger perspective in which we see our tasks and in another sense the spiritual dynamic for handling them with courage and confidence. When we use the phrase, "This nation under God," in a Christian church we are not simply saying that it would be well if everyone believed in a supreme being of some sort. Rather when we say "under God" in a Christian church we mean under the sovereignty of the Almighty as his purpose is revealed to us in and through the saving life, death, and eternal mission of Jesus Christ our Lord.

III. Like the men of faith recalled in Hebrews we can be led to see our daily responsibilities as paving blocks on the king's highway and our long-range dreams as ways by which we, like them, "desire a better country, that is, a heavenly one." Then indeed we can make our own the faith of the writer who said, "God is not ashamed to be called their God (indeed our God), for he has prepared for them (and for us) a city." —Charles D. Kean.

Topic: Our Stake in Democracy
TEXT: Mic. 4:3.

I. The first reason why the church has a stake in democracy is that Christians believe that men are good enough to make democracy possible. Those who have followed Jesus Christ have always been impressed by the fact that men can rise to great heights of character. Indeed Christians are so impressed by this that they believe men are made in the image of God.

II. The second reason why the church has a stake in democracy is that men are wicked enough to make democracy necessary.

III. The third reason that the church has a stake in the survival and spread of democracy is that men are alike enough to make democracy universal.— Robert J. Arnott.

Topic: On Loving or Leaving America
SCRIPTURE: Amos 7:10–17.

I. What does it mean to love your country? What does it mean for a Christian who professes to love God to say that he loves his country? What motivates the widespread use of the slogan to love America or leave it?

(a) Love, we are told and probably know from experience, is often blind to the faults of the beloved. But in the long run it is a weak love that cannot face reality.

(b) If it is suggested that we should leave America rather than challenge the ills of the nation, then we are being called to an infantile love, to live by illusions, and to ignore the seed of destruction already growing.

(c) Surely to love our country does not require that we refuse to confront grievous problems, the blemishes which disfigure the face of our nation, the malpractices which distort justice.

II. Does love of country require that I leave the country rather than speak out?

(a) The fact is that many people who say "America: Love It or Leave It" are not thinking of America at all, not the real America. Nor do they love their country. They are thinking of themselves, of their own comfort, their own pleasant spot. They feel that they have it made, and they do not want anything to upset their personal plans for the future or undercut what they have stashed away. They would like to put everything disagreeable out of sight.

(b) If anyone begins to press for action the whole prospect of dragging the evils into the open is so upsetting hat they would rather the critics would leave the country.

III. Many of the men and women whom our children are taught to regard as the great lovers of their country are people who during their lifetime were treated as disturbers, cranks, and dangerous.

(a) This was the story of the prophets who deeply loved their country and who criticized it not because they wished its destruction but because they wanted it saved for the purposes of God. The prophet Amos went with some reluctance to Israel. He was not the kind of person who loved a fight, the kind who has to stir up trouble so as not to be bored. He delivered his message in an attempt to persuade Israel to become a nation under God. He was not thanked for putting his finger on the sore spots of the nation's body. (See Amos 5:10–12.)

(b) Such talk was not what was wanted. For many people the times were prosperous, they had never had it so good, and they did not want to make adjustments for the sake of justice in the land. (See Amos 6:4–6.)

(c) They were not grieved over the ruin of their nation. They professed to care for their country, to love it, but in reality they loved only themselves and what the country was doing for them. Consequently they found Amos a disturber and sought to get rid of him. In very self-righteous terms they told Amos to love Israel or leave it.

IV. Our Lord was bitterly attacked by people who wanted everything to remain just as it was. It became clear that if his teachings were to be followed the old order would have to change.

(a) To get rid of him the charge was made that he was not a friend of Caesar, which was another way of saying that he was not loyal to the government. He was charged with breaking with tradition. He was told in effect to love Jerusalem or leave it.

(b) Can there be any doubt now as to who truly loved Jerusalem? He wept over the city of his love because he saw it rejecting its salvation and hope.

V. We now come to a day of national remembrance of the days and events which gave this nation its birth.

(a) We are forced to ask what it means to love our country. We profess to love God with all our hearts if we are Christian. How do we get love of country and love of God together? We are churchmen; we are citizens. How are we one and the other at the same time? Being a churchman on Sundays and a citizen on Monday has been tried, but it breaks down, for there are many situations in which the only way we can show our love for God is by doing our duty as a citizen.

(b) Let us ask if it is America we love or whether we love our own comforts and securities. America is more than mountains and streams. America is people of many classes and races. Some of them are victimized, many are exploited. These are God's people.

(c) We pledge allegiance to "this nation under God." Love of God and love of country need not be in conflict. Love for God will be manifest in our attempt to realize the ideal of a nation reflecting the righteousness of God.

(d) To love my country requires that I seek to make known to all men the nature of God revealed in Jesus Christ. That means witnessing to the lordship of Jesus Christ and his call to repentance and faith. I can do that only as I also seek to take responsibility for citizenship which will extend love through justice to all men. The work of evangelism and the work of social righteousness are wed in the gospel of Jesus Christ.—Wayne K. Clymer.

ILLUSTRATIONS

NEVER-ENDING STRUGGLE. An abiding love of our country is founded on some of the noblest concepts that have ever come from the mind and pen of man, all of which were clearly stated in the Declaration of Independence that gave birth to our nation and were later incorporated in its Constitution. Needless to say those concepts and ideals have not been fully realized over the intervening two hundred years, either in our country or in the many others that have incorporated them in their founding documents.

It is in the nature of such concepts and ideals to be a goal toward which men struggle and the more noble they are, the more difficult to achieve. The glory of a people is in the struggle to achieve them. It is a never-ending struggle and one that each generation must take on from those preceding it.

It is a struggle that should bring joy to those that undertake it as they envision in it the great opportunities for service it holds out to them and the challenge to advance further toward an idealistic goal.—George A. Newbury in *The Northern Light*.

OLD GLORY.   For more than ninescore years I have been the banner of hope and freedom for generation after generation of Americans.

Born amid the first flames of America's fight for freedom, I am the symbol of a country that has grown from a little group of thirteen colonies to a united nation of fifty sovereign states. Planted firmly on the high pinnacle of American faith, my gently fluttering folds have proved an inspiration to untold millions.

Men have followed me into battle with unwavering courage. They have looked upon me as a symbol of national unity. They have prayed that they and their fellow citizens might continue to enjoy the life, liberty, and pursuit of happiness which have been granted to every American as the heritage of free men.

So long as men love liberty more than life itself; so long as they treasure the priceless privileges bought with the blood of our forefathers; so long as the principles of truth, justice, and charity for all remain deeply rooted in human hearts, I shall continue to be the en-

during banner of the United States America.

CHALLENGE OF HISTORY.   Some nation has got to rise and answer the challenge of history. Some nation has got to say to the listening earth: "We have decided in an age that has turned its back on God to live as God wanted men to live. We reject the concept that man created God and now can abolish him. We accept humbly, hopefully, the truth that God made man and now can change him and lead nations and continents in the paths of peace."—Peter Howard.

GREAT TRADITION.   So long as the English tongue survives, the word Dunkirk will be spoken with reverence. For in that harbor at the end of a long battle the rags and blemishes that have hidden the soul of democracy fell away. There, beaten but unconquered, in shining splendor she faced the enemy.

It was not so simple a thing as courage, which the Nazis had in plenty. It was not so simple a thing as discipline, which can be hammered into men by a drill sergeant. It was not the result of careful planning, for there could have been little.

It was the common man of the free countries, rising in all his glory out of the mill, office, factory, mine, farm, and ship, applying to war the lessons learned when he went down the shaft to bring out trapped comrades, when he hurled the lifeboat through the surf, when he endured poverty and hard work for his children's sake.

This shining thing in the souls of free men Hitler cannot command or attain or conquer. It is the great tradition of democracy. It is the future. It is victory.—*The New York Times*.

RISING SUN.   Whilst the last members were signing it Doctor Franklin looking toward the President's Chair, at the back of which a rising sun happened to be painted, observed to a few members near him, that Painters had found it difficult to distinguish in their art rising from a setting sun. "I have," said he, "often and often in the course of the Session, and the vicissitudes of my hopes and fears as to its issue, looked at that behind the President without being able to tell whether it was rising or setting: but now at length I have the happiness to know that it is a rising and not a setting Sun."—James Madison.

THE LADY WITH A LAMP. A man once took his little granddaughter with him on a New York visit. They rode the ferry out to see the Statue of Liberty. The child was awed by the sight of the great arm holding up the huge torch. On the return boat to Manhattan she kept looking back at the statue. That night when she could not sleep her grandfather asked if something was troubling her. "I keep thinking of the lady with the lamp," she said. "Don't you think somebody ought to help her hold it up?"—Robert E. Goodrich, Jr.

IF THEY'D PLAYED IT COOL IN THE YEAR 1776. Nathan Hale never saw his twenty-second birthday. He could have blamed George Washington and have lived to a ripe old age.

Paul Revere could have said: "Why pick on me? It is the middle of the night. I cannot ride through every Middlesex village. Besides I am not the only man in Boston with a horse."

Patrick Henry could have said: "Yes, I am for liberty, but we must be realistic. We are small compared with the British, and someone is going to get hurt."

George Washington could have said: "Gentlemen, you honor me. I am just getting some personal matters settled and have much to do at Mount Vernon. Why don't you try General Gates? Also you might say I have served my time."

Benjamin Franklin could have said: "I'm over seventy-five years old. What you need as a Minister to France in these strenuous times is a younger man. Let a new generation take over. I want

to rest." Instead he negotiated most brilliantly the Treaty of Alliance.

After Appomattox, Robert E. Lee could have said: "I've gone through the worst strain a man could endure. I've lost the cause, and my personal affairs have suffered. I could cash in on my reputation and put myself and my family into continued wealth." Instead he turned down the most lucrative offers.—James E. Palmer, Jr.

CIVIC DUTY. A citizen has a complex duty. He ought to learn to express his opinions and to make up his own mind on the principal public issues. He ought never to miss the ballot box. And when he casts his vote for somebody he should weigh that somebody in the scale of morals, which includes intellectual integrity.—Herbert Hoover.

THEN AND NOW. It struck me that with the American people preparing to recapture the spirit of '76 and eager to become immersed in a nostalgic recognition of their past, we should become aware of what the American was two hundred years ago and what we are now.—Eric Sloan.

FROM THE STEPS OF THE LINCOLN MEMORIAL. I say to you today, my friends, even though we face difficulties today and tomorrow, I still have a dream. It is a dream deeply rooted in the American Dream. I have a dream that one day this nation will rise up, live out the true meaning of its creed: "We hold these truths to be self-evident, that all men are created equal." I have a dream that one day on the red hills of Georgia, sons of former slaves and sons of former slave-owners will be able to sit down together at the table of brotherhood. . . . I have a dream that my four little children will one day live in a nation where they will not be judged by the color of their skin but by the content of their character.—Martin Luther King, Jr.

NATION UNDER GOD. The Declaration

of Independence, as originally presented to Congress, contained three references to God: the first in the opening paragraph where "the laws of nature and of nature's God" are invoked; the second in the next paragraph where "We hold these truths to be self-evident, that all men . . . are endowed by their creator with certain unalienable rights"; and the third where the signers appeal to "the Supreme Judge of the world for the rectitude of [their] intentions."

The draft presented to Congress closed with this sentence: "And, for the support of this declaration, we mutually pledge to each other our lives, our fortunes, and our sacred honor." Congress amended this sentence by inserting after the word "declaration" the clause "with firm reliance on the protection of Divine Providence."

In the midst of the Constitutional Convention, when that document was finally adopted, there were many times when it appeared that the Convention was doomed to failure. Then Benjamin Franklin made one of the greatest speeches of his distinguished lifetime. He spoke of the apparent inability of the Convention to solve the problems confronting it and stated his faith in an "overruling Providence" and in the power of prayer.

He said: "I have lived, sirs, a long time, and the longer I live the more convincing proof I see of this truth: that God governs in the affairs of men. And if a sparrow cannot fall to the ground without his notice, is it possible that an empire can rise without his aid?"

He continued: "We have been assured in the sacred writings that 'except the Lord build the House, they labor in vain that build it.' I firmly believe this; and I also believe that without his concurring aid we shall succeed in this political building no better than the builders of Babel. We shall be divided by our little partial local interests; our projects will be confounded, and we ourselves shall become a reproach and byword down to future ages. And, what is worse, mankind may hereafter from this unfortunate instance despair of establishing governments by human wisdom and leave it to chance, war, and · conquest.

"I, therefore, beg leave to move that henceforth prayers imploring the assistance of heaven, and its blessings on our deliberations, be held in this Assembly every morning before we proceed to business, and that one or more of the clergy of this city be requested to officiate in that service."—Daniel L. Marsh.

THE SPIRIT OF LIBERTY.   What is the spirit of liberty? I cannot define it; I can only tell you my own faith. The spirit of liberty is the spirit which is not too sure that it is right; the spirit of liberty is the spirit which seeks to understand the minds of other men and women; the spirit of liberty is the spirit which weighs their interests alongside its own without bias; the spirit of liberty remembers that not even a sparrow falls to earth unheeded; the spirit of liberty is the spirit of him who nearly two thousand years ago taught mankind that lesson it has never learned but has never quite forgotten, that there may be a kingdom where the least shall be heard and considered side by side with the greatest; the spirit of an America which has never been, and which may never be, nay, which will never be except as the conscience and courage of Americans create it.—Alan Geyer.

AMERICAN CULTURE.   No land has ever before drawn upon so many diverse cultural elements for its population as America, and there can be very little doubt that a great part of the vitality which is so characteristic of the American scene is due to the static generated by so many different cultural charges. The sparkling character of American culture is like a high-tension wire free at one end and discharging a continuous stream of dancing multicolored sparks. No other display of fireworks has ever equaled it. It is this liveliness of the social atmosphere that continually replenished the energies of Americans.—Ashley Montagu.

LIVING WITNESS.   It is not merely for today but for all time to come that we should perpetuate for our children's children that great and free government which we have enjoyed all our lives. I beg you to remember this, not merely for my sake but for yours.

I happen, temporarily, to occupy the White House. I am a living witness that any one of your children may look to come here as my father's child has. It is in order that each one of you may have, through this free government which we have enjoyed, an open field and a fair chance for your industry, enterprise, and intelligence, that you may all have equal privileges in the race of life with all its desirable human aspirations.—Abraham Lincoln.

ASSESSMENT.   On Hay Island during the Revolutionary War some hungry and dispirited soldiers dragged themselves and their wounded comrades into an old barn. The tide of battle was against them, and they were discouraged.

At that moment General George Washington entered the barn and gave the men the truth about their situation as he said, "I promise those who will follow me further, no chance of victory, for by my God, I see none; no glory or gain, or laurels returning home, but rather wounds and death, cold and disease and hunger, winters to come such as this, with our bloody trail in the snow, and no end to it till you shovel each other in with those at Valley Forge!"

As the weary soldiers prepared to bury a dead comrade, General Washington faced them with thoughtful and almost bitter words: "This liberty will look easy by and by when nobody dies to get it."

DEEPEST EMOTIONS.   The spirit of nationalism springs from the deepest of human emotions. It rises from the yearning of men to be free of foreign domination, to govern themselves. It springs from a thousand rills of race, of history, of sacrifice and pride in national achievement. In our own country does not the word "America" stir something deeper within us than mere geography? Does not the suffering and the sacrifice of our forebears who fought for our independence flash in our minds with every mention of the word "America"?—Herbert Hoover.

PRAYERS

SENATE PRAYER.   Lord God of heaven, who hath so lavishly blessed this land, make us thy people to be humble.

Keep us ever aware that the good things we enjoy have come from thee, that thou didst lend them to us.

We say that in God we trust, yet we worry and try to manage our own affairs.

We say that we love thee, and yet we do not obey thee.

Wilt thou reach down and change the gears within us—that we may go forward with thee.

Sanctify our love of country that our boasting may be turned into humility, our pride into a ministry for men everywhere.

Help us to make this God's own country by living like God's own people.—Peter Marshall.

FOR HERITAGE AND PEOPLE.   God of all nations, thou art the God of our nation. We thank thee for America, for this, our inheritance, a beautiful and bountiful country; for fields of grain and tall mountains and restless seas. But most of all for people—for Americans of all classes, of all colors, of all creeds. We are grateful for workers in industry, for farmers, for doctors and nurses and ministers. And we thank thee for soldiers and sailors and airmen who guard and protect us day and night. Make us more effective witnesses of thee, our Father, in word and in deed. Give us the courage to face our difficulties unafraid, putting our trust, O God, in thee.—*The Link*.

INAUGURATION PRAYER.   Almighty God: we make our earnest prayer that thou wilt keep the United States in thy holy protection; that thou wilt incline the hearts of the citizens to cultivate a spirit of subordination and obedience to government; and entertain a brotherly affection and love for one another and for their fellow citizens of the United States at large. And, finally, that thou wilt most graciously be pleased to dispose us all to do justice, to love mercy, and to demean ourselves with charity, humility, and pacific temper of mind which were the characteristics of the Divine Author of our blessed religion, and without an humble imitation of whose example in these things we can never hope to be a happy nation. Grant our supplication, we beseech thee, through Jesus Christ our Lord.—George Washington.

GRATITUDE AND CONFESSION.   Almighty God, the earth is yours and the nations your people. Remind us of your good provision in this lovely land with its cloud-wrapped mountains and pounding surf, with its tall timber and green meadows, with its productive farms and teeming cities, with its pure air and water, its fertile soil, and its plentiful harvest. We thank you for honest government and freedom of religion, for quality education, dedicated teachers, and eager students.

Thank you for the capable leaders of our land and its faithful folk. Thank you that ours is one nation under God, for patriots who trained and sacrificed, for citizens who defend our liberties, for our free press and liberty of conscience, for law and justice with mercy.

We confess our indifference to your good gifts and our unthankful hearts. Forgive our blind trust in power and private possession. Forgive our man-made divisions and prejudices, our indifference to those who hurt and are in need, and our lack of concern for our neighbors across the sea and across the city.

Eternal God, before you nations rise and fall. They have their day of glory and eclipse. Remind us of your plan for the ages. Give us a glimpse of the city of God which you have under construction. Never let us forget our dual citizenship. We pray for peace of heart, of home, and of nations. Forgive our sins and accept our gratitude, through Jesus Christ our Lord.—Alton H. McEachern.

SECTION XI. *Sermon Outlines and Homiletic and Worship Aids for Fifty-two Weeks*

SUNDAY: JANUARY FOURTH

MORNING SERVICE

Topic: Beginnings

TEXT: Phil. 3:12–14 (RSV).

I. There are no permanent victories. (a) One of the most disconcerting lessons of life is to discover the illusion of arriving. There is never a point in life when we can truthfully say, "Now I have arrived." Sooner or later we wake up to the stark realization that regardless of our successes, achievements, or honors, there are no permanent destinations in our earthly pilgrimage, only intersections.

(b) There are temporary destinations we reach. But upon arrival we find it is not the end at all. It is not even the beginning of the end. It is merely the end of the beginning. There is forever a hidden agenda of unfinished business between us and God and each other.

(c) This unfinished business begins with birth. Birth is quite an event. I am forever impressed with the miracle of it. There is no greater miracle, but there is nothing conclusive about it. At best it is merely the end of the beginning. Birth is a process, not an event.

(d) Graduation from any level of a formal educational institution is an auspicious event, but commencement is a far more accurate term. I once had the naïve notion that I would have it made upon graduation from a theological seminary. Success would be automatic. Sermons easy to prepare. I would have it made. What an illusion. It has not turned out that way.

(e) There is a great distance between the prologue of the wedding and mature love. Much of marriage is covered with the dust of dailyness. Yet Mrs. Browning's phrase, "And if God choose, I shall but love thee better after death," is intriguing.

(f) What we call death is as traumatic as birth but seems so much more final. It isn't. At the heart of Christian faith is the conviction that death is not the end. It is only another intersection in the road beyond which the soul is no longer visible because it has been released from its temporary habitation which we call the body. Onward it journeys to a new horizon, there to be equipped with a new instrument which God provides even as he provided life and its instrument in the beginning.

(g) There is never ground for complacency. After we accept the fact that our destinations are temporary and our victories fleeting, that we cannot possibly remain where we are, we are in the correct frame of mind to accept the fact that to settle down or be self-satisfied with any relationship or achievement is the essence of sin or defeat.

II. We are compelled to get our sense of satisfaction and significance, meaning and fulfillment out of the journey itself. This is what Paul realized when he wrote the words in the text.

(a) This is our reason for participating in Holy Communion. This experience symbolizes the eternal process of birth and rebirth. There is a beginning which is common to every experience, the point of decisiveness when we turn to God and each other with a new attentiveness, a new openness to our possibilities.

(b) We have a new beginning every time a significant person or significant experience comes to us. At each intersection of life we are born again. The deep satisfactions and fulfillments of life are realized in relationship with each other. What Sigmund Freud called the "will to pleasure" and Alfred Adler described as the "will to power" and Viktor Frankl terms the "will to meaning" can be met only in relationships. Abiding meanings come to us only in interpersonal relationships.

(c) So we are here to seek that quality of life that relates us creatively to the Creator, that moves us from self-centeredness to centeredness in God and others, away from values that use people to those that love people.

(d) "After all, being on the way forms in some sense the goal of life" (Winifred B. Garrison). "The authentic individual is neither an end or a beginning but a link between ages, both memory and expectation. Every moment is a new beginning with a continuum of history. It is fallacious to segregate a moment and not to sense its involvement in both past and future." (Abraham Heschel.)

III. How wise and wonderful are the designs of our Creator! (a) He asks us to live life amidst the uncertainties of our tomorrows. He calls us to live a day at a time and to trust, hope, love, and live by faith. He rewards our affirmation with wonder and surprise and fills life with challenge rather than with physical security. We live and move into a future that is always unknown but with foundations and resources that give us inner strength.

(b) God has more truths for us to learn, more victories for us to win, more persons for us to love, more rivers to cross, more loads to lift, more kingdoms to conquer. We've only just begun to live.—Ralph B. Johnson.

Illustrations

OPPORTUNITY. The year begins, and all its pages are as blank as the silent years of the life of Jesus Christ. Let us begin it with high resolution; then let us take all its limitations, all its hindrances, its disappointments, its narrow and commonplace conditions, and meet them as the Master did in Nazareth with patience, with obedience, putting ourselves in cheerful subjection, serving our apprenticeship. Who knows what opportunity may come to us this year?—George Hodges.

HEAVEN AND HELL. Hell is not related to an evil life as a spanking is related to disobedience, for a spanking need not necessarily follow disobedience. Rather hell is related to an evil life as blindness is related to the plucking out of an eye. And heaven is not related to a good life as a medal is related to a school examination; it is rather related to a good life as knowledge to study. Some say, "We have our hell on this earth." We do. We can start it here, but it does not finish here. Heaven also has its beginnings here in a true peace of mind in union with divine life, but it does not finish here either.—Fulton J. Sheen.

Sermon Suggestions

THE ART OF MAKING DECISIONS. Text: Luke 10:18. (1) Make your decisions in the light of long-range goals instead of short-term desires. (2) Make your decisions on the basis of moral principle instead of personal popularity. (3) Make your decisions at the level of your responsibilities instead of your desires.—Charles M. Crowe.

PROCRASTINATION. Text: Acts 24:25. (1) It is dangerous and foolish to say tomorrow because it is easy and natural to procrastinate. (2) It is dangerous and foolish to say tomorrow because it gives to tomorrow a false value. (3) It is dangerous and foolish to say tomorrow, to ask for a more convenient season, because of new conditions and new circumstances which surround us. (4) It is dangerous and foolish to say tomorrow, a convenient season, for tomorrow may never come.—Clarence Edward Macartney.

Worship Aids

CALL TO WORSHIP. "Great is the Lord, and greatly to be praised; and his greatness is unsearchable. One generation shall praise thy works to another, and shall declare thy mighty works." Ps. 145: 3–4.

INVOCATION. O God, whose name is great, whose goodness is inexhaustible, who art worshiped and served by all the hosts of heaven: touch our hearts, search out our consciences, and cast out of us every evil thought and base desire; all envy, wrath, and remembrance of injuries; and every motion of flesh and spirit that is contrary to thy holy will.

OFFERTORY SENTENCE. "Thy prayers and thine alms are come up for a memorial before God." Acts 10:4.

OFFERTORY PRAYER. Our Father, we bow in humble gratitude that as a new year dawns we may call on thee to guide, strengthen, bless, and forgive, and that through these gifts we may share thy love with all who call upon us and thee.

PRAYER. Eternal God, in whom there is no beginning or end, no daylight or darkness, and who is the same yesterday, today, and forever, individually and corporately we stand in constant need of your renewing presence and forgiving love. We are like travelers through a desert, and you, O God, are a welcomed oasis. Spiritually we are dry and parched and need the living water that only you can give. Let us drink deeply of your well of righteousness. Fill us, O Lord, with power and purpose so that we can continue to be travelers for good in your world.

Lord God, we confess that we have not always traveled on your behalf. Shamefully we admit that we have taken many journeys on our own behalf and haven't even bothered to consult you, but the law of diminishing returns always sets in and we find ourselves used up, depressed, and feeling flat.

Spirit of the living God, come into our lives with *love* that we may journey forth as reconcilers, that we may go to our neighbors in their need and give them a cup of cold water in your name.

God of the ages, come into our lives with *joy* that we too may be able to share the good news of your eternal life with those who are cringing in fear at the threat of death.

Father of our Lord Jesus Christ, come into our lonely lives and fill us with *peace*—your peace that passes all understanding—and when we are filled with peace, send us out to be peacemakers in a world where brother is pitted against brother. May each of us be girded with Christlike power, and may we use this power purposefully, to witness to your kingdom which in part we have experienced here this morning.—George L. Earnshaw.

EVENING SERVICE

Topic: The Comprehension of the Gospel

SCRIPTURE: I Cor. 3:1–4.

In the verses before us Paul is speaking of the comprehension of the gospel. He anticipates the question as to how people can know spiritual initiation, illumination, and interpretation and yet be infantile in their understanding of the things of God. Contrasting carnality as against spirituality in the Christian life, he shows that carnality is the real cause of division in the church of Jesus Christ. Three aspects of carnal Christians are brought to our attention.

I. *The category of carnal Christians* (v. 1). Paul introduces us to three categories of people here upon earth. He speaks of the natural man who receiveth not the things of the Spirit, for they are foolishness unto him. Such an individual may be educated and refined, but he is still lost and undone. Then there is the man who possesses not only physical life but spiritual life, and because he feeds on spiritual foods he matures accordingly. The carnal man is a person whose spiritual life is dwarfed and therefore whose spiritual walk is defeated. In Corinth the saints were for the most part carnal.

II. *The capacity of carnal Christians* (v. 2). The capacity of carnal Christians is pathetically limited to an infantile formula. Paul describes this diet as milk as against meat. Through lack of growth and experience in the word of righteousness, there is no discernment of truth. And being unable to appreciate truth, carnal Christians are also incapable of appropriating the meat of the Word.

III. *The conduct of carnal Christians* (v. 3). In this word picture of spiritual babyhood Paul tells us that the believer who never seems to pass the childish stage is carnal in all his behavior. His conduct is characterized by unhealthy discontent, discord, and division. How repelling are these traits of the uncrucified flesh. As we examine ourselves in the light of this exposition, how it makes us want to grow until we have left spiritual babyhood behind! (See I Cor. 13:11.)—Stephen F. Olford.

SUNDAY: JANUARY ELEVENTH

MORNING SERVICE

Topic: Bad Deal but a Good Lord

TEXTS: Gen. 50:20; Gal. 3:13–14 (RSV).

Joseph was dealt a bad deal in life. His brothers turned on him and sold him into slavery and then outwitted their father into thinking that he had been killed by a wild beast. If anyone ever got a raw deal, certainly this talented young man did. If anybody ever had reason to be bitter, certainly Joseph had reason. If anyone ever had an excuse to become a cynic, he did. Who could condemn him if he were to seek revenge upon his scheming brothers? But Joseph did none of these things.

His response is one of the high points of spiritual greatness in the Old Testament. It revealed a remarkable spiritual maturity in Joseph to be able to say to those who had once wanted to kill him that somehow God was working out his purpose even through their mean-ness. His insight should give us the strength to believe that no matter how evil the circumstance in life, God can make even the evil of men glory him.

I. We must accept, as Joseph did, that evil is a fact of life in our world. It is here and it is here to stay.

(a) Joseph made no attempt to persuade himself that what his brothers had done to him was anything but an evil act. He did not blame it on the fact that they were weaned from their mother too early or dropped on their head as a child, nor did he conclude that their actions were a reflection of their being culturally deprived. He said to their faces that "you meant evil against me.' This they could not deny. (See Rom 7:15.)

(b) Evil is loose in our world, and we dare not hide our heads in the sand from this fact. We had better accept the fact that evil is a very present reality in all of us and in all we do. Certainly the cross of Christ is a reminder of what sin can do to goodness in our world.

II. We still have the difficulty of "why?" (a) If we could have asked Joseph what he thought as he was being carried away to Egypt, he would probably have confessed to being troubled over this obvious act of injustice. "Why me, O Lord? What did I ever do to you? I don't deserve this. I never hurt anybody. I've been a good boy." Many years later after he had a chance to see how strangely and wonderfully God works he could say God meant this for good. He did not pretend to know the whole mind of God, but he did come to see that somehow God had his own reasons for making the world as he did and that in God's own good time his purpose would come clear.

(b) Trouble is one of life's best teachers. The farmer knows that weeds make him more alert and attentive to his crops. The creeds of the church were hammered out in the sharp conflict between orthodoxy and heresy. Most of the convictions that you and I hold most strongly have been won through our own struggles with trouble, despair, defeat, and disaster.

(c) We must learn to say with Jacob as he struggled with the angel who had come to teach him a profound lesson after his sin against Esau, "I will not let you go, unless you bless me." If we approach every conflict with evil in this way, determined to wring a blessing from it and to learn another lesson of life, we will surely discover that God has good reasons for permitting so much evil to exist in his world.

III. How can you possibly grow through an evil experience? We grow only when we gain perspective on it. We must remember that many experiences, events, and words are evil only by our definition and not by God's. We define a weed in a garden as evil only because we define the growth of the plant as good, and anything that interferes with it is evil.

(a) The love of money has often been called the root of evil, and it is for millions of people who worship it as their god and sacrifice all other values at its altar. But money in the hands of a responsible, dedicated, spiritually disciplined person can bring untold blessings.

(b) Sex is neither good nor bad in itself. When expressed within the context of marriage it is a divine blessing for which we can thank God, but when it is taken out of context and used selfishly it is one of the worst of life's curses.

(c) Old age is neither good nor bad. If we have been deceived into thinking that youth is the high point of life, then all that follows is a miserable anticlimax. But if we look forward to "the last of life, for which the first was made," old age can be the rich fruit of years of preparation.

(d) Nor is death good or bad in itself. (1) Certainly in biblical times it was thought that to die on a cross was a curse. Our text quotes the Old Testament law that says, "Cursed be every one who hangs on a tree." When Jesus was nailed to that tree it was meant as an act of hatred toward him. Through this evil act the blessing of God has come upon us all that "we might receive the promise of the Spirit through faith."

(2) What those people meant for evil against Jesus, God meant for good. While they thought they were killing Jesus they were really bringing him to life for good. While they thought this would put an end to that small band of followers who called themselves Christians it turned out to be only the beginning. While it may have been a "bad deal" for Jesus to die in such a manner, a good God was able to turn this evil act into an opportunity for eternal life for you and me.—C. Thomas Hilton.

Illustrations

ALL CREATORS. You must recognize yourself as being in a sense the "creator" of the world around you. No matter what the disposition quirks and character failings of other people, you and I must face the fact that we do "create" an atmosphere around us. Only God is the lone Creator, but we are all little "creators" in that we create friction or peace, rest or strain, reality or "phoniness" in the area immediately surrounding us. What kind of vibrations does your personality set up in your home? In the office where you work? In the church? Are the people with whom we live free to be their best selves? Are they free to be themselves at all?—Eugenia Price.

PROBLEM NEIGHBORS.   A sheepman in Indiana was troubled by his neighbors' dogs who were killing his sheep. Sheepmen usually counter that problem with lawsuits or barbed wire fences or even shotguns, but this man went to work on his neighbors with a better idea. To every neighbor's child he gave a lamb or two as pets; and in due time when all his neighbors had their own small flocks they began to tie up their dogs, and that put an end to the problem. —J. Wallace Hamilton.

Sermon Suggestions

TO OBEY GOD IS TO BE MISUNDERSTOOD. Scripture: Matt. 10:16–22. (1) Misunderstanding is inevitable because the ways of God are not the ways of man. (2) It is also desirable. To have our faith challenged is good for us for it is only then that we discover that we have a faith at all. (3) When a great faith is subjected to misunderstanding and persecution it becomes communicable and, like molten lead, can flow into the life of another.—Daniel D. Walker.

DYNAMIC LIVING FOR DIFFICULT DAYS. Three things are essential for living in difficult days. (1) The presence of an inward power to motivate. (2) Homes which produce strength, stability, and security. (3) A recognition that the individual holds the key to the abundant and dynamic life.—Fred M. Wood.

Worship Aids

CALL TO WORSHIP.   "O come, let us sing unto the Lord: let us make a joyful noise to the rock of our salvation. Let us come before his presence with thanksgiving, and make a joyful noise unto him with psalms." Ps. 95:1–2.

INVOCATION.   Our Father, we thank thee for thy Word and for the eternal truths which guide us day by day. We thank thee most of all for the living word, Jesus Christ, and the sureness of his presence. Teach us how to turn unto thee so that thy thoughts may be our thoughts and thy ways our ways.

OFFERTORY SENTENCE.   "What shall I render unto the Lord for all his benefits toward me? I will pay my vows unto the Lord now in the presence of all his people." Ps. 116:12–14.

OFFERTORY PRAYER.   Help us to remember, O Lord, that a life is a more persuasive testimony than words, that deeds are more effective than arguments, and that these gifts are only a portion of the loyalty thou dost require of us.

PRAYER.   O God, whose riches toward us in Christ Jesus are unsearchable, whose love is beyond our knowledge, whose peace passeth all understanding, and who art able to do exceeding abundantly above all that we ask or think, we praise thee for the resources which are ours in Christ: for reserves of power upon which we can draw without limit, for a patience that fainteth not neither is weary, for a perseverance which seeks until it brings the wanderer home, for an understanding which knows us far better than we can know ourselves, for a reverence for us that trusts and honors us when we have lost self-respect and forfeited all confidence from others, for a forgiveness which stops at nothing, for a grace which is able to save unto the uttermost, for a love which beareth, believeth, hopeth, endureth all things and never faileth, for a fullness from which we receive grace upon grace and know that from its supplies we shall still receive until we are filled unto all the fullness of God. Oh, how great is thy goodness, which thou hast laid up for them that obey thee in Christ Jesus, which thou hast wrought and workest even until now in Christ for them that follow him among the sons of men. Thanks be unto thee for thine unspeakable gift.—Henry Sloane Coffin.

EVENING SERVICE

Topic: Total Christian Stewardship
TEXT: II Cor. 8:2, 5 (LNT).
I. *What it is.* What is involved in stewardship? Life itself, mind, talent, skill, personality, time, one's whole self. All of these are the possessions which have been put into our care by the God who made us. Have you ever paused to consider how rich you really are? You exist as a live, personal being. You have reality; you are an entity that can think, can imagine, can invent, can produce. Your very life is a gift; you did not produce it; it was given you by God.
II. *How it works.* The best way to learn how total Christian stewardship works is to observe the actions of those people mentioned in II Cor. 8:1–5.

(a) They dedicated themselves to the Lord.
(b) They gave of their means "because they wanted to."
(c) They invested their poverty because of their joy in the Lord. They invested what they had, not what they did not have.
III. *What it produces.* Is it wrong to ask what good will come from my stewardship? No, because the scripture actually speaks of it. (See II Cor. 9:8, 10.)
(a) There will be the benefit of personal sufficiency. God will bless what we are and what we do.
(b) People will praise God because they will come to know him and have peace with him through your witness. (See II Cor. 9:12.) That is evangelism.
(c) They will thank God because you have helped to meet their need. That is humanitarian service.
(d) You vindicate your profession. (See II Cor. 9:13.) That is a reward and an honor that is difficult to duplicate.
(e) People who have come into a living faith in God will pray for the one who made it possible. (See II Cor. 9:13.)
—Paul P. Fryhling.

SUNDAY: JANUARY EIGHTEENTH

MORNING SERVICE

Topic: Responses to the Gospel (Missionary Day)
SCRIPTURE: Acts 17:1–18.
I. *Rejection.* (See Acts 17:1–5.) (a) One would have expected the Jews to become immediate followers of Jesus. Many favorable points should have drawn them to him: he was a Jew; he spoke highly of Abraham, Isaac, and Jacob; he spent much time in the temple and synagogues; he taught important truths about the Almighty God whom the Jews worshiped. In spite of many logical reasons for believing, the Israelites continually rejected Christ.
(b) An important lesson is provided here to every person who witnesses for Christ. We cannot logically predetermine

who will respond favorably to the gospel. Every soul-winner will testify that many of those persons whom he considered "good prospects" turned a cold and indifferent shoulder. And some "poor prospects" responded favorably.
(c) Rejection is difficult to withstand. It brings discouragement to the believer. Assuming that such rejection is typical and to be expected in all cases, we are tempted to quit witnessing. But we dare not overlook a most important fact: "some of them believed" (Acts 17:4).
(d) Jesus Christ faced the rejection of the world in order that some might be saved. Paul was rejected by many, but a few were converted. Should we expect a different response? (See John 15:20.)
II. *Sincerity.* (See Acts 17:10–14.) V. 11

provides three admirable traits of the Bereans.

(a) "They received the word with all readiness of mind." Many modern language translations describe the Bereans' response as one of "great eagerness." Theirs was not a unique reaction. Some people have always been eager to learn the Word. The psalmist declared, "How sweet are thy words unto my taste! yea, sweeter than honey to my mouth" (Ps. 119:103). Substantial increases in the numbers of Bible sales and Bible study groups bear witness that a great many people share the Bereans' and psalmist's feelings.

(b) "Searched the scriptures daily." We suspect the faith of the Bereans was strong because it grew out of the Word of God. (See Rom. 10:17.) A great temptation confronts modern Christians. Religious publications fill our bookshelves. Church libraries continue to grow. Each piece of literature provides an opportunity to read something other than God's Word. Every available tool can be used in understanding the Bible. But we would do well to duplicate the Bereans' example and study the scripture each day.

(c) "Whether those things were so." Can you imagine anyone thinking the word of the spirit-filled apostle Paul should be investigated? The Bereans refused to be gullible recipients of every word they heard. If a message withstood the test of scripture they would believe it. Fewer strange doctrines would exist today if followers of Christ had always been this careful.

III. *Skepticism.* (See Acts 17:15–18.) (a) Many people delight in doubting. Their joy in life seems to come from a practice of tasting all philosophical dishes but devouring none. A bite here and a bite there, always suggesting that they know how such a dish could have been made tastier.

(b) The men of Athens departed from this earth long ago. But their spirit lives on, ready to listen, ready to discuss, ready to argue, but never ready to search for the truth. Theirs is a sort of mental gymnastic, the primary goal of which is to develop the muscles of the mind.

(c) Such men tempt us to turn our backs and walk away. There came a time when Paul did depart (17:33). But before leaving Athens the apostle gave these skeptics an opportunity to hear the gospel. Paul's action should be carefully considered. The philosopher, the doubter, the cynic all need Jesus. We must give each one an opportunity to learn of salvation through Christ. Some will become believers. (See Acts 17:33.) —Jerry M. Paul in *The Lookout.*

Illustrations

BIG AND LITTLE PRAYERS. The great soul prays, "Lord, make me as big as my problem"; the little soul prays, "Let me off easy."

The giant soul says, "Lord, give me strength sufficient for a hard day"; the small soul begs, "Lord, give me a lighter load."

The great heart prays, "Lord, let me stand firm when the fight is the hardest"; the fearful heart cries, "Lord, let me escape."

The crusader soul sends up the prayer, "Lord, stand with me until I finish my task."—*The Anglican Digest.*

MILLIONS OF VOICES. I can only speak of what I know, and what I know is that if Christians made up their minds to it, millions of voices, millions I say throughout the world, would be added to the appeal of a handful of isolated individuals who, without any sort of affiliation today, intercede almost everywhere and ceaselessly for children and men.—Albert Camus.

Sermon Suggestion

CHURCH COMMITMENTS. (1) To worship God publicly. (2) To foster Christian character. (3) To remake human nature. (4) To Christianize social institutions. (5) To build a universal church. —Robert J. McCracken.

Worship Aids

CALL TO WORSHIP. "We are laborers together with God: ye are God's husbandry, ye are God's building. Let every man take heed how he buildeth. For other foundation can no man lay than that is laid, which is Jesus Christ." I Cor. 3:9–11.

INVOCATION. Almighty and everlasting God, whom the heaven of heavens cannot contain, much less the temples which our hands have built, but who art ever nigh unto the humble and the contrite: grant thy Holy Spirit, we beseech thee, to us who are here assembled; that cleansed and illumined by thy grace, we may worthily show forth thy praise, meekly learn thy word, render due thanks for thy mercies, and obtain a gracious answer to our prayers.

OFFERTORY SENTENCE. "Therefore, my beloved brethren, be ye steadfast, unmoveable, always abounding in the work of the Lord, forasmuch as ye know that your labour is not in vain in the Lord." I Cor. 15:58.

OFFERTORY PRAYER. God of our fathers, dearly do we cherish the blessings which thy church brings to us and dearly do we covet the privilege of sharing through these gifts the proclaiming of thy Word until all of the earth shall praise thee.

PRAYER. Help us, our Father, we pray, to comprehend more fully the prayer thy Son has taught us. Give us an understanding of every petition.

We have prayed, "Hallowed be thy name." May we understand that all our relationships, our struggles and temptations, our dreams and desires must be endowed with reverence. Direct our powers in dignity and quietness; may our every action be in thy name.

We have prayed, "Thy kingdom come." Help us to remember that thy kingdom will come upon the earth as first one soul and then another submits to thy rules of life. Help us to say unreservedly, "Here I am, use me."

Our Father, we have prayed, "Thy will be done in earth as it is in heaven." Help us to enter into a new and deeper relationship with thee, knowing that only as our small purposes become part of thy great purpose can we share in thy redemption of the world. May we be willing to say, "Not my will, but thine be done."

Our Father, we have prayed, "Give us this day our daily bread." Help us to know that thou wilt supply our every need. Above all we pray thee for thy rich, unfailing gifts of the living Water and the living Bread.

Our Father, we have prayed, "Forgive us our trespasses as we forgive them that trespass against us." We need to be reminded that our sins are forgiven only as we forgive others, that the gifts we bring to thy altar can be offered only if we are at peace with our brothers.

Our Father, we have prayed, "Lead us not into temptation, but deliver us from evil." May we know with certainty that in the frictions, the ceaseless demands, the clashes of wills which engulf us we may turn to thee as our sure bulwark. Lead us, our Father, out of fear and confusion into thy peace.—Sue Weddell.

EVENING SERVICE

Topic: Creed for a Congregation (Week of Prayer for Christian Unity)
TEXT: I Cor. 4:17.

I. This church is not a rival of any other church. We do not boast that our preaching, our teaching, our friendliness, our program, our music, our building are better than those of other churches. Remembering that "they who compare themselves among themselves are not wise," we strive to be a church worthy of the Christ whom we honor.

II. This church does not criticize any other church. We believe that "to his own Master a man stands or falls."

There is so little time to spread the gospel throughout the world that we dare not waste any of it by pausing to condemn others.

III. This church stands ready to share any of its vision or methods with other churches, prays for other churches, and rejoices when any other church shows an excellence for us to pattern after.

IV. This church stands in awesome recognition that it is part of the body of Christ and must strive to do the "greater things" which he promised when his own work was completed.

V. This church invites anyone who is seeking a savior and a means of serving him to be in fellowship with us.— Glenn A. Asquith.

SUNDAY: JANUARY TWENTY-FIFTH

MORNING SERVICE

Topic: Why Does God Allow It?

SCRIPTURE: John 9:1–12 (RSV).

If God has all power on earth and in heaven why does he allow tragedy to strike into our lives at what must always seem the least opportune moment? Why aren't we better prepared for what is to come? Why are widows left with small children when the father of the family is so badly needed? Why are the wicked allowed to live and to prosper when the good so often die young? There's no end to the number of questions that rush into the mind in an hour of trouble.

I. It may be that God has allowed sorrow to come into your life in order to point out some new pathway.

(a) We are often hard to teach. Learning comes only through the difficult experiences. We are happy with our minor routines, our little private worlds. It takes a shock to dynamite us out of them.

(b) The disciples would have been content to wander the dusty roads of Palestine with Jesus for the rest of their days. They cringed from facing the crisis that developed at Jerusalem. They fled in terror and hid trembling during the days of the crucifixion and resurrection. But the effect of all their suffering and mental turmoil was to rouse them from their complacency. "It is to your advantage that I go away," Jesus had said. Finally they realized that God had taken from them the staff on which they leaned in order to make them stand on their own two feet, powerful and unafraid.

II. There may be some ultimate purpose which we can see only dimly from this side of the veil of eternity.

(a) God's ways are different from ours. We cannot think with his mind; it is too great for us. But we know that change is the order of his universe. One generation succeeds another. Death is only one facet of that continuing change.

(b) Fortunately we have been endowed with a spirit facile enough to meet and accept the changes which are bound to occur in our lives and in our world. If they do not always seem to be changes for the better we can only rely on a trustworthy God to make them so in his good time and according to his eternal program.

III. It may be that we have allowed some earthly form of security to befog our vision of God and need a sharply clarifying influence to come into our lives.

(a) Once when the disciples were walking in a city with Jesus they saw a man born blind and began to speculate on the cause of his tragedy. "Did he sin, or was it the fault of his parents?" they asked Jesus. "Neither," was Jesus' astonishing reply. "It was done that the works of God might be made manifest in him. . . . As long as I am in the world, I am the light of the world."

(b) Our limited vision may make us wonder how the personal tragedy of a man doomed to walk in darkness most of his life could possibly be considered a means of glorifying God or manifesting his works. But what is more important, after all, to see earth's beauties or to see God? When the darkness of tragedy and sorrow descends it may be a blackout of human security in order that the light of God can shine in your life.

(c) The blind man was healed through a miracle performed by Jesus. But that doesn't happen often. Even when Jesus walked on earth there were many blind people who were not healed. We don't know in any special case why God allows suffering and sorrow. There are times when it seems that the cause of righteousness and peace, both personal and national, could better be served if we did not have to endure quite so much hardship. We think we could praise God more if we walked upon a rose-strewn path rather than on a path of burning coals.

(d) God has the power to change things if he chooses, and his choice is always wise. If it were not he would not be our loving Father, and we could bow our heads in utter despair. "The Lord disciplines him whom he loves," says the old Book. But it also tells us that he loves us with an everlasting love that seeks only our good.—Albert P. Stauderman.

Illustrations

PARABLE.   An engineer said to me one day: "I think I have a sermon idea for you. When we build a bridge we figure on three loads the bridge must bear: the dead load, the live load, and the wind load. The dead load is the weight of the bridge, the live load is the weight of the traffic on the bridge, and the wind load is the pressure of the wind on its superstructure."

This is a parable of life, for life can be defined in terms of successfully meeting these three pressures which bear upon every life. Life's "dead load" is concerned with managing oneself. Its "live load" is the pressure of daily wear and tear. And its "wind load" is adversity and unalterable circumstances.—Carl F. Lueg.

COMMENTARY ON PHIL. 2:3.   Behind the Greek word which is translated "lowliness" is our word "tapestry," and I think I shall not be far away from the apostle's mind when I say that he counsels us to lay our life down like a soft tapestry carpet—in kindly thoughts and gracious sympathies and helpful services in order that the weary, bruised feet of other people may find ease and comfort on the road. For some of the ways of life are very rough and flinty, and the sharp, jagged edges of circumstances cut the feet most sorely, and "going" is for many people a matter of ceaseless pain. It is the blessed privilege of Christians to lay a soft surface on the roads by spreading over them the graciousness of tender compassion, so stooping that other pilgrims can "walk over us" and so forget the hardships of the way.—John Henry Jowett.

Sermon Suggestions

DOES GOD USE PAIN?   Text: II Cor. 7:10 (GOODSPEED). (1) God uses pain when we let him, and God guides pain. (2) God uses pain as a danger signal. (3) Pain which we allow God to guide can turn us to himself. (4) If we will let God guide the pain we can enter into new appreciation of others and can actually deepen and widen our love. (5) God uses pain when we cooperate with his life-giving spirit to make us better persons.—David A. MacLennan.

A KNOCK AT THE DOOR.   Text: Rev. 3:20. (1) Christ knocks at the door of life when one looks out on the years and considers life's possibilities. (2) Christ knocks at our door with opportunity. (3) Christ knocks at the door of grief.—Halford E. Luccock.

Worship Aids

CALL TO WORSHIP.   "Thou wilt keep him in perfect peace, whose mind is stayed on thee: because he trusteth in thee. Trust ye in the Lord for ever: for in the Lord Jehovah is everlasting strength." Isa. 26:3–4.

INVOCATION. Out of our darkness we are come to thee for light; out of our sorrows we are come to thee for joy; out of our doubts we are come to thee for certainty; out of our anxieties we are come to thee for peace; out of our sinning we are come to thee for thy forgiving love. Open thou thine hand this day and satisfy our every need. This we ask for thy love's sake.

OFFERTORY SERVICE. "We then that are strong ought to bear the infirmities of the weak, and not to please ourselves." Rom. 15:1.

OFFERTORY PRAYER. Our heavenly Father, help us to remember that though Christ does offer his companionship, yet to us belongs the decision as to whether or not we will follow him. May we through these gifts and our witness share with all the world the blessedness that comes to us through thy grace.

PRAYER. Our most gracious heavenly Father, thou whose spirit meets us in the valley of shadows as well as on the mountaintop of triumph, we come before thee in this hour of worship, praying that thou wouldst sustain our spirits this day.

Sustain us as we seek to understand ourselves. We pledge ourselves to the cause for which thy Son gave himself, but then in unguarded moments we reveal attitudes and actions that are unworthy of his love. Speak to our hearts of thy forgiving grace, set our minds on the lofty heights of fulfillment, and send us on our way.

Sustain us, O Lord, in our relationships with our fellow men. Plant within our hearts the seeds of trust that will allow us to reach out unafraid to those around us. Give us vision to see the refinement that is a part of every heart, though it might not be perceived at first glance. Remove from us, O Lord, feelings of suspicion, bitterness, mistrust, and cynicism that rise against our souls like waves that pound the rocky shore.

Sustain us, O God, in life at home with our families. So often we close the door of our minds when we enter the sanctuary that is our dwelling place. Alert us, we pray, to the intimate needs that go unnoticed day after day because we are preoccupied with less important concerns. Let love flow unchallenged through the dry, parched land that we might glimpse what it means to speak of the redemptive love of Christ.

Sustain this nation, our Father, for we are fast becoming aware that the saving power is not within our grasp. Remove the weeds of bitterness that have strangled our sensitivity to the needs of other people. Show us what reconciliation really means and help us to understand it when we see it.

Sustain thy church, O Lord, and help us to prepare ourselves for the other that lies ahead within thy vineyard. Hold our tongues when we would speak pious but empty words. Let actions and attitudes stand side by side so that others will know that the church is indeed alive and at work in this world.

Sustain our spirits now as we come before thine altar in prayer. Hear our innermost thoughts and bring thy healing spirit forth to meet the uncountable needs that are ours this day. —Charles H. Sanders.

EVENING SERVICE

Topic: Evidences of God
TEXT: II Cor. 5:7.

I. *There are evidences of God from nature.* (a) Scientists state that there are 100,000 different types of plants and trees, 600,000 kinds of insects, and thousands of species of animals. Over God's creation is man, the crown of God's creation. All these things came by definite acts of God's creation. (See Gen. 1:1–2.)

(b) God's design is seen in nature with all its wonders, giving evidences of his power. (See Ps. 139:14.)

II. *There are evidences of God in the Bible.* God gives a declaration of himself in the Bible. The words "God said" and "Thus saith the Lord" are mentioned 3,808 times in the Bible. "The word of God" occurs 525 times in the Bible. It is God speaking in the whole Bible. The Bible reveals prophecy as fulfilled in history. The Bible reveals God's faithfulness, his loving care, and his rulership over all mankind. (See Acts 17:25–28.)

III. *God has revealed himself in Jesus Christ.* (See Heb. 1:1–2.) By a definite new birth, which comes by faith in Christ and by accepting his atoning death upon the cross, men may know God in Christ. Millions of persons have believed in Christ as Savior and have learned to know God. (See John 17:3.) Without the acceptance of Christ as Savior men cannot know God. (See Heb. 11:6.)

IV. *God has been revealed in history.* (a) God was revealed in the history of Israel in the Old Testament and in the church, which Christ established nearly 2,000 years ago. Witness also the historical books, the testimony of the four gospels, and the Book of Acts.

(b) God's hand was seen in the battle of Tours when Charles Martel with Austrian Franks stemmed the tide of Mohammedanism in A.D. 732. This victory changed the whole course of human history and preserved Christianity.

(c) God was seen in the Thirty Years' War of 1618–48 when finally Gustavus Adolphus with 30,000 Swedes defeated Wallenstein at the battles of Leipzig and Lutzen (1648). This led to the "Peace of Westphalia" and saved Protestantism from defeat.

(d) God gave victory to George Washington and the colonial armies, which made possible the United States as a nation and as a haven for the oppressed of many nations. Who can deny that God was with Washington in his prayer meeting in Valley Forge?

V. *God is revealed in the experiences of men.* God is revealed in the spiritual experiences of millions of persons that have trusted him through the centuries. The Holy Spirit convicts of sin, converts the soul, brings assurance and comfort to the penitent heart. He gives his joy, his peace, his presence, with an abiding faith in God. Such vital experiences have made Christianity what it is. God has become real in the midst of trials, giving victory over sin and Satan.

VI. *God has proved himself to be alive by answering prayer.* (a) Prayer is the basis for fellowship with God and his Son. God challenges men to seek his face. (See II Chron. 7:14; Jer. 33:3; John 14:13–14.) Prayer for daily guidance, wisdom, strength, and victory over temptations has surely been answered by God our Father.

(b) More is wrought by the prayers of God's people than by any other force known to man. Jesus Christ set the example of prayer and invites his own to follow.—Joseph T. Larson.

SUNDAY: FEBRUARY FIRST

MORNING SERVICE

Topic: Fulfilling Our Purpose in Life
TEXT: Phil. 2:5.

Paul challenged us to have that mind in us which was in Christ Jesus. As we think of these things three persistent

questions demand our honest consideration.

I. *Who are we?* (a) In every area of life it is important to know who you are! But nowhere is it so important as when you seek to fulfill your purpose in life.

(b) What a heartening faith—that we are creatures made for God, that our spirits are restless until they find their rest in him, that only in God's will is our peace, that we carry the hallmark of God as we live our earthly life.

(c) The clue to understanding who we are is not to be found in the world of nature beneath us but in the world of God above us. When we look to Christ we see mirrored in his eyes of love the person we are meant to be. When we know whose we are we know who we are!

II. *Why are we here?* (a) There is some time in every man's life, we may safely say, when he is a philosopher and queries "Why?" We are not content just to make a living; we also want to make a life! We sense that life holds a purpose even though the purpose is not clear to us.

(b) We come from God, we live for God, and we return to God. God has a purpose and plan for everyone. Not the years in our life but the life in our years is of supreme importance. When we live for God we find life illumined by the wonder of his friendship and we know why we are here.

III. *Where are we going?* (a) Does life have a destination as well as a direction? Is our activity purposeful in the sense that we are going somewhere or is it like the scrambling of little feet in a squirrel cage, much energy but no progress?

(b) If we live for God we know that heaven is our destination. God not only lifts a standard beneath which we march; he also flings before us the vision of his eternal world where the good life finds fulfillment in the perfect fellowship of moral love.

(c) To understand earth we must know heaven. It is the light of eternity that lights our pilgrimage in time. This is a good world, and our life in it has a glorious goal.

(d) A world in which we can shape life on eternal lines is a good world in which to live. If we turn to God to learn what we are to do with our life,

our experience in this world will become, as St. Paul describes it, an earnest or foretaste of the eternal happiness of the heavenly life.—Lowell M. Atkinson.

Illustrations

GOD CARES FOR ME.   My life too is fashioned and guided by the same hands that beckoned the stars and the flowers at the world's dawning and made the day and night. If he knows that the earth with its plants and animals need rain and therefore separates the waters under the firmament, he will also know all the needs of the Queen of England, the orphan child in a children's home, and the aged pensioner. If a thousand years in his sight are but as yesterday then in his eyes even my little cares will weigh no less than the immensities of Sirius; then for him the tiny stretches of my daily journey, for which I ask his blessing, are just as important as the light years that measure the reaches of cosmic space.—Helmut Thielicke.

COMPLICATED TOY.   We are like a child who has been given a beautiful mechanical toy as a Christmas present. His father says to him, "Come along, and I'll show you how to make it go." The child replies, "No, I want to do it myself!" He tries, gets angry and sulky, takes it to pieces, damages it, and finally admits his incompetence. Defeated, he hands it to his father saying, "There, you make it work."

We too have received a beautiful and very complicated toy: life. We try to make it work on our own. We think we are having some success, but then things begin to go wrong and we run into personal or social disasters. The more we struggle to put things right with our own strength, the worse does the situation become, until at last we come back to God, and offering our lives to him, say: "Take over; I can't manage it on my own."—Paul Tournier in *The Person Reborn.*

Sermon Suggestions

LIVING HIGH. Text: Jer. 31:21. (1) Living high is living in fellowship with God. (See Exod. 24:12.) (2) Living high means working in partnership with God. (See I Cor. 3:9.) (3) Living high is living by the royal law of love. (See Matt. 5:44; 22:39.)—Gwynn Mc-Lendon Day.

YOU DON'T KNOW IT ALL. Text: I Cor. 13:8–12. (1) Human knowledge and understanding are partial and incomplete. (2) Our security and our certainty are in God as we know him in nature generally and in Jesus Christ specifically. (3) Through the response of our hearts we can enter into a saving and satisfying relationship with God through Christ. (4) Our experience of God and our knowledge of him are limited. The closer we come to him, the more we realize how far away we are; the more we know of him, the more we realize how much there is yet to be known. (5) We should never tire in our pursuit of truth and be ever willing to listen to God and our fellow man.—Frank H. Epp.

Worship Aids

CALL TO WORSHIP. "Thy word is a lamp unto my feet, and a light unto my path. I have sworn, and I will perform it, that I will keep thy righteous judgments. Quicken me, O Lord, according unto thy word." Ps. 119:105–107.

INVOCATION. Eternal and ever-blessed God, grant this day light to the minds that hunger for the truth and peace to the hearts which yearn for rest. Grant strength to those who have hard tasks to do and power to those who have sore temptations to face. Grant unto us within this place to find the secret of thy presence and to go forth from it in the strength of the Lord.

OFFERTORY SENTENCE. "Unto whom-soever much is given, of him shall be much required: and to whom men have committed much, of him they will ask the more." Luke 12:48.

OFFERTORY PRAYER. Help us, dear Father, to be cheerful givers of our time, means, talents, and self to the Master that he may use us in the up-building of his kingdom.

PRAYER. Father, as we go to our homes and our work this coming week we ask you to send the Holy Spirit into our lives.

Open our ears to hear what you are saying to us in the things that happen to us and in the people we meet.

Open our eyes to see the needs of the people round us.

Open our hands to do our work well, to help when help is needed.

Open our lips to tell others the good news of Jesus and bring comfort, happiness, and laughter to other people.

Open our minds to discover new truth about you and the world.

Open our hearts to love you and our fellow men as you have loved us in Jesus.—*Service Book* (The United Church of Canada).

EVENING SERVICE

Topic: Three Worlds
TEXT: John 8:23.

We live in three worlds: the world of the spirit, this present world, and the world to come. We cannot live a full life if we neglect or disregard any of these.

I. The world of the spirit is our inner world, our inner space. This is our inner life where we have our deepest resources of being and our guidance system for all our values and all our conduct. The teaching in the Bible about the indwelling presence of the Holy Spirit, our fellowship with Jesus, and God's energizing power concerns the inner world. Prayer, meditation, quietness, and his Word are our means to feel and know him in this inner world of the spirit.

II. This present world, the social world surrounding us, is the world where our lives rub together. Here we are tried and tested as to whether our inner world has enough strength to meet the demands of the outer world. Our theories of goodness and conduct are thrust daily into this crucible of practical living. We come forth as gold or shrivel like straw in this crucible depending upon what we really are. People are falling every day into violent, selfish behavior because, lacking spiritual resources, they cannot stand the heat of this crucible of life.

III. Neither of these worlds has ultimate meaning in itself. A hermit might live a very self-satisfied existence in his inner world, never being challenged or tested in rubbing life against life. A social activist might by a constant whirl of activity anesthetize himself to all reality but the present. But saints have always known that it is the world to come that measures our efforts here and gives meaning to our inner life and our conduct. Saints have sought "the city whose builder and maker is God."

IV. The inner life alone is power without application. The outer life alone is application without principle or meaning. The world to come alone is an escape from God's call to grow and serve. We live in all three worlds if we live as Christians.—George Alder in *The Lookout*.

SUNDAY: FEBRUARY EIGHTH

MORNING SERVICE

Topic: A Plea for Integrity
TEXT: Ps. 7:8.

Integrity is a searching word. It probes us at every level of our personal, social, and religious life. The high summons of God is that we become truly integrated personalities.

I. Emotional integrity is an imperative. (a) Parents and teachers alike have been too little concerned about this aspect of life. The disciplines of home and school have been aimed to promote social behavior but have neglected the emotions which determine behavior. Children have been taught how to think but not how to feel.

(b) As a result the emotional life of a multitude is an anarchy. Love and hate, fear and confidence, desire and aversion are in perpetual conflict.

II. Intellectual integrity is too often neglected if not scorned. (a) We use our minds to discover the facts which please us and ignore those which disturb our complacency. We put interpretations on our experiences which inflate our spiritual pride but which are not justified by critical intelligence. We do not set our wits to work on a problem at all, trusting God to guide us, and fail to realize that God has never offered to be a guide to lazy minds.

(b) Loving God with all our minds means using our minds to discover truth. Unless we love truth we do not love God, for God is truth. Unless we accept our responsibility to learn his truth for ourselves and to receive truth from whatever source we do not love God, for all truth is God's truth. Frightened obscurantism and blind faith are not integrity but the absence of it.

III. Moral integrity is often less realized though perhaps more appreciated. (a) We are all sinners. Some find it difficult to admit that. The Pharisee is still among us: "God I thank thee, that I am not as other men." But most of us are ready to confess moral failure. That confession is both intelligent and honest. But it, alas, means that we have not achieved integrity; a part of us condemns what the rest of us indulges, and that is a wretched state of soul. No one is so miserable as the man who must point an accusing finger at himself. No scorn wounds like self-scorn. No accusation slays like self accusation. (See Rom. 14:22; I John 3:21.)

(b) Abraham Lincoln knew the transcendent importance of moral integrity: "I desire so to conduct the affairs of this administration that if at the end I have lost every other friend on earth, I shall at least have one friend left, and that friend shall be down inside of me." When one is his own friend, when one can be at home with himself, all of himself, then one knows the true meaning of integrity. Then one can be a friend both to God and to men.—Albert E. Day.

Illustrations

OVERTONES OF VICTORY. The strings of a violin in order to produce tones of music must be stretched between two poles until some tension is exerted on them. If they hang loose they will emit only a dull flapping sound. But when connected to the tailpiece on the lower end of the instrument and to the tuning pins on the upper neck of the instrument and drawn tight, their overtones become delightful when controlled by the musician. Likewise when we connect our faith to the eternal God above us and fasten it securely in the depth of our nature, allowing God to remove all of the slack by his skilled hand, then an overtone of victory will be the order of the day.—Raymond C. Kratzer.

THE MISTAKES OF MAN. The Roman philosopher and statesman, Cicero, listed the six mistakes of man: (1) The delusion that personal gain is made by crushing others. (2) The tendency to worry about things which cannot be changed or corrected. (3) Insisting that a thing is impossible because we can-

not accomplish it. (4) Refusing to set aside trivial preferences. (5) Neglecting development and refinement of mind and not acquiring the habit of reading and study. (6) Attempting to compel others to believe and live as we do.

Sermon Suggestions

WHAT IS YOUR RELIGION?   Text: John 18:34. (1) Is it a voice or is it an echo? (2) Is it a conviction or is it an opinion? (3) Is it an experience or is it an argument? (4) Did you get it out of a book or did you get it out of life?—Joseph R. Sizoo.

BASIC LIFE PRINCIPLES.   (1) Cooperation: cheerfully work with others. (2) Ambition: work toward a goal. (3) Initiative: think of things to do. (4) Originality: use imagination. (5) Perseverance: do not quit too soon. (6) Reliability: be a person who can be counted on. (7) Enthusiasm: nobody wants a half-dead person around. (8) Persuasion: study to put across your ideas. (9) Consideration: realize that there are other people. (10) Character: have something inside.—Douglas E. Lurton.

Worship Aids

CALL TO WORSHIP. "Know therefore that the Lord thy God, he is God, the faithful God, which keepeth covenant and mercy with them that love him and keep his commandments to a thousand generations." Deut. 7:9.

INVOCATION. Almighty God, who of thy great mercy hast gathered us into thy visible church: grant that we may not swerve from the purity of thy worship, but may so honor thee both in spirit and in outward form that thy name may be glorified in us and that our fellowship may be with all thy saints in earth and in heaven.

OFFERTORY SENTENCE. "Verily I say unto you, Inasmuch as ye have done it unto one of the least of these my brethren, ye have done it unto me." Matt. 25:40.

OFFERTORY PRAYER. Dear Father, may we ever give thee a definite, consistent, and heartfelt service.

PRAYER. Almighty God, eternal spirit, we for whom thou art the only hope of life acknowledge our need of thee now.

By the skill of head and hand, man has shortened the distance between the homes of his fellows, till all on our globe are now neighbors.

Help us, O God, joyful spirit of universal love, to make this new closeness a blessing to us all. Help us to believe in our heart's core that none of us can know joy, safety, content, if others do not know hope.

By the skill of head and hand, man has brought forth such wealth of material goods as no other generation has known. Help us to know that none of us is safe in the enjoyment of our man-made wealth if all cannot have a share.

Almighty God, move us to put our whole trust in thee and thy all-powerful spirit of love. May we draw from thee that faith in the human spirit which alone gives meaning to efforts for the common good. Inspire us with that universal faith in the might of goodness, which means wholeness and life for all human souls.—Dorothy Canfield Fisher.

EVENING SERVICE

Topic: The Church and Scouting

I. *What scouting offers a church.* (a) A program that belongs to the local church and is administered by the church.

(b) Evangelistic possibilities for reaching, teaching, and training boys and strengthening the church of today and tomorrow.

(c) A program that challenges men to take responsible action on behalf of boys in the church and community.

(d) A cooperative program by which

the church, the school, and the home can work together as partners.

(e) Effective training for leaders selected by the church to guide its boys in the scouting program.

(f) Abundant and helpful literature and program aids for the leader.

(g) Service and counsel from professional and volunteer scout leaders available to every community.

(h) The assistance of a local council office functioning as a service station and as a medium of cooperative effort to all sponsors of scout units.

II. *What the church can provide through scouting.* (a) A program of boy activities that has been hammered out on the anvil of more than four decades of experience and which has reached more than twenty million boys.

(b) Opportunities for vocational exploration under capable guidance through the merit badge program.

(c) Responsibilities that train boys in developing initiative and leadership skills.

(d) A church-centered program of religious instruction and service that gives the adolescent boy a sustained and personal relationship with his pastor through the God-and-country program.

(e) A program that is geared to boy needs and designed especially for the three distinct age groups found in the ages 8 through 10 (Cub Scouts, pack, den), 11 through 17 (Boy Scout troop, patrol), and 14 through 20 (Explorer Scouts post).

(f) Membership in a worldwide movement for boys which fosters international understanding and cooperation.

III. *Scouting, a resource of the church.* The church has become deeply concerned about providing a program under Christian leadership that reaches into the boy's own world to guide his conduct and mold his character as he engages in leisure-time activities. Churches are finding that the Boy Scouts of America offers such a program. Scouting is an ideal resource available to churches to complement or expand their work in the multifaceted ministry to the youth. —*ABC Fellowship News.*

SUNDAY: FEBRUARY FIFTEENTH

MORNING SERVICE

Topic: **Putting Off and Putting On** (Brotherhood Week)

SCRIPTURE: Col. 3:5–14.

One commentator says that the theme of this passage is the transformation of the Christian in character and conduct. Paul here uses the method of contrast to make his point; he contrasts the old and the new, the good and the bad. His point is that the gospel completely transforms the believer, making him a new person.

I. *Being a Christian requires a "putting off."* (a) This is a foundation of everything Paul understood by the Christian faith. He believed deeply that one who becomes a Christian must put some things behind him. Christianity is a new way of life. It means giving up some former practices or attitudes, a change we call "conversion."

(b) However obvious this may seem, it is often at this point that the church fails. When someone comes to unite with the church we welcome him, we congratulate him, and surely we should do this. But how often do we confront him with the real and difficult demands of the gospel? How often do we say, "There are some things you have to leave behind?" We hardly ever speak so bluntly. We don't wish to offend.

(c) Paul was not timid about this. He spoke plainly and clearly: "seeing that you have put off the old nature." We should be so blunt with ourselves. Have we put off some things? Are we done with the type of things Paul lists: anger, slander, foul talk? Paul is right in saying that those who are Christian ought to be rid of these things.

II. *Being a Christian requires "a putting on."* (a) Paul was not content to be negative. He was not concerned with only reminding Christians what they must give up. He said also that the Christian must "put on the new nature," must become a new person in Christ.

(b) There is an important lesson here. We tend to define Christianity in terms of what we don't do. We don't curse, we don't cheat on our spouses, we don't steal from our customers, and we don't tell lies. This misses the whole point. The Christian should be known by the positive things his life stands for. His life should be an indication of the freedom that was evident in Jesus, the freedom from the law that Paul constantly referred to.

(c) To put on the new nature was, to Paul, a positive thing. What are the positive evidences of the new birth? Paul lists some of them: compassion, kindness, lowliness, meekness, patience, and love. These are the things by which the Christian ought to be known.

III. *The result of this is brotherhood.* (a) Paul's point is that putting on the new nature has great results. Those who are truly changed will give evidence of it in their relationships with others. Because they are Christians they will regard all men in an entirely different light.

(b) What is the result of becoming Christian? It is brotherhood. For the Christian such distinctions as Jew and Greek, slave and free man do not hold any longer. In our time the Christian looks at another without seeing a red man or a black man or a poor man or a foreign man. He sees a brother. The classifications so casually applied are no longer valid. Christians see "Christ in all," in Paul's words.

(c) Paul pointed to what we ought to see, what we need to see, but what we often refuse to see. The relationship of men to Christ overcomes all human relationships and destroys the barriers we have built to separate us from our brothers.—John Rutland, Jr.

Illustrations

BARRIERS AND BRIDGES.   There are two drives in man: one is to build barriers.

This is not all bad, for our sense of autonomy requires some space between ourselves and others. The other drive is to build bridges. The first is expressed by the word "will" which is our need to be independent. The second is characterized by the word "love" which is our need to trust and be dependent or interdependent.—Robert B. Wallace.

MANWARD AND GODWARD.   No man dare say that he loves God unless he also loves his fellow men; and no man can really and truly love his fellow man unless he sees that the true value of a man lies in the fact that he is a child of God. Without the manward look religion can become a remote and detached mysticism in which a man is concerned with his own soul and his own vision of God and nothing more. Without the godward look a society can become a place in which, as in a totalitarian state, men are looked on as things and not as persons. Reverence for God and respect for man can never be separated from each other.—William Barclay in *The Ten Commandments for Today* (Harper & Row, 1974).

Sermon Suggestions

ALL GOD'S CHILDREN.   Text: Rom. 12:2 (PHILLIPS). We are in a new day. What can we, as individual Christians, do to affirm the inclusive nature of the gospel? (1) I can help create the right atmosphere. (2) I can keep a spirit of compassionate understanding. (3) I can keep moving forward. (4) In faith and practice we must draw closer to God.—Edward L. Tullis.

WHAT DO YOU BELIEVE IN?   (1) The humanity of all mankind. (2) The sacredness of life. (3) The divinity of joy. (4) The beauty of the present creation. (5) The celebration of God—now. (6) The unity of love.—Bob Kuntz.

Worship Aids

CALL TO WORSHIP.   "Hereby perceive we the love of God, because he laid down his life for us: and we ought to lay down our lives for the brethren. Let us not love in word, neither in tongue; but in deed and in truth." I John 3:16, 18.

INVOCATION.   Merciful God, forgive the halting nature of our discipleship. We confess that so little of thy love has reached others through us and that we have borne so lightly wrongs and sufferings that were not our own. We confess that we have cherished the things that divide us from others and that we have made it hard for them to live with us. And we confess that we have been thoughtless in our judgments, hasty in condemnation, grudging in our forgiveness. Forgive us, we beseech thee.

OFFERTORY SENTENCE.   "Offer the sacrifices of righteousness, and put your trust in the Lord." Ps. 4:5.

OFFERTORY PRAYER.   O eternal God, may these gifts represent an inner commitment to love thee above all else and to love our brethren in need because they are loved by thee.

PRAYER.   Dear God our Father, we thank thee for all human relationships. Teach us to find the richness of these relationships in the often unexplored places, the majesty of a human spirit set down in a sphere of life racially or economically or socially unknown to us. Let us know where beauty is. Grant that we shall seek truth and cleave to it as a way of life. Hasten the day when distinctions of class and race will lose their meaning and the relationships of people will be governed by perfect love. Make strong in us the ideal of the brotherhood of all thy children. Strengthen our hand as it clasps the hand of another and another and another until we too have caught the indelible wisdom of that new earth where all nations and kindreds and peoples and tongues shall stand before thy throne as brothers.—*Fellowship in Prayer.*

EVENING SERVICE

Topic: God's Love Affair (St. Valentine's Day)

God is altogether alive, altogether unmanageable, altogether uninhibited in his behavior. And the Bible is specifically a book about God's love affair, his stormy, passionate, and heartbreaking marriage with an oddly matched wife and covenant partner.

I. The church is God's wife. (a) He has married himself to her "for better or for worse." According to the church's history in the Bible and in subsequent ages, it is frequently "for the worse." She suffers from selfishness, self-righteousness, stuffiness, timidity, and the cruelties that spawn out fear and prejudices.

(b) God's wife suffers from the womanly temptation to want to settle down. She craves a place to shelter and entrench herself, her children, her knickknacks. Incidental to all this, she secretly determines to reform her husband, to domesticate him, to tie him down.

II. God cannot be tied down. (a) He is free. He is a missionary, pioneer, explorer, frontiersman, a creator of that which has not been before. He shakes the status quo. He tears the old times off the world's calendar so that every age is a new age and every day is an adventure into an untrodden future. He is a turbulent husband. He keeps moving on, and he keeps calling to his wife to follow him.

(b) The church wants to settle down. She wants security. The church knows in her secret heart how dangerous it is to follow her Lord. One can get killed going where God goes and doing things his way.

III. Where does God want to go, and what does he want to do? Some people act as though all God wanted to do was "go to church." He "goes to church" but just long enough to have a quick, no-foolishness chat with his wife, a briefing session on "what's cooking." He pays her loving, deeply understanding, husbandly attention. But then all too soon he says: "Come on, old girl. Let's get moving. We've got work to do."—Louise Mohr.

SUNDAY: FEBRUARY TWENTY-SECOND

MORNING SERVICE

Topic: Facing Life's Calamities
TEXT: I Kings 22:48.

On the Gulf of Aqabah there was once a city called Ezion-geber. It was built there by Solomon for a special purpose. Solomon needed a refinery or smelting area for copper and iron. After Solomon's death the city went into eclipse, but we read in the Book of Kings that Jehoshaphat wanted to restore the splendor of Solomon's reign, and he chose to reopen the port and the smelting process. The Tarshish ships mentioned, which were smelting ships, were in the harbor being loaded to be sent to Ophir. Something tragic happened. We do not know what, but the ships were wrecked, possibly by strong winds or by an insurrection. Soon afterward Jehoshaphat dies and sleeps with his fathers.

How did he face this calamity? Did it cause his death? Did it bring the great disappointment that what he wished to do he was unable to accomplish? At least this introduces us to a human situation that we know quite well, the existence of life's calamities. The ships that carry the traffic of our own lives may indeed at some point be wrecked, and we must seek to make some sort of recovery.

I. *It is good sense to avoid catastrophe when we can.* (a) We can by the use of wisdom and faith and common sense do just that many times. We ask did Jehoshaphat miscalculate? Was he pressed for money? Did it push him to an untimely venture? Was he too anxious? We do know that in all probability he was certainly not as wise as Solomon. One can miscalculate and bring upon himself grief and harm.

(b) The tragedy of so many people in our time is that they pursue certain ends that are destructive. They never consider the consequences of what they do.

(c) Sometimes we think too late about the consequences of what we do. Too often we think that God's strong warnings to us are just old hat. We conclude that there is a new day, a new liberation, a new individuality. One can discard with a sort of carefreeness the things that we have learned through the ages about God and his will for us.

II. *There are calamities not of our own making for which we are responsible.* (a) Adonijah, son of David, first after Absalom, wanted the throne. He was a spoiled man. His father had not disciplined him, we are told. He was egotistical. His father's lack of influence was destructive to him. Another, Abijam, "walked in all the sins which his father did before him." Many a young person has been marked by the lack of concern, the lack of wisdom, lack of spirituality of the family in which he grew up.

(b) Adonijah and Abijam suffered misfortune through the hands of others, and their reaction was to respond in destructive ways. Whatever our misfortune, we must learn to accept responsibility for who we are and what we are. It is not enough to keep repeating that old proverb, "The fathers have eaten sour grapes and the children's teeth are set on edge."

III. *There are some calamities which are beyond our control.* (a) The fleet of Jehoshaphat at Ezion-geber may have been wrecked in a storm. The unpredictable winds of life blow, leaving us with tragedy. Immanuel Kant had a congestion in his chest. It stayed with him as long as he lived. He had no control over the fact that this was a part of his fate. Robert Louis Stevenson had tuberculosis, never to be well.

(b) It is possible that one can be ill because of mistakes in diagnosis or treatment. This is possible because those who treat us are human beings. They do the best they can, but often the best is not perfect. One can also go through economic stress and failure. He may see the stock market hit the bottom.

IV. What do you do with calamities you make for yourself, those that are made for you, and those over which you really have no control?

(a) You can be defeated by them, or you can confront them with human courage. Enduring courage comes from God. In the Book of Kings there is a picture of Hezekiah. Isaiah comes to him one day and tells him to get his house in order for he is about to die. Hezekiah turned his face to the wall and prayed and wept. Because of that God added fifteen more years to his life.

(b) All calamity may not be removed. God may heal us of our diseases. He may lift us from our depression. He may help us to restore a lost fortune. But sometimes calamity comes to stay. We must live with it or die in it. In either case we may do so in faith. Robert Louis Stevenson lived with his tuberculosis, Beethoven with his deafness, Immanuel Kant with his chest congestion, and Lord Byron with his club foot. Others have died like saints when the end has come. The point is that we can do something with our tragedies. We can rise in triumph over them if God is with us.—Tom A. Whiting.

Illustration

ENCOURAGEMENT. Ernest Gordon recounts an experience from his years as a prisoner of the Japanese during World War II. In the Changi Prison for civilian internees at Singapore there was a man whose friend was sentenced to solitary confinement. He asked, "What can you do to help him?" The obvious answer was "Nothing." His friend was locked in a tiny cell in a section of the prison which was so heavily guarded that none could get in.

One day the Methodist Bishop of Singapore saw him trying to cut another prisoner's hair. "Hello, John. I never knew you could cut hair." "I can't. It's something I've never done. I'm just learning." "Why?" "My friend is in solitary. He is allowed to have his hair cut once a month. So I thought I'd apply for the job." Some time later the Bishop heard that John had been appointed as the barber of those in solitary. He asked him how things were working out now that he could see John once a month. "Oh, I'd say fair." "You can't bring him anything, I know that. But can you speak to him?" "No." "Well, what can you do?" "This is what I do. While I'm snipping away at his hair, I keep saying to him, 'Please keep your chin up, keep your chin up.' The guards think this has something to do with the barbering trade, so I'm allowed to say it—and I do, over and over."

Sermon Suggestions

TAKING LIFE AS IT COMES.   Text: John 16:33. How can you meet life joyously and constructively? (1) You must grow in faith in one greater than yourself. (2) You must never be content to let life stay as it is. (3) Become active in a Christian fellowship, the fellowship of believers, that is called the Christian church. (4) Keep in constant fellowship with the Christ who has promised, "In the world ye shall have tribulation. . . . In me ye might have peace."—Theodore F. Adams.

WHY CHRISTIANITY SATISFIES.   (1) It gives us a sense of the conscious favor of God. (2) It gives us the consciousness that God has made us good. (3) It gives us the consciousness that God has made us good for something. (4) It gives us the assurance that no matter what happens to us all is going to be well with us.—William Booth.

Worship Aids

CALL TO WORSHIP.   "If a man love me, saith Jesus, he will keep my words: and my Father will love him, and we will come unto him, and make our abode with him." John 14:23.

INVOCATION.   Eternal God, in whom we live and move and have our being, whose face is hidden from us by our sins and whose mercy we forget in the blindness of our hearts: cleanse us, we beseech thee, from all our offenses and deliver us from proud thoughts and vain desires, that with lowliness and meekness we may draw near to thee, confessing our faults, confiding in thy grace, and finding in thee our refuge and our strength.

OFFERTORY SENTENCE.   "Therefore, as ye abound in every thing, in faith, and utterance, and knowledge, and in all diligence, and in your love to us, see that ye abound in this grace also." II Cor. 8:7.

OFFERTORY PRAYER.   O God, help us so to practice by our gifts and our lives the divine principle of good will that in our homes, our communities, and among all the nations of the earth, men may enjoy the boon of peace.

PRAYER.   O God, our heavenly Father, high above all thought, far beyond all earthly vision, yet nearer than we dare to believe, closer than any earthly friend, we need great help in understanding this strange experience of thy spirit moving in our hearts.

We are of time, and our little world is marked by space. Thou art timeless, and for thee there are no boundaries that we can comprehend. Yet, though we fail to fathom so great a mystery, help us in humility and with great thanks to accept thy presence.

Amid our limitations, create within us a place wherein thy limitless love may find a home. Banish confusion of thought that causes such conflict within our minds. Free us, O Father, from false and cruel ways into which we may have slipped through loss of insight into others' needs or strange unwillingness to recognize our own.

Build up in us, we pray, that life through which thy presence may find fit expression and thy purpose march on toward ultimate triumph.—S. Ralph Harlow.

EVENING SERVICE

Topic: The Fruit of the Spirit
TEXT: Gal. 5:22–23.

I. *Love.* This is the supreme quality which forms the foundation to the whole structure of life. This love is the love of I Cor. 13 which is based on nothing and thus includes all.

II. *Joy.* Jesus desired for the disciples and for us that our joy might be full and that his joy might remain in us. (See John 15:11.)

III. *Peace.* "It is the repose of a spirit right with God. It is the serenity of a secured soul, deaf and blind to circumstances."

IV. *Longsuffering* (or patience). This is God's attitude toward man. In our lives, in our attitude to and dealings with our fellow men we must reproduce this loving, forbearing, forgiving, patient attitude of God toward ourselves.

V. *Gentleness* (or kindness). A gentle person is one who is submissive to the will of God. A gentle person is one who is not too proud to learn. A gentle person is one who is considerate. The Holy Spirit produces all three qualities in life.

VI. *Goodness.* A good person is one who does what is right toward people in a right spirit in an active life.

VII. *Faith.* It involves a complete abandonment to God and an absolute dependence upon him. It is a perfect antidote to fear, which causes worry, anxiety, and pessimism. A person who has Spirit-inspired faith will be faithful and dependable. "When the Spirit is in control, life goes forward under the full conviction of God's ability and power."

VIII. *Meekness.* The natural man is proud, haughty, arrogant, egotistical, and self-centered, but when the Spirit fills the life of an individual he will be humble, mild, submissive, and easily entreated.

IX. *Self-control.* It is the picture of a long-distance runner who will forego any pleasure to keep himself in condition. The Spirit-filled man will be one that is consistent, dependable, and well-ordered.—Bill Duncan.

SUNDAY: FEBRUARY TWENTY-NINTH

MORNING SERVICE

Topic: Christ's Marching Orders
SCRIPTURE: Luke 9:1–5.

I. Jesus wanted to extend his work and to reach people he could not reach himself. How bold for a carpenter from Nazareth with no credentials to think that he could send out twelve men into the world to start a mission that would eventually be worldwide! We take it for granted, we are so accustomed to it, but what a bold thing it was when he gave those first marching orders to a dozen men.

(a) He started something in the world. He was here on a mission, but he did not try to do it alone. He began with a dozen men. Since then how many do you suppose there have been? When you think of the people who have gone out to preach the gospel and to heal the sick, to the lepers in Hawaii, to the untouchables in India, to the underprivileged in Africa, to the Indians in the United States, to people in South America, to the Eskimos in Alaska, how many people do you suppose there have been from that time until now?

(b) His mission is still alive. It has quite naturally its ups and downs. It has waves of success and defeat; it has times of growth and shrinkage. It is still alive, and I am convinced that nothing will ever destroy it.

(c) The test of a man's greatness is the number and the quality of the disciples he leaves behind him. By that measurement alone the stature of Jesus is greater than most men can comprehend.

II. Let us look at these marching orders. Notice three things that Jesus did not do.

(a) He did not wait until the men were ready before he sent them out.

(1) If he had waited until they understood him and his message, until they knew the answers to all the questions and were completely equipped and entirely ready to do the work, if he had waited for that he would never have sent them. If I had waited until I was ready to be ordained I would never have been ordained. If I had waited until I knew all the answers and was sure of all the principles and knew exactly what I was doing I would never have done it at all.

(2) If you wait until you are ready to be confirmed, that is, commissioned to go out into the world, you will never be confirmed. You will never know all the answers. You will never be completely satisfied with the church as it is. You will always have questions. If you wait until you are completely ready you will never do anything. Might we put it this way? There is a time to prepare; no one questions that; but there is a time to proceed, and the wise man is the man who knows when the time to proceed has come, who knows when the time to march has arrived.

(b) He did not give them a constitution and a set of bylaws, nor did he make them officers of an organization. To be sure, it is one thing to deal with twelve men; it is quite another thing to deal with twelve thousand men. You cannot do anything on a large scale without some organization. If you try to do that you have nothing but confusion. The mission could not continue without some form and structure. We know that.

(1) You and I are living in what I suppose is the most highly organized society that has ever existed. Everything is "packaged." Everything is organized and mechanized. The mail is now sorted by machines, not by people, and the telephone is operated by machines, not by operators. This makes for efficiency. It facilitates a great many of our daily activities, but you cannot deny the fact that it makes life much less personal.

(2) The church is in danger of the same thing. The danger in the church is that the organizations become more important than the work for which the organization is designed. Preach the gospel? Heal the sick? I don't have time to do that. I am too busy running the departments, keeping the wheels going. I speak with feeling because I, like all other clergy, am involved in this, and I keep out of it only by very considerable effort, and I do not always succeed.

(3) Jesus sent his men out to preach the gospel and to heal the sick. He did not send them out to promote his mission. He sent them out to do it. And when the church becomes so organized that it has no energy left to do the things that it is sent on earth to do, then it ought to reexamine itself in the light of these marching orders.

(c) Jesus in these marching orders did not say anything about himself. He told them to preach the kingdom of God and to heal the sick.

(1) Preach the kingdom of God and tell the people about the kingdom of God. The word "king-ship" of God would be more accurate. Tell the people that God is supreme. Tell the people that money is important, but money is never supreme, and when people make it supreme they deteriorate. Tell the people that food and clothing and shelter and education are all important, but they are never supreme. God alone is supreme. Tell the people that political power and prestige are important but not supreme. God, who is the disposer of events, the God of righteousness and life, alone is supreme, and unless his supremacy is recognized and all these other important things are consumed under his supremacy they lead us to destruction.

(2) Heal the sick. Make people whole.

Take the broken bits of humanity and put them together. If I may say so in all humility I have healed the sick. God has healed the sick through me. I have seen people who were broken, not able to bear the pain and the suffering that was torturing their bodies, and I and thousands of others like me have been able to make those people whole and to heal them; if not to cure them, to give them the courage to bear what they have in such a way as to make their pain incidental.

(3) In all this, you see, he said nothing about himself. He did not have to. Wherever his disciples went they told the people about him. They couldn't help it, and eventually he became the center of their message. He never underestimated his importance—"Follow me," "Come unto me," "Take my yoke upon you," "Learn of me," "No man cometh unto the Father but by me"—but he gave no sign that he was starting a mission for his own glorification. His glory lies in the fact that he did not know that he had any.

III. Listen now to the marching orders. See the splendor of the one who gave these severe, simple, selfless orders to a dozen working men. Then he called the twelve together and gave them power and authority over evil spirits and the ability to heal diseases. He sent them out to preach the kingdom of God and to heal the sick with the words of our scripture.—Theodore P. Ferris.

Illustrations

ASH WEDNESDAY. Every day is Ash Wednesday and life itself, though some do not know it, is a priest continuously whispering in man's ear, "Remember, man, that thou art dust and unto dust thou shalt return." These are humiliating words, but "the streets," as Emerson said, "are full of humiliations for the proud." And humiliation—that this body should grow old, sicken, and die; that we should not get our due; that full recognition of what we are is withheld—humiliation, if we do not bitterly rebel

against it, ushers us into the presence of God. There every man is Job discovering that over against God there is no justice. There every man is Jacob with a handful of worthless credentials. There every man is the Baptizer, Peter, the prodigal, saying, "I am not worthy." There every man is Browning's Count Guido, appealing at first to his nobility, his ancestry, his influence, his friends, his good works, but at last crying to his judges, "Sirs, my first true word all truth and no lie is—save me notwithstanding." But for the penitent there is another judge, another priest—the Great High Priest—who makes the sign of his cross not on the forehead but in the heart, not in cold ashes but in cleansing fire, not in removable smudges but in the shedding of his indelible blood.—*The Christian Century.*

PROMISE. When Robert Moffat, the great missionary to Africa, was ready to leave home for the first time, his mother said to him, "Robert, I want you to promise me one thing, sight unseen." After much persuading by her, he agreed. She said, "Robert, promise me that you will start each day with God and close each day with God." Moffat said later, "My mother added a continent for God in one sentence. It shaped my life."—William Fisher.

Sermon Suggestions

CHRISTIAN DISCIPLESHIP. Text: Luke 9:23. (1) A Christian disciple is a believer *in* Christ. (2) A Christian disciple is a learner *from* Christ. (3) A Christian disciple is a creator *for* Christ.—Claude Young.

CHRISTIANITY IN FOUR WORDS. (1) Admit. (2) Submit. (3) Commit. (4) Transmit.—Samuel Wilberforce.

Worship Aids

CALL TO WORSHIP. "Wait on the Lord: be of good courage, and he shall strenghen thine heart: wait, I say, on the Lord." Ps. 27:14.

INVOCATION. O God, who makest thyself known both in the stillness and in the flurry of life: come to us as we seek to come to thee, in this place of prayer. In music, word, and song lift our hearts to thee, and so purify our thoughts and strengthen our resolves that we shall go forth into the world of tomorrow, confident that thou art with us.

OFFERTORY SENTENCE. "This is the thing which the Lord commanded, saying, Take ye from among you an offering unto the Lord: whosoever is of a willing heart, let him bring it, an offering of the Lord." Exod. 35:4–5.

OFFERTORY PRAYER. Dear Lord and Savior of us all, may we become obedient to thy will both in the dedication of our tithes and of our talents.

PRAYER. O God, who art the creator, sustainer, and preserver of life, God of our fathers, God of ourselves, we pause before thee for strength and steadiness. We know that the heavens declare thy glory and the earth speaketh thy praise, that science and art and music are man's response to thy leading, that conscience and character and brotherhood trace out the unfolding of thy purposes in us. And in the strong persuasion of Jesus Christ we see the mighty thrust of thy holy love. Our Father, it is vision we would seek, the vision of thee and thy universe, of mankind in thee, of Jesus as thine own.—Elmore McNeill McKee.

EVENING SERVICE

Topic: The Secret of Creative Solitude (Ash Wednesday)

SCRIPTURE: Matt. 4:1–11.

I. *Creative solitude is willed.* (a) After his baptism Jesus deliberately sought the solitude of the desert. He needed time to reflect on such a profound religious experience. He needed solitude to decide what type of messiah he would be, for there had been many who claimed messiahship.

(b) Throughout this gospel narrative Matthew pictures Jesus constantly withdrawing from the teeming crowds for periods of solitude. In spite of their need for him, he never apologized for it, but he determined to be alone.

(c) Solitude does not come naturally in our society. It must come from an act of the will. It must be carried out by careful planning and scheduling, else solitude will be devoured by the mad rush of people and responsibilities. You may find that your solitude must be more mental than physical. Isaiah was in a crowded temple when he saw the Lord "high and lifted up." He was experiencing mental solitude, and he was never again the same because of it.

II. *Creative solitude is dangerous.* (a) The testing Jesus experienced in the wilderness was not designed to make him fall but to make him stand stronger. He was severely tested. It is important to notice, however, what kind of testing took place. Satan tested not the *fact* of his calling but the *nature* of his calling. Nothing could silence that voice still ringing in his ears: "This is my beloved son, with whom I am well pleased." Jesus knew he was called to be a messiah. The question was, what type of messiah?

(b) Should he become an economic messiah and give bread to the hungry? Should he be a miracle-working messiah and astound the people by throwing himself down from the temple? Should he be a military-political messiah by leading a vast rebellion against the tyrannical Roman government? These are the questions which plagued him for forty days and nights. But when it was all over Jesus had rejected Satan's security for God's sealed orders.

(c) The obvious fact is that in creative solitude you cannot escape the danger of that subtle tempter. He tests not so much the fact of your Christianity but the nature of your faith. What kind of Christian will you be?

III. *Creative solitude prepares for a mission.* (a) Creative solitude must have controls, else we could be like the Zen Buddhist meditating on a tree for hours. After the period of solitude Jesus turned immediately toward his mission: "From *that time* Jesus began to preach" (Matt. 4:17). He was not aloof from the world but vitally involved in the task of life. His creative solitude led him to positive action. (See Luke 4:18.)

(b) Creative solitude is only complete in the giving of oneself. Paul caught it when he made the appeal "to present your bodies as a living sacrifice, holy and acceptable to God, which is your reasonable worship" (Rom. 12:1). In a sense the wonderful surprise of creative solitude is the fact that it is not the end but only a beginnig. In creative solitude God prepares you for a mission.—Thomas McKibbons, Jr.

SUNDAY: MARCH SEVENTH

MORNING SERVICE

Topic: Learning to Pray (Lent)
TEXT: Matt. 6:9.

I. We pray because we cannot help to do otherwise. We have a basic need, as real as our need for food or water. Bishop Emerich's tract, "Not to Eat Is Silly," is not about food but about prayer. It is silly not to eat enough to live and work; it is likewise silly not to pray, for as Jesus said, "Man does not live by bread alone" (Matt. 4:4). No one can keep himself from the innate longing to be in touch with God, to know him, to be close to him, and to seek to do God's will. God searches us out; he yearns for us as we yearn for him.

II. Jesus' disciples made the simple request, "Lord, teach us to pray" (Luke 11:1). That is our plea too. Jesus leads us into the wonder of prayer, ever deepening, ever widening, ever growing as we persist and as we mature. Childish prayers are a good beginning, but as grown-ups we should know how to pray as mature men and women, never satisfied with merely asking for favors. We are content only when we can offer our total selves to God as a living sacrifice. This we do, first, through prayer, and secondly, we follow up our prayer with effective action.

III. Prayer is not an optional in life. Prayer is not a panic button to press only when in extreme trouble. Prayer is conversation with God, presenting ourselves honestly before God. Prayer is listening as we hear what God wants to tell us. Prayer is practicing the presence of God in every moment.

(a) Jesus revealed that God is a loving friend as well as eternal judge. So prayer should be as easy and as natural and as irresistible as conversation with a friend whom one knows and trusts.

(b) One can pray anywhere and at any time, but it is only in the fellowship of faith that we hear God's Word and respond to God's initial acts of undeserved kindness. We Christians are protected from our whims of devotion by regular worship through the life of the church.

IV. There is much about prayer that we do not understand. Most puzzling is the question many people ask, "Why are my prayers not answered?" We dare not assume that there is only one answer to prayer, the answer we want to hear. God does not always deal with us that way. Nor do we give our children everything they ask for. Sometimes we must say "No." Sometimes we must say, "Perhaps later, but not yet." I believe that God does answer our every prayer, though it may not be in the way we expect or desire.

V. Surely God must yearn for conversation with us not only when we ask him for the necessities of life but also when we are thankful, when we are joyous, when we are filled with adoration

tion and praise, and often when we must say we are sorry.

(a) The best way I know to begin to grow in the life of prayer is to pray for someone in particular who needs help. Pray for the sick, the afflicted, the troubled, the lonely. Quickly you will see how blessed, how fortunate you must be by comparison and how much more appropriate is your prayer of thanksgiving rather than one more request for yourself.

(b) It has been said that anyone who spends more time before a mirror than he spends on his knees in prayer is in love with himself. And that is a rejection of what the Christian religion is all about. The complications and troubles of life begin to get sorted out and straightened out when we can put God first, others second, and ourselves last. That is not easy.—Herbert M. Barrall.

Illustrations

MAN AT PRAYER. In a large eastern city where a church stood open daily for prayer, it was observed that a certain man regularly would enter, kneel for the briefest of moments, and then be on his way. One day the priest met him, and it seemed appropriate to speak. "Young man," he asked, "when you kneel down so briefly, what do you say?" He replied, "When I come in here at noon, I simply say, 'Jesus, this is Jimmy.'"— John H. Townsend.

TIMES OF PRAYER. It is a great delusion to think that the times of prayer ought to differ from other times; we are as strictly obliged to adhere to God by action in the time of action as by prayer in the season of prayer. I made this my business as much all the day long as at the appointed time of prayer; for at all times, every hour, every minute, even in the height of my business, I drove away from my mind everything that was capable of interrupting my thought of God. As for my set hours of prayer, they are only a continuation of the same exercise.—Brother Lawrence.

Sermon Suggestion

STEADFAST IN HIS COVENANT. Text: Gen. 6:18. (1) It is a covenant to worship God in spirit and in truth. (2) It is a covenant to study, to show ourselves approved unto God, to engage in searching and systematic study of the Bible. (3) It is a covenant of dedicated discipleship which involves (a) the way of witnessing and (b) the way of the committed life.—Oliver deW. Cummings.

Worship Aids

CALL TO WORSHIP. "It is good for me to draw near to God: I have put my trust in the Lord God. . . . God is the strength of my heart, and my portion for ever." Ps. 73:28, 26.

INVOCATION. Almighty God, whose chosen dwelling is the heart that longs for thy presence and humbly seeks thy face: deepen within us the sense of shame and sorrow for the wrongs we have done and for the good we have left undone. Strengthen every desire to amend our lives according to thy holy will. Give light to our wills and rest to our souls that we may do those things which are pleasing in thy sight.

OFFERTORY SENTENCE. "Of every man that giveth willingly with his heart ye shall take my offering (saith the Lord)." Exod. 25:2.

OFFERTORY PRAYER. Awaken us to the claims of thy holy will, O God, and stir us with a passion for thy kingdom, that we may respond at this time with our gifts and also with our lives.

PRAYER. O God, who art perfect in righteousness yet who comest with the mercy of love to every sinner: we praise thee that in Christ thou art our savior. Through his suffering and death thou hast spoken to us as through none other. When the fallen were despised he brought the forgiveness and healing of the kingdom. While he was homeless he revealed the dwelling place of our souls. When his heart overflowed with sorrow he brought thy comfort, O God, for the troubled in heart.

Dwell among us this Lenten season with the spirit that was in Christ. Make us aware that thy Word made flesh came also for us to reveal the things that are pure and true. His holy presence disturbs our complacency and pretensions. When the Man of Sorrows sets his face toward the cross a strange evil nature within us shrinks from his way. The temptations of the world deceive and attract us. Lord of all Gethsemanes, visit us with heavenly strength in our trials. By thy mercies, O Christ, help us to present ourselves as a living sacrifice acceptable unto thee. Let thy love which was despised and rejected of men and which endured pain and death for our sake triumph in us.

Inspire us to seek earnestly to follow as disciples who love thee. Help us to rejoice in the lives of the faithful who have been a benediction to us. Aid us to be a good example to our youth. In the hush of pleading hearts let thy consolation come to the weak and bereaved until they recognize thy gracious spirit. In good and evil hours lead us to take up our cross and to follow thee.—Samuel J. Schmiechen.

EVENING SERVICE

Topic: The Appeal of Lent
The Lenten period has one of the truly sound and appealing messages of the gospel. People love the services of Lent, Palm Sunday, and Easter. There are four great reasons for this being the real stirring series of our Christian calendar.

I. There is the call for discipline. People do not respond to a call of weakness or complacency. They need a challenge. Down deep we all know that there are demands and denials to any worthy call or way of life. It is true in sports, in work, in marriage, in citizenship, and in our faith.

II. There is pageantry in the triumphant entry into Jerusalem, and likewise there is triumph in Christ's coming into our lives. Our emotions are stirred and our hearts and minds are refreshed and made to sing and ring with joy and glad hallelujahs.

III. There is a cross on which our Lord cared and shared. When folk know that another sacrifices and loves, then they listen and follow. This is the season to tell how Jesus loves all and the time to tell pictorially and devotedly how he lived and gave his all for all of us. It has depth and reach and power.

IV. Easter is triumph. We sing and proclaim a message of vitality and hope. The loud amens and the words "he is risen" is the most positive message people have heard in months. This season is not negative, gloomy, piously articulated, or subdued by defeat and theological pessimism. If we will take a lesson from this glorious season and proclaim its message and reveal its spirit for the next ten months we will find a new joy in our souls and a more enthusiastic church.—Paul V. Galloway.

SUNDAY: MARCH FOURTEENTH

MORNING SERVICE

Topic: Salt and Seed: The Church at Work (Lent)
TEXT: Matt. 28:18–20 (RSV).
A church does not cease to exist when the benediction is pronounced Sunday morning and the congregation leaves the sanctuary for home and the activities of the week.

(1) A church is as real when she is scattered as when she is gathered. She is as real when she is an invisible corporate body as when she is a visible congregation or ecclesiastical institution.

(2) When the church is scattered,

when she is invisible, she is doing the work to which Christ sends her. This is implicit in Christ's analogy of his disciples as salt (Matt. 5:13) and seed (Matt. 13:37–38). Salt and seed are useless in their gathered form. When they are put to use they are scattered, and they disappear—salt into food, seed into soil.

(3) Awareness and acceptance of this reality are pressing needs among believers today. Most of our thinking, talking, planning, and programing presupposes the church in her gathered, visible, corporate form. Her influence in the world is measured on this basis by result-oriented and result-obsessed administrators, and failure to see "success" in these terms intimidates and discourages many pastors and lay people.

(4) This inadequate view of the church and her mission is nowhere more apparent than in the conventional response to the great commission.

I. The focus of the commission traditionally has been on the word "go." The emphasis, the challenge, the pressure, the mandate has been "go!"

(a) The measure of a local congregation's faithfulness in mission has been the number who have gone from its fellowship to preach and teach somewhere else, or it has been the amount given to others who go somewhere else to preach and teach.

(b) The word "go" has been identified almost exclusively with a relatively few professionals (the "missionaries"), who take specialized training for a work somewhere else. Generally speaking, lands beyond an ocean have been thought of as the primary mission field, the place where those who "go" go.

(c) "Go" is not the big word, the mandate, in the great commission. Nor was it intended that a relatively few "professional missionaries" be the only ones to take it seriously, unless we assume it was intended only for the Eleven. The mandate in the great commission is "make disciples . . . teaching them to observe all that I have commanded." The measure of our response is in terms of making disciples, not the number of converts or baptisms which are tallied.

II. The word "go" as it is used in Matt. 28:19 is for all the people of God, as demonstrated in Acts 1:8 and in Acts 8:1, 4.

(a) The word "go" is addressed to all the peoples of God with reference to their dispersion. It is as if Jesus said, "Going" or "Wherever you are . . . make disciples."

(b) Here is the exciting strategy of our Lord Jesus Christ. He scatters his church like salt and seed everywhere to accomplish his purposes. And everywhere she is dispersed she is enlisting and teaching followers of Christ. This is the work of the church, and it involves every single member.

(c) He is not alone, for Christ has promised to be with him with all authority. Christ has equipped his servant with all he needs to do his work in the person of the Holy Spirit.

III. Why is the believer there? To make disciples. (a) As a witness to Jesus Christ he is to share his reconciling, redemptive love. As an ambassador of Christ he is to beseech those nearby, in Christ's stead, to be reconciled to God. He is there to share all he knows and has experienced with others, that they might receive the benefits of the love of God for the world and conform to God's will.

(b) This is something every believer can do. As he learns he transmits his knowledge to another; as he grows he shares his life with another. Think of the network of believers at any given moment scattered everywhere, literally encircling the earth, penetrating all the institutions like salt in food, like seed in soil.

(c) In the economy of God every believer is called to full-time service for Jesus Christ. He should accept his daily task as his holy vocation and accept the place he is as the locale where he is to do it. The work of the ministry belongs to all believers, and those who are "specialists," such as apostles, prophets, evangelists, pastors, or teachers, are to equip them for this work. (See Eph. 4:1, 7–8, 11–12.)—Richard C. Halverson.

Illustrations

VOICE OF PROPHECY. The church's mission to the world is to keep it from getting bogged down in the present. When the world is swallowed up by hopelessness or is bored by its stagnant present, the church can lift up public symbols of the future that generate new possibilities in the present. The church is needed as the voice of prophecy in the world to regenerate the social and political images that inspire the world to change for the better. The church cannot limit its mission in history to salvaging individuals from a meaningless world; it works not only in history but for history, not only in culture but for culture, not only for persons but for communities, not only in the present but toward the ultimate future.—Carl Braaten.

PILLAR OF FIRE. Every church has its "Back to Egypt Committee." Each church must basically decide whether the thrust of its mission is to "return to the good ol' days" or be led by a "pillar of fire" into the promises and trials of the future.—Jameson Jones.

Sermon Suggestions

A FAITH WORTH SHARING. Text: Heb. 11:24. (1) A faith that shows maturity. (2) A faith that chooses the right. (3) A faith that leads to action. (4) A faith that suffers hardship. (5) A faith that leads to triumph.—Harold B. Kuhn.

ARE YOU A DRIFTER? Text: Heb. 2:1 (PHILLIPS). (1) Are you drifting away from a life of vital communion with God through prayer? (2) Is the Bible as the Word of God losing its command over your life? (3) Are you one of the many who are drifting away from the practice and custom of public worship on the Lord's Day? (4) Are you on speaking terms with Jesus Christ? Do you know him as a daily, present companion, guide, and master in your life?—Aaron N. Meckel.

Worship Aids

CALL TO WORSHIP

Come, you who are weak,
     but would be made strong;
Come, you who are weary,
     but want a new song.
Come, you who are seeking
     the joy of creation,
Come into the fellowship
     of this congregation—
Who also are seeking,
     even as you,
The heart of the good,
     the noble, and true;
In times overwhelmed
     by furor and strife
To find God revealed
     in everyday life.

—Thomas Roy Pendell.

INVOCATION. Blot out, we humbly beseech thee, O Lord, our past transgression; forgive our negligence and ignorance; help us to amend our mistakes and to repair our misunderstanding; and so uplift our hearts in new love and dedication that we may be unburdened from the grief and shame of past faithlessness, and go forth to serve thee with renewed courage and devotion.

OFFERTORY SENTENCE. "God is not unrighteous to forget your work and labor of love, which ye have showed toward his name, in that ye have ministered to the saints, and to minister." Heb. 6:10.

OFFERTORY PRAYER. O Lord, upon whose constant giving we depend every day, teach us how to spend and be spent for others that we may gain the true good things of life by losing every selfish trait.

PRAYER. O God, who hast redeemed us through the mystery of the cross: we bow before thee in reverent gratitude for the revelation of thy love declared in Jesus Christ. We praise thee that he shared our common life and humbled himself and became obedient unto death, even the death of the cross. We bless thee that he bore our griefs, carried our sorrows, and triumphed over sin and death. We glorify thee that through his perfect and sufficient sacrifice on the cross there is pardon for the penitent, power to overcome for the faithful, and transformed life for all who truly turn to him.

Give us grace to yield ourselves in glad surrender to the Lord Jesus. May we share his spirit of obedience to thy will, his consecration to the welfare of humanity, and his passion that thy kingdom may come and thy will be done on earth as it is in heaven. So may Christ dwell in our hearts and reign there as our divine Redeemer.—Carl A. Glover.

EVENING SERVICE

Topic: **Life in Christ**
TEXT: John 14:6.
I. *Jesus, the way of love.* "I am the way" witnesses that love bears and endures all things. Love is more than a feeling; it is a decision of the will involving a deep commitment. There is too often an idolatry of feelings in our day. Love, like God, is a verb, a very active verb. Love as an active commitment of the will which bears and endures all is definitely witnessed to us in the way Jesus gave his life for us even to the cross. His life witnesses to us the extent to which our love should bear and endure all things. The fullest example of our way of love is Jesus.
II. *Jesus, the truth about love.* "I am the truth" witnesses that love believes all things.
(a) I suppose the greatest gift a parent can give a son or daughter is the gift of believing in him in the sense that you come to know that whatever you do, wherever you go, whatever happens to you, love is there. Somehow you just know that it's there. If we believe that someone believes in us like that then we can never totally lose confidence in ourselves.
(b) God believes in you and me, even if nobody else does. Jesus witnessed this time and again as he told people they were the salt of the earth, ministers, disciples, servants, and "friends, because I have told you everything I heard from the Father" (John 15:15). He believes in you and me so deeply and endlessly that he frees us to live in our own integrity as we see it. He frees us to risk our lives and even to fail. But he's always waiting for us right in the middle of that failure to help us get up and begin again.
III. *Jesus, the life in love.* "I am the life" witnesses that love hopes all things.
(a) Love is living in the hope that there is a seed of resurrection buried at the heart of every little and big death we experience. Love is living in the hope that there are more possibilities than we have yet discerned in every specific trap we think we're in. It is realizing that there are always new choices of attitudes and feelings and responses that we can make. It is living with the confidence that our past does not need to bind us, that the future holds the possibilities of new life.
(b) God has witnessed such love for us in Christ. He loves us and this gives us hope for new life. His love hopes all things for us in spite of our past, for Jesus has shown us the way of life.—W. Benjamin Pratt.

SUNDAY: MARCH TWENTY-FIRST

MORNING SERVICE

Topic: **Not My Will but Thine (Lent)**
SCRIPTURE: Mark 14:32–42.
I. *Our Lord's suffering.* (a) *The place.* In the darkness of the night Christ and eleven of the disciples went to the Garden of Gethsemane, the place to which he frequently retired for the purpose of prayer, to make additional preparation for the storm that was about to break upon him and around them.

(b) *The pressure.* Christ felt the pressure of the testing even before he prayed. (See vv. 33–34.) But as he began to pray the anguish was so deep and the sorrow so intense that it pressed him to the earth. Bearing the pressure of the world's guilt for sin, sweat-drops of blood fell from his brow. (See Luke 22:44.)

(c) *The prayer.* Communion with the Father was a necessity in Christ's life and his resource in every hour of need. Prayer was as much his habit as was breathing. The scene in Gethsemane is solemn, sacred, and sad. Alone in the deep recesses of the garden, in the dead of night, prostrate upon his face and pleading with the Father was our blessed Lord. At the time of his deepest distress the human companionship which he craved was denied him because even his dearest earthly friends slept while he suffered and prayed.

(d) For what did he pray? That the hour might pass from him. That the cup might be removed from him. That the will of God might be done.

II. *Our Lord's submission.* (a) When the cup of human guilt was held out to Christ, his tender and pure heart revolted from the pain and the shame of it. Dreading the ordeal which he was facing, Christ prayed earnestly that, if it were possible, the cup might pass from his lips. With him the Father's will was the ultimate authority, so he prayed and then adjusted or yielded to that blessed will uncomplainingly and gladly. His prayer was a marvelous expression of prompt and complete submission to God's will. Christ was determined to conform to it in every respect.

(b) While Judas Iscariot was in the city making arrangements to betray our Lord for thirty pieces of silver, eight of the apostles were at the entrance of the garden, sleeping. The other three, Peter, James, and John, were just "a stone's throw" from Christ, and they were sleeping also. Because he was eager for human sympathy and companionship our Lord had taken them into the garden of his impending crisis, but they were not interested enough to remain awake.

(c) Returning to the three, Christ found them fast asleep. They had not anticipated the imminent arrest of their Lord. After awakening them Christ chided them by saying, "Watch ye and pray, lest ye enter into temptation." That was his way of warning them of the more challenging hours that were yet to come. His words were unheeded, for each time he returned the Lord found the disciples asleep.

(d) Even though no man stood by our Lord in Gethsemane, the Father was with him. He talked with the heavenly Father, trusted him implicitly, and yielded himself fully and completely to his will. From him he obtained the blessed assurance that he would receive all of the strength and help which he would need for the accomplishment of God's will.—H. C. Chiles.

Illustrations

TOTAL FAITH. The trust implied is not that of a person who sits with folded hands and peace of mind because he is confident that everything will turn out all right. It is better symbolized by the attitude of the deep-sea diver who, trusting his equipment and supporting crew, drops into the sea and explores the ocean floor. Yet it is more than this. The diver may regard the significance of his life and even the soundness of his decision to go down into the sea as assured even if the air hose may, in fact, become fouled, causing his death. The risk is a sound one, even if it is a risk. Faith in Paul's sense is total. In faith the Christian stakes his all, even the very meaning of his existence, as well as his life, happiness, and hope, upon the action of God in Christ. This total commitment of life to God in trust and steadfast loyalty is the distinctive and full meaning of Christian faith. Every other meaning is subordinate to this.—L. Harold DeWolf in *Teaching Our Faith in God.*

JRNING FIRES.   Our sin scorches us
hen it comes under God's forgiveness.
 scorches us then. We do not see sin
r what it really is except in the
arning fires of God's forgiveness.—
arl Barth.

ermon Suggestions

IE TESTING OF LOYALTY.   Text: Matt.
5:35. How is our loyalty to Christ
sted today? (1) It is tested at the
oint of our independence in answering
s call. (2) It is tested at the point
 our friendship. (3) It is tested at the
oint of our action.—Phillips Packer
lliott.

IE SUPREMACY OF WILL.   Text: John
15-16. (1) The will to know opens
ae door to knowledge, especially
aowledge about God. (2) The will to
aoose follows out of the will to know.
) To be "lights in the world" and to
eflect "the beauty of Jesus" requires
will to obey. With that will-ing comes
avariably the knowledge of how it is
a be done and the power to do it.—
aul P. Fryhling.

Vorship Aids

ALL TO WORSHIP.   "He that dwelleth
a the secret place of the most High
aall abide under the shadow of the
lmighty. I will say of the Lord, He
 my refuge and my fortress: my God;
a him will I trust." Ps. 91:1–2.

VOCATION.   Eternal and ever-blessed
od, come to us this day as we wait
pon thee; and banish every evil
aought, and restrain every wandering
aought, that we, being pure in heart,
aay see thee.

FFERTORY SENTENCE.   "Walk in love,
a Christ also hath loved us, and hath
ven himself for us as an offering and
acrifice to God." Eph. 5:2.

FFERTORY PRAYER.   O heavenly Father,
e pray that thy blessings, which are

as countless as the stars, may be so used
as to bring light and love to thy
children everywhere.

PRAYER.   O God, our Father, we lift
to thee our grateful praise. Thou art
our strong deliverer. In hours of darkness thou hast been our support and in
joy our companion. From thy hand
comes every good gift. For family and
friends, for beauty and laughter, for
work and prayer, we give thee thanks.
Above all we thank thee for the gift
of thy blessed Son for our redemption.

Forgive, O Lord, the littleness of
our return for thy great bounty. Save
and deliver us from the sins that so
easily beset us: our selfishness, our
pride, our anxiety, our envy, our eagerness to be praised, our resentments,
our unkindness, our narrowness of
vision, our complacency before the
agony of the world. By thy grace heal
our unholy divisions of nation, race,
and class and unite thy church to serve
thee by serving all mankind.

Create in us, O God, clean hearts
and a right spirit. Give strength for the
daily task, and help us to see each duty,
however small, as a service done for
thee. Let us feel thee near in whatever
may befall us. Thou knowest our cares;
grant us thy peace. Knit us together in
love and labor and use us by thy spirit
for the healing of the nations.—Church
Women United.

EVENING SERVICE

Topic: A Message to Youth
TEXT: Eccl. 12:1.

I. *Whom to remember?* Remember
your creator. This implies that man
has a creator. It would be strange if
he didn't have, seeing that all else have.
This creator is God, the one true and
living God, the Almighty One, the
maker of the universe. This creator is
Christ as well. (See Col. 1:16.)

II. *When to remember?* In the days
of youth, Solomon says. In fact the
scripture writers are unanimous in

urging the early knowledge of the spiritual. (See Moses' words in Deut. 31:33; David's words in Ps. 34:11; Christ's words in Matt. 6:33.) The creator is to be remembered not only by youth. The notion that spiritual things, while proper for childhood or youth, are neither demanded by nor becoming in manhood is vain delusion. No age is exempted or unsuitable.

III. *Why remember?* (a) He is infinitely worthy of being remembered. Without him there is no real happiness here and no salvation hereafter. He is to be remembered because the human heart is so prone to forget.

(b) Youth, being the formative time of life, is the most important time for acquiring spiritual habits. Youth, as the happiest time of life, is also the time when God can most easily remembered and sought. In youth th days of too much business concer worry, and temptation, of sin, afflictio and sorrow, of disease and decay ha not yet come. It is the time for th shaping of one's afterlife. "As the tw is bent, so the tree will grow."

IV. *How to remember?* By thinki of his person. Of the wicked it is sai "God is not in their thoughts" (I 10:4). But a good man "remembers G upon his bed and meditates upon hi in the night watches." By receiving hi as savior. By reflecting on his characte By acknowledging his goodness. I meditating upon his Word. By keepi his commandments. By loving a serving and following him.—C. Reube Anderson.

SUNDAY: MARCH TWENTY-EIGHTH

MORNING SERVICE

Topic: The Terrible Burden of Love (Lent)

SCRIPTURE: I Cor. 13:4–8 (RSV).

I. Paul tells us that love is faithful to the end. "Love suffereth long and is kind." It never gives up. It is the eternal spirit brooding over life's brokenness, bringing light out of darkness, reducing chaos to order. Paul does not say that love is never discouraged, never makes mistakes; he simply says, "Love never ends." It is deathless.

(a) During the excavations of the ruins of Pompeii it is reported that the workers came upon the skeletal remains of a mother and her child, with the mother's arm under the child. There in the darkness and the dust, through centuries and centuries they lay, symbolic of the unending love of a good mother. "Ah, the terrible burden of love!"

(b) In the story of the prodigal son the father knew the dreadful burden of love. After months and months of wandering in a foreign environment, spending his resources foolishly agair his father's wishes, the lad came himself. We are told that in the trava of his soul he decided to go back hon and hopefully he might be accept as one of his father's servants. Wh happened upon his return? The fath saw him at a distance and went o to meet him. The love that had suffere long was now *kind*. What an opport nity to have chastised the lad! B there was not a word of bitterne "Love keeps no score of wrongs." F love it was a time to rejoice. "Th my son was dead, and is alive; he w lost, and is found." The family on broken was made whole again. A that which made it whole again w the endless love of a good father wh had suffered long and was kind. "A the terrible burden of love!"

II. Let us note another dimensi of love: "Love believes all things." T some this may seem like credulity. T person who literally believes all thin must be confused; a weak mind that easily exploited. Moffatt's translatic from the original Greek helps us to clearer understanding of Paul's thinking. "Love is always eager to believe the best." That makes sense.

(a) Admittedly this is a difficult standard to embrace. Psychologists have shown us that there is something within our nature which makes it easy for us to believe the worst. We have an appetite for bad news. At worst we may become scandalmongers and talebearers, dispensers of half-truths. There is something within human nature that makes it easy for us to rejoice in the failure of another human being. It was against such temptation that Jesus directed his warning, "Judge not lest you be judged."

(b) This tendency to believe the worst has more than individual application. Some there are who look at the whole of life in this manner. It is a destructive approach to life. But love, not blind to the failures and weaknesses of man, is always eager to believe the best. This is the creative force in life. Love begets love; it evokes good will and trust. Jesus was aware of the creative nature of love. He encouraged his disciples to take the tiny flowers of love and faith and hope and to nurture them so that they could multiply and conquer the evils of hate and discord.

(c) When Jesus selected those who would be most closely associated with him in kingdom work, he looked for people with obvious weaknesses as well as strengths. Peter, a rough, impulsive man, under the love and teachings of the Master blossomed into greatness of character. Love that is eager to believe the best is the redemptive force that often saves us from surrendering to the beast that is within us. We draw strength from those about us who are eager to believe the best about us.

III. Consider this demand which love makes: "Love bears all things." In Weymouth's translation we find another way of articulating this truth: "She can overlook faults." Moffatt renders it, "Love is always slow to expose." The idea suggested here is that love is intel-ligent. It knows that there is a time to expose and a time to refrain from exposing, a time to speak and a time to refrain from speaking. Love is sensitive. It knows how to be silent in moments of great suffering.

(a) To say that love knows when to remain silent is not to belittle speech. Words are the vehicles for feelings and ideas that link soul to soul. I have the greatest admiration for those who are skilled in the gift of the right use of words. But words are powerful and can be dangerous. There are emotionally charged words that can excite to violence or that can rob another human being of his will to live. And there are great empowering words which, spoken at the right time, can heal and inspire.

(b) Paul tells us that love knows how to overlook faults, to keep silent in those moments when it would be far easier to form words to vent our anger or disappointment. Every parent knows that there are times in relationship to the growing child when the temptation to speak in anger is great. And surely everyone must fail, perhaps many times, to live up to the high standard. But after each failure love will rededicate itself to the high resolve: bear all things, overlook faults, slow to expose. "Ah, the terrible burden of love!"

(c) This dimension of love that calls upon us to bear all things is a hard saying, but then the best things of life are bought with a price. As one psychiatrist says, "It is easier to hate, but healthier to love." What is needed is a religion that knows how to be firm without being inflexible, that hates the sin but loves the sinner, that is able to forgive and trust and respects individual differences. This is the love that bears all things.

IV. There is a further dimension to love that we must consider: "Love hopeth all things" or as Moffatt renders it, "Love is always hopeful." It never gives up. The good father is always hopeful that the prodigal will come home again. Man cannot live without hope. He must always be able to hope that in any difficulty things will right themselves.

(a) Small wonder that the other name we have for God is love. For love is the spirit of hope brooding over the darkness, coaxing light out of the shadows, giving form to that which is without form and void. It is the agglutinator that holds the world together, the organizing principle.

(b) Love is the positive force, playing over the darkness, yet never giving up. Even over the grave love never ends. After everything visible has been telescoped into the invisible, three things abide, faith, hope, love, but the greatest is love. It never gives up; it always begins again.

(c) When the wholeness of life is threatened love is the silent cohesive force that is always hopeful. It is the greatest force for good in the world for, in the language of an early Christian, "Love is of God, and he who loves is born of God and knows God." So we confidently say, "Our hope is in God," for God is love and love never ends. Teilhard de Chardin said, "Someday, after mastering the winds, the waves, the tides, and gravity, we shall harness —for God—the energies of love. And then, for the second time in the history of the world, man will discover fire."— Charles F. Jacobs.

Illustrations

SOMETHING FOR NOTHING. Rebecca West in *Black Lamb and Grey Falcon* describes the "something for nothing" person with painful accuracy: "Gerda has no sense of process. She wants the results without doing any of the work that goes to make it. She wants to enjoy the position of a wife without going to the trouble of making a marriage. She wants to enjoy motherhood without taking care of her children. She has no sense of what goes to buy people love or friendship or reward. Therefore, she wants the results that belong to other people. She is able to look at a loaf of bread and not realize the miracles of endurance and ingenuity that had to be performed before the wheat grew and the mill ground and the oven baked."

HUNGER FOR LOVE. We all hunger for love. More eagerly than a blind man seeking for light, a drowning man for air, or a starving man for food; more ardently than a Christopher Columbus looking for a new route to the East; more yearningly than a homesick boy dreaming of home, we hunger and thirst for love—that sweet mystery of life that turns darkness into light and keeps the light from going out, that turns evil into good and keeps the good from spoiling.—Lance Webb in *Discovering Love.*

Sermon Suggestions

AFFIRMATIONS ABOUT GOD'S LOVE. (1) Divine love is magnetic. (2) Divine love has a strange, transforming power. (3) Divine love is personal. (4) Divine love is eternal. (5) Divine love will triumph. —Robert V. Ozment.

WHAT DID JESUS DO? Text: John 20:30–31. (1) He embodied the Word. (2) He emboldened the disciples. (3) He empowered the believer.—Norman R. Lawson.

Worship Aids

CALL TO WORSHIP. "Lord, who shall abide in thy tabernacle? Who shall dwell in thy holy hill? He that walketh uprightly, and worketh righteousness, and speaketh the truth in his heart." Ps. 15:1–2.

INVOCATION. Almighty and everlasting God, who givest to all who desire it the spirit of grace and supplication, deliver us, O Lord, from all coldness of heart, from all indifferent wandering of the mind, that we may fix our affection upon thee and upon thy service. Fill us with holy, peaceful, and beautiful thoughts, that with steadfast minds and kindled affection we may worship thee in spirit and in truth.

OFFERTORY SENTENCE. "For ye know the grace of our Lord Jesus Christ, that though he was rich, yet for your sakes he became poor, that ye through his poverty might be rich." II Cor. 8:9.

OFFERTORY PRAYER. O Father of our Lord Jesus Christ, we dedicate these offerings to the fellowship of him, whom to know aright is life eternal.

PRAYER. O God, the light of all that is true, the strength of all that is good, the glory of all that is beautiful, we thank thee that thou hast put within our minds some spark of the eternal flame, some desire after goodness, some enjoyment of whatsoever things are lovely. We thank thee for the strength of reason and for all the inner kingdom of the mind, for every thought that lifts us to thyself, for every noble desire, for every holy impulse. We thank thee that thou hast so framed our hearts that our deepest instincts anchor us to thee, that thou hast so created everything that he who loves the truth can never miss thee at the last. In all our thoughts, save us from anxiety, presumption, and fear. Deliver us from all falsehood, error, and prejudice. And as we have gathered ourselves to seek thee afresh may all our doubts vanish before the shining of thy face, and as our thoughts are hushed to silence now, may we find thee moving upon our minds, higher than our highest thought, yet nearer to us than our very selves. Inspire, uplift, and comfort us, and manifest thyself, O God.—William E. Orchard.

EVENING SERVICE

Topic: The Man Who Is God

I. Jesus claimed to be the Son of God. (See Matt. 26:63–64; John 5:18; 10:36; 11:4.)

II. Jesus refers with unmistakable clarity to his preexistence with God. (See John 5:18; 8:23, 58; 10:30; 17:5.)

III. Jesus claimed divine supremacy in both worlds. (See Matt. 13:41; 25:31, 34; 28:18; John 3:13; Rev. 1:18.)

IV. Jesus claimed indisputable power in dealing with every moral duty and destiny. (See Matt. 7:24; 12:3–8; 28:20; Rev. 2:1; 3:21.)

V. Jesus asserted full possession of the power to forgive sins. (See Matt. 9:6; Luke 7:48; John 8:36.)

VI. Jesus claimed the power to raise his own body from the grave and to raise all the dead at the last great day. (See John 2:19, 21; 5:28–29; 6:40; 10:18.)

VII. Jesus claimed to be the source of life that is real and eternal. (See John 4:14; 5:21; 6:35, 40, 53, 58; 10:28; 11:25–26; 14:6; 15:4; 17:1–3.)

VIII. Jesus declared he had power to do all his Father's works. (See John 5:17, 19; 10:37–38.)

IX. Jesus claimed to know the Father uniquely. (See Matt. 11:27; John 7:29; 8:55; 17:25.)

X. Jesus claimed to reveal the Father flawlessly. (See John 12:45; 14:9; 15:23; 17:21.)

XI. Jesus claimed to obey the Father perfectly. (See John 5:30; 6:38; 8:38, 40; 12:49–50; 14:10.)

XII. Jesus unequivocally demands faith in himself. (See Matt. 10:32; John 8:24, 36, 51; 10:9; 11:26; 14:1.)—Seth Wilson.

SUNDAY: APRIL FOURTH

MORNING SERVICE

Topic: Was Jesus Mad? (Passion Sunday)

TEXT: John 10:19-21.

For months now the critics had been standing on the fringe of the crowd muttering and murmuring, jabbering among themselves. Then emotions exploded. Angry cries shattered the air: "Jesus has a devil. He is mad!" Jesus' contemporaries were not the only ones to consider him mad. There have always been persons—some bound by tradition, others protecting vested interests, still others saturated in their materialistic cultures—who have vigorously questioned the "workability" of the Christian way of life. And if we are honest with ourselves we will admit that there are some of us who, if not explicitly, at least subconsciously, do not believe that the gospel can be realistically applied to the complexities of global conflict and the down-to-earth details of daily life.

I. Maybe we can better understand our own purgatory of doubt if we ask ourselves why Jesus was rejected by people in his own time. What did he say, what did he do, that brought him at last to a cross?

(a) *He insisted that he and his God lived in perfect union.* (See John 10:30; 14:9.) "I and my Father are one," he said. "If you have seen me you have seen the Father." Those who heard him saw his peasant garb, they saw how young he was, and they cried: "What presumption! He has a devil. This man is mad."

(b) *Jesus proclaimed the primacy of love.* He said that love summarized the law's commands. When man has loved God with all of his energies and has loved his neighbor as himself he has fulfilled life's requirements. To illustrate the point, Jesus made the hero of the world's most famous short story a Samaritan, a member of the hated "mongrel" race. And the self-righteous sneered and contemptuously cried: "This man is dangerous. He has a devil. He's mad."

(c) *Jesus presumed to forgive sins.* In the fishing village of Capernaum a sick man was brought to the Master. Sensing the deep roots of his illness, Jesus calmly said, "Son, thy sins be forgiven thee." Eyebrows shot up. Mouths dropped open. A Pharisee spat out the words: "This is blasphemy. Who can forgive sins but God only? This man has a devil. He is mad."

II. Was he mad? Different? Yes. Disturbing and disruptive? Yes. But mad? Think for a moment. If we choose to reject him and his ideas what remains?

(a) *Is separation from God sane?* Jesus said, "I and my Father are one." Delete the Father from that phrase and see what happens. Jesus was never more sane than when he prayed for mankind to be one with God even as he was. If our own lives are not to become hollow shells and if the mad scramble of the world's jigsaw is to be pieced back together, then life—all of life—must be integrated about the central fact of God.

(b) Jesus insisted that the human must somehow be joined with the divine. In proclaiming the primacy of love he pointed the way. We come to know God as we express unselfish love. Does that sound insane? *Rather is it not madness for us to continue in ways of hostility and aggression?* Jesus said, "Love one another." Is love madness? Or is it rather the only answer to the needs of our splintered, fearfilled time?

(c) And what about forgiveness? Was Jesus mad when he presumed to forgive? The apostle Paul, peering into the depth of his own spirit, cried out, "Wretched man that I am, who can save me from this doom?" But trusting divine love, he went on to say: "Thank God! It is done through Jesus Christ" (Rom. 7:24–25). Forgiveness brings to the experience of the Christian not a morbid doctrine but a glorious freedom.—James Armstrong.

Illustration

THREE CROSSES. When Francis of Assisi had an audience with a Muslim ruler he had to approach the potentate by walking on a carpet decorated with crosses. The Muslim taunted him for having trodden on the symbol of his Lord, but Francis replied: "There were three crosses on Calvary. I have walked on the other two."

The cross of Jesus Christ was unique among all of the instruments of execution devised and used by humans in that it was the scene of God's mighty work of reconciling man to himself. In fact it was unique not only in the sense that nothing else like it ever happened before or since but also because what took place there was *ep' hapax*, once for all. In the words of the Book of Common Prayer, Jesus Christ "made there, by his one oblation of himself, once offered, a full, perfect, and sufficient sacrifice for our sins and the sins of the whole world."

Yet as the confrontation between Francis and the Bey of Tunis indicates, in another way Jesus' cross was not at all unique. There were three on Calvary, and thousands lined the Roman roads when rebellious slaves were put to death. In that sense the cross was common, all too common, and the remarkable thing about the cross of Jesus is not the singularity of his suffering or the cruelty of his death but who he was and is and the absolutely unique effect of his death.— *Christianity Today.*

Sermon Suggestion

THE SIGN OF THE CROSS. Text: Gal. 3:1 (MOFFATT). (1) The cross points upward, toward the heights, like the finger of God. (2) The cross goes straight down into the ground, the dimension of depth. (3) The cross goes deep as the grave. (4) The cross is extended wide with arms that outstretch in invitation and embrace the world. (5) The cross is a signpost bidding us take up our direction from what Christ did that day on Calvary.— David A. MacLennan.

Worship Aids

CALL TO WORSHIP. "Having therefore, brethren, boldness to enter into the holiest by the blood of Jesus, by a new and living way, which he hath consecrated for us, let us draw near with a true heart in full assurance of faith." Heb. 10:19–20, 22.

INVOCATION. Almighty and merciful God, who hast created us for thy service and glory: we confess in thy holy presence that we have broken thy commandments and sinned against thee. We have offended by our deeds, by our thoughts, and by the sinful impulses and desires of our hearts. In the greatness of thy love, shed abroad in us a holy sorrow for all our transgressions and make our wills obedient to thy perfect love revealed in Christ Jesus our Lord and Savior.

OFFERTORY SENTENCE. "If any man will come after me (saith Jesus), let him deny himself, and take up his cross daily, and follow me." Luke 9:23.

OFFERTORY PRAYER. O God, who hast given us thy Son to be an example and a help to our weakness in following the path that leadeth unto life, grant us so to be his disciples that we may walk in his footsteps.

LITANY. O God of grace and glory, we acknowledge before thee our unpayable indebtedness; we are the children of sacrifice; our choicest benedictions have been bought with the price of other blood and tears than our own; thou hast given us the inheritance of them that feared thy name,

O Lord, make us thankful.

For all saints and martyrs, prophets and apostles; for all soldiers of the common good who served thee in scorn of consequence and fell on sleep unashamed, of whom the world was not worthy,

O Lord, make us thankful.

For the cross of Christ and his exceeding bitter sacrifice; for the truths which there were brought to light, the love unbounded which there was freely given, and the costly salvation which there visited thy people,

O Lord, make us thankful.

By his loneliness in the garden; by his betrayal and his trial; by the humiliation of his people's hate, the mockery of his thorny crown, and the bitterness of scourging; by the anguish of his cross; by his unfailing faith in thee and love for man,

O Lord, make us thankful.

Eternal God, may we, who owe our spiritual blessings to so great a cloud of witnesses, who have suffered before us, and to Christ, whose cross is our peace, walk as becomes those who are debtors to thy grace. From ingratitude, pride, hardness of heart, and all manner of evil requiting,

Good Lord, deliver us.

From neglect of blessings dearly purchased; from selfish use of opportunities for which good men died; from growing within our hearts the venomous roots of covetousness; from pampering ourselves with vain superfluities; and from all spendthrift wasting of our costly heritage,

Good Lord, deliver us.

Gird us, we beseech thee, with gratitude and fidelity; devote us to the service of mankind with more courageous zeal; free us from the detaining reluctance of our fear, selfishness, and unbelief; and at this altar of remembrance, may we, O Christ, join afresh the honorable company of thy true servants who in sacrificial living share the fellowship of thy cross.

Lord, have mercy upon us and grant us this blessing.—Harry Emerson Fosdick.

EVENING SERVICE

Topic: The Big Fisherman's Worst Hour

SCRIPTURE: Mark 14:53–72.

I. *Peter's mistakes.* (See v. 54.) (a) He disregarded warning. Jesus had warned Peter, "You will deny me three times" (v. 30). In reply Peter had protested that he would die for his Lord before he would deny him. Instead of protesting, he should have been listening. When we think we know more than the Lord knows we always get into trouble.

(b) He followed afar off. Our only hope in the Christian life is to keep close to Christ. Peter thought it was safer to keep his distance, but he got "hooked." Following afar off always leads to failure.

(c) He warmed himself at the enemy's fire. After swinging his sword at a servant of the high priest and cutting off his ear (John 18:10, 26), Peter took a big risk in sitting down with the servants in the courtyard ("palace") of Caiaphas. The way of comfort ("warmed himself") is not always the best life.

II. *Peter's denials.* (See vv. 66–71.) (a) The four accounts of the denials differ somewhat in detail, though they all agree that Peter denied his Lord three times. Probably there was considerable confusion with several people "chiming in" to accuse the apostle.

(b) All four accounts agree that he was first questioned by a maidservant of the high priest. Mark's account suggests that she recognized him in the light of the open fire. He was vigorous in denying that he knew Jesus.

(c) The second time it was a "maid" who told the bystanders, "This is one of them" (v. 69). So the KJV. But the Greek clearly says, "And when the maid saw him, she began again to say to those standing by." Peter didn't know enough to remove himself from the spotlight.

(d) The third time it was a general chorus: "Surely you are one of them, for you are a Galilean" (v. 70). They recognized him by his Galilean accent. Poor Peter! He was always opening his mouth and getting himself into trouble.

(e) In answer to his final accusation Peter "began to curse and to swear." This has sometimes been interpreted as meaning that he used vulgar language and thus proved that he was not a loyal follower of Christ. But this is judicial terminology here. What Peter was saying was this: "Let me be cursed if I am not telling you the truth; I declare under oath that I do not know this man." So he was guilty of perjury.

III. *Peter's repentance.* (See v. 72.) Just then the rooster crowed. Peter remembered Jesus' prediction, "Before the cock crows twice you will deny me thrice." It struck him hard! "And when he thought thereon, he wept." This is only three words in the Greek, only two after "and." The first of the two, a participle, could mean that he "covered his head" or "flung himself out." In any case, he wept bitter tears of repentance.—Ralph Earle.

SUNDAY: APRIL ELEVENTH

MORNING SERVICE

Topic: Christ Enters in Triumph (Palm Sunday)

SCRIPTURE: Matt. 21:1–9.

I. On the first day of the week in which he died Jesus did a surprising thing. He entered Jerusalem in triumph and accepted the acclamation of the crowds. Why did he do this?

(a) It is easy to see why he chose the place and the time. Jerusalem was the center of the national life of Israel, and if anyone had a claim to make, Jerusalem was the place to make it. The time was the season of the feast of the Passover. There were more people in Jerusalem during Passover than at any other time of the year, and if anyone were seeking to make a claim to the largest possible number of people, Passover was the time when they could be found in Jerusalem.

(b) What Jesus did he did deliberately. He had made arrangements ahead of time for the donkey on which he was to ride. He sent two of the disciples ahead, telling them where they would find the animal tied and instructing them how to answer if anyone questioned their taking it. They were to say, "The Lord has need of him." That would identify them. They followed these instructions, and they were allowed to take the animal as Jesus had told them they would be. The whole thing had been planned ahead of time.

(c) It is clear that Jesus entered the city as he did in order to fulfill the conditions of an ancient prophecy. (See Zech. 9:9.) Jesus planned his triumphal entry in such a way as to make it impossible for people to miss the point. He was deliberately claiming to be the Lord of life whose coming had been prophesied in the scripture.

II. This kind of public demonstration strikes us as uncharacteristic of Jesus. (a) He was not the sort of person who liked to draw attention to himself. Indeed he seems most of the time to have tried to turn attention away from himself. His triumphal entry into Jerusalem strikes us as uncharacteristic of the Jesus with whose personal modesty we have become familiar in the gospels.

(b) One feature of the triumphal entry is highly characteristic of Jesus. That is that it was a demonstration rather than an argument, and Jesus regularly used demonstration rather than argument to make his point. (See Matt. 9:5–6; 12:10–13; 26:26–28; Luke 10:37.)

(c) The triumphal entry is not so uncharacteristic of Jesus as it seems at first glance. When the time came for him to offer himself to the people as the promised Lord for whom they had been waiting, he did not make a political speech; he performed an act of public demonstration and put it squarely up to those who witnessed the demonstration to decide whether they were going to stand with him or against him.

III. We all know how it turned out. On the day when Jesus entered the city of Jerusalem in triumph the crowds acclaimed him. They spread their garments in the road to serve as a royal carpet and bestrewed the way with branches from the trees. But the enthusiasm of the crowd was of the moment only. Most of them did not really want the kind of life that Jesus offered. And as the succeeding days unfolded it became increasingly clear that the majority of those to whom he offered himself wanted no part of him.

(a) I have heard it said that the same people who on the first Palm Sunday cried, "Hosanna! Blessed is he who comes in the name of the Lord," shouted, "Crucify him! Crucify him!" on the succeeding Good Friday, but I do not think there is any real evidence for that. What seems to have happened is that another group, more numerous and more powerful, took over in the meantime, and those who had welcomed Jesus were overwhelmed. Perhaps they were frightened off. They were certainly drowned out.

(b) I have heard it said that if Jesus were to come into the world again today the same thing would happen all over again. I do not believe that. The fact that Jesus lived was not without its effect on men. His teaching has deepened the dimensions of our moral thinking, and his life and death and resurrection have enlarged the horizons of our understanding of the things of the spirit. We have changed since Jesus first walked among us. We have changed because he walked among us.

(c) If he came to us again, as he came to men on that first Palm Sunday, I think he would find many more men and women who were ready to accept him and to stand by him to the end. He would not find that all Christians had forsaken the gospel or that all businessmen were dishonest or that all government officials were corrupt or that all our citizenry had fallen prey to the worship of material comfort or worldly success. There are those who, to use St. Paul's phrase, have "put on Christ" and have become "a new creation."

(d) What his coming again would do would be to divide the world into two groups. There would be those who would stand with him and those who would stand against him. The question is, which group would we belong to?—Charles H. Buck, Jr.

Illustrations

KILLED BY FRIENDS. I suppose, after we get over the first refusal to admit it, that we shall have to confess finally that we killed God. By "we" I mean most explicitly we Christians. We domesticated God, stripped him of awe and majesty, cornered him ecclesiastically, taught him our rules, dressed him in our vanity, and trained him to acknowledge our tricks and bow to our ceremonial expectations. After some time it was difficult to see any difference between God and what we believed, what we did, what we said, or what we were. God was killed by his friends.—Samuel H. Miller in *The Dilemma of Modern Belief*.

A WAITING AGE. Thomas Kelly has said that we live in "a waiting age." He feels that the land is full of seekers, and the church also is full of seekers. Many people are looking for something "vastly deeper" than they heretofore have found. This, says Kelly, is not due to weakness but to vision. He explains that "over the horizon men dimly see something glorious, they know not what. But what they see is Christ walking again in lowly, simple love, recapturing the church and the world for himself, rebuking the scribes and the Pharisees who sit in Moses's seat, tenderly leading men to share in his immediacy and enthrallment in God."—John H. Townsend.

Sermon Suggestion

A STUDY IN CONTRASTS. (1) The excitement of the people and the quietness of Jesus. (2) What the people wanted and what Jesus wanted. (3) The joy of the disciples and the sadness of Jesus.—Theodore P. Ferris.

Worship Aids

CALL TO WORSHIP. "God hath exalted

him, and given him a name which is above every name: that at the name of Jesus every knee should bow, of things in heaven, and things in earth, and things under the earth; and that every tongue should confess that Jesus Christ is Lord, to the glory of God the Father." Phil. 2:9–11.

INVOCATION. Our Father, thou who wast received amid the shouts of an earlier day, open our hearts and journey into our inward parts. Help us to lay aside all prejudices, forsake all sins, and overcome all biddings that might bar thy entrance. Let thy entrance into our hearts be triumphant. Conquer our fears, silence our unbelief, quicken our faith. Lead us, through thy spirit, to spiritual victory and conquest.

OFFERTORY SENTENCE. "Give unto the Lord, O ye kindreds of the people, give unto the Lord glory and strength. Give unto the Lord the glory due unto his name: bring an offering, and come into his courts." Ps. 96:7–8.

OFFERTORY PRAYER. As thy faithful disciples blessed thy coming, O Christ, and spread their garments in the way, covering it with palm branches, may we be ready to lay at thy feet all that we have and are, and to bless thee, O thou who comest in the name of the Lord.

PRAYER. For this day of victory we thank thee, O God. Men lifted up the Man of Galilee and set him high upon his throne. In this day of triumph we pause to render our loyalty to the King of kings. Thrill us as we remember that in his name children have been blessed, women's load has been eased, men's cruelties have diminished, the aged have been comforted, the sick healed, the dumb given speech, the blind enabled to see, the ignorant taught to know, the bitter have found love, the cynics have learned to believe, the despairing have been given faith, the weak have found strength, and the fearful have learned how not to be afraid.

Let this day be a victory for us. May we too be triumphant. Let it be a day when we earn our laurels as we subdue our fears, conquer our weaknesses, hurdle obstacles, and invigorate faith. Cleanse us of cheapness, purge us of sordidness, take deceit from our hearts, remove gossip from our lips, dislodge bitterness from our minds, and expel hatred from our souls. Send us into this week with a sense of victory for Christ, for the church, and for ourselves.—Fred E. Luchs.

EVENING SERVICE

Topic: Don't Fence Me In (Good Friday)

TEXT: Luke 23:33.

I. They nailed him to a cross and let him die. And that was that or so they thought. They built a fence around him and shut him out. This man who had come so that men might have life more abundant, this man who had given God his chance at him and who, in turn, wanted his chance at other men, they didn't quite know what to do with him, so they crucified him. They strung him up on a crude, wooden cross. It was better that way or so they supposed.

II. For 1,900 years the world has tried desperately to build a fence around Jesus. The first fence was a cross. But that way did not succeed nor could it succeed.

(a) They could kill the body; they could not kill the soul. They could destroy the flesh; they could not destroy the spirit which the flesh incarnated, especially a spirit which in the hour of its greatest hurt cried out, "Father, forgive them, for they know not what they do."

(b) The cross having failed, the world turned to a far more subtle way of disposing of Jesus: it worshiped him. It put him up on a high altar with its ornate and costly symbols and fenced him in there. It said to him: "Stay there. That is where you belong. Stay there, and when Sundays come, we shall worship you."

III. All the while Jesus keeps pleading: "Don't fence me in. Let me down from your crosses. Let me down from your altars. Let me out of the four walls of your churches. Let me into your minds and hearts. Let me into your homes. Let me into your offices and your marts of trade. Let me into your communities and the councils of your statesmen. I want to get back where I first started, walking in the common ways of men and talking with them about how to live and how to live together. Give me my chance. Don't fence me in."—Harold W. Ruopp.

SUNDAY: APRIL EIGHTEENTH

MORNING SERVICE

Topic: Easter Changes Everything (Easter)

TEXT: Col. 3:1–4.

Though he was not one of the original disciples, though he did not witness the events of the first Easter Day, the apostle Paul was obsessed with the event of Easter. For Paul the Christian drama begins on Easter Day. All Christian theology is an exposition of Easter. All the truths that really matter derive from Easter, and one of those truths is that Easter changes everything. It can be a liberating truth if we can understand what it means for our personal lives.

I. *Easter changes your past.* (a) That seems impossible, doesn't it? The past is a closed book. What we have written we have written. We wish we could rewrite a few pages or even rip them out because they make unpleasant reading and not private reading either. Your life story is not in a private diary but in a public library; and the whole world can get a glimpse of what W. E. Orchard called "those sad turned pages which some chance wind of memory blows back again with shame."

(b) Imagine yourself standing before some heavenly tribunal to explain the record of your life upon earth. After you have confessed what you think to be your worst sins, an angelic presence asks, "Any extenuating circumstances?" You reply: "None. I want to be forgiven." The angel leafs through the pages of a great golden book, then surprises you by saying: "There is nothing to forgive. We have no record of such sins." "No record?" you protest. "But there must be. Did you get the name right? Look it up again." "The name," replies the angel, "that isn't here either. Oh, yes, there used to be such a person, but he died, so we closed his account. Your record begins after his death."

(c) According to Paul, that's how Easter changes your past. Paul believed, and his own experience confirmed the belief, that the death and resurrection of Christ represent the operation of God's grace and power in every man who becomes by faith a man in Christ. God kills that man, kills the person he is, buries him, and erases his name from the book of life; then God raises that man, brings him to life again, makes him a new creature with a new identity and a new name who need not be ashamed of his past because he has no past to convict him.

(d) God says to the human race through Christ: "Take my life. I give it to you. And hand your life over to me so that I can carry all your sins away." That's how Easter changes your past, and that's what Paul means when he says, "For you have died and your life is hid with Christ in God."

II. *Easter changes your present.* (a) We should like to believe it, of course, because a change in present circumstances is just about the biggest thing that some of us want. Do you know anyone outside a barnyard who feels perfectly satisfied with the way that things are? Most people, especially as they come to middle age, wish they could change their jobs which have reached a dead end, or their marriages which have degenerated into tired friendships, or their economic status which denies them many of the good things of life, or their whole life-style which seems dull and friendless; but who climbs out of a coffin after the lid has been nailed down?

(b) Paul says in effect, "Identify with Jesus in his death and resurrection, and that will change everything." It will change your present circumstances because it will change you, make you a different person with a new mind and hence a new way of looking at life, new eyes that can see in all the old tasks and relationships hidden glimpses of loveliness and meaning. You might even be like Don Quixote, that dreamer of impossible dreams, who saw things not as they were but as he wanted them to be. Where others saw a wayside inn he saw a castle, where others saw a rabble of peasants he saw an assembly of lords, where others saw a common prostitute he saw a virtuous lady, where others saw a stable he saw a chapel. Don Quixote with his guileless mind had a different view of reality, a different standard of values, a different criterion of happiness and success. Therefore he could dream the impossible dream. His mind was set "on things that are above, not on things that are on the earth." That's how Easter changes everything.

(c) Someone has said that in life's crises we look within ourselves and become confused or we look above us and become calm and serene. Easter makes that change in our present circumstances. When we have added up all the factors in any situation there is still the factor of God, and we are different people if we believe that he is the God who raised Jesus Christ from the dead.

III. *Easter changes your future.* (a) That also seems to fly in the face of facts. If we have any resentment about growing old it's not because we have lost our youthful appearance and vigor or even because we know that life's major experiences are behind us. It's because we know that our time is running out. The past gets larger and the future gets smaller like the sand in the top of an egg timer, until one day the last grain will have dropped and there will be none left. How can we change that?

(b) We can think life through instead of stopping, as we usually do, at the blank wall of death. We can hold the hope, held by intelligent people of all cultures and civilizations, that there is life beyond that wall, which means that we could have a future even on the day that we die. Easter awakens that hope and confirms it. Easter is the historical event of a man whose friends saw him after he was dead because God raised him from the dead. Paul believed that what God did for Christ he does for us if we are identified with Christ: "When Christ who is our life appears, then you also will appear with him in glory."

(c) Paul Tillich recalled that in the Nuremberg war-crime trials a witness appeared who had lived for a time in a Jewish cemetery in Poland. It was the only place where he and many others could hide after they had escaped the gas chamber. During this time he wrote poetry, and one poem described an unusual birth. In one of the graves a young woman, assisted by an elderly gravedigger, gave birth to a baby. When the infant uttered his first cry the old man prayed: "Great God, hast thou finally sent the Messiah to us? For who else than the Messiah can be born in a grave?" The old gravedigger spoke the truth in a larger sense than he realized. The Messiah, the Christ, was born in a grave, a grave in a garden from which he came forth on Easter Day to fill the world with his presence and to live in the world eternally. The grave is not the place of our death if we are men in Christ but the place of our birth. We don't die there; we are born there. Our future in eternity has begun.— Leonard Griffith.

Illustrations

WHAT IS EASTER? Easter is many things. It is the time of singing birds and blooming of flowers. It is the promise of dawn—the watching for sunrise. It is the light heart of a little girl dressed in pink organdy or a little boy munching chocolate candy. Easter causes all creation to burst forth in the singing of a grand antiphonal, "Up from the grave he arose!" It provides the basis for the sermon regarding the fact and the significance of the resurrection of Christ from the grave.

Easter always brings with it the renewal of hope to gladden the heart of mankind. It is the wellspring of zeal on the part of the church. It motivates the conversion of the sinner. It maintains the faithfulness of the saint.

The eternal vindication of Jesus Christ as the Son of God, the savior of the world, the lord of life, the judge of all creation—this is Easter. He lives! And because he lives we too shall live. This is the Easter promise.—*The Lookout*.

SPIRITUAL RESURRECTION.   There are men in whom the resurrection begun makes the resurrection credible. In them the spirit of the risen Savior works already, and they have mounted with him from the grave. Their step is as free as if the clay of the sepulchre had been shaken off, their hearts are lighter than those of other men, and there is in them an unearthly triumph which they are unable to express. They have risen above the narrowness of life and all that is petty and ungenerous and mean. They have risen above fear. They have risen above self. In the New Testament that is called the spiritual resurrection, being "risen with Christ."—Frederick W. Robertson.

Sermon Suggestions

THE RESURRECTION: AN EVENT AND A PERSON.   Text: John 11:25 (NEB). (1) Our faith centers not in a dead man but in one whom God raised from the dead. (2) Our faith hinges not on the teachings of a mere moralist but on the power of the living Christ to transform us into new creatures. (3) Our faith reaches out not to call attention to ourselves or to exploit others but helpfully to give concrete expression to the love Christ has implanted in us.—Russell Q. Chilcote.

EASTER AND THE ROLLING STONES.   Texts: Luke 19:40; 24:2. Easter rolls some stones away from our lives. (1) The stone of our earthbound lives. (2) The stone of defeat. (3) The stone of finality. —C. A. McClain, Jr.

Worship Aids

CALL TO WORSHIP.   "Blessed be the God and Father of our Lord Jesus Christ, which according to his abundant mercy hath begotten us again unto a lively hope by the resurrection of Jesus Christ from the dead, to an inheritance incorruptible, and undefiled, and that fadeth not away, reserved in heaven for you." I Pet. 1:3–4.

INVOCATION.   O God, we thank you this Easter morning for the eternal beauty and everlasting power of the resurrection of Jesus. We pray that these days shall see our Christ emerging from the tomb in which our generation has placed him—a tomb which we have closed with the stone of our selfishness and sealed with our hardness of mind and heart. Fill us this day with the spirit of reverence and humility because we are permitted to sing your praise. Help us to remember that we are your children living in your divine presence in our human lives. Make us faithful to duty and worthy of your love, through Jesus Christ our risen Lord.

OFFERTORY SENTENCE.   "Greater love hath no man than this, that a man lay down his life for his friends." John 15:13.

OFFERTORY PRAYER.   Eternal God, give us a vision of thy glory that no sacrifice may seem too great, and strengthen us in every step we take from selfishness to generosity.

PRAYER. Our Father and our God, it is Easter again, and we are gathered in this congregation to worship thee. Give us the will to worship thee in spirit and in truth. Help us to be made ready to be found by thee; help us to prepare ourselves to be confronted by thee. Thou didst create us, and thou hast given us life and a world in which to live. Thou dost love us with a love we find it hard to understand; thou didst give us the power to determine our own destinies, even the power to reject thee, to rebel against thee.

We have misused the world thou hast given us. Instead of beautiful gardens, we have too often created slums. Too often we have exploited the resources of thy world to our own selfish advantage.

We have failed also in our relationship with the people in thy world. Instead of creating a climate of love we have created a climate of bitterness, suspicion, prejudice, and hatred. Instead of building a world of justice for all we have allowed pockets of injustice to flourish.

As we look upon the cross, help us to realize the pain and agony our waywardness has caused. Help us to know the cost of our separation from thee. Help us to understand the pain and agony thou dost suffer because of our rebellious willfulness.

But as we look at the resurrection and realize that all our sin, selfishness, prejudice, hate, bitterness, and willfulness cannot defeat thy purpose for us, cannot overcome thy love for us, cannot finally separate us from thee, grant that we may give thanks for thy mighty love that will not let us go.

May we stand tall this day, ready to accept thy love, ready to be renewed, ready to reach toward our potentialities with thy very real and ever-present help. Lift us up that we may together sing the alleluias, "Christ is risen," and celebrate the death of our self-centered selves and the birth of our new life in thee.—Lyle V. Newman.

EVENING SERVICE

Topic: What Is Left after Easter?

TEXT: Col. 3:1.

I. The first new possession we ought to have from Easter morning nearly everybody does lay hold on: new assurance of the life everlasting.

(a) The first Easter did not bring as a new thing belief in immortality. From the beginning of the Hebrew faith belief in life after death was present. "He is the God of Abraham, Isaac, and Jacob" is a frequent expression in the Old Testament. This reference means that these individuals were thought of as still being alive.

(b) What Easter brings us is confirmation of belief in life beyond the grave through the living demonstration which Jesus made of this fact in his resurrection appearances. As David Wesley Soper puts it, "The resurrection is the future in the present." In the resurrection, Dr. Soper says, God rolled back the curtain between earth and heaven and showed us a fleeting glimpse of the life beyond.

II. Following the resurrection the early Christians, observed Edgar J. Goodspeed, had a new and glorious conviction that they were in living communion and communication with the risen Christ.

(a) Jesus was not only living after death as the early Christians expected that he would be. He was living in their own experience to their tremendous surprise. Dr. Goodspeed called this awareness the most precious possession the first Christians had.

(b) After Easter every follower of Christ should have this conviction and inspiration in personal life. Easter should mean, as George Stewart said it in the title of one of his books, *The Resurrection in Our Street*.

III. After Easter the church should possess a sense of fullness through the living presence of Christ in it. Borthwick gave the world a sad but significant painting entitled "The Presence." The scene is of the sanctuary of a great cathedral with a few worshipers down front. Unknown to any of the worshipers, Christ has entered to console a poor woman on the back row. The church, of course, knows that Christ is present with it, but the church is not responsive to this fact to the extent it should be.

IV. After Easter the church should come to fruition in witness for Christ. This began to happen to the disciples when they were visited by Jesus on the evening of the day of the resurrection. They were then huddled together in fear because of what the world might do to them because they were followers of Jesus. Coming to awareness that Christ was with them, they began to move on to confidence and bravery and witness to Christ. The contemporary church huddles too often and too long in fear of what the world will think and do if the church completely follows Christ. After Easter we should be vigorously engaged in seeking to bring to be on earth those things which God in Christ wills for earth.—Herschel T. Hamner in *The Methodist Christian Advocate.*

SUNDAY: APRIL TWENTY-FIFTH

MORNING SERVICE

Topic: The Withdrawal of God
SCRIPTURE: John 16:16–19.

I. The great affirmation of Easter, reinforced by the sequence of his resurrection appearances among his disciples, was that Christ had not left them alone. Good Friday came, but three days later Christ left an empty tomb. The disciples huddled together in the secret of a hidden room, fearful of the powers which crucified their Master; but into their midst came the Risen Christ, saying, "Peace be unto you." Whenever the disciples felt alone and forsaken, as if God had abandoned them and the cause of the heavenly kingdom, there Christ came in the breaking of bread and the blessing of the cup.

(a) In holy communion Christ comes. It is the same today, just as it was in the days of the apostles. We may be anxious or discouraged or disquieted of heart. But when we come to the altar of the Lord anticipating a renewal of his abiding presence we discover him afresh in this breaking of bread and the blessing of the cup. The miracle happens. Suddenly we find ourselves forgiven. We sense communion with him and with our fellow men. We know that we are not alone but are in the company of the saints.

(b) This is only one part of the story. The other part consists of all those other times in between when God seems to have evaporated from our lives. We find ourselves insecure and sometimes afraid. We sense the uneasiness like that of a little child who suddenly has lost her mother in the press of the supermarket shopping crowd. We are tempted to panic.

II. In that moment of lostness and loneliness we feel as if suddenly we must face life alone with only our own resources to count upon. When we experience this kind of situation certain truths may sustain us.

(a) You're in good company. Your experience is probably a universal one in the religious life. The disciples knew precisely this same experience. One minute Christ is with them in the breaking of bread; in the very next moment he has withdrawn from them. So baffling is this experience to the disciples that Jesus finds it necessary to explain, "A little while and ye shall not see me, and again, a little while and ye shall see me." Saints in every generation through the long Christian centuries can testify to the same thing.

(b) We may safely assume that it is not due to some special sin or fault or lapse in vigor on our part which is the root cause. In other words we need not become too defensive or filled with a sense of personal guilt. This withdrawal is God's doing, and in his wisdom he undoubtedly has good reasons for it. He begins by surrounding us with his love which confirms within us a sense of basic security. He then periodically allows us to be on our own, so to speak, to try our own wings, in order that we may grow in spiritual strength and in the "independence" of true spiritual maturity. No parent, including God, can pamper his child if the youngster is to develop.

(c) God is never very far away from us. Our loving parents who have left us at home alone for the first time have not abandoned us. Despite their physical absence, they continue in their concern for us and are in control of the possibilities of the total situation. Likewise, God is God, and he is in control of man's existence. He still loves us and cares for us, and underneath are his everlasting arms.

(d) There are times when the withdrawal of God from our lives is more than we think we can bear. We are tempted to question his goodness as well as his wisdom. At such moments we must continue to trust God in faith, leaving all things in his judgment, in his hands.

(1) Often personal tragedies and deprivations, personal disappointments and sorrows dominate the immediate outlook of our lives. These are real and inescapably painful. I would never for a moment want to minimize them.

(2) Often we lose perspective because of the subjective manner in which we handle them. We may hug these pains to our hearts. We may wallow in self-pity. We may allow these to rob our lives of joy and purpose, of meaningful pursuit of the creative and the contributing life.

(3) God has an uncanny way of bringing blessing to us in ways we may not expect or desire or consider possible. In the faithful living of life in trust and obedience, his will is fulfilled in our lives.—Russell K. Nakata, Jr.

Illustrations

THE ABSENT GOD. It is the spirit of God that removes God from our sight. We live in an era in which the God we know is the absent God. Sometimes when our awareness of him has become shallow, habitual—not warm and not cold—when he has become too familiar to be exciting, too near to be felt in his infinite distance, then he becomes the absent God. Then the Spirit shows us nothing except the absent God and the empty space within us which is his space. The Spirit has shown to our time and to innumerable people in our time the absent God and the empty space that cries in us to be filled by him. And then the absent one may return and take the space that belongs to him, and the Spiritual Presence may break again into our consciousness, awakening us to recognize what we are, shaking and transforming us.—Paul Tillich in *The Eternal Now*.

AT GOD'S GRAVE. We have buried God. But we haven't been the same since. We don't talk much about it, but we laugh lots louder than we used to, and we don't like to be left alone, not even for a minute. We get along all right in the daytime. We amuse ourselves with the many devices which our clever age affords. But the moment it gets dark, as soon as it is night, we go out and we howl over God's grave.—Edna St. Vincent Millay.

Sermon Suggestions

THE RESURRECTION VICTORY. Scripture: John 20:19–29 (NEB). (1) Jesus imparted to the disciples the blessings of peace. (See v. 19.) (2) Jesus charged them with the responsibility of a mission. (See v. 21.) (3) Jesus conferred the power of the Holy Spirit. (See v. 22.) (4) Jesus gave authority to proclaim forgiveness of sins. (See v. 23.)—Vernon O. Anderson.

THREE VOICES FROM HEAVEN. (1) God's

approval of his Son. (See Matt. 3:17.) (2) God's call for obedience to Christ. (See Matt. 17:5.) (3) God's promise to glorify Christ in his death and resurrection. (See John 12:28.)

Worship Aids

CALL TO WORSHIP. "O send out thy light and thy truth: let them lead me; let them bring me unto thy holy hill, and to the tabernacles." Ps. 43:3.

INVOCATION. Most holy and gracious God, who turnest the shadow of night into morning: satisfy us early with thy mercy that we may rejoice and be glad all the day. Lift the light of thy countenance upon us, calm every troubled thought, and guide our feet into the way of peace. Perfect thy strength in our weakness and help us to worship thee in the spirit of Jesus Christ our Lord.

OFFERTORY SENTENCE. "Remember the words of the Lord Jesus, how he said, It is more blessed to give than to receive." Acts 20:35.

OFFERTORY PRAYER. Dear God, help us to become unobstructed channels that thy love may flow through us to others and our gifts may be used for the proclamation to all men of thy saving goodness.

PRAYER. O Lord our God, each time we worship thee we are stricken by a consciousness of the poverty of the lives we offer thee. We have not loved thee with all our hearts. We have loved ourselves too much and our neighbors too little. The life we live is not like the life of Jesus, and the mind in us is not the mind of the Master. Let the piercing light of thy truth so shine into our lives this day that we shall see ourselves as thou dost see us.

Uncover, we beseech thee, O Lord, all the little falsehoods whereby we lull ourselves into complacency. Prick our consciences awake to the heroic needs of the day in which we live. Set o[] sights higher so that we may not [] satisfied with lives conformed to t[] standards of this world. We hunger wi[] an appetite that is not eased by an[] thing less than the bread of heave[] Give us, we pray thee, both the wisdo[] and the strength to live as those w[] aspire to be thy children.

We pray this day for thy holy chur[] universal. Let the labors of those w[] would persecute her from without [] dishonor her from within be co[] founded. Let the barriers of creed a[] practice that keep her members apart [] broken down to a height where we c[] see over them and know that all Chr[] tians are brethren in allegiance to th[] common Christ. May thy church [] true to her high calling and her vo[] be raised against violence and injusti[] and misery until thy world is at peace.[]

Be in this fellowship this day, O G[] for we have gathered together in t[] name. Let this be a fellowship of he[] ing for the downcast, strengthening f[] the weak, and for all of us one of f[] giveness and reconsecration to the gr[] task that is our common mission, ev[] the bringing in of thy kingdom. [] Nathanael M. Guptill.

EVENING SERVICE

Topic: The Sacrament of Preaching
TEXT: II Tim. 4:2.

I. Preaching uses visible and outwa[] signs to set forth an inward and spiritu[] grace.

(a) For one thing it uses personali[] "Preaching is truth through personality[] But let us remember what makes [] the total personality of the sermo[] There is the man—his dress, his ma[] ner, his mind, his experience, the rea[] of his soul. Is he aware that he is de[] ing with things too great for utteranc[] Besides the man there is the buildin[] Daniel Webster speaking in a hayfie[] was moving, but Daniel Webster spea[] ing from the tribune of the Senate w[] compelling.

(b) In the sacrament of preaching []

the visible things of church architecture shadow forth the whole faith of Christians: the revelation of God in the Bible, in history, in saints and prophets who have trusted in him, in Jesus himself? Do those visible things lead the mind and the eye to the cross of Christ?

(c) There is the order of worship. Does it guide the congregation from idea to idea, from one act of devotion to another act of devotion, until the holy of holies is reached? What is the content of worship? A historic faith, a living Christ, a redeeming cross?

II. Preaching uses words to say what words cannot express. (a) One of the abiding mysteries of this universe is the power of language to awake and charge the mind. It uncovers insights, stimulates feeling, and calls to depths far below the surface of life. Each of us is familiar with this experience. There was a time when our minds and hearts were leaden and lifeless. Then we read a great poem, a moving novel, some sacred scripture. And from the language there came the living word. Memory was quickened; thought after thought darted from the brain like sparks from a wheel of emery. Almost before we were aware of the transformation, the heart and soul were alive.

(b) Here lies the argument for biblical preaching, use of biblical language, biblical associations, biblical imagery. "The Lord is my shepherd"; "he that dwelleth in the secret place of the Most High"; "though I speak with the tongues of men and of angels"—the majesty of those words, the very rhythm of those phrases, creates an authority which modern speech does not possess.

III. Preaching is directed to the imagination as well as the reason; its purpose is to suggest, not to exhaust.

(a) Good preaching plants the seed of faith; it does not attempt to transplant the full-grown tree. We ought to turn often to poetry, especially the religious poetry of the scripture. The poet lets the imagination of his reader feed and nurture the seed he plants until truth springs full-blown in the soul.

(b) When the seed is planted, something not ourselves tends and cares for it. God is in the hearts of men and women, moving "in a mysterious way his wonders to perform." Over and above the work of man there is in the sacrament the work of God. That fact should give great hope and great courage to every one of us. All our clumsiness, our inadequacy, our imperfections cannot permanently obscure the God of truth.— Paul Austin Wolfe.

SUNDAY: MAY SECOND

MORNING SERVICE

Topic: **Honorable Parents (National Family Week)**

Text: Col. 3:20–21 (RSV).

I. When the Bible commands children to honor their parents, it is at the same time calling parents to recognize that the task of being a parent is tremendously significant. The only way to maintain this point of view in these dehumanizing days is to immerse yourself in the Bible, for there children are clearly considered some of the most important people in the world.

(a) Children are a "heritage from the Lord." They are real people, not just little organisms on the way to becoming important. They are important from the very beginning of their existence. They are image bearers of the Almighty.

(b) Just because they are smaller than adults does not mean that they are less important to God. Nor does it mean that they have less right to being treated respectfully and with the deepest consideration. Children are really people not fully mature, admittedly, but then most adults are not nearly so mature as they think they are either.

II. When God commanded children to honor their parents he obviously expected these parents to take their responsibilities toward their children extremely seriously. Parents are to love their children in the deepest way possible. Often parents use their children.

(a) They have them in the first place because they want their children to supply something that is lacking in their homes.

(b) They expect the children to perform in a way that will never bring shame to the parents.

(c) They often establish unrealistic goals for their children that are meaningful to the parents rather than for the children.

(d) They lay standards of conduct on their children which they violate in their own lives.

(e) They worry and fret over their children, not so much because they are genuinely and deeply concerned about their children's welfare, but because they desperately hope that their children will do nothing that will reflect badly upon the parents.

(f) Parents who receive their children from the Lord as real, developing people and who accept their children in love for what they are will be able to be parents who are worthy of their children's honor and respect.

III. The parents whose attitudes about all of life and about their children have been formed through their contact with Jesus Christ are equipped to rise above all the problem-oriented discussion of children and see children for what they really are. They are the little people God has entrusted to them for such a little time.

(a) Parents who have themselves knelt at Jesus' cross and confessed their sins are able to accept the lack of perfection within their children. They learn to join with their children in prayer for forgiveness.

(b) Parents who know Jesus as their Savior and who know that they have received their task as parents from him also have the astonishing experience of having their very own children minister to them. For God speaks to children too and children sometimes have insights into life that are far clearer than their parents' foggy vision.—Joel H. Nederhood.

Illustrations

MARY AND MARTHA.   St. Bernard has a remark in which he says, "Happy is the home where Martha complains of Mary." Happy is the home where the contest is between working for Christ and listening to Christ. Like the good Samaritan, Martha is a practical Christian: she does for others. Yet it is something else that is important: listening to Christ to grow in love for Christ; learning from Christ to grow in faith in Christ. The final combination of Mary merged into Martha—of doing directed by faith—would be unbeatable. —*Dimension.*

HARMONY.   Successful family living strikes me as being in many ways rather like playing chamber music. Each member of the ensemble has his own skills and his own special knack with the part he chooses to play, but the grace and strength and sweetness of the performance come from everyone's willingness to subordinate virtuosity and personal ambition to the requirement of balance and blend.—Annis Duff.

Sermon Suggestions

WHAT IS LOVE?   (1) Outreaching good will. (2) All-embracing good will. (3) Creative good will. (4) Constructive good will.—Winifred Rhoades.

A FAITH TO LIVE BY.   Scripture: Ps. 27:1–14. (1) It must give the assurance that the future is worth the facing. (2) It must give the confidence that we are not alone. (3) It must give us stability in the midst of all the instability that surrounds us. (4) It must reward us now and then with some evidences that it, too, is real and dependable.—Jerry Hayner.

Worship Aids

CALL TO WORSHIP.   "Lift up your heads in the sanctuary, and bless the Lord. The Lord that made heaven and earth bless thee out of Zion." Ps. 134:2–3.

INVOCATION.   O God our Father, who dost dwell in the high and holy place, with him also that is of a humble and contrite heart: grant that, through this time of worship in thy presence, we may be made the more sure that our true home is with thee in the realm of spiritual things, and that thou art ever with us in the midst of our common walk and daily duties; that so the vision of the eternal may ever give meaning and beauty to this earthly and outward life.

OFFERTORY SERVICE.   "And whatsoever ye do in word and deed, do all in the name of the Lord Jesus, giving thanks to God and the Father by him." Col. 3:17.

OFFERTORY PRAYER.   Our Father, we thank thee that thou art so generous to us. All that we have is a gift from thee. Help us to serve one another so that we may reflect thy spirit and goodness.

LITANY.   Let us thank God for all of his blessings. For the wonders of your creation, for the beauty of the earth, for the order you did bring out of chaos, for life itself:
We thank you, O Lord.
That within the created order and for your own purpose you did ordain and establish the sacred order of marriage and the family:
We thank you, O Lord.
That as we have been loved by your Son and have been instructed by your Spirit in the ways of love, both human and divine:
So perpetuate your love within our hearts that we may love you fully and that we may love one another freely and sincerely.
That our homes may be built upon our trust in you, that our marriages may be strengthened by bonds eternal,

and that our children may be brought up to know you and to love you:
We beseech you to hear us, good Lord.
That within our homes your Word may be heard with reverence and appreciation, that your Son may reside with us, and that your Holy Spirit may dwell within our hearts:
We beseech you to hear us, good Lord.
That our homes may be happy and that therein our children may find security, understanding, patience, joy, gentleness, self-control, godliness, and the infinite riches of your grace:
Be our strength and guide, good Lord.
That as husbands and wives we may be as one with our mates, that we may encourage each other in faith and discipleship, and that we may share the dreams, hopes, nobility, and the excitement and adventure of the Christian pilgrimage:
Be our strength and guide, good Lord.
That as sons and daughters we may honor, obey, and revere our parents, that we may build upon the foundations they have laid for us, and that we may never willingly cause them grief or distress but that we may ever be to them means of joy and grace.
Be our strength and guide, good Lord.
—William M. Everhard.

EVENING SERVICE

Topic: An Amazing Way of Life
TEXT: John 12:24–26.
I. *Only by death comes life.* (See v. 24.) The grains of wheat never produce so long as they are sacked up in a dry storage bin. Only when the grains are placed in the soil where they die to themselves do they produce the multiplied harvest. The great struggle of our time or of any age is not that struggle between men; the great struggle goes on in the human heart to determine who is Lord in your life.

(a) The Jews thought of conquest by armies; Jesus thought of surrender of the will. The Jews thought of national identity; Jesus thought of identity with the Father's will.

(b) Jesus did not fit the pattern that his people had prescribed for him; he was content to follow the will of his Father. It will be by death to personal desire and ambition that we begin to identify with the kind of life that Jesus spoke about for his followers.

II. *Only by losing life do we retain it.* (See v. 25.) One who loves his own life only is selfish and vain. We may call it desire for security, but our only wish is to keep what we have gained. We may boast about our life, seek to protect our life, or even try to hoard our life and exist, but we will never really live like this.

III. *Only by service comes greatness.* (See v. 26.) Those whom we remember in love are those who have served others. Jesus comes to us with a new way of life—life through denial and death. He sees glory in a cross, and he was willing to bear his. Now he asks us to assume our cross as a symbol of discipleship. —Keith Wilson.

SUNDAY: MAY NINTH

MORNING SERVICE

Topic: Homemade Religion (Mother's Day)

SCRIPTURE: Luke 2:39–52.

I. Christianity is certainly "homemade" religion. Jesus received much of his insight into the nature of God, his will and character and purpose, in the home from Joseph and Mary.

(a) Jesus' almost exclusive term for God was "father" or "my father." It is only a symbol, of course, as is any idea of God we may have.

(b) To speak of God as father is to use the most adequate symbol we can find. What was Jesus' source of this conception of God? He was not the first to speak of God in this way, but it became for him almost the exclusive name for God, and this must be the result of his experience in the home in Nazareth in his relationship to Joseph and Mary. For Jesus "father" denotes not only love but majesty, power, and the right to command.

II. Jesus learned in the home to depend upon the power of love. This meant respect for each individual as such in the light of his particular age and responsibility.

(a) A true family will reveal concern for the real welfare of each member. This is something more than the permissiveness about which we hear so much today. It is not sentimental indulgence. God is like a father, not like a sentimental, indulgent grandfather.

(b) Parents who really love their children will hold them to high standards and will live by those standards themselves. Standards and values are better lived than uttered.

(c) The goal of the family must be to bring the children to maturity, to help them develop independent judgment and run the risk of making mistakes and learning from them, so that they may become responsible persons able to face life without dependence upon either mother or father.

(d) Hegel said that the purpose of a family is to destroy itself. This seems a harsh thing to say but not if we realize what it means: the purpose of a family is to help children to become completely independent and responsible persons. They should continue to love their parents and will if their parents have earned the respect of their children by integrity and holding them to high standards, but they will be able to go out into the world and establish homes of their own without dependence upon their parents.

III. The home taught Jesus faith in the laws of growth and patience, the value of freedom for the individual, and the need for personal understanding and appropriation. Individuals must learn *for* themselves, but this does not mean to learn *by* themselves.

(a) Wisdom and understanding cannot be forced. There is need for personal insight and adventure and the securing of a point of view, a faith, for ourselves.

(b) The most difficult task of a parent is to remain silent while a child or a young person makes a decision for himself or learns something for himself. It would be so easy to tell him what to do on the basis of the experience we have gained, but this is fatal to the individual's development as a mature person.

IV. Homemade religion requires more than direct teaching. Teaching by example is more effective always than teaching by precept.

(a) We should remember that it was said of Mary and Joseph: "It was the practice of his parents." This could not have failed to make a real impression on Jesus and his sisters and brothers.

(b) Table talk is most important. Unkind criticism of members of other races or other religious groups or other nationalities will undo all the teaching parents can give about all men and women being children of the one Father.

(c) Children learn much from the ways their parents meet and face difficulties, how they treat each other, upon whom they depend for strength and guidance, their readiness to forgive or the lack of it, what they value most as demonstrated by their actions and reactions.

V. The family must not become an end in itself. Not only must the family look forward to being destroyed in the sense that each of the children moves out to establish his or her own home and to assume responsibility for his or her own life but also because of the first loyalty of each member of the family to God's cause.

(a) We learn in the family that God wants the whole human race to be like a family, that the principles that we appreciate in the home are those that should determine the social order.

(b) The home will always be dear to each of the members if it has succeeded in developing mature and independent young people who will always be grateful for the wisdom and love of their parents.—Nenien C. McPherson, Jr.

Illustrations

A RECOLLECTION FROM COLLEGE DAYS. My dear mother used to post me a little box of flowers each week. The picture of my mother, with the thousand demands and worries of a large school for small boys on her hands, finding time to gather, pack, address, and post each week with her own hands so fleeting and inessential a token of her love, has a thousand times arisen in my memory and led me to consider some apparently quite unnecessary little token of my love as being well worth the time and trouble.—Wilfred T. Grenfell.

CARING.   A woman who was caring for her aged and semi-invalid mother was asked why she did it. "Why shouldn't I?" she replied. "When I couldn't walk my mother helped me. When I couldn't feed myself my mother fed me. When I couldn't clothe myself she clothed me. When I couldn't bathe myself she bathed me. Why shouldn't I do all these things for her now? Besides," she smiled, "I love her."—William Fisher.

Sermon Suggestions

GET YOUR HOME IMPROVEMENT LOAN HERE.   Text: I John 5:4. (1) The home is a place where one can fail and experience forgiveness. (2) The home is a place where one can fight and experience reconciliation. (3) The home is a place where one can know fear and doubt and find a faith to overcome.—Glenn K. Ioder.

AN IDEAL MOTHER AND HOME.   Scripture: Prov. 31. Verse 1 tells us that this chapter was written by King Lemuel and were the words his mother taught him. Perhaps this is the way his mother looked to him. (1) He saw her as a virtuous woman. (See vv. 10, 12.) (2) He saw her as a good worker. (See vv. 13–19.) (3) He saw her as a good neighbor. (See v. 20.) (4) He saw her as a good homemaker. (See vv. 21–27.)—Wilbert Donald Gough.

Worship Aids

CALL TO WORSHIP. "Now in Christ Jesus ye who sometimes were far off are made nigh by the blood of Christ. For he is of our peace, who hath made both one, and hath broken down the middle wall of partition between us. Now therefore ye are no more strangers and foreigners, but fellow citizens with the saints and of the household of God." Eph. 2:13–14, 19.

INVOCATION. O God our Father, creator of the universe and giver of all good things: we thank thee for our home on earth and for the joy of living. We praise thee for thy love in Jesus Christ, who came to set things right, who died rejected on the cross, and who rose triumphant from the dead. Because he lives, we live to praise thee, Father, Son, and Holy Spirit, our God forever.

OFFERTORY SENTENCE. "As every man hath received the gift, even so minister the same one to another, as good stewards of the manifold grace of God." I Pet. 4:10.

OFFERTORY PRAYER. As we bring our offering today we thank thee, O God, for the happiness of our earthly life, for peaceful homes and healthful days, for our powers of mind and body, for faithful friends, and for the joy of loving and being loved. We pray that these blessings may come to abound throughout all the world and to all people.

PRAYER. Almighty God our Father, thou who didst first love us, make us to love thee. We stand in awe of thee and thy quiet concern for us, thy wavering children. Come out of the distance and stand near as we seek to view thy face. O Lord our God, we bow before thee, our creator and redeemer.

Take from us all that would hinder our clear view of thee. Forgive us for equating size with significance: give us the sight to see to the heart of life. Forgive us for looking for thee where thou art not: give us to discern thee in the daily walk of life. Forgive us for becoming sentimental over life's deepest experiences: discipline us to motivate the right deed while it is still day.

May our concern for those closest to us sharpen our effort to love those far away. Bless, we pray thee, the family and the families of men. Thy children need thee even as they have needed thee in the past. They need thee even though they deny it. Grant unto all of us thy blessing and thy leadership, even though we may be unworthy. Without thee our worship is blasphemy; with thee it is a blessing. Without thee our acts are hollow pretense; with thee they are progress toward thy goal.—Herman N. Beimfohr.

EVENING SERVICE

Topic: Challenges when Growing Old
TEXT: Job 42:12.

I. I will not become grouchy, complaining, and critical. Even if I must disagree occasionally, I will try to disagree agreeably, still accepting as persons those with whom I differ. When the wires are all down and all the central places of one's heart are covered with the snows of pessimism and the ice of cynicism, then one has grown old.

II. I refuse to become a chronic worrier. (See Rom: 8:38–39.)

III. Instead of dwelling upon the peculiarities of others, I will study my own and try to improve myself.

IV. I will love and believe in young people. In our youth we want to change the world. In old age too often we want to change youth. Realizing that in many cases the perspective of young people may be different from my own, I will trust and respect them, knowing that there are still many fine and wholesome youth. Hardening of the heart ages people more quickly than hardening of the arteries. Those who love deeply never grow old; they may die of old age, but they die young.

V. I will try not to bore people by talking about "the good old days" before the world started "going to the dogs."

VI. I will try to maintain an active interest in the world around me and in what is going on in it. In whatever way I can, I will strive to contribute to the world and its betterment.—Ray L. Koonce in *United Methodists Today*.

SUNDAY: MAY SIXTEENTH

MORNING SERVICE

Topic: Four Questions for the Graduate (Commencement)

TEXT: II Tim. 2:7.

I. *Have you discovered your mental aptitude?* (a) Have you been engaged in that most important job of research, more important to you than all the research of the world—the discovery of what you really want to do and what you are best fitted to do? Young people frequently either drift from one place to another or, having taken a place unsuited to them, do not have the initiative or courage to lift themselves out of it. Be careful not to misplace yourself. You must discover your own aptitudes; you must pilot your own ship. It should not be your purpose after commencement to be content with mediocrity.

(b) Train yourself for leadership. The world needs leaders. It needs young men and women like you to guide it. Learn to make decisions. Learn to bear responsibility. You can direct the destiny of your own and future generations. Remember the world you build today is the world you will live in tomorrow.

(c) Let the honest intent to serve others have a larger place in your life for yourself. The individual who lives for himself is a failure, but the individual who lives for others has achieved true success. Life is a measure to be filled instead of a cup to be drained.

(d) The best way to find purpose for tomorrow's world is to live well today. The best method of preparing for today is to see yourself and your world in the light of eternity. Tomorrow grows out of today just as today fades into the memory of yesterday.

II. *Have you learned the truth of freedom?* (a) Freedom is not a mere word. It is indefensible if it stands alone. Freedom must be coupled with recognition of the moral law and of the fact that men's rights carry with them duties to their fellow men.

(b) The Christian faith has at all times emphasized the duty of man to his fellow man, and that duty is a fundamental of our heritage. The moral law is sublimely reflected by the Ten Commandments and by the injunctions: "Thou shalt love the Lord thy God with all thy heart, and with all thy soul, and with all thy mind" and "Thou shalt love thy neighbour as thyself." Christ particularly emphasized these two commandments.

(c) Freedom is an opportunity for fellowship rather than an opportunity for private indulgence. If personal freedom is exercised without regard to the fate of others, then it becomes socially intolerable; in fact it will disappear. Without the discipline of the moral law, freedom becomes chaotic and men accept the order of slavery.

III. *Have you learned how to get*

the most out of life? (a) The age-old question that has occupied much of man's thoughts is that of getting the most out of living. Over this question philosophers have speculated, theologians have pondered, and psychologists have experimented.

(b) Christ looks on the materialistically minded, physically tired, mentally bored life and offers a cure. He does not seek to remove the appetites in man, but he would redirect them. He would give man new ideals and new goals. He would say, "He that loseth his life for my sake shall find it." To get the most out of your life you must seek to put much into it. When your desire to give is greater than your desire to receive you are on the sure road to successful living.

IV. *Have you learned how to make your life meaningful?* (a) Life should be dominated by a great purpose, an ideal, or a cause in which you can lose yourself. "Jesus," said E. Stanley Jones, "was obsessed with the idea of the kingdom of God." You must be obsessed by some worthwhile purpose and lose yourself in that cause. The meaningful life is a life loyal to some great cause. He who sides with some profound issue is bound to find life full of meaning. Put your heart and soul into a mission that is so big that, come what may, the mission will mean more than anything else to you. Get behind a purpose that is so vast that you lose yourself in it.

(b) This cause of making life meaningful must be one that gives purpose and coloring to life and demands your best and finest. When you find a course that offers new lands to discover, greater contributions to be made, new ideas to be translated into action, you find life brimful of meaning.

(c) Find some good in the world in which you live. Cultivate the habit of finding good in people and beauty in the world around you. Beauty and value are found in everything about you if you but train yourself to detect them.—C. Raymond Spain.

Illustrations

DIVIDING OUR TIME. It was recorded of Beau Brummell, the famous "dandy" and authority on dress in the England of the eighteenth century, that "it took him four hours to get dressed and he dressed three times a day." No one else has ever turned out so flawlessly. Three times four hours equals twelve hours. That did not leave any time for anything else. We do not spend so much time on our clothes. But the statistics of Beau Brummell do bring us the question—how do we divide our time? Do we give too much time to trivialities compared to the really important things? Do we put first things first?—Halford E. Luccock

WORLD IN QUESTION. While sitting in his study one Sunday morning pondering the message he was to preach that day, J. Winston Pearce was interrupted by a member of the youth department who was looking for a globe. Knowing that there was one in the pastor's study, the youth asked facetiously, "Pastor, if you're not going to do anything with the world this morning, could you give it to the young people?" This changed the gusto and direction of the minister's message forcing him to ask himself, "What am I doing with my world?"—Jerry Hayner.

Sermon Suggestions

DEVELOPING A CHRISTIAN LIFE. Text: Luke 2:52. (1) Remember that Christianity is a religion of fellowship. (2) Read your Bible regularly. (3) Learn how to pray. (4) Be a tither. (See Mal 3:10.) (5) Rely on the help of God in your daily life. (See Phil. 4:13.) (6) Remember always that the emblem of the Christian is love. (See John 13:35.) (7) Always be a witness for Christ.—Charles L. Allen.

A TIME FOR GREATNESS. Text: John 12:27-28. (1) Great days call for great faith. (2) Great days require great courage. (3) Great days require great sympathy and understanding. (4) Great days call for great consecration. (5) Great days call for great sacrifice.— Edward Hughes Pruden.

Worship Aids

CALL TO WORSHIP. "They that wait upon the Lord shall renew their strength; they shall mount up with wings as eagles; they shall run, and not be weary; and they shall walk, and not faint." Isa. 40:31.

INVOCATION. Almighty God, who hast given us minds to know thee, hearts to love thee, and voices to show forth thy praise, we would not know thee if thou hadst not already found us: so assist us again to know thee with pure minds, to love thee with warm hearts, and to praise thee with a clear voice, world without end.

OFFERTORY SENTENCE. "Every one of us shall give account of himself to God." Rom. 14:12.

OFFERTORY PRAYER. Our Father, help us who claim to be Christians to bring forth fruit consistent with our profession of faith. May these tithes and offerings be so used that others may hear the glad story of thy redeeming love.

PRAYER. Father of all mankind, throughout this day help us to remember that a very real portion of thy kingdom has been placed in our keeping. Therefore teach us to love thee:

With all our hearts that we may love those whom thou lovest, giving back to the most unlovable and difficult thine own everlasting mercy and compassion;

With all our souls that we may seek fresh ways in which thy divine power may surge through our commonplace routine from morning till night;

With all our strength that our hands may work the works of him who sent us, that our energy may be poured out for the needs of thy family, until all we own or earn or gain may be spent in a stewardship of loving kindness;

With all our minds that we may think thy thoughts after thee from moment to moment, making beautiful and significant each expenditure, always placing thee first, that thy kingdom may come through our sharing, our caring, our daring.—Margaret T. Applegarth.

EVENING SERVICE

Topic: Weight Watchers
TEXT: Job 31:6.

There are three sets of balances it would be wise for us to remember daily:

I. How much do you weigh in your own private scales? Paul said, "Let a man examine himself" (I Cor. 11:28). What about your "secret sins"? The true desires of your heart? What is the real motivation of your life? The primary purpose of your life? What you weigh in your own scales can bring you happiness or heartache, peace of mind or a troubled mind, self-respect or suicide, abundant life or a living death.

II. How much do you weigh in the scales of others? These are the scales you cannot see but family and friends can. Our influence does show for better or for worse. We are to be responsible stewards of our Christian influence. The Christian life is supposed to attract, not repel. Are people blessed because they know you?

III. How much do you weigh in the scales of God? These scales are of eternal importance and are the ones about which Job is talking. His desire was that God would weigh him in an even balance so that God might know his integrity. How many of us would want God to do the same to us? How many of us would want others to look at God's scales when we are put in that even balance? If God were to put us in his balances today and on the other side place what he has called us to become, what we should be, would there still be an even balance?—Bob Maddux in *The Baptist Record*.

SUNDAY: MAY TWENTY-THIRD

MORNING SERVICE

Topic: Air, Water, Soil — and God (Rural Life Sunday)

SCRIPTURE: Gen. 1:26–31 (RSV).

I. The first page of the Bible tells us that God created man in his own image. What does this mean?

(a) To be created in God's image does not refer to a special intellectual capacity or moral ability or spiritual nature. To be created in God's image means that we are made so that God can talk with us and enter into a personal relationship with us. He speaks and we answer. We can say "Yes" or "No."

(b) The other creatures have to be what they were made to be, but in the creation of man God did something special. He made man free to fail and to fall, free to love and to obey. He so related himself to us that we can respond. We are given a responsibility.

II. What is our responsibility as creatures made in the image of the Creator? "Be fruitful and multiply, and fill the earth."

(a) The census records suggest we have done well here, maybe too well in the past few decades. The world population never reached one billion until 1850, but in 1930 it reached two billion, in 1965 three billion, and by 2000 it should hit seven billion. Every four seconds the census clock ticks off a new American. Every generation the number of mouths on the planet is doubling, so we are faced with agonizing hunger and mass starvation soon. Either the supply of food must increase or the supply of people decrease.

(b) Then God adds the other part of our responsibility which limits the first: "Subdue [the earth]; and have dominion over the fish of the sea and over the birds of the air and over every living thing that moves upon the earth." So we are to rule, to be in control of our environment. We are to reflect the Creator and be his representative in maintaining his claim to dominion. Many today read their horoscope in the daily paper as if the stars were in control. But God the Creator is in control, and he calls on us to share in the control of the world. He gives us responsibility for our environment.

III. The revolution in technology is an expression of obedience to God. As scientists open up secrets of the world around us and master the space above us, we can be glad that they are doing the will of the Creator, whether they know it or not. But you say, isn't the pollution of air and water and soil the result of so-called progress made through science and technology?

(a) The question pushes us deeper into the Genesis story where creation is pictured as being in balance. All plants and all animals were under man, with certain plants specified for animal food. This suggests to me a kind of interdependence between organic and inorganic, between man and the rest of nature. When one part gets out of balance other parts are affected, and as we are seeing in our day we suffer the consequences. When we upset the ecological balance we are in trouble with our air and water and soil. A proper balance is necessary for our environment to be called good.

(b) Its goodness depends on all men sharing properly in the care and joy of creation. When every other part of nature had been prepared, man came on the scene. The environment was made for man, not man for the environment. But what man or what group of men? The word for man in this

Genesis story is the Hebrew for mankind or humanity, A-D-A-M. The responsibility for rule belongs to all, and the benefits are to be shared by all. No one group can claim exclusive control, for every man and every woman is included in Adam. You are represented by Adam.

IV. We who are created in the image of God are to reproduce and to rule our environment in a way that maintains balance and involves all people. In the words of Adlai Stevenson in his final speech to the United Nations: "We travel together, passengers on a little space ship, dependent on its vulnerable resources of air and soil; all committed for our safety to its security and peace; preserved from annihilation only by the care, the work, and the love we give our fragile craft."

(a) But something has gone wrong in our travel together on spaceship earth. The pollution of air, water, and soil indicates we have failed to tend the world God gave us. By arrogance or ignorance we have neglected to maintain the balance and to share with all people. Instead of controlling the elements, we are being destroyed by them. So God meets us in judgment through dead lakes and dirty rivers, through smoke and smog and slums. As Pogo puts it, "We have met the enemy and he is us."

(b) Why have we failed in our responsibility to our environment? Why have we allowed America the Beautiful to become America the Ugly, America the Dirty? Harvey Cox sees our failure rooted in the sin of sloth, that is, the sin of laziness or the sin or irresponsibility. He points to the second and third pages of the Bible with that ancient story of the fall where the basic sin is not pride but sloth, of leaving matters to take their own course. Eve shares with Adam the responsibility to master all the creatures. She eats the forbidden fruit, but before that fatal nibble she listens to the snake and allows this creature to lead her astray. The basic sin was sloth, the failure to be faithful as a trustee of creation. Cox writes: "Adam and Eve are the biblical Everyman and Everywoman. Their sin is our sin. We fritter away our destiny by letting some snake tell us what to do."

V. Since we are made in the image of God we can do better than listen to a snake. Though that image has been distorted, we can try to listen again to the God who created us.

(a) If you have trouble listening to him from the first page of the Old Testament, maybe a glance at the first page of the New Testament will help. Here the God of creation is seen in the person of Jesus. We look at him and see the true "image of God" and get a clearer clue as to our role. We listen to his stories about stewards and trustees, about being faithful with talents and time, with air and water and soil, with all of creation. We learn that God who "in the beginning" was busy creating the world is now busy calling you and me to rule under his rule.

(b) "I believe in God the Father Almighty, maker of heaven and earth," and I rejoice that "the maker of heaven and earth" is not only "almighty" but "God the Father Almighty."—Wade P. Huie.

Illustrations

SIN AND SOCIETY.   Society has no soul except in a sentimental sense. It cannot sin nor expiate the sins of its components. Nor can it rise to heroic levels of self-change except as its individuals rise. Only as men sin does community sin; only as men achieve does society achieve; only as men consciously unite does community cohere. The land fares ill only as men decay.—Edwin McNeill Poteat.

BEAUTY NEARBY.   I should always distrust the man who raves of beauty in distant lands and under foreign skies and yet has never awakened to the beautiful within five miles of the place where he is living.—George H. Morrison.

Sermon Suggestions

WHO AM I?   Scripture: Ps. 8:1–9. (1) I am a person created in the image of God. (2) I am a person created for fellowship with God. (3) I am a person created to be God's trustee over the rest of creation. (4) I am a person created to glorify God with every fiber of my being. (5) I am a person whom God knows and loves because I am of infinite worth in his sight.—William E. Hungate.

ECOLOGY: PART OF THE MISSION OF THE CHURCH.   Text: Gal. 6:9. The covenant in Gen. 9:13 was not made with man alone but with the whole of creation. In Rom. 8:19–21 Paul says that not only men but all creation will ultimately be redeemed. (1) The ecological task is part of the ongoing mission of the church, and Christians must not become weary in our well-doing. (2) If we saw pollution as a sin against God we would be more thoughtful of ocean and air. (3) Man owns nothing on this earth. His dominion is that of tenant. His responsibility is to leave it in as good a condition as it was when it was entrusted to him. (4) The renewed emphasis on the spiritual aspect of ecology should help us to see more clearly just how much of our own souls we are destroying along with creation. —Richard M. Wilson.

Worship Aids

CALL TO WORSHIP.   "I will lift up mine eyes unto the hills, from whence cometh my help. My help cometh from the Lord, which made heaven and earth." Ps. 121:1–2.

INVOCATION.   Heavenly Father, we are grateful for this beautiful world thou hast created for us; for the singing birds, the radiant flowers, the blue sky, the soft breeze; for the dark night which gives way to a bright dawn; for the good earth which, when tilled by the plow, shoots forth the wheat, the corn, the beans that our hungry bodies may be fed; for the trees which will fruit and a thousand gifts which come from thy bountiful hand. Help us to share this wealth, this treasure, with all who are in need.

OFFERTORY SENTENCE.   "Every man hath his proper gift of God, one after this manner, and another after that." I Cor. 7:7.

OFFERTORY PRAYER.   Almighty God, whose loving hand hath given us all that we possess: grant us grace that we may honor thee with our substance, and remembering the account which we must one day give, may be faithful stewards of thy bounty.

PRAYER.   Almighty and eternal God, whom we seek to find and sometimes meet in the inward heart but often think we fail to see at all, we thank thee for every sign of thy coming to men. We give thee praise that thou dost speak to us in the coolness of those mornings when all the symphony of heaven and earth is pouring forth the word that this is thy world, in the fellowship of kindred minds when the touch of life on life renews our knowledge that in the beginning thou didst make us as we are, in the record of the years gone by when history confirms our faith that only truth can triumph or justice long endure.

Thou knowest that we do not always seek thee with the faithfulness thou dost deserve. Thou knowest how much our sin has dimmed the windows of our souls until no sudden need of thee can bring the sight of thee for which we long. Yet we turn to thee in trust because thou wast at Gethsemane when the sweat of thy Son was like great drops of blood falling down upon the ground; and thou wast at Calvary when the cross was raised on the windy hill; and knowing our weakness, thou knowest no less the weight of the load and the length of the climb.

Purge us of the fear that shortens our

vision. Strip us of the pride that saps our strength. Cleave us from the greed that wastes our life in the effort to save it. Grant that we may be sensitive to thy people everywhere, but spare us the folly of not seeing what lies close at hand. Make us generous in helping those across the seas, but lead us also to help the man next door. Guard us against hating our enemies, but protect us from neglecting our friends. Give us grace to toil for peace among the nations, but allow us no contentment until we end the wars in our homes.

We pray for ourselves, our Father, but as we grow in strength and sight, we pray that we may also grow in eagerness to serve thy will for other men. Accept us as thy servants, Lord, that we may be thy sons and daughters too. Bend us in thy bondage that we may at last be free. And vouchsafe that in the end we may not slow thy kingdom's coming to the earth.—Roy Pearson.

EVENING SERVICE

Topic: The Offense of the Familiar
TEXT: Matt. 13:55.

Jesus was "hometown folks" to the people of Nazareth. They knew his family; they certainly expected no more of him than other Nazareth-dwellers. So when great claims began to be made about him they "took offense" (Matt. 13:57). They rejected him because they knew him well. This is the offense of the familiar.

I. *The offense of the familiar can affect our worship of God.* On a typical Sunday we may come to church at the same hour, wear the same suit, sit in the same seat, hear the same preacher, greet the same people—everything is so familiar. And we may fail to hear the mighty God speaking to us because we expected nothing more than business as usual.

II. *The offense of the familiar can affect our study of the Bible.* Most of us know parts of the Bible so well that our minds shift to neutral when we read them or hear them. A new translation may help. Still, like the people of Nazareth, it's easy to say "we've heard that before." And sameness is deadening. God may become "a very old gentleman living in heaven," while Christ remains a "pale Galilean" (J. B. Phillips).

III. *The offense of the familiar can affect our Christian fellowship.* Just because we've been around a person for some time doesn't mean we really know him. The familiarity of a person's face may hinder us from looking deeper. We may go to the same church, but our lives touch only as marbles in a bag—superficial contact. We may have nothing more in common than spectators at a drive-in movie.—Edward C. Briggs in *Baptist and Reflector*.

SUNDAY: MAY THIRTIETH

MORNING SERVICE

Topic: Giving and Receiving Criticism
SCRIPTURE: Matt. 5:11, 7:1; Rom. 12: 14–18.

I. There are those who would claim that there is no such thing as Christian criticism. Most certainly all would agree that criticism which is destructive of other persons is completely inconsistent with the way of Christ. Jesus himself was a critic of others. I think there is no way for you and me to live this life without criticizing others, but woe to us if we are not careful in making our criticism to others.

(a) All criticism which is Christian must be made in the context of love for the person criticized. Paul uses the word "edification." That means "building up" other persons. Jesus never criticized any person except to lift and improve the other's life.

(b) All Christian criticism is built on

complete honesty and justice. You can never know all of the facts about another person. You must be honest enough to get as many of the facts as you can if you truly desire to make any criticism Christian.

(c) Christian criticism always leaves the door open for the criticized to improve. No criticism that you and I ever make can be final. Only God can make final judgments. If your criticism is really to be constructive and helpful to other persons then it ought to challenge, to inspire those persons to newer and greater heights. Other persons will live up or down to the expectations we have of them.

(d) Christian criticism must always be in a spirit of humility. No matter what you may criticize in another person, you stand just as much in need of help as does he, even though perhaps in some other area of life. Christian criticism is never made from the level of superior to inferior. Christian criticism is always one sinner standing with another sinner on level ground beneath a cross.

II. It is difficult to criticize others in a Christian spirit in a constructive way, but how much more difficult it is to receive criticism in a Christian manner.

(a) Evaluate the criticism to see if there is anything valid in it at all, if there is any truth, profit from it. Use it as an experience of growth.

(b) Take your criticism, realizing that you are not on this earth to please men. It does not really matter whether you ever please another person, be he a critic or not. (See Gal. 1:10.)

(c) As criticism comes at you realize that by taking it you may be able to help those who criticize you. There are persons who need to get rid of the hostility which is in them. God's spirit cannot work in the life of a man who is on the defensive. So if you can become like a blotter and absorb the critic's hostility this may be opening the door for God to work in his life.

(d) As criticism is shot your way be certain you keep a sense of humor. Humor always cushions the shock of criticism. As Jesus faced his critics, the scribes and Pharisees, he tinged his replies with humor. In reality humor is the ability to get off and objectively look at self and laugh about it.

(e) When you face the criticism which comes to you in this society, don't be surprised. Jesus has promised that you are going to be criticized. Take it in humility, but don't take it with humiliation. Don't let it crush you. Don't let it steamroller you. Stop to understand that Jesus has promised that all who live according to Christian convictions will be criticized. He even says that you will be happy or blessed when you are "persecuted for righteousness' sake."

(f) Even if you can follow all of these principles in facing criticism, there is one more important principle: pray for those who criticize you. (See Matt. 5:44.) Never forget that two wrongs do not make a right, two hates do not make a love, but sometimes when hate is followed by your love the result can be two loves.—Thomas L. Jones.

Illustrations

GOD'S WILL.   It is easy enough to tell the poor to accept their poverty as God's will when you yourself have warm clothes and plenty of food and medical care and a roof over your head and no worry about the rent. But if you want them to believe you, try to share some of their poverty and see if you can accept it as God's will yourself.—Thomas Merton.

TENDERNESS.   The highest expression of civilization is not the art but the supreme tenderness that people are strong enough to feel and show toward one another.—Norman Cousins.

Sermon Suggestions

GOD'S UNFAILING LOVE.   Scripture: Rom. 8. (1) A new liberty. (See vv. 1–11.) (2) A new relationship. (See vv. 12–17.)

(3) A new hope. (See vv. 18–25.) (4) A new assurance. (See vv. 26–30.) (5) A new security. (See vv. 31–39.)—Earl Stallings.

THE HEALING OF OUR TENSIONS.   Text: Ps. 37:7. (1) Nothing can so effectively remove the tensions that bother us as a firsthand experience of the renewing, cleansing grace of God. (2) Ask God to fill you with unfeigned love and good will for your fellow men, and irritability will stop tying you into knots. (3) We need to get more of the hint of the Eternal into our day-by-day living and to do all things for the glory of God.— Aaron N. Meckel.

Worship Aids

CALL TO WORSHIP.   "We have thought of thy loving kindness, O God, in the midst of thy temple. According to thy name, O God, so is thy praise unto the ends of the earth." Ps. 48:9–10.

INVOCATION.   Almighty God, fountain of all good, kindle in us insight and aspiration, that this hour of prayer may be a moment of time lived in eternity. Open our ears that we may hear. Soften our hearts that we may receive thy truth. Reveal thyself to us here that we may learn to find thee everywhere.

OFFERTORY SENTENCE.   "Seek ye first the kingdom of God, and his righteousness, and all these things shall be added unto you." Matt. 6:33.

OFFERTORY PRAYER.   O thou source of all light, open our blind eyes to see the beauty of the world as thy gift, and grant us the will and wisdom to do our part in bringing thy light into dark places.

PRAYER.   Almighty God our Father, thou who hast made us the heirs of faithful men and women of all generations who gave themselves to great endeavor and made life nobler by having walked this earth, we thank thee for every memory that crowds around and for every experience that causes us to come to thee in worship.

We thank thee for life with all of its privileges and responsibilities. We thank thee for those influences that have supported us and made us strong. We thank thee for those individuals who have inspired us and instructed us in ways of righteousness and service.

We would remember the faith that led our fathers to settle this country, establish its laws, fight its battles, share its goods, and declare its faith. Whatever was true in their lives, whatever was honorable, whatever was just, whatever was pure, whatever was lovely, whatever was gracious, whatever worthy of praise, let us think on these things and be thankful.—G. Curtis Jones.

EVENING SERVICE

Topic: The Gospel of Ascension Day
TEXT: Acts 1:11.

Ascension Day brings into the songs of the church militant the final note of victory. Ever since then the church has kept looking up and will do so until he comes again, as come he will. Meanwhile the church should sing, "Glory, glory to our King!"

I. *Glorious in direction.* Twice our text says "up into heaven." In the light of Ascension Day our prayers ascend in the assurance of God's love. By faith we now have up there the one who lives to intercede for us, the one exalted far above all earthly things, able to govern his church and finally lead her to glory forever.

II. *Glorious in meaning.* (a) For our King this was coronation day. At the end of his earthly sojourn it was fitting that he should return to heaven in triumph. For those who now walk the way of the cross and with all their heart believe that no one cometh to the Father but by him, the ascension of Christ has built a free bridge to heaven.

(b) The ascension is the crowning finale of all his words and works for our salvation. Here is the final and complete assurance that God the Father has accepted the work of his Son for the redemption of men from the guilt and punishment of all their sins.

III. *Glorious in hope.* For believers here on earth the highest blessings of the ascension may be in the realm of hope. Hope is the keynote of our text.

(a) The idea of our Lord's return was not new. But in view of the ascension the message of the angels brought to believers a new impetus both to work and to wait for the Savior's second coming. Time for the winning of souls is limited. God wants all believers to be filled with the sort of energy reflected in the words of his Son: "I must work the works of him that sent me, while it is day, for the night cometh, when no man can work."

(b) We call this our hope, and "we are saved by hope." Hope here means faith as it concerns the future. To be of lasting worth one's hope must have a sure foundation.

(c) If any man says, "My hope is built on nothing less than Jesus' blood and righteousness," that man has a blessed hope. It rests on the everlasting Rock of Ages, Christ and his unchanging Word.—Henry George Hartner.

SUNDAY: JUNE SIXTH

MORNING SERVICE

Topic: To Hoist a Sail (Pentecost)
TEXT: Acts 2:2–3.

I. "What is the wind?" a little lad asked his grandfather, a wise and hardy sailor. "I don't know, my boy," answered the old man of the sea, "but I can hoist a sail."

(a) On Pentecost the Holy Spirit descended like the sound of a mighty rushing wind. The 120 people gathered in prayer, waiting for something to happen, did not question the miracle of the coming of that tremendous lifesurge.

(b) They hoisted a sail, gave God their lives, responded to the miracle of God's inspiration, and went out to transform the world. The church was born out of a group of bewildered individuals, lamenting the loss of a dead leader. And then, because they could not help it, they became leaders, charismatic individuals with the same dynamic that had first drawn them to Christ.

(c) A miracle took place in the upper room where they had gathered to worship. Something new breathed into their lives, and they were never quite the same again. A happening occurred and continues to take place wherever men have faith enough to hoist a sail.

(d) It is fitting that the symbol of the church through the years has been a ship plowing through the sea of life, sails unfurled, driven on by the mighty power of the force of God himself.

II. Leonard Griffith calls the Spirit "the truth of the invisible God in action." That is a good description of the stupendous surging energy unleashed that day, setting in motion far-reaching forces still undiminished.

(a) "But how do I know the power is real?" someone asks. By what happens. Said the little lad to his grandfather, "What is the wind?" "I don't know, my boy, but I can hoist a sail." Evidence of the unprovable fact. For the seaman it is wind in the sails. For the Christian it is life in the soul. To the sailor it means lifting a piece of canvas to catch the power of the indescribable miracle. To the Christian it is the set of the soul, the waiting expectancy, the openheartedness that says, "Come, Creator Spirit."

(b) Every one of us has been inspired: some spoken word, a soft refrain, some thunderous majesty of nature, a crisis we felt we couldn't conquer but did, the silent thought that gripped us thoroughly, an act of adoration, some confrontation in which all conviction was called on to respond and something out of nowhere, it seemed, possessed us, fired us, strengthened us, lifted us, pushed us, calmed us, helped us, healed us, restrained us, restored us, until we were not only ourselves but inspired by the Holy Spirit we found what we couldn't do on our own, God helped us do.

(c) That was the force that created the church. That is the force which creates new lives. That is the strength that makes saints. The same power that created man out of nothing, that created the living church out of a group of mourning disciples deals equally with people. No less divine than the miracle of birth is the miracle of rebirth, the new life in Christ.

III. The supreme work of the Holy Spirit is to convince people and to convict them, to cleanse and renew them and make them over in the likeness of Christ.

(a) Paul lists the "fruit of the spirit": love, joy, peace, patience, kindness, goodness, faithfulness, gentleness, and self-control. The apostle would have us know that we do not make Christians of ourselves, cultivating the Christian graces, manicuring our souls, and pulling ourselves up by the moral bootstraps. Rather we open our lives in faith to the cleansing, renewing breath of God, and the Spirit produces these graces within us as naturally as a tree produces fruit.

(b) Is that so difficult to understand? Perhaps it sounds too mystical and unreal, so we shy away. We raise our credibility guard against what we do not understand spiritually. But we don't with the physical. "What is the wind, grandfather?" "I don't know, my boy, but I can hoist a sail."

IV. Pentecost is a day of implicit challenge and crisis, as it was in the weeks following the execution of Jesus.

(a) We live in a revolutionary age, full of unrest among students, people of other colors, and the poor. These are days of turmoil, demonstration, polarization, fragmentation, and frustration. Pentecost comes again to remind us that a handful of people utterly transformed a sick society and gave it new life. What they did then is equally possible today. The church has not failed nor has God. We are the church as individuals, and God makes himself known to us as individuals. We are co-operators with God.

(b) Knowing God and doing his will, we become part of the leavening influence of which our Lord spoke. To pray earnestly, to serve despite the cost, to worship as an act of faith, to give as an expression of loyalty, to study the Word as discipline for the soul, to let the mystery of the sacraments speak —these mean to hoist a sail, leaving the rest in the providence of Almighty God.—Allan J. Weenink.

Illustrations

THE SPIRIT IN THE EARLY CHURCH. Each Christian was able to serve and help the church through the working of the Spirit in his life. Indeed the Spirit's ministry was so rich and varied that all needed gifts were present, and all worked together to make the one church fully equipped for mutual help and effective world witness.—Floyd Filson in *Jesus Christ the Risen Lord.*

RAISON D'ETRE. The church is the only society which makes total demands upon its members without being totalitarian, because it is not and never claims to be a self-determining sovereign power. It is entirely subordinate to ends beyond itself—the ends of Christ. Those ends transcend the interest of the church, for Christ is the Savior not of the church alone but of the world. The church, which is his body, is interested in the salvation of the world and in no lesser end. Its ultimate reason for existing is the glory of God.—C. H. Dodd.

Sermon Suggestions

PENTECOST: OUR REMINDER. (1) Pentecost is our reminder that the church contains within herself the power to renew herself. Because of the Holy Spirit within her the church can speak more loudly of the kingdom of God, serve more effectively, teach more compellingly, and proclaim more boldly. (2) Pentecost is our reminder that the church has a beginning that never grows old and that the church blazes with a Spirit that never dies out. (3) Pentecost is our reminder that each of us has a part to play for the building up of the kingdom of God. We are part of history; we are part of God's church.—*Dimension*.

THE BIRTHDAY OF THE CHURCH. Scripture:. Acts 2:1–13. (1) Pentecost was a fulfillment of prophecy. (See Joel 2:28.) (2) Pentecost marks the completion of the revelation of the godhead. (See John 4:23–24; John 14:16.) (3) Pentecost produced changed disciples. (4) Pentecost marks the beginning of a world fellowship.—J. Manning Potts.

Worship Aids

CALL TO WORSHIP. "I will praise thee with my whole heart. I will worship toward thy holy temple, and praise thy name for thy loving kindness." Ps. 138: 1–2.

INVOCATION. Almighty God, regard, we beseech thee, thy church, set amid the perplexities of a changing order and face to face with new tasks. Fill us afresh with the spirit of Pentecost that we may bear witness boldly to the coming of thy kingdom and hasten the time when the knowledge of thyself shall encircle the earth as the waters cover the sea.

OFFERTORY SENTENCE. "Give unto the Lord the glory due unto his name: bring an offering, and come before him." I Chron. 16:29.

OFFERTORY PRAYER. We praise thee, O God, for thy countless blessings and pray that thou wilt accept these gifts of gratitude in Jesus' name.

PRAYER. Great God our Lord, we thank thee today for thy church. It is

thy glory and sometimes, we are sure, thy despair. Yet thou hast entrusted to her the nurture of the saints, the training of children, the proclamation of the faith, the witness to holy living and confident dying. Give her the courage to speak judgment upon every unrighteousness of community and nation, as well as winsomeness in telling and living the gospel to the ends of the earth. May she continue to know the joy of binding up the wounds of mankind and pouring in oil and wine.

Keep clear to believers the assurance that all are priests of the Most High, mediating to their fellows the benediction of faith that is transforming their own lives. Make her pastors true shepherds, her scholars clear thinkers, her teachers inspiring trainers, and her preachers great prophets. We pray in the name of the one who loved the church and gave himself for it, Christ Jesus our Lord.—Hillyer H. Straton.

EVENING SERVICE

Topic: The Wonderful Works of God
SCRIPTURE: Acts 2:1–4, 11.

I. Where there is *a surrendered heart,* there is a wonderful work of the spirit. (a) A phrase in v. 1, "one accord," is indicative of the surrendered hearts that were present. Whatever their disagreements, their agreements were more important. We are not to assume they were in accord on all things but on the item that mattered most, their surrender to the Spirit.

(b) Whatever the phrase may suggest, it established their accord about one thing: Jesus was Lord of life. They laid aside all to follow him. Their following led to an upper room. Through surrender they became the recipients of God's Spirit.

(c) Their accord, their unity, centered around the possibility that God was going to do something in their lives. There's something about believing that the best is yet to be, with God, that ignites a man's faith and opens the way for God to work. When a man thinks all his great, exciting, meaningful experiences are behind him, his spiritual experiences are over.

(d) The believers in the upper room surrendered their *belief* to God. Not until this last part of our being is given over to God are great things possible.

(e) Because the upper room followers surrendered their belief to God there was a sense of expectancy. Anytime you and I effect that combination of obedience with God's call or that mixture of our faith with God's promise, that stirring together of our wills and God's plan, we may expect the wonderful works of God.

II. Where there is *a sharing heart*, there is a wonderful work of God. (a) "We all are witnesses" (Acts 2:32) could well be the summary of the second stage of Pentecost, which was sharing, the first stage being receiving.

(b) The authenticity of an experience is somewhat validated by the urge, the need, the desire to share. The Pentecost event was never just heresay, because the receivers became sharers.

(c) Wherever they shared, the wonderful works of God continued. Acts 2:41, 47 speak of souls being added to the church.

III. Where there is *service*, there the wonderful works of God continue. (a) Acts 2:41–47 tells us something about the growth of the early church. Notice the words "continued" in v. 42 and "continuing daily with one accord" in v. 46. They suggest obedience.

(b) The obedience it suggests combines three things—service, sharing, and surrender. These three responses bring the wonderful works of God.—C. Neil Strait.

SUNDAY: JUNE THIRTEENTH

MORNING SERVICE

Topic: Four Things God Wants Children to Know (Children's Day)

TEXT: Eph. 6:1–3.

Paul's key word or words for you in relation to your parents is *obedience* and *honor*. The word "obedience" literally means to listen to or to give respectful attention to; this is your duty. The word "honor" is the translation of the Greek word *timao* and pertains to your basic disposition or attitude toward your parents. There are four great truths for you in these verses from Ephesians. This is not all that God's Word says to you about your parents, but it does contain a great deal.

I. *Obedience and honor must have a spiritual basis.* (a) Eph. 6:1 states that obedience is "in the Lord." The idea is that if you have a good relationship with the Lord, a healthy spiritual life, then you will have a proper relationship to your parents. You cannot speak about a good relationship to Christ if you do not have one with your parents.

(b) When you listen to your parents and give them the honor due to them you are at the same time pleasing the Lord. So many young people miss this point and thus fail to be a good testimony to their parents.

II. *Obedience and honor are commanded.* (a) The verb "obey" and the verb "honor" are both in the imperative mood. That means they are commands. If a person is under authority—and you are to your parents—then you must obey their commands.

(b) The verbs are in the present tense. That means that obedience and honor must be given all the time. There are no holidays or vacations. This obedience and good attitude must be present regardless of whether you like or agree with the command given. It is not what pleases you that counts but what your parents command. Surely they should be commanding in love and consideration, but whether they do or do not is not the basis for your good response. God asks you to respect your parents, and because he does you must obey and honor them regardless of the difficulty involved.

III. *Obedience and honor are related to God's system of order in the family.*

The end of Eph. 6:1 states: "For this is right." That means that your obedience and honor to your parents is part of the plan for family life as God has set it up. Jesus' response to his parents illustrates this. In Luke 2:51 we read, "And he went down with them, and came to Nazareth, and was subject unto them." If Jesus, none other than God's Son and God himself in human form, was obedient to his parents, then certainly we should be.

IV. *Obedience and honor carry a promise.* (a) "Honour thy father and mother; which is the first commandment with promise; That it may be well with thee, and thou mayest live long on the earth" (Eph. 6:2–3). The Greek word for well is *eu* and carries with it the idea of having a sense of well-being, of prosperity, of something well done. It means a relaxed inner confidence that you have given your parents their proper due.

(b) It is true that the second part of the promise offers a bit of a problem, for many children have at least seemed to honor their parents and have not lived long. However, this does not set aside the fact that God assures you personal inward peace and good feeling when you obey.

(c) It is the will of God that you walk in obedience to his Word. The truths that speak of your relationship to your parents are for your good. God does not ask children to do certain things just because he wants to command you, but he desires what is best and good for all of us in all areas of our lives. If there is the need of confession and adjustment, be willing to take the necessary steps. Then, starting today, walk in obedience and honor toward your parents, for this is the will of God for you.—A. W. Jackson.

Illustrations

HAPPY HOMES.   Six things are requisite to create a "happy home." Integrity must be the architect and tidiness the upholsterer. It must be warmed by affection, lighted up with cheerfulness; and industry must be the ventilator, renewing the atmosphere and bringing in fresh salubrity day by day; while over all, as a protecting canopy and glory, nothing will suffice except the blessing of God.—James Hamilton.

GREATEST GIFT.   We should remember that our greatest gift to our children is to give them the ability to stand on their own two feet so that they no longer need us.—Bennett Olshaker in *What Shall We Tell the Children?*

Sermon Suggestions

THE FOUR BASIC EMOTIONAL NEEDS OF THOSE YOU LOVE.   Text: I Tim. 5:8. (1) Intimate response. (2) Adventure. (3) Security. (4) Recognition.—John A. Huffman, Jr.

GOD'S REDEEMING GRACE.   Scripture: Eph. 1:1–14. (1) God the Father: provider of grace. (See vv. 3–6.) (2) God the Son: provision of grace. (See vv. 7–12.) (3) God the Spirit: applier of grace. (See vv. 13–14.)—Frank M. Bozeman.

Worship Aids

CALL TO WORSHIP.   "Both young men, and maidens; old men, and children: let them praise the name of the Lord: for his name alone is excellent; his glory is above the earth and heaven." Ps. 148:12–13.

INVOCATION.   Our Father, we give thanks for Jesus Christ our Savior. Help us to receive the fullness of thy salvation. Grant us grace to live joyful, obedient, and triumphant lives as thy children in this thy world. May the spirit of peace reign within our hearts and invade the nations of the world.

OFFERTORY SENTENCE.   "Give unto the Lord the glory due unto his name: bring an offering, and come before him:

worship the Lord in the beauty of holiness." I Chron. 16:29.

OFFERTORY PRAYER. O living Christ, help us to know the ecstasy of thine everlasting lordship that we may more perfectly become cheerful givers.

PRAYER. Almighty and ever-living God, we praise thee for the strong consolation that we find in thy love. We rejoice in the thought of thy aggressive grace, ever seeking us, ever giving us blessings if we open our hearts to receive them. We gather together to praise thy name in this time of holy worship, to honor thee as our living God and the God of all the universe. We praise thee in the name of our Savior who is the Lord of lords and King of kings. We praise thee in the name of thy Holy Spirit dwelling in our hearts as comforter, strengthener, and friend and guiding us in the way of life.

We thank thee for the privilege of being called to be thy colleagues in strengthening and advancing the holy cause of the kingdom of Christ in our time. Wilt thou give us guidance and direction. Wilt thou give us spiritual strength that we may see what is to be done and have the power to do it. Above all wilt thou give us that deathless spirit of love which was in Jesus Christ and grant that as we love thee and love our Savior we may learn to love one another and make this a world after the pattern of thy holy will.

We would ask thy special blessing upon those of our fellowship who are sick. We thank thee for the privilege of turning to thee for healing and help, and now we ask that thy blessings may come into the lives of those who have distress, who have physical illness, who have depression of spirit or problems of mind. Wilt thou be a healer and helper to all, and through the very hours of trouble wilt thou bring the shining light of an eternal hope.— Lowell M. Atkinson.

EVENING SERVICE

Topic: How Long Is a Child a Child?
TEXT: Luke 7:31-32.

I. Until he knows that others are also human beings with rights, privileges, and ideas.

(a) A babe is born into a world in which he is the very center. All activity points toward him and everyone does for him. He is fed, changed, bathed, burped, cuddled, and made faces at, as though he were the only important person on earth.

(b) Adults know that other persons are real, that their energy is limited, that they have other responsibilities, and that they too are endowed with certain inalienable rights. An adult knows that his freedom is limited by the personal rights and the property rights of others. He knows too that the world is not a benevolent grandmother put on earth to rock his cradle. If he really outgrows childhood he discovers that true riches are available only on a do-it-yourself basis. In this respect it is quite a journey from the child to the man.

II. Until he becomes mature enough to know that life consists of more than the moment and that there will be a tomorrow.

(a) Youth talk much about being part of the now generation. Everybody should be alive now; this is a time to live. But to confine life exclusively to today is to return to infantilism.

(b) An infant knows only the moment; tomorrow is no part of his experience. If he's hungry he says with a cry, "Feed me now." The now is all he knows. In contrast an adult is aware that there will be a tomorrow and that it will be conditioned by today.

III. Until his emotional response has a larger base than that of his own physical circumstance.

(a) There is "a time," says Ecclesiastes, "to weep, and a time to laugh; a time to mourn, and a time to dance." Weeping and laughing, mourning and dancing for adults are the heart's response to real life situations. In referring to their play, Jesus was pointing up the shallowness of children. "We wailed and you did not mourn." You missed the cue. "We piped and you did not dance." Did you think it was a dirge?

(b) People need to laugh. "The world is too much with us"; it seems to be saying, "Heavy, heavy hangs over thy head." How does one experience the joyous spontaneity of laughter? Our need is not for laughter induced by being tickled or entertained. That is the laughter of children. You can tickle an infant and make him laugh, but even then you cannot always be sure whether its a smile or a gas pain.

(c) How old are you? One test is, what makes you laugh? What a joy when we learn to laugh at the very processes of life, to see ourselves and our frailties, to laugh at our own clumsiness. Adults laugh at themselves and with others. That is different from the laughter of a child.

(d) What makes you weep? A child cries when he gets hungry. A man cries when he looks out across the world and sees millions of children who will never have a full stomach. A child cries when he has a pain; a man when he feels the pain of others. A child cries when he doesn't get his way; a man cries when he looks out over the world and sees millions who by the imprisonment of poverty or ignorance or ruthless tyranny will never know freedom.

IV. Until he is able to subdue his own wants in behalf of another's needs.

(a) A child has no basis for separating needs from wants. An infant has no experience by which to detect wants other than his own. In contrast a grown-up is able to distinguish between needs and wants, and if he is mature he subdues his own wants in favor of another's needs.

(b) Jesus could do "mighty works," but his greatest strength was his ability to do without. He had power to deny himself. (See John 10:17–18.) Two questions arise: How much power do you have? How free are you?—Wesley P. Ford.

SUNDAY: JUNE TWENTIETH

MORNING SERVICE

Topic: Checklist for Fathers (Father's Day)

TEXT: Luke 11:11.

"What should I have done differently? If your children were small again what would you do?" These words burst from the burning heart of a father sitting across from me. His eyes pleaded for help. He was suffering the awful, empty, deathlike feeling a man senses when his son has strayed. He felt he had failed as a father.

And his words stay with me. Although they came to me in a direct and blunt way that day, they are not the words of a lone father. In them are the questions which are uppermost in the minds of many couples, if they take parenthood seriously. I've pondered these questions and a few suggestions have surfaced.

I. If I were starting my family again, *I would love the mother of my children more.* That is, I would be more free to let my children see that I love her.

(a) To let my child know I love his mother I would seek to be faithful in doing little loving things for her. True love is visible. I would show special kindnesses such as opening the car door, placing her chair at the table, giving her little gifts on special occasions, and writing her love letters when I'm gone from home. I would take her hand as we stroll in the park. And I would whisper loving words about her in the ears of my children. I would praise her in the presence of my children.

(b) When a child knows parents love each other there is a security, stability, and sacredness about life which is gained in no other way. A child who knows parents love each other and who hears them expressing words of love for each other needs little explanation about God's character of love or the beauty of sex.

II. If I were starting my family again *I would listen more.*

(a) Most fathers find it hard to listen. We are busy with the burdens of work; at the end of the day we are tired when we arrive home. A child's talk seems like unimportant chatter at such times, yet we can learn so much more by listening than by talking, especially from our children.

(b) I would listen when my child shares his little hurts and complaints, his joys, and what he is excited about. And I would try to refrain from words of impatience at the interruption. Such times can be the best times to show love and kindness.

(c) I would seek to keep from staring into space when my child is talking to me. I would try to understand what my child says because I now believe that the father who listens to his child when he is small will find that he will have a child who cares what his father says later in life. And the father who takes time to understand what his child says when the child is small will be able to understand his child later in life.

III. If I were starting my family again *I would seek more opportunities to give my child a feeling of belonging.*

(a) A sense of belonging is essential for a child's security and feeling of worth. And when a child feels he belongs in his family and is of real worth there, it is not a big step also to feel accepted, loved, and of worth to others and in God's sight.

(b) How are feelings of belonging generated? By doing things together. By sharing common concerns. A child feels he belongs when he is invited to be involved in the responsibility and work of the family. Celebration of birthdays, when the person rather than

the gifts is central, creates a sense of belonging. A sense of belonging is built into the child when he hears prayers prayed on his behalf, when his opinions are really listened to and valued.

(c) No part of child guidance is more important than assuring the child by action and word that he is important for the family and he has a place in the affections of the family.

IV. If I were starting my family again *I would express words of appreciation and praise more.*

(a) Children are reprimanded for making mistakes, but many children seldom hear words of commendation and encouragement when they do a job well or exhibit good behavior.

(b) Probably no other thing encourages a child to love life, to seek accomplishments, and to gain confidence more than proper, sincere praise, not flattery but honest compliments when he does well.

V. If I were starting my family again *I would spend more time together.* In every father's week there are 168 hours. He probably spends about 40 hours at work. Allow another 15 hours for overtime, lunch, and driving to and from work. Set aside 56 hours for sleep. That leaves a father 57 hours each week to spend elsewhere. How many are actually spent with his family?

VI. If I were to start my family again *I would laugh more with my child.* (a) Oscar Wilde wrote, "The best way to make children good is to make them happy." I see now that I was much too serious. While my children loved to laugh I, too, often, must have conveyed the idea that being a parent was painful.

(b) I remember when I laughed with my children—at the humorous plays they put on for the family, at the funny stories shared from school, at the times I fell for their tricks and catch questions. I recall the squeals of delight when I laughed with them and shared in their stunts on the lawn or living-room floor. And I remember the times they told of these experiences with joyful expressions years later. I know when I laughed with my children our love was enlarged and the door was open for doing many other things together.—John M. Drescher.

Illustrations

ONE DAY. In his youth Brooks Adams, son of onetime ambassador to Great Britain, Charles Francis Adams, made this entry in his diary: "Went fishing with my father. The most glorious day of my life." So great was the influence of that one day's personal experience with his father that for thirty years thereafter he made repeated references in his diary to the glowing memory of that day. The rest of that story is pathetically sad. Charles Francis Adams, the boy's father, made this comment in his diary: "Went fishing with my son. A day wasted."—Jerry Hayner.

CORNERSTONE. The family is the cornerstone of our society. More than any other force, it shapes the attitudes, the hopes, the ambitions, and the values of the child. When the family collapses it is the children that are usually damaged. When it happens on a massive scale the community itself is crippled.—Lyndon B. Johnson.

Sermon Suggestions

GIFTS MY FATHER GAVE ME. Text: I Cor. 13:4. (1) My father gave me a good bill of health and by his own choice a good mother. (2) My father taught me the dignity of honest work. (3) My father gave me the quality of endurance. (4) My father gave me an interest in books and an open mind. (5) My father gave me a dream. (6) My father gave me a deep and abiding faith in God.—Charles F. Jacobs.

THE FAMILY THAT PRAYS TOGETHER. Text: I Thess. 5:17. (1) Prayer provides power for the home: (a) to stay close by Christian convictions, (b) to repel from without, and (c) to sustain from within. (2) Prayer provides protection from the evils of the world. (3) Prayer provides the patience necessary to accept and understand, partially, the trials and the problems that come to the home. (4) Prayer gives the presence of God in the home.—Ralph Stults.

Worship Aids

CALL TO WORSHIP. "Oh that men would praise the Lord for his goodness, and for his wonderful works to the children of men! For he satisfieth the longing soul, and filleth the hungry soul with goodness." Ps. 107:8–9.

INVOCATION. Most gracious Father, who withholdest no good thing from thy children and in thy providence hast brought us to this day of rest and of the renewal of the soul: we give thee humble and hearty thanks for the world which thou hast prepared and furnished for our dwelling place, for the steadfast righteousness which suffers no evil thing to gain the mastery, for the lives and examples of those who were strangers and pilgrims and found a better inheritance in peace of soul and joy in the Holy Spirit, and above all for the life, teaching, and sacrifice of thy Son our Savior Jesus Christ.

OFFERTORY SENTENCE. "He that hath a bountiful eye shall be blessed; for he giveth of his bread to the poor." Prov. 22:9.

OFFERTORY PRAYER. Cleanse and accept these our gifts, O God, and may they be used according to thy will to redeem, restore, and renew the ministries within thy kingdom.

PRAYER FOR PARENTS OF TEEN-AGERS. My God, here are my children; I give them to you. Reach out and touch them with the finger of your love so they will stop where you are, sense your presence, and turn to you. Take them and make them what you want, not what I want; call them to adventures you have planned for them, not what I aspire to for them. Keep them from sin, but if they sin draw them back to you. Keep them from smallness of spirit. Help them to know themselves and enjoy the person you created them to be.

Help them to use their gifts to serve you. Help them to plunge deep into the mystery of their union with you and to love you above all things.

As for me, help me to love them without possessiveness. Help me to be firm and protect them when I must. Help me to be patient while they find themselves. Help me to respect them for what you made them to be. Help me to love letting them go. When the work is done and they are formed and raised and gone, help me to turn them back to you. Let them be your children and continue the journey, wiser and more understanding of you and your way with men.—*The Church Militant.*

EVENING SERVICE

Topic: A Decalogue in Affirmations
TEXT: I John 2:8.

I. Thou shalt enjoy this lovely world which God has made: sun, moon, and stars; fields, flowers, and trees; wind, warmth, and rain; earth, sea, and sky.

II. Thou shalt enjoy the gift of love from parents, sweethearts, wife, the love which goes on loving when you are most unlovely.

III. Thou shalt enjoy home where you do not visit but belong, where your absences means a gap which no one else can fill.

IV. Thou shalt enjoy the trustfulness of little children and their adoring belief that there is nothing you do not know and nothing you cannot do.

V. Thou shalt enjoy friends, their loyalty and fellowship, their constancy in sorrow, and their unprotesting acceptance of your timely help.

VI. Thou shalt enjoy wholesome laughter, the ludicrous incident, and the sidesplitting joke.

VII. Thou shalt enjoy art, music, the cinema, literature, eloquence, animals, singing, rhythm, games.

VIII. Thou shalt enjoy the privilege of helping others: the poor and sick, the aged and maimed.

IX. Thou shalt enjoy peace. This peace shall not attach only to your circumstances; it shall abide in your heart.

X. Thou shalt enjoy God: the knowledge that he is there, that he is love, and that he cares for all.—W. E. Sangster.

SUNDAY: JUNE TWENTY-SEVENTH

MORNING SERVICE

Topic: Giving and Receiving
TEXTS: Acts 20:35; II Cor. 5:15 (JER).

I. Giving is not enough as an expression of Christian stewardship and concern. (a) A husband gives generously to his wife and children and easily assumes that they ought to be happy and content that he is so thoughtful a provider. What he does not admit to himself or to others is that his family must come almost on hands and knees to beg for his beneficence and that in every way he uses his power of the purse to exalt himself and demean others.

(b) Parents oftentimes dole out allowances to children and in the process do nothing to build up their sense of self-respect and responsibility but make them even more dependent and immature.

(c) The rich can take pride and even joy in helping the poor and in so doing destroy their personal dignity, shame their poverty, and demand that they ever be beholden to them.

(d) How many missionaries, social workers, and teachers literally "give their bodies to be burned" in their concern for the underprivileged and dispossessed yet resent it when the objects of their zeal can finally stand on their own feet and deal with them as equals?

(e) How often do the tentacles of racism and distorted patriotism destroy the relationships between men and nations, when one is quite willing to give aid so long as the other feels himself inferior and weak?

(f) This kind of giving is no blessing but a curse. We cannot hide behind a facade of generosity to cloak our lack of love for the other person.

II. The only kind of giving worth the name is the kind that is driven by love, the love for others that rises from the ashes of the death of self-love. (See II Cor. 5:14–15; cf. I Cor. 13:2.)

(a) Love is the basic ingredient that knits men together and creates that blessedness or happiness of which both Jesus and Paul spoke. Love is a giving and a taking, a mutuality that is essential in Christian fellowship.

(b) A person who gives but finds it impossible in turn to receive is indulging in an act of paternalism that is recognized and resented. We have too readily put a halo around the one who has and dressed the one who has nothing in sackcloth and ashes.

(1) However the debate goes on women's liberation, surely much must depend on the willingness of both sexes to recognize and respect each other for the gifts that God has given to all. There can be no equality where one side claims that it is the only active initiator, giver, and provider.

(2) However confused we are by the misunderstanding and enmity that fester among the old and young of our day, surely reconciliation can come only as we recognize that each has gifts, aspirations, and goals that are valid in themselves and has freedom of expression and realization.

III. Sometimes it is more blessed to allow another person the happiness of giving to us, as Christ did by dying for us and giving us the opportunity to die for him.

(a) We always run the risk of confronting the withholding of gifts from those who say, "Well, if our giving is causing so much unhappiness, we will just stop giving!" Yet as we read the gospel and realize how free and joyful those people were who were the objects of Jesus' love, we cannot cater to our pride and self-sufficiency. Love presupposes that both parties are open, are trustful, and are expectant.

(b) In Christian love we give not to enslave but to free. There is a mutual sharing of ourselves in free and open association.

(1) If we are troubled about our motives in giving or receiving, recall St. Paul's standard of judgment: "Put love first."

(2) In fulfilling this declaration the church has gone into the world raising men up to new dignity and self-respect. Faithful people have joined hands with multitudes in professing their brotherhood and fellowship.

(3) Healing has entered into the experience of husbands and wives, children and parents, neighborhoods and communities as they have declared their intention to live joyously and freely in common concern and mutual benefit.—John Melville Burgess.

Illustrations

THINGS THAT CANNOT BE KEPT. Some things can be preserved and pickled. But the real things in life cannot be kept. Try to keep love and watch it turn to lust. Try to keep peace to yourself and see it degenerate into passivity. Try to keep money and watch it change into mammon. Try to keep beauty and you become a mummy. Keep a vision and you become a visionary. Try to keep Christ and you become a bigot.—Theodore P. Ferris.

LIFEBLOOD. One day Kagawa was in conversation with Mr. Okamura, secretary of the Kobe, Japan, YMCA. The YMCA was going through hard times. Debts had accumulated, programs and services had been curtailed, all for lack of money. As they talked Kagawa reached into his pocket and took out a letter. The letter contained a check which Kagawa that morning had received from a publisher in payment for a book of his that was about to be published. He handed the check to Okamura. Okamura said, "I can't possibly take it." Kagawa said, "You must," and literally forced it on him. Okamura went home and wrote a letter to Kagawa trying to get him to take the money back. "You mustn't give money away like that," he wrote, well knowing the poverty in which Kagawa lived. The saintly man wrote back: "Why shouldn't I? When your friend is dying there is only one thing to do—give him your lifeblood."

Sermon Suggestions

THE DIVINE ALPHABET.   Text: Rev. 1:8. "Alpha" was simply the first letter of the Greek alphabet, and "omega" was the last letter of that alphabet. So what Jesus said was simply this: "I am A and Z." (1) It is the most sublime revelation ever given of the inexhaustibility of Jesus. (2) It is the most sublime revelation ever given of the indispensability of Jesus. (3) It is the most sublime revelation ever given of the invincibility of Jesus. (4) It is the most sublime revelation ever given of the adaptability of Jesus.—Frank W. Boreham.

FROM MANIPULATION TO CELEBRATION. Text: Eph. 5:30. (1) Manipulation is when we use another; celebration is when we share. (2) Manipulation is when we flatter; celebration is when we compliment. (3) Manipulation is when we control; celebration is when we offer the other a gift of freedom. (4) Manipulation is when we love only the lovable; celebration is when we love the unlovable.—C. A. McClain, Jr.

Worship Aids

CALL TO WORSHIP.   "Ye shall know truth, and the truth shall make you free. God is a Spirit: and they that worship him must worship him in spirit and in truth." John 8:32; 4:24.

INVOCATION.   Grant, O Lord our God, we beseech thee, that now and every time we come before thee in worship and in prayer we may be vividly aware of thy presence, become conscious of thy power and a sense of thy protection, and finally know in our hearts and minds and souls the wonder and the grace of thy peace.

OFFERTORY SENTENCE.   "To do good and to communicate forget not: for with such sacrifices God is well pleased." Heb. 13:16.

OFFERTORY PRAYER.   Dear Father, help us to be ever concerned to find thy way for our lives, and may we never be satisfied to give thee our second best in return for thy great gift of love.

PRAYER.   Eternal God, source and giver of life, in whom we live and move and have our being, we praise thee for him who is the savior and redeemer of our lives. In his name we bring before thee in true repentance all those sins and dispositions of our lives which make for evil and our death. Forgive us for every choice of wrong instead of right. Our sins have often been deliberate and presumptuous. We have sought only our own pleasure and happiness and have failed in the service of others. We have transgressed the laws which thou most graciously hadst written upon our hearts. Overcome, O God, the evil in us with the good and renew a right spirit within us.

We thank thee, our Father, that Jesus came to give us abundant life. Help us to accept his grace. May evil men discover their folly and turn to the Christ, becoming agents of righteousness. May the indifferent and complacent be stirred in their hearts to seek the higher ways of life. May good men be filled with thy spirit, becoming powerful in the world. May all of us by thy grace become men and women of finer character, higher vision, and nobler achievement.

By the life surging within us through the grace of Christ may we be assured of life eternal. By that assurance may we live as children of God and unto thy glory.—M. K. W. Heicher.

EVENING SERVICE

Topic: Maturity and the Cross
Text: Gal. 2:20.

Four crucifixions are mentioned in the Bible.

I. *The crucifixion of Jesus Christ.* (a) Here spiritual perspectives and attitudes are first formed. The redemptive work of Jesus on that cross makes possible the beginning of spiritual life. Later when the measure of maturity is made it will be according to "the fullness of the measure" of that Christ.

(b) Paul approached the "babes" in the Corinthian church with the following words: "I determined not to know anything among you save Jesus Christ, and him crucified" (I Cor. 2:2). Paul pointed them to the measuring rod by which they could see their shortcomings and to the guiding truth by which their maturity could be realized.

II. *The crucifixion of self.* (a) "I am crucified" is a past tense judicial position provided by God's action and attitude. That the believer has been crucified with Christ is a divine fact.

(b) Maturity of the believer demands that his crucifixion be accepted, appreciated, and applied in daily conduct. Thus when selfishness and self-centered living are abandoned in favor of "crucified" living a person has greatly matured spiritually.

III. *The crucifixion of the flesh.* (See Gal. 5:24.) (a) A physician said the newborn baby first cries because of its fleshly discomfort. That is good because it serves a purpose in birth. These cries bring mother's quick response to meet that need and sustain that life which is so precious. But when that baby has grown physically into adulthood and still demands that pampering physical attention to the flesh it is known as immaturity.

(b) Fleshly appetites and desires become gauges to maturity. Jesus said he came not "to be ministered unto, but to minister, and give his life a ransom for many." (See Rom. 8:13.)

IV. *"The world is crucified unto me"* (Gal. 6:14). Christian maturity is certainly measured by one's attitude toward the world. (See Jas. 4:4.) A mature Christian will limit himself to the priorities of the Lord. We are in the world but not of the world. Of necessity our life-style will be fashioned by the systems of the world, but we are to be agents of our Lord, introducing the people of this world to the life-changing powers of our Lord. Maturity is discerned in this transaction and this attitude.—William C. Burns.

SUNDAY: JULY FOURTH

MORNING SERVICE

Topic: Do We Deserve Democracy?
(Independence Day)
Text: Mark 12:17.

I. What is utterly unique and distinctive about America? What is the source of our life? On what base has our national life and our political institutions been erected?

(a) To some it may seem trite, but to the thoughtful it is the profoundest thing we can say about America. America begins where the Bible begins, "In the beginning God. . . ." Such is the testimony of our instruments of government, and such the message of our authentic spokesmen.

(b) We cannot understand American history except as a spiritual movement. The eternal God is the source of this nation, we have said, and his spirit the guide of its development. This nation was founded upon theistic—not atheistic, secular, or humanistic—presuppositions.

(1) This was the American consensus at the beginning. The American people covenanted with God, not as a local, continental, or racial deity, but as the living universal God who, while being the God of all people, becomes in a special sense the God of all those who accept his purpose and do his will in human life. Although there were not as many formally acknowledged church members then as now, there can be no doubt about the pervasiveness of religious faith and the certitude of theistic presuppositions.

(2) The vast entity we call America had a spiritual origin. When true to her genius she has a spiritual destiny—a sense of mission derived from faith in the sovereign God. The religious spirit has been mediated to American life by a wide variety of religious denominations. In some individuals the spiritual element has been personal, profound, and dynamic; in others it has been an attitude derived from the cultural atmosphere and climate which religion produced. There can be no question that the religious spirit—the God-hypothesis, the awareness of deity in all of life—has been emphatic and pervasive in our land.

II. It is the base of life which has made the difference. (a) Democracy is a high faith in the capacity of the common man—which means most to us—in his spiritual capacity to discern truth, to see and accept and live by ideals. Where does that come from? Out of the Hebrew-Christian tradition.

(b) Democracy is belief in freedom of speech and assembly and press, recognizing that perhaps many untrue and foolish things may be said; and it is quite possible we may say some of them. Where does that come from? Emphatically, that privilege arose out of the Protestant Reformation.

(c) Democracy is the belief that individuals have a high moral dignity because of their relation to their Creator and as his sons their personalities are of highest value. What hurts personality is wrong; what enriches is good. What is the source of that? Emphatically, the Christian religion. This belief in the value and welfare of persons means also that majorities have a responsibility for the needs and welfare of the minority, especially if that minority is disinherited or voiceless.

(d) Democracy believes that man with such splendid spiritual origins and capacities can be inspired and led to put the general good above his own selfish interests and ambitions and that he finds his true happiness in service. Where do we get that? Out of the Christian faith and primarily out of the Reformation.

(e) Democracy as we know it is so much a child of the Christian religion that there is no reason to suppose that where Christ has ceased to grip and inspire men the foundation of democracy can be maintained.

III. Does the Christian have a responsibility as a citizen? The more Christian he is the more obligation to participate in the processes of government.

(a) We have obligations to our common life which today probably transcend all previous ages.

(1) There is the obligation to think. We have need to listen, to see, but not to become victims of slogans or the mass media. What you see on the television screen is what some person wants you to see or thinks you want to see. There is the need of analyzing, evaluating, assessing. We need to do some sorting—to analyze the analyzers. We need to do some hard thinking.

(2) We have an obligation to discuss issues and concerns with others. None of us has a monopoly on sensitivity or morals or patriotism. An exchange of

observations and views with our friends is fruitful in the democratic process.

(3) We have an obligation to vote. To fail to do so is to forfeit a high privilege and to forego the very participation on which a democratic society depends. For Christians to refrain from voting may be to vacate the destiny of the nation to the demagogue or scoundrel.

(4) We have the obligation to pray for and encourage our leaders in coming to wise conclusions.

(5) In a republican form of government we have the obligation to accept the verdict of all who participate in it.

(b) As we have yielded ourselves to the lordship of Jesus, let us give our best to our nation that this nation may fulfill its mission to itself and to all mankind.—Edward L. R. Elson.

Illustration

NEW LIGHT. The dawn will come. Disappointment, sorrow, and despair are born at midnight, but morning follows. "Weeping may endure for a night," says the psalmist, "but joy cometh in the morning." This faith adjourns the assemblies of hopelessness and brings new light into the dark chambers of pessimism.—Martin Luther King, Jr.

Sermon Suggestions

TO BE REALLY FREE. Text: John 8:36. (1) To be free is to be related. (2) To be free is to be committed. (3) To be free is to open your life to God and to give yourself to God.—Charles L. Copenhaver.

BY THE GRACE OF CHRIST. Text: Rom. 5:15. (1) By the grace of Christ there is education in the land. (2) By the grace of Christ there is healing in the land. (3) By the grace of Christ there is benevolence in the land. (4) By the grace of Christ there is worship in the land.—M. K. W. Heicher.

Worship Aids

CALL TO WORSHIP. "Let all those that put their trust in thee rejoice: let them ever shout for joy because thou defendest them: let them also that love thy name be joyful in thee." Ps. 5:11.

INVOCATION. Beget in us a thirst for thy presence. Kindle in us the impulse to pray. Tear out our pride; rip away our fear; and persuade us to kneel in our need that we may rise in thy strength. In this nation grant that we may show our love for thee by working loyally toward justice in every touch of man upon his fellow man. In this church grant that we may willingly become a part of that body wherein again the Lord is made flesh and dwells on the earth.

OFFERTORY SENTENCE. "Bring ye all the tithes into the storehouse, saith the Lord, [and I will] open the windows of heaven, and pour you out a blessing." Mal. 3:10.

OFFERTORY PRAYER. We thank thee, O God, for another anniversary of our nation's independence and pray that this rich gift may be an opportunity to serve one another in love.

PRAYER. Almighty Father, as we recall once again the story of our nation's birth we would be mindful of our great heritage of freedom. We thank thee today for freedom of thought, liberty of expression, and opportunity to worship thee according to the light that is within us. Grant, we pray, that the light of freedom in our land may never grow dim.

Help us to understand that freedom's light is holy and that apart from a knowledge of thy sovereignty it will flicker and fade. As we think of the liberty of their children we would not forget the faith of our fathers. Like them, we would be brought by obedience to Christ unto a right use of the opportunities granted us. In service we would find the goal of existence. In worship we would discover how to use our heritage of freedom to thy glory.

Save us from boastfulness and pride that hide beneath the banner of patriotism. Keep us from any exercise of selfishness that hinders the larger experience of brotherhood. Keep us aware of our responsibility to all men, and protect us from the illusion that our country can do no wrong. In our national life give us the courage to proclaim thy moral law and the desire to obey it. Raise up stalwart leaders among all nations, men and women who respect thy truth and hold thy name in reverence.

Lord God of hosts, renew our faith in thee that there may be ground for confidence in one another. Permeate with thy saving truth our group life as well as our individual lives, our social attitudes as well as our personal devotions. Keep us from attaining any semblance of greatness that hides our sin from us. Where we have lusted for power, increase our desire for purity.— Marion C. Allen.

EVENING SERVICE

Topic: Stand-By Ideas

The history of opera and the theater is marked by great and dramatic hours here and there when an unknown "stand-by" was summoned to the stage and from there to stardom. This came to mind when I read: *"Actors waiting to go onstage. A 'stand-by' is an actor who does not have to appear at the theater every night, as an understudy does, but calls in thirty minutes before the curtain goes up to see if the performer he might have to replace is all right. If he is, the stand-by leaves a phone number and must be able to reach the theater in twenty minutes in an emergency. Just now there are a number of good actors standing by in New York."*

At this very moment in history, there are many good "stand-by" ideas that are waiting to move center stage. We ought to consider summoning them to the spotlight, for surely some of our presently performing ideas in this society need to be replaced. Indeed it can be claimed that many of them have created a kind of emergency situation on various levels of our common life. So let us bring on the "stand-by" ideas that we have neglected much too long.

I. The resources of this world are precious and must be used responsibly. For too long we have been existing with the idea that this is a "throw away" world in which everything is disposable. The junk-heaps which blemish our landscape are monuments to our profligate waste. Now out of necessity we are beginning to allow a stand-by idea to gain the spotlight: energy itself, in present forms, is not inexhaustible. Not even oil.

II. The character of a people is more crucial to the issue of national strength than military or material power alone. We remain an industrial giant, and we retain an awesome military might. And yet our standing among the nations of the world has slipped strikingly. No one can deny that something serious seems to have happened to the American character. Surely it is time to let this "stand-by" idea step on stage: the quality of our character as a people is the most decisive factor for our future in history.

III. Every society lives by root-values which sustain it. If you promiscuously tear up the deep roots in the value-system of a people, you end up with a cut-flower civilization. Cut-flowers may be pretty for a time, attractive to the eye, but then they wilt and wither away. Let a "stand-by" idea come center: nurture the deep roots for they alone can uphold a people.

IV. Nothing is free, and everything worthwhile carries its price. You get what you want if you are willing to pay for it and nothing more. And yet we have allowed a "something for nothing" attitude to take over. It didn't work, and it won't work. A better "stand-by" idea stands ready in the wings: take what you want, and be willing to pay the price.—Charles L Copenhaver.

SUNDAY: JULY ELEVENTH

MORNING SERVICE

Topic: Waiting on the Lord

TEXT: Isa. 40:31.

When you understand the circumstances out of which Isa. 40 was written you begin to appreciate the message proclaimed by the prophet. Isaiah with his fellow countrymen are in exile in Babylon. They have been in captivity for many years. They have grown weary of their difficult lot. As year after weary year goes by without any hope of deliverance, their discouragement deepens. Their identity as a people is all but lost. They are even becoming cynical about faith in God and cry out: "My way is hid from the Lord, and my right is disregarded by my God." Their despair approaches despondency, for they do not feel that God cares anymore.

But in the darkness of the night the prophet places a new star in their firmament or points to one they had forgotten. Perhaps they had not looked up for a long time. "They who wait for the Lord shall *renew* their strength."

I. "Wait for the Lord!" To wait for the Lord the prophet contrasts with merely watching current events. At this time the world was rocking under the conquests of Cyrus. The Jews with their neighbors were asking, "What next?" To such inquiry the Bible always answers "the living God." Events are never bare events but advents of the eternal God.

II. To wait for the Lord is to wait in faith. The original word used here means to "fully trust" or "strongly hope." Our waiting for the Lord is a trusting in God. I read a statement that has lingered with me: "We would rather hustle than pray, which is proof that we really trust ourselves more than God." A fellow seminary student once said to me: "We pray to God, but we do not really *trust* him."

III. Waiting on the Lord is ultimate trust, but it is also recognizing that life is of grace.

(a) Life is not to be taken by force it is to be received. We pray in the Collect, "In returning and rest we shall be saved, in quietness and confidence shall be our strength."

(b) If we were to characterize the renewal that comes in waiting on the Lord we would probably invert the order that the prophet has used: "They shall walk . . . they shall run . . . they shall mount up with wings like eagles." But the prophet sees that life sometimes is lived with greater enthusiasm and we mount up with wings like eagles sometimes we are very excited and will run eagerly, but ordinarily life is lived at a slower pace, walking, or even plodding. Not just in high moments or on special occasions but in the every day the resources of the eternal God reach us as we wait upon him. And we can walk and not faint.—John Thompson.

Illustrations

FRUIT OF LEARNING. It would seem to me that the finest fruit of serious learning should be the ability to speak the word "God" without reserve or embarrassment, certainly without adolescent resentment; rather with some sense of communion, with reverence, and with joy.—Nathan M. Pusey.

MEMORY AND HOPE. The Christian faith is a blending of memory and hope. But the memory is such as to provide incentive and daring for the needs of today. And the hope has no validity except as it is grounded in the brave and faithful performance of contemporary responsibilities.—Truman B. Douglass.

Sermon Suggestions

IMPLEMENTING LIFE.   Text: I Cor. 16:13. (1) We may withdraw from life. (2) We may compromise with life. (3) We may mold life.—W. Earnest Calkins.

DIVINE COMPANIONSHIP.   (1) Walking before God. (See Gen. 17:1.) (2) Walking after God. (See Deut. 13:4.) (3) Walking with God. (See Gen. 5:22.)—Alexander Maclaren.

Worship Aids

CALL TO WORSHIP.   "Let us search and try our ways, and turn again to the Lord. Let us lift up our heart with our hands unto God in the heavens." Lam. 3:40–41.

INVOCATION.   Eternal God, in whom we live and move and have our being, whose face is hidden from us by our sins and whose mercy we forget in the blindness of our hearts: cleanse us, we beseech thee, from all our offenses and deliver us from proud thoughts and vain desires, that with lowliness and meekness we may draw near to thee, confessing our faults, confiding in thy grace, and finding in thee our refuge and our strength.

OFFERTORY SENTENCE.   "If thou draw out thy soul to the hungry, and satisfy the afflicted soul; then shall thy light rise in obscurity, and thy darkness be as the noonday." Isa. 58:10.

OFFERTORY PRAYER.   Our Father, help us to trust thee more fully and to accept our responsibility toward thy work and thy children who are our brethren in Christ.

AFFIRMATION OF FAITH.   I believe that beliefs are true only when confirmed in the life-style and behavior of the believer.

I believe that God is spirit; his spirit is power; his power is love.

I believe his love was made real to me in the person and teachings of Jesus.

I believe that in accepting God's love for me through Jesus, my life has taken on meaning and purpose, which bring a sense of joy deeper than any human reward.

I believe that living in the style and spirit the Christ means that I be a person for others, which summons me to have a vital concern for persons and for justice in society.

I believe that being a Christian challenges me especially to care for those of God's children for whom my culture cares the least.

I believe in the church as the community of supportive people, who mutually encourage each other in living out their Christian beliefs.—Keith I. Pohl.

EVENING SERVICE

Topic: Spiritual Vagrants
SCRIPTURE: Matt. 7:13–28.

I. Houses need deep and firm foundations. Any building must be built solidly or else it will not stand up long under the stress and strain of rain and snow and cold and heat and in our day air pollution and tornadoes.

(a) Why do we have so many people in and outside of the church who build their lives on shaky foundations? Who think that what matters are surface appearances? Who think "It's what's up front that counts" and not what's underneath holding up "what's up front." Who are concerned with surface values that are here today and gone tomorrow on the wings of some new fad? Who sacrifice in order to drive an up-to-date car and live with all the modern conveniences and yet will not bring their faith up-to-date and modernize it?

(b) Many of us are spiritual vagrants. A vagrant is a person who has no visible means of support. His whole life is built around visible things. Some of us actually think that "man's chief end is to buy everything we want and to enjoy it forever."

II. Spiritual vagrancy is a malady that has spread like wildfire throughout our churches because its remedy involves work. Its remedy involves personal commitment. Its remedy involves investing ourselves in study groups, book discussions, Bible reading, prayer, Sunday school classes, and regular worship.

(a) It is so much easier to build on sand and so much less trouble and disturbing. It is easier to drift along and postpone decisions that should be made. It is easy to think that I know better than any church's teaching. It is even a little comforting to think that I am the final authority on any religious subject and I don't need Bible reading or sacraments or trained ministers to explain passages of scripture to me. Once I enthrone myself as the authority, I can reject all other authorities.

(b) The world of today is confirming the truth of the 100-year-old hymn:

"Change and decay in all around I see; O thou, who changest not, abide with me." It is a time when we are discovering that too many of us have been living with only visible means of support and when they give way or change we are left without a reason for living. For many of us the visible supports have all failed, and we know not where to turn.

III. Isaiah said, and I believe it, that God gives us power for the living of these days. Isaiah said, and I believe it, that they who wait for the Lord shall renew their strength. Jesus said, and I believe it, that when we live in love, when we live for the betterment of our fellow men, when we sacrifice for their good, when we go out of our way to do them a favor, when we live in obedience to his commandments and follow his way and not ours, then we shall have a rocklike foundation to our lives, we shall have an invisible means of support for life that no misfortune can ever shake or catastrophe erase.— C. Thomas Hilton.

SUNDAY: JULY EIGHTEENTH

MORNING SERVICE

Topic: Tempted in the Wilderness
TEXT: Matt. 4:1–11.

The three temptations were in one way unique to Christ because of his supernatural powers as Son of God, yet they are also common to us in his sharing with us as Son of Man. (See Heb. 4:15.) So we may learn from him the force and direction of temptation and how to meet it. There are different ways of classifying these temptations.

I. *Tempted to misdirect priorities.* (a) At first sight the first temptation seems to be the insinuation that Jesus might be mistaken as to his status as Son of God. (See v. 3.) But Jesus sees the temptation for what it is: the misdirection of priorities, the greater concern for himself than for his Father, the using of his spiritual powers for

his own ends rather than for the kingdom. It is thus self versus God.

(b) If Christ weakens here he will be far weaker later when involved in his exhausting ministry. If he weakens here what of the cross? The battle itself was not over a small item, a loaf of bread, but over a fundamental issue. When such a fundamental issue is won, then the next battle along the same line is much easier to win. (See John 4:34.) It is not that food is unimportant. "Man shall not live by bread *alone*." It is a matter of priorities.

(c) How easily too we can use the church to our own ends of merely providing what we want—friends, activities—rather than for the fully orbed relationship with Christ in his body or use his gifts to us merely for our own purposes or advancement.

II. *Tempted to misuse promises.* (a)

The pinnacle of the temple sequence again produces the "*if* you are the Son of God" idea and the suggestion of a test to see if Jesus is what he thinks he is. The basis suggested is a promise of the Word. But the promise is, as so often with the devil, misquoted. The words "to guard you in all your ways" are missed out from this quotation of Ps. 91:11–12. They make quite a difference. It is not a text for special tests but of the Lord's hand upon our daily living.

(b) How easily we can misquote promise texts: "Lo, I am with you" of Matt. 28:20 without its context of being for those in service for Christ; or Rom. 8:28 where often the first phrase alone is quoted; or Eph. 3:20 where the limiting factor of "according to the power at work in us" is omitted. It is a misleading practice but more serious when it leads to sensation seeking. There are many who misinterpret the "greater works than these will you do" text and want greater miracles, reporting some incident on a far-off Pacific island as if it proved the text. But we do not see Christians walking on the water or stilling storms at a word. For this text was shown on the day of Pentecost as meaning spiritual results, when 3,000 were converted on one day, a result that had never happened in the ministry of Jesus.

(c) The "give me a miracle" emphasis is off course. Jesus' word is firm here: "You shall not tempt [put to the test] the Lord your God." God's promises and power are not to be treated as a plaything but to be constantly trusted and drawn upon in all their inexhaustible richness in all our ways, and very often we shall marvel at his miraculous blessing.

III. *Tempted to misunderstand power.*
(a) Where does power really lie? The devil sweeps God aside in his claims to authority over the world. Christ later called him the prince of the world. Yet the devil's authority is a pseudo-power. All true power belongs to God.

(b) The devil has lured so much of mankind to live, work, and sell their souls for mere earthly power, honor, or possession. In the midst of all such pressures in our twentieth-century society we have to keep our sights quite clear and our eternal perspective fresh. Jesus says, "Begone, Satan! you shall worship the Lord your God and him only shall you serve." There was to be no compromise, and because Jesus would not compromise he went to the cross. If we follow him it means our taking up the cross and for us too that means "no compromise."

(c) So the Son of God faced the full force of the devil's attack. These temptations are common to man, yet we are given assurance in I Cor. 10:13. How wonderful that the Lord we worship has "been through it," suffering every kind of temptation. (See Luke 4:13.) He is not distant and remote but a Lord who can sympathize and understand, a Lord who can help, a Lord who shows us how to face temptation and conquer in his strength. Each time Christ answered, "It is written." Let us hammer out the principles of our lives from the word of God and look to him for power to stand and withstand.— Michael Baughen.

Illustrations

CONSISTENT UNIVERSE. Someone asked Albert Einstein what would happen to human morals if intelligent life were found on other planets. "Is morality merely based on the accumulated experience of mankind and, therefore, limited to our earth?" the questioner asked. "The universe is fully consistent," Einstein replied. "It is a unity. The same physical laws that regulate the movements of our planet control also the most distant stars. Likewise," the great scientist continued, "the moral law that governs us holds sway in the farthest reaches of the universe."— William Fisher.

EASY ALTERNATIVES. Satan attempts to get us to bring in God's kingdom by methods so alien to him that it turns out to be the very antithesis of all that Jesus came to be and to do; it is the hallmark of antichrist. Today we have the choice of the same easy alternatives offered to Christ 2,000 years ago: (1) win men by ministering to their bodily and social needs alone, (2) gain a cheap success by conjuring tricks and manipulations of what is claimed as compelling evidence, and (3) pursue the line of freedom and peace but deny it by the methods you employ. That is exactly how Jesus saw Satan's insinuations and why he rejected them as denying the lordship of God and the fulfillment of his will *in his way.*—Ralph P. Martin in *Eternity*.

Sermon Suggestions

STEPS INTO SALVATION. (1) Belief in a record. (2) Faith in a person. (3) Trust in a promise. (4) Obedience to a Lord.—A. T. Pierson.

WHAT CHRIST MEANS TO ME. (1) Pardon. (See Matt. 9:2.) (2) Peace with God and the peace of God. (See Rom. 5:1; Phil. 4:6–7.) (3) Purpose. (See Phil. 1:21.) (4) Power. (See Phil. 4:13.) (5) Provision. (See Phil. 4:19.) (6) Prospect. (See John 14:19.)—Vance Havner.

Worship Aids

CALL TO WORSHIP. "They that wait upon the Lord shall renew their strength; they shall mount up with wings as eagles; they shall run, and not be weary; and they shall walk, and not faint." Isa. 40:31.

INVOCATION. Eternal God, who committest unto us the swift and solemn trust of life, since we know not what a day may bring forth but only that the hour for serving thee is always present, may we wake to the instant claims of thy holy will, not waiting for tomorrow, but yielding today. Consecrate with thy presence the way our feet may go, and the humblest work will shine, and the roughest places be made plain.—James Martineau.

OFFERTORY SENTENCE. "Offer unto God thanksgiving; and pay thy vows unto the most High." Ps. 50:14.

OFFERTORY PRAYER. We give thee thanks, O Father, that through our tithes and offerings thou dost give us an opportunity to illuminate the dimness of the future and to glorify our present life with the word of him who is the Light of the world.

PRAYER. Lord, we would this day lay in thy hands all that we have and are, that our bodies and souls may become fair temples of thy indwelling. We desire with a great desire, O our God, that our wills may be utterly possessed by thy will, that our eyes may look out on this world as thine eyes look, that our being may be filled by thy being, that through our feeble hearts may beat a pulse of thine eternal love, and in our narrow souls may dwell a spark of thine eternal joy.

For, Master, what have we in heaven or earth but thee? Yet not as an external possession do we desire thee; come not in condescension from above; come not in glory and power from without; come not as a belief to be comprehended; come not as a wave of emotion to be felt and forgotten, but come as the indwelling spirit within our souls, transforming them into thine own divine nature, creating in them thine own joyful and loving will.

May we know with an immediate and ineffable knowledge that in thee we live and move and have our being. May we prove before men, in daily practice of devoted living, in peace and joy, patience and fortitude, humility and love, the fact that thou art our Father and their Father.—J. S. Hoyland.

EVENING SERVICE

Topic: Our Spiritual Universe
TEXT: Phil. 2:5.

The mind of Christ and the mind of the believer should be one. Jesus is the pattern; we should be like him. For Jesus that meant emptying himself in obedience to God the Father. For us it means centering our lives upon Christ.

I. For thousands of years before Copernicus men thought that the moon, the sun, the planets, and the stars revolved around the earth. This was the Ptolemaic system. And it was a good system, much better than most people of our day imagine. It could foretell the hours of sunrise and sunset. It could chart the general alteration of the heavens. But it was wrong.

(a) Because the sun is the center of our solar system and not the earth, as Ptolemy imagined, it was inevitable that the Ptolemaic system would have defects. Simply speaking, it had two defects.

(b) It was not always accurate, particularly in charting the position of the planets. Under the strain of providing corrections for these movements, the system eventually broke down.

(c) Second, it did not allow for progress. New discoveries always went against it. It was only under the system of Copernicus that Newton's theories of gravity could be developed. And it is only under this system that the flight of space ships beyond the earth is possible.

II. Do you see the application? You live within a spiritual solar system that is as fixed as the one that fills our heavens. Christ is the center of this system, but many people today, perhaps even you, imagine that they are the center of the system. As far as they can see the system works quite well. They serve themselves and generally get what they desire. If they work hard enough for a home they will get it, particularly if circumstances are with them. If they work hard enough at their job and ability they can count on a certain measure of success. Like the proverbial Englishman, they are self-made men who worship their creator.

III. This man-centered system has defects, just as the Ptolemaic system of astronomy had. (a) It is not quite accurate. It predicts a certain measure of success, but it does not account for failure or for the inevitable letdown when the person actually gets the thing for which he has been working. Similarly the system of the natural man does not allow for progress. Man is limited, and any system that makes man the center of life is limited also.

(b) It is not this way for Christians, for those who see things the way God wants all men to see them. Before God, man is abased and Christ exalted. Christ is the center of the system, the center of the spiritual universe. The Bible tells us that in this system there is infinite progress, for it is based on reality and on the nature of an infinite God. Do you know where you stand before God? Will you accept Christ's place within this system?—James Montgomery Boice.

SUNDAY: JULY TWENTY-FIFTH

MORNING SERVICE

Topic: The Service of Silence
    TEXT: Ps. 4:4 (KJV).
Other translations prefer the word "silence." For our noise-numb age could anything be more timely? A silence pregnant with God makes you feel that even one audible word would be sacrilege. What then is the service of these quiet yet creative interludes in the life of God's child?

I. *An aid to memory.* When we are still, the past comes back to haunt us, perhaps to humble us, or to make us happy. In the psalm when David is quiet his memory goes to work. He looks back on troubles at the time seemingly unbearable but troubles that have left him a bigger man with a richer soul and a finer faith. Silence is the setting in which memory has its best chance and does its noblest work.

II. *A response to mystery.* Before any mystery "stand in awe, and sin not." Among the mysteries consider the holiness of God. Do we stand in awe of it? "As he who has called you is holy," cries Peter, "so be ye holy in all matters of conduct." There is a hushed response that should be evoked by the unsullied holiness that our poor eyes behold in God. This response is a part of worship, of penitence, of sensitive discipleship. In the presence of such mysteries how useful to be silent! When no other response is ready, "in silence reflect."

III. *A form of ministry,* not least to ourselves. Without some such concern against evil and protest against it, something is missing from our moral fiber. Silence is even more a form of service to others. In another sometimes a hurt is too deep for words; it calls for loving silence. Often I have gone to a funeral parlor or to a home to face a friend to whom grief has just come. My first ministry there has been no smoothly turned sentence, no glib, conventional condolence. No, just a clasp of my hand and whatever of Christ's tender care I could convey with my eyes. When a heart is throbbing with its most acute anguish it is not speech that is needed but our Lord's healing silence.

IV. *A symbol of mastery.* When Christ hung upon the cross, how did he reply to cruel taunts? With a silence so noble and noteworthy that the centuries reckon with it as sublime. Like the Savior, we too cannot escape occasions when the noblest weapon of moral dignity is silence. Let no one think silence useless. Give it a larger and a more meaningful place in your soul. Whatever you do, don't treat Christ with such carelessness and flippancy that he can return you nothing but his awful and dooming silence. His silence to you can be terribly fatal. Your silence to him may be tremendously fruitful.—Paul S. Rees.

Illustrations

HIGH RELIGION. Religion should seek to make itself as intelligent as science, as appealing as art, as vital as the day's work, as intimate as home, and as inspiring as love.—Edward Scribner Ames.

REALITY. If we spend sixteen hours a day with things and not five minutes in the presence of the spiritual, things will seem 200 times more real than God.—W. R. Inge.

Sermon Suggestions

IF WITH ALL YOUR HEART. Text: Phil. 4:11–13. Christ will share these blessings of which Paul speaks, if with all your heart you truly seek him. But there are conditions. (1) Put your faith in God. (2) Keep it there. (3) Forget yourself in the love of God.—Glenn E. Hanneman.

CASTING SHADOWS. Text: Acts 5:15. (1) We may cast malevolent shadows. (2) We may cast benevolent shadows. (3) We may cast transforming shadows. —Fred R. Chenault.

Worship Aids

CALL TO WORSHIP. "Trust in [God] at all times; ye people, pour out your heart before him: God is a refuge for us." Ps. 62:8.

INVOCATION. O God of mercy, in this hour in thy house have mercy upon us. O God of light, shine into our hearts. O thou eternal goodness, deliver us from evil. O God of power, be thou our refuge and our strength. O God of love, let love flow through us. O God of life, live within us, now and forevermore.

OFFERTORY SENTENCE. "Take heed what ye hear: with what measure ye mete, it shall be measured to you: and unto you that hear shall more be given." Mark 4:24.

OFFERTORY PRAYER. Dear Lord, as we travel the highways of life give us a generous and sympathetic spirit for all people in all circumstances of life.

PRAYER. Almighty God, who art supreme power working invisibly among us, suffering no barrier to deter thee or obstacle to deflect thy course, we give thee thanks that thou hast not been thwarted by the thoughtless ways of men. When we remember that some of our fathers sought the false god of power, we are grateful that thou didst overrule their erring ways and command thy faithful ones to stand for the truth that is in thee.

We thank thee for the Bible, which shows us the pattern of thy redeeming love. We thank thee that thy Word is a lamp unto our feet and a light unto our pathway. Through its power our stagnant lives are renewed and we are made conscious of thy never-failing and all-encompassing benediction. May we not fail to trace thee through the recorded Word given us by thy prophets and apostles who meditated upon thy precepts and found thee clearly in the cross.

We thank thee that in thee and not in ourselves is our salvation. May we know of a surety that we are justified, not by the activity of our hands or the hasty movement of our feet, but by faith in thee, the most high God. Send us to our knees that we may in supplication discover thy will for us. Thou great and merciful Father, teach us to look to thee that we may learn thy message of redemption. Reveal to us the good news of thy salvation.

We thank thee that each of us is thy priest coming to thee in a quiet place and finding thee willing and eager to favor us with thy blessing. We thank thee that thou hast not given us dominion over others but hast placed a demand upon us to give to all men a staff for their journey and a sign of hope as they move toward the heavenly city.—Albert Buckner Coe.

EVENING SERVICE

Topic: The Master's Joy
TEXT: John 15:11.

I. *Jesus found joy with his family at Nazareth.* There had to be much love and laughter and happiness in that home, or he would never have prayed to God as his Father and introduced a new kind of kingdom patterned after the human family.

II. *Jesus found joy in a good meal.* Some of the greatest lessons he taught were spoken as he broke bread and drank wine with his friends around the dinner table.

III. *Jesus found joy in the laughter of children.* He watched them dancing in the street and compared the new kingdom of his love to the happiness of these children.

IV. *Jesus found joy in friendship.* The hours spent with Mary and Lazarus and Martha in Bethany were treasured moments snatched from the busy ministry he came to fulfill.

V. *Jesus found joy in his work.* He took seriously the task God called him to do, but the touch of humor was always there, even when he was teaching and healing and challenging his enemies.

VI. *Jesus found joy in his vacations.* When he was physically exhausted from the pressures of the crowds that pushed upon him, he would get into a boat and pull away from the shore on Lake Galilee, as he was lulled to sleep by the lapping of the waves.

VII. *Jesus found joy in helping fallen men stand on their feet.* His most beautiful parable about a father's love that forgives and welcomes home a penitent son closes with the preparations for a veal barbecue and a dance to celebrate his homecoming.—*The Texas Methodist.*

SUNDAY: AUGUST FIRST

MORNING SERVICE

Topic: Your Turn at Bat
TEXT: Col. 1:23–24.

I. *Reaction.* (a) Perhaps strange to us is the fact that Paul's reaction to suffering was rejoicing. "Now I rejoice in my sufferings for you." Recall that the apostle wrote this letter from a Roman prison. From this same prison he wrote Philippians, whose very theme is joy.

(b) He might have complained and whined as so many of us do. He who had served the Lord so completely might have accused God of being unfair, of deserting him. Rather he found it an occasion for joy. For to him it was a means of growth in Christian grace. In his reaction he depicted the words of an old Chinese proverb: "The gem cannot be polished without friction nor man perfected without trials." And he looked beyond the moment to the heavenly reward. As Longfellow said, "What seems to us but dim funereal tapers may be heaven's distant lamps."

(c) Suffering may be either a stumbling stone or a steppingstone. You may fall flat on your face or you may use the stone as a staircase toward heavenly bliss. It all depends upon you and your reaction to it.

II. *Regard.* (a) Paul had a proper regard for suffering. He said that he must "fill up that which is behind [lacking] of the afflictions of Christ in my flesh."

(b) What did he mean by this? Certainly he did not mean that Christ's suffering on the cross was insufficient for his salvation. We may be refined through our sufferings, but we certainly are not saved by them. Yet Paul clearly said that he must "fill up" in his body that which was lacking in the sufferings of Christ.

(c) The sufferings of Christ to which he referred were those that Christ endured not on the cross but prior to it. Among other things in his earthly ministry Jesus endured hardships, privation, hunger, thirst, exhaustion, loneliness, criticism, and persecution. Paul said that in his ministry for Christ he should expect no less.

(d) The word rendered "fill up" means to fill up in turn. To use a baseball term, in his earthly ministry Jesus had his turn at bat. Now Paul says that it is his turn at bat. He also must suffer as he fulfilled his ministry in proclaiming Jesus' redemptive work for lost men.

(e) Each of us must do the same. We do so knowing that we as Christians are fellow heirs of Christ's suffering as well as his glory. (See Rom. 8:17–18.)

(f) Jesus' sufferings did not include sickness and disease in his own perfect body. Still he did and still does bear the infirmities of others. But because of evil, man's body is subject to sickness and disease. However, it should also be remembered that God does not will that we shall so suffer. He permits it but does not perpetrate it. Nevertheless, he has promised to be with us in such sorrow. In tender love he promised never to forsake us in our trials.

III. *Reason.* (a) The apostle took his turn at bat joyfully because he also recognized the reason for his sufferings. It was "for his [Christ's] body's sake, which is the church."

(b) This does not mean that he saw any atoning value in his sufferings. Only Christ suffered for sin. Paul saw his suffering as an experience in which he was building and strengthening the church as the body of Christ. In his death Christ provided the means whereby men might be reconciled to God. Thus he gave meaning to the gospel of salvation.

(c) In his turn Paul proclaimed that gospel. It called for total dedication on his part. One has but to recall Paul's life as an apostle to see how in this dedication he suffered at the hands of evil men. (See II Cor. 11:16–33.) His present imprisonment was due to no criminal act but to his faithfulness in declaring the gospel of salvation by grace through faith.

(d) Paul referred to his sufferings not to gain sympathy but to encourage his readers in their trials for the purity of the gospel, and it has given heart to Christians down the ages.

(e) If and when you suffer let it be to the end that you may glorify Christ. Rather than turn your face to the wall in rebellion and doubt, let it be in your turn to fill up the sufferings of Christ. Determine that others shall see that Christ makes the difference. Know that when God allows you to enter the furnace of affliction, he is with you in it.—Herschel H. Hobbs.

Illustrations

PROCLAIMING GOD. There is not a flower that opens, not a seed that falls into the ground, and not an ear of wheat that nods on the end of its stalk in the wind that does not preach and proclaim the greatness and the mercy of God to the whole world. There is not an act of kindness or generosity, not an act of sacrifice done, or a word of peace and gentleness spoken, nor a child's prayer uttered that does not sing hymns to God before his throne and in the eyes of men and before their faces.—Thomas Merton.

ANSWERED PRAYER. I have never prayed sincerely and earnestly for anything but it came to pass sometime. No matter how distant the day, somehow, in some shape, probably the last I should have advised, it came.—Adoniram Judson.

Sermon Suggestions

THE SHEPHERD'S PREPOSITIONS. Scripture: Ps. 24. (1) With me: "my shepherd." (2) Beneath me: "green pastures." (3) Beside me: "still waters." (4) Before me: "a table." (5) Around me: "mine enemies." (6) Upon me: "the anointing." (7) After me: "goodness and mercy." (8) Beyond me: "the house of the Lord."—P. H. McSwain.

THE ANSWERS JESUS GIVES. Scripture: Luke 8:49–56. (1) The answer Jesus gives to life's problems. (See v. 50.) (2) The answer Jesus gives is an assurance that life has possibility. (See v. 52.) (3) The answer Jesus gives reflects authority over life's predicaments. (See v. 54.)—C. Neil Strait.

Worship Aids

CALL TO WORSHIP. "The kingdoms of this world are become the kingdom of our Lord, and of his Christ; and he shall reign for ever and ever." Rev. 11:15.

INVOCATION. O thou who art the light of the minds that know thee, the life of the souls that love thee, and the strength of the wills that serve thee, help us so to know thee that we may truly love thee and so to love thee that we may fully serve thee, whom to serve is perfect freedom.

OFFERTORY SENTENCE. "The end of the commandment is charity out of a pure heart." I Tim. 1:5.

OFFERTORY PRAYER. Our Father, enable all Christians to know that their lives may be lived with Christ in God and that their gifts are means by which thy love in Christ may reach into the lives of wayward and needy persons everywhere.

PRAYER. O sevenfold Spirit of God, come thou into our dwelling place this day and make thine abode with us.

O comforter, leave us not comfortless but fill our sadness with thine eternal joy.

O rushing, mighty wind of God, stir up and quicken and cleanse us and fill our souls with thy breath of life.

O flame of holy fire, burn up the evil that is in us, kindle our coldness, enlighten our darkness.

O giver of holy voices, reach us to speak to others in the language of their own hearts with the gifts of wisdom and understanding.

O spirit of truth, guide us into all truth that we may worship nothing lower than the holiest one.

O spirit of remembrance, keep in our hearts and minds the things of the kingdom that we may not forget and fall away from them.

O dove of peace, descend upon us and abide with us now and evermore.

EVENING SERVICE

Topic: The Old-Time Religion
TEXT: Ps. 22:4.

I. We need to recapture some of the old-time puritanism. (a) Some may shudder at that, for with it they associate all the narrow religious sects and habits of our early settlers. They think only of blue Sunday and witchcraft and what-have-you. This makes it necessary for us to recapture what the word originally stood for. Puritanism was a protest against dictatorship or bureaucracy in church or state, and it stood for the application of the principles of the Christian faith to daily living. The Puritans got into disrepute because they stood up against dictatorship.

(b) Three essentials are at the very heart of puritanism. (1) God is the center and end of all life. No nation can

have that faith and tolerate a dictatorship.

(2) God had to be worshiped in daily business as well as in the church. Frugality, sobriety, and honesty were business concepts.

(3) Puritans believed that each person had a personal accounting to give to God.

II. They had in the old-time a missionary emphasis. (a) Christianity is not a church; it is a movement, and if we do not keep it moving forward it is going to move backward. The kind of teaching Christ gave us will never stand still for long in any community. The fact is that the church does not exist to keep a gospel; it exists to give a gospel.

(b) What a chance for the church of God to proclaim its Christ! Here is a world where people are awakening to the fact that might and power are not enough. Here is a world where people are awakening to the fact that there is such a thing as a soul. It is a world where people are unhappy and broken down inside.

III. The old-time religionists had a way of placing emphasis upon their confession of faith. They said what they believed, and they believed what they said. What a thrill it is to hear a person come right out with words such as those of Paul: "I know whom I have believed" or "For me to live in Christ." I wonder if this is not a great part of our trouble: our faith is punctuated by question marks while the old-timers had theirs punctuated by exclamation marks. —Carl J. Sanders.

SUNDAY: AUGUST EIGHTH

MORNING SERVICE

Topic: The Meaning of Repentance
SCRIPTURE: Acts 2:37–41.

There is scarcely a word that is less pleasant to us than the word "repentance," "conversion." (1) It is this door to which we are stubbornly, clearly

pointed in the holy scriptures when we ask about the way. It goes through that, and only through that; there is no other way to this goal, just as there is only this one way through the *couloir* (passage) to one particular mountain peak.

(2) If we are serious enough about this to act so that we may receive the

Holy Spirit and become children of God, truly human, then we must get in through here, through this *couloir*, and through no other place. We must repent.

I. To repent is to talk with God—I should say, aloud and on one's knees in a quiet room or outside in the forest where no one will surely hear it—just as a child talks with his or her father and tells him everything, what disobedient, unfaithful creatures we are.

II. To repent is not to speak great words but to lament to God from the heart our sorrow about ourselves, in which we tell him quite particular things that we have thought, said, and done, of which we certainly know that they are not right before him, and by which it becomes clear to us that we have a disobedient heart. Repentance is acknowledgment of sins but such an acknowledgment that it grieves us heartily, not only that we have done that but that we are such who could do that.

III. To repent is to have a hearty remorse and to shame ourselves before God who has done so many good things for us and whom we have rewarded with such unthankfulness. That is why repentance necessarily flows into the prayer for forgiveness of sins and for an obedient heart.

(a) Why is this repentance so important? Quite simply because only so can we encounter God. As one can lay no gift in a clenched fist, so God cannot lay his love in an unrepentant heart.

(b) Repentance is the opening of the heart, that is, the whole person for God, the decramping of the heart that was previously cramped, in love with itself or gone mad about itself.

IV. To repent is really nothing else than to become honest before God and to see oneself as one is in the mirror of God. Only when one becomes honest before God can one really receive God's word of grace. Only when one hates the disobedience in his disobedience can one be filled by the love of God. Thus we want to bow down, all the way down, with one another before God and tell

him how it is with us so that he may help us to a new life.—Emil Brunner.

Illustrations

POSITIVE COMMANDS. It is commonplace in traditional Christian moral thinking that negative commands are easier to obey than positive ones. If I tell someone not to do this or that and he complies with what I have said, the matter is over and done with. On the other hand, if I give him a positive injunction—and if this injunction is also broad in its expectation—he will never fully live up to all the possibilities in view and he will certainly find it difficult to do even those which he undertakes.—Norman Pittenger.

PROFOUNDLY CHANGED. I challenge anyone anywhere to expose his inner life to Jesus Christ in repentance and faith and obedience, and I will tell what will happen—tell with an almost mathematical precision. Such a person will be changed, profoundly changed, in character and life; and he will know it in every fiber of his being.—E. Stanley Jones in *A Song of Ascents*.

Sermon Suggestions

BELIEFS ARE CREATIVE. Text: Jer. 2:4–5. (1) Our faith in God, our faith that we are a part of God, and our faith that he is our Father and that we are his children. (2) Our faith in Jesus Christ in whom our faith is incarnate. (3) Our belief not only in rights but also in duties and obligations. (4) Our faith that all work needs to be consecrated, all work dedicated to the good of God's children. (5) Our belief in cooperation, bringing our best gift and linking it with the best gift of others.—Roy A. Burkhart.

CHRIST THE REDEEMER. Text: Matt. 20:28. (1) Christ the redeemer of the world. (2) Christ the redeemer of the church. (3) Christ the redeemer of you and me.—Joseph M. Applegate.

Worship Aids

CALL TO WORSHIP. "Be strong and of a good courage, fear not: for the Lord thy God, he it is that doth go with thee; he will not fail thee, nor forsake thee." Deut. 31:6.

INVOCATION. Almighty God, our heavenly Father, who reignest over all things in thy wisdom, power, and love: we adore thee for thy glory and majesty, and we praise thee for thy grace and truth to us in thy Son our Savior. Grant us the help of thy Holy Spirit, we beseech thee, that we may worship thee in spirit and in truth.

OFFERTORY SENTENCE. "It is God who is at work within you, giving you the will and the power to achieve his purpose." Phil. 2:13 (PHILLIPS).

OFFERTORY PRAYER. Accept, O Lord, these offerings thy people make unto thee and grant that the cause to which they are devoted may prosper under thy guidance, to the glory of thy name.

PRAYER. Eternal God, who art the beginning and the end of all things, shine with thy morning upon our souls and grant that when evening falls we may not be shamed either by memories of evil deeds or by ghosts of missed opportunities. We are conscious how little we can earn and how much we are given. We thank thee for thy love which all our foolishness has never tired. Keep us from the shabbiness of complaining and deepen our gratitude.

Eternal God, who from chaos didst create the world, who from a weak and wandering people didst bring forth thy people, and who from a cross didst give redemption, look thou with pity on our torn and troubled world. We confess that by our hatreds we have alienated ourselves from our neighbors and from thee, by our preoccupation with ourselves we have lost confidence in ourselves, by our failure to seek after thee we have lost thee. Yet thou hast not lost us, and always thy loving care sustains an unworthy world. We ask that in grateful response we may find the way to worship thee with undivided heart and to serve our neighbor's needs with eager hands. Save us alike from arrogant speaking and compromising silence, and grant us a holy impatience with all that hinders the coming of thy kingdom. For our confusion give clarity, for our callousness give commitment, for our doubt give faith.—William Croft Wilson.

EVENING SERVICE

Topic: The Big Little Man
SCRIPTURE: Luke 19:1–10.

Zacchaeus did not seek for excuses not to see Jesus. He transformed his disadvantage—small stature—into advantage. He "sought" earnestly to get through "the press" of the crowd to "see Jesus." He was greatly rewarded for his persistent effort to find the Master.

I. The spirit of the mob: "They all murmured." The crowd was filled with curiosity and excitement to see Jesus. The mob showed an unintended praise for the Master. The public mob complained and "murmured" because of Jesus' attention to a chief of sinners.

II. The spirit of the man: "He sought . . . Jesus." (a) He was determined to find Jesus. "He sought" (v. 3). "He ran" (v. 4). "He climbed" (v. 4). We will find Jesus only when we are fully determined.

(b) He received him joyfully. His heart was touched as Jesus "looked up" (v. 5). His heart leaped for joy as Jesus spoke, "Come down." "He made haste, and came down" (v. 6).

(c) He made restitution. He was a sinner. "For the Son of man is come to seek and to save that which was lost" (v. 10). He repented. "If I have taken any thing . . . I restore" (v. 8). A yielded heart. "Lord, the half of my goods I give" (v. 8).

III. The spirit of the Master: "Come . . . I must abide." (a) The invitation:

"Make haste, and come down" (v. 5). "Come," "for the harvest is ripe" (Joel 3:13). "Behold, now is the accepted time . . . the day of salvation" (II Cor. 6.2). "Come; for all things are now ready" (Luke 14:17).

(b) The command: "I must abide" (v. 5). The Master's desire to abide with all is so great. God's will is an imperative to a happy life. God's only dwellingplace is the hearts of men.

(c) The gift: "This day is salvation come to this house" (v. 9). The reward is to all who accept the Master's invitation. Salvation is life's most glorious gift. It is an immediate experience of grace—"this day."

IV. The spirit of the mob will never change from the spirit of the majority. The spirit of man must always change in repentance with the minority. The spirit of the Master cannot change from his assurance of salvation and grace to the seeker.—J. Walter Hand, Jr. in *The Preacher's Magazine*.

SUNDAY: AUGUST FIFTEENTH

MORNING SERVICE

Topic: Self-Inflicted Wounds
TEXT: I Sam. 31:6.

There are wounds which we inflict upon ourselves. We make deliberate choices for which we must take the consequences. This is indicated in the life of Saul. He was Israel's first king. True, he started out with a great deal against him. He was a foil in God's hands against the disobedient Israelites. The Israelites annoyed God by crying, "Give us a king who can lead us in our battles and increase our fortunes." So God said to Samuel the prophet, "Give them a king, and let them see what living under a king is like." He ordered Samuel to find Saul, the son of Kish, and to anoint him king. But even here Saul might have made it had he not succumbed to those inflictions he imposed upon himself. The final chapter indicates all the rest. Surrounded by Philistines, fear and melancholy in his heart, and wounded with arrows in his stomach, he commands his armor bearer to run him through with his sword lest the uncircumcised Philistines capture him and mock him before death. The bearer refused, so Saul took his sword and fell upon it. This ancient scene provides us with some unforgettable lessons. We inflict ourselves needlessly.

I. *Saul began his destruction when he forgot God*. That is more likely when one has much of this world's goods. Being a king is heady business. Saul, a head taller than his countrymen and very handsome, was at first humble and teachable. He resisted being made king and even hid himself when Samuel came to anoint him at Mizpah. He protested to the prophet: "Why do you pick on me? 'I am the least of the tribe of Benjamin, one of the smallest of the tribes of Israel.'" But he did consent, and soon he became proud and arrogant, sure of himself and unsure of God. He forgot God, played the fool, and was unwilling to confess his sins. He grew moody and morose.

II. *Saul was wounded by his indiscretions*. We are hurt when we turn our backs on God. We wound our spirits, and they are sometimes difficult to heal. An unrepentant sense of guilt is what Saul had. It is an emotional wound which is more painful than a stab in the flesh. Saul had been wounded in battle but nothing like this. "There is no peace for the wicked," says the scripture. The reason is that sin is an unclean wound, and unless we repent of it and move on to loving and serving God it will never heal. It can get into the mind and produce melancholia or fear; it can make one nervous or jittery; it can cause loss of appetite and weight; it can affect health both mental and physical.

III. *Saul had some attitudes that were destructive.* (a) He was filled with jealousy and envy. Had Saul been a good king we might never have heard of David. When David contested the Philistines and won, on his return the women sang, "Saul has killed his thousands; but David his tens of thousands." This made Saul angry. It put jealousy in his heart, but David honored and loved him. One day David was entertaining the king with his harp. Saul became angry, reached for his javelin, threw it as hard as he could toward David who barely escaped with his life.

(b) Very near to jealousy is bitterness. It is a dead-end street. Whether it be a reaction to an unfortunate marriage, a business failure, or a personal disappointment of some sort, it will destroy, drive the blood pressure up, produce ulcers and mental problems. Let me ask you, have you forgiven the past? That is crucial. Saul couldn't. Jealous and bitter, he was filled with rage and in a corner he nursed his wounds.—Tom A. Whiting.

Illustrations

WHAT FAITH MEANS. To have faith in God is not to pray that two and two equal seven. It is not, as a recent humanistic declaration caricaturing faith stated, that to be religious is to give up the struggle and turn everything over to a divine problem solver. It is rather to insist and proclaim that the universe means something and means well; that the creator of the vast universe is the father of our spirits; that he is alpha and omega, the beginning and the end; and that his will must become our way.—William M. Thompson.

KNOWING AND DOING. While we must beware of the man who is able to explain everything, we must also beware of the man who insists on having everything explained. Our difficulties are not in knowing God's will for our lives—we know it all too well—but in doing it. Our difficulties with the Bible are not with passages we do not understand; our difficulty lies with the passages that we understand all too well.—Peter Marshall.

Sermon Suggestions

THE CHURCH CHRIST LOVED. Text: Eph. 5:25. (1) If Christ loved the church we cannot love Christ without loving the church. (2) We cannot love the church without loving the real, existing churches. One cannot love intellectual abstractions. (3) We cannot love the churches at large without loving one local, particular church, the church on our doorstep, in reach. (4) We cannot love the local church without loving its people, its work, its services, its good name.—R. E. O. White.

PREACHING TO THE CONVERTED. Text: Rom. 1:15. (1) The purpose of preaching to Christians is to preach the gospel. (2) The purpose of preaching to Christians is to teach the gospel. (3) The purpose of preaching to Christians is to apply the gospel. (4) The purpose of preaching to Christians is to experience the gospel before their eyes.—Ronald A. Ward.

Worship Aids

CALL TO WORSHIP. "I will bless the Lord at all times: his praise shall continually be in my mouth. O magnify the Lord with me, and let us exalt his name together." Ps. 34:1, 3.

INVOCATION. Almighty God, the giver and lord of life: we bless and praise thee for thy merciful keeping and gracious care, for all the gifts of thy providence and grace, and for all the blessings which manifest thy fatherhood. We thank thee for the faith which sustains us, the hopes which inspire us, and the light by which we daily walk. We thank thee for Jesus Christ, who, by the life he lived, the temptations he conquered, the gospel he taught, and the cross he bore, has brought us nigh to thee and closer to one another.

OFFERTORY SENTENCE.   "Seeing ye have purified your souls in obeying the truth through the Spirit unto unfeigned love of the brethren, see that ye love one another with a pure heart fervently." I Pet. 1:22.

OFFERTORY PRAYER.   O Christ, may we walk constantly in thy way and work fervently for those causes which are dear to thee.

PRAYER.   Most gracious God, who hast made us stewards of thy bounty and trusted us with the use of thy gifts: we lift our hearts in thanksgiving for the manifold tokens of thy surrounding love. We thank thee for life and the joy of it; for health and all the powers with which thou hast endowed us; for the wondrous world about us; for the greater world within us and every gleam of light which turns our minds toward thee; for the love of friends and kindred and their belief in us; for the way over which we have come and all that has been good in it, for the way that lies untrodden before us and our chance to make it the way of peace and right-eousness; for thy companionship all the way and our assurance that thou wilt guide our steps aright. For all that thou art to us and all that we may be to thee, we give thanks unto thee, the author of goodness, and bless thy name for thy mercies which endure through-out all generations.—Morgan Phelps Noyes.

EVENING SERVICE

Topic: Judgment: True and False
SCRIPTURE: Rom. 2.

I. *The judgments of man.* (a) Man condemns himself who judges (v. 1). (b) Man often does the same things (vv. 1, 22–23). (c) Man must remember he shall be judged (v. 3). (d) Man despises the riches of God's goodness (v. 4). (e) Man treasures up wrath against himself (v. 5). (f) Man is legalistic (v. 17). We feel we are right; we fancy ourselves leaders of the blind and teachers and preachers of the knowledge of God.

II. *The judgments of God.* (a) According to truth (v. 2). (b) Inescapable (v. 3). (c) Follows only after forbearance, long-suffering, goodness (v. 4). (d) A righteous judgment (v. 5). (e) Rendered according to man's deeds (v. 6). (f) Glory, honor, peace, immortality, eternal life to the righteous (vv. 6–10). (g) Tribulation and anguish for the impenitent and wicked (vv. 8–9). (h) Those by law who have sinned in the law (v. 12). (i) The secrets of men (v. 16) according to the gospel of Jesus Christ.

III. *True judgment is inward, not outward.* (a) Not the keeping of the law alone (v. 25). (b) Keeping the righteousness of law as keeping the law (v. 26). (c) Not by letter nor by circumcision (v. 27). (d) You are of the Israel of God when such inwardly and only then (v. 29). Of the heart, of the spirit; then the praise of God is incurred.— Ed Irwin.

SUNDAY: AUGUST TWENTY-SECOND

MORNING SERVICE

Topic: Jesus Christ: Servant-Lord
TEXT: John 13:13.

We perceive by faith, faith tested and being tested, by scripture, tradition, reason, and experience, that Jesus Christ is Servant-Lord. He is God with us in the realities of our common life. Within these realities he claims authority over our corporate and personal thoughts, words, deeds, and relationships, but he does not force our obedience. He challenges us to choose between his servant-lordship over us and all the lesser lords who seek to manipulate and control us. In short, he calls us to be born into free life under his authority and to go on to perfection with his Holy Spirit "resourcing" and directing our going.

I. He is Servant-Lord of *all creation*. The whole created order from atoms to universe is sacramental because it is permeated, perhaps almost saturated, with his efforts to provide an adequate life-sustaining context for communities and persons who are traveling by his gracious favor from sin to salvation, from death to life, and from the old earth to the "new heaven and new earth." Through the whole creation are traces of the Servant-Lord at work on our behalf.

II. He is Servant-Lord of *nations*. The great commission in Matt. 28:18–19 deserves more careful exegesis than it usually gets. In it the risen Lord said: "All authority in heaven and on earth has been given to me. Go, therefore, and make disciples of all *nations*." This text says only by inference, "Go, make disciples of persons." It says directly, "Go, make disciples of nations." The word for "nations" in the Greek text means literally "multitudes associated or living together; a company, a troup." We perceive, therefore, that Christ is Servant-Lord of nations, communities, groups, and that he expects to be recognized as one who creates, re-orders, and sustains kingdom-directed social and systemic values.

III. He is Servant-Lord of *persons*. In John 20 there is the record of Thomas and his doubting but also of Thomas and his confessing. When the disciple recognized Christ, risen and present, in the company of disciples, he exclaimed, "My Lord and my God!" We perceive that individuals, as well as nations, may come consciously under the Servant-Lord and there find new life status. We believe we participate in this everywhere that we work.—Paul Washburn.

Illustrations

HEART'S DESIRE. This universal Chris[t] with the chameleonlike gift for adapt[ing] himself to every place and epoc[h] makes things too easy for us. Anyone ca[n] find in him not only his heart's desir[e] but also a judicious blend of all th[e] virtues he hopes to see vindicated i[n] his own time. Our ideals about Jesu[s] tell us more about ourselves than the[y] do about him. I search the gospels fo[r] a freedom fighter and Jesus strides ou[t] sword in hand. The pacifist looks ther[e] for the great advocate of nonviolenc[e] and is rewarded by a glimpse of th[e] triumph of suffering love. As Georg[e] Pfister wrote, "Tell me what you fin[d] in your Bible, and I will tell you wha[t] sort of person you are!"—Colin Morri[s]

OPENING OF SPRINGS. You cannot b[e] filled with the Spirit and be indifferen[t] to the claims of the suffering and th[e] poor. If the baptism of the Spirit we[re] given to us in the fullness of its powe[r] the result would be the opening o[f] springs from which rivers of pity an[d] passion would flow to every provinc[e] of sorrow and human distress.—R. W[.] Dale.

Worship Aids

CALL TO WORSHIP. "How beautifu[l] upon the mountains are the feet of hi[m] that bringeth good tidings, that pub[-] lisheth peace; that publisheth salvation[,] that saith unto Zion, thy God reigneth!" Isa. 52:7.

INVOCATION. Teach us, good Lord, i[n] our days of rest to put our worship an[d] prayer first, and may we never let th[e] services of the church be crowded out o[f] our lives. Keep before us the vision o[f] thy dear Son Jesus Christ, who in hi[s] boyhood days worshiped with his famil[y] and may that vision inspire us and a[ll] men to unite as members of the churc[h] universal in witness, in worship, an[d] in love.

OFFERTORY SENTENCE. "Every good gift and every perfect gift is from above, and cometh down from the Father of lights." Jas. 1:17.

OFFERTORY PRAYER. Our Father, help us this day to remember that we do not live in our own strength but that thou art our help and that from thee cometh even these gifts which we consecrate in Christ's name.

PRAYER. Lord Jesus, draw near in pity to us. The nearer we come to thee the further we feel away. Each upward step we take shows us greater distances still to tread. Forgive us if we have sought our own sanctification and ignored the needs of the world. Forgive us if the love we had for others and which we fancied so pure was tainted with self-concern; if we loved them because we wanted them to think what we think, do what we do, and not for themselves alone. Enlarge our narrow hearts. Give us to yearn with thee over our lost race. Help us, even when we feel the pain of the world's sin, not to feel superior to it or forget that so much of it is done in ignorance. Change our nature into thine and so save us in every part of our being that wherever we go thy mighty heart may be beating in us, thy purposes shaping themselves in our eager minds, and thy holy will directing us into wider fields of service. —W. E. Sangster.

EVENING SERVICE

Topic: The Church in a Changing Society

TEXT: Eph. 3:21.

Great churches come in all sizes and places. Their greatness is determined by their ministry under the circumstances of their existence. Here are eight principal kinds of churches, each great to the extent of its outreach and ministry.

I. *The large, downtown church.* Steeped in history and tradition, it includes in its membership the town's wealth and those who determine its destiny. It must aggressively engage in mission endeavors at the community level while giving support to world missions. Its work must match its money. Otherwise it turns inward, baptizing only its children and shutting out the world.

II. *The church in the growing suburbs.* Carefully conceived and strategically located, it can hardly avoid numerical growth. Its problems are not so much enlisting new members as recruiting sufficient leaders for its programs and planning far enough ahead for future buildings. Its opportunity to achieve greatness is not limited to head counts and buildings. It must engage in programs of spiritual enrichment and be a fellowship seeking God's purpose.

III. *The country church.* Well out of town and far removed from any city, this church quite likely is old. Its membership is static, with neither gains nor losses more than slight. Complacency is its worst enemy as it ministers to changing needs in a seemingly changeless setting.

IV. *The country church in change.* This church is beset by problems and confronted by new opportunities. It is rooted in a rural past, but it has been overtaken by the sprawling residential areas that reached out from the city. Its worst mistake would be to ignore the reality of change or reject its new opportunities. It must seek out every new resident, ministering to him and enlisting him in turn to minister to others.

V. *The city church in a rezoned community.* As its neighborhood changes from homes to businesses this church is almost certain to suffer heavy membership losses. Its future may be in doubt. It has a God-given responsibility to weigh against other alternatives its obligation to those remaining in the membership. Its finest hour can be a rearguard action against premature abandonment of a changing community.

VI. *The church as the community changes from white to black.* Quick population shifts have left dozens of white churches in black communities. A church must show Christian brotherhood in such change. It can welcome anyone to its services, it can initiate programs of service across racially sensitive lines, or if its membership dwindles it can seek to sell its buildings to the new residents of the area.

VII. *The closed community church.* This church is far along in change or in deep trouble because the closed community, be it textile, military, maritime, or other, is gone. It has only two options: to become truly a community church or to disband. The measure of its greatness, as in all churches, can be seen in how truly it accepts new members into the fellowship.

VIII. *The relocating church.* This takes the faith of Abraham and the wisdom of Solomon. If for any of the reasons cited or others a move is contemplated, the need for a church in another place must be weighed against the need for one in the former location. A move can be a spiritual pilgrimage under God's leadership.—John E. Roberts in *Baptist Courier.*

SUNDAY: AUGUST TWENTY-NINTH

MORNING SERVICE

Topic: Holy Worldliness
TEXT: John 17:15.

I. The question with which we are faced daily as we seek to walk the pilgrim's way is the question of our relationship to the world. There are two extremes of approach and, as we might expect, one as wrong as the other.

(a) To withdraw from the world. (1) When we become pilgrims we are separated men and must live as such. The world is evil and any compromise with it or its ways will only lead us to disaster and deprive us of our inheritance in the kingdom. The world can only taint us with its evil or, at the very least, distract us from the things of the spirit. Therefore, it is said, we must be otherworldly. We are, after all, as the scripture assures us, strangers and pilgrims on the earth.

(2) The result of such a philosophy is, of course, to have fellowship only with other believers, themselves strangers and pilgrims. The next step of exclusiveness is to have fellowship only with some of those other believers. Ultimately none would be good enough for communion with us save God alone. This is the final temptation of the medieval hermit, but surely no one tries to live this way today.

(b) To be swamped by the world. Failing to recognize our purpose we become so attracted by the ephemeral and the temporal that we not merely lose our identity but we are conquered and possessed. This can happen to the church as it becomes more highly organized and sometimes hardly distinguishable from a successful social club or, at best, a service organization.

II. Somewhere between the extremes lies the truth. (a) Our text is found in the context of what is called the high priestly prayer of Jesus. According to the fourth evangelist, these were the thoughts nearest to the heart of our Master on the last night of his earthly life. Seldom are we nearer to the meaning of the Master, to his desire for his disciples, than when he prays for them on that last occasion of fellowship.

(b) Here his very purpose is crystallized as the mission of the church in the world is set forth in unmistakable terms. Jesus speaks of their unity with him and one another. He acknowledges again that the travelers on the pilgrim's way must live by a different standard of values than those ordinarily known as worldly, but he surely also makes abundantly clear that the place of the church and of the Christian is neither in a hermit's cell nor in succumbing to the seduction of the secular.

III. In doctrinal terms this is a truly incarnational theology, that is, it is what the coming of Jesus was about. It is what his life was about. It is what the church is about; holy worldliness rather than otherworldliness.

(a) The Word, a spiritual concept, entered the flesh, a material concept, and in doing so wiped out all the false distinctions between temporal and eternal, secular and holy, heavenly and worldly.

(b) "The more you are interested in the Incarnation the more you must be concerned about drains" (Henry Scott Holland). Drains and slums and disease and hunger and poverty; not in some condescending pity that would offer a touch of soothing ointment for the symptoms of a deep-rooted disease but rather because God so loved the world.

(c) It is because all things are ours. We are in the world and must live in the world which is God's creation and which he sent his Son to redeem, and the Christian church is there as his body.

IV. "The life of Christ is contained in history and contains it. It is the supreme explanation and the final standard by which everything is measured from which history itself takes meaning and justification." (Henri Daniel Rops.)

(a) Only a willful misreading of that life would see him as an ascetic, a hermit, a member of some exclusive brethren. Rather he gives us the unmistakable example of involvement or immersion in the carpenter shop at Nazareth; at a wedding in Cana of Galilee; in the day-to-day life of the countryside, the villages, and the towns. Yet there is never any question but that he is living by a different set of values.

(b) Holy worldliness is to say that we live in one world. If we would be holy it is in the world we must be holy, that indeed immersion in the world is the only way to holiness just as it is

the only way to relevance for the church. To walk the pilgrim's way is not to be separated from the world but immersed in the world, kept from the evil.—J. Ernest Somerville.

Illustrations

FUN IN RELIGION. The price of romance in religion is the price of romance everywhere else—singlemindedness. You can't pursue a dozen ways of life at once nor serve a dozen spiritual masters. There is fun in religion—heaps of it— quantities of it—for those who go far enough for the fun.—Samuel M. Shoemaker.

KNOWING PEOPLE. You don't know people through psychology, philosophy, or sociology. You can catalogue certain facts, analyze them, but you don't really know them until you love them.— Erich Fromm.

Sermon Suggestions

MOUNTAIN-MOVING FAITH. Text: Matt. 17:20. (1) Faith power is stronger than will power. (2) We are entitled to have faith in ourselves only because we have faith in God. (3) It is our business to nurture faith, and the food of faith is prayer.—John A. Redhead.

PORTRAIT OF A CHRISTIAN. Text: Gal. 6:17. (1) The mark of character. (2) Living radiantly and confidently. (3) Making a sincere effort to see the good in life. (4) Concern for human need.— Elbert E. Gates, Jr.

Worship Aids

CALL TO WORSHIP. "Worthy is the Lamb that was slain to receive power, and riches, and wisdom, and strength, and honor, and glory, and blessing." Rev. 5:12.

INVOCATION. O God, in glory exalted and in mercy ever blessed, we magnify thee, we praise thee, we give thanks unto thee for thy bountiful providence, for all the blessings of this present life, and all the hopes of a better life to come. Let the memory of thy goodness, we beseech thee, fill our hearts with joy and thankfulness.

OFFERTORY SENTENCE. "Give unto the Lord the glory due unto his name: bring an offering, and come before him: worship the Lord in the beauty of holiness." I Chron. 16:29.

OFFERTORY PRAYER. Our heavenly Father, may thy kingdom be uppermost in our minds, our hearts, and our lives. Accept our gifts and with them the rededication of all that we are and have to thy greater glory.

A PRAYER FOR STUDENTS. Thou fountain of all wisdom, wilt thou hear us as we pray for those who are called to the discipline of learning in schools, colleges, and universities. Inspire them with the desire for reality in thought, that they may know thee, the Ultimate Reality, whose thoughts they can but think again. Deliver them from the mind which is closed to new truth, from the ignorance which is content with half-truth, and from the pride that thinks it knows all the truth. Give them diligence in their studies, loyalty to their teachers, an earnest desire to excel, and the humility to rejoice in one another's success. Inspire them with great hopes and ideals and with pure and unselfish ambition that in due time they may give freely of what they have received. Spirit of all counsel and knowledge, guide the feet of thy servants into the paths of eternal life. May their souls be lamps of thine, burning and shining with the truth, dimmed by no evil passion, darkened by no deadly sin. Teach them the secret of Christ, which is the secret of wisdom and without which all other learning is but dust and ashes. To him alone, whose is the image of the eternal God and whose spirit leads us into all the truth, be the glory and the praise forever.—Leonard Griffith.

EVENING SERVICE

Topic: Profile of the Early Church
SCRIPTURE: Acts 2:42–47.

I. The early church was marked by *doctrine*. It was a church with great emphasis upon learning. The people gave heed to the teaching of the apostles. Doctrine is teaching. Every day in a believer's life should witness new truth, deeper penetration into the wisdom and grace of God. The religion of the Lord a moving experience that tends to cause one to lift up his eyes and ever look toward the sunrise rather than the sunset.

II. The early church made much of *fellowship*. This means that the people experienced and shared a sense of to-Christ is not a static thing but rather getherness which had great meaning for their lives. The church was a real brotherhood. When Nelson was asked to explain one of his great victories he is said to have replied, "I had the happiness to command a band of brothers."

III. Believers made much of *prayer* in the early church. They were a praying people. "Lord, teach us to pray," said one of the disciples to Jesus, "even as John also taught his disciples" (Luke 11:1). Little wonder that the disciples prayed, for Jesus had set them the perfect example. We know that on one occasion he went out into the mountain to pray and "continued all night in prayer to God" (Luke 6:12).

IV. The early church was marked by *reverence* and there were *signs* and *wonders*. Luke says, "And fear came upon every soul." The word translated "fear" carries the idea of "awe and reverence." The Christian looks upon the whole earth as "the temple of the living God, for God is the creator and the owner of the universe." In the words of Paul, "He is before all things, and in him all things consist" (Col. 1:17).—R. Paul Caudill.

SUNDAY: SEPTEMBER FIFTH

MORNING SERVICE

Topic: A Faith for Monday Morning (Labor Sunday)

Text: Phil. 2:15 (RSV).

I. *Faith for Monday morning is a faith in its working clothes.* (a) God has so ordained life that we have periods for rest and for spiritual refreshment. We take time out to meditate, to worship, and to find restoration for our souls. Then we go forth to serve in life's ordinary ways. We are called upon to spend and be spent in serving God and our fellows in the world. We were never meant to be hermits but to share the common life of mankind.

(b) This is where our faith must be put to work. When we leave church after worship we do not shelve our faith until we return again. If meditation and prayer and praise nurture our souls then the world is to be the proving ground where our faith is tested.

II. *Faith for Monday morning is something the world sorely needs.* (a) Hear again the words of the apostle: "In the midst of a crooked and perverse generation." What an apt description of the topsy-turvy world of unending conflict and of evil casting its dark shadows everywhere.

(b) When Paul told his friends that in that kind of a world they were to shine as lights he used a very strong word. He was not suggesting the candle or lamp which might flicker in the variable wind. The word he used for light suggests the light such as a star, a constant gleam with steady power to penetrate the dark.

III. *Faith for Monday morning is a farsighted faith.* (a) We are not time-bound creatures. The meaning of life is not cramped into the days on the calendar. God does not work on a little human time table. He has long-range purposes which he calls us to share. The witness and the work of Christians must have this long-range outlook. Only with this kind of spiritual perspective can we steady our souls.

(b) This farsighted faith helps us when evil seems to win the day. The forces set against Paul's friends in Philippi were very great, yet it was in that kind of situation they were to bear their witness to Jesus Christ. Many of us feel that never before have there been so many things to overwhelm us. On every hand there are hatred, violence, and deadly strife. There are wars and rumors of wars. One can easily be discouraged if he has no faith. The Christian in his moments of desperate need recalls the words spoken about our Lord in John 1:5.

(c) We need this farsighted faith when the results of our labors are hidden from our eyes. Parents never see the immediate results of their training and discipline in the lives of their children. They seek to do the best they can and then wait. The teacher does not see the immediate results in the response of his pupil, but he may open doors and vistas of truth that will guide that student through lifetime. What we are and what we do as Christians seldom bring immediate results. The important thing is that we are to be bearers of the light. Jesus calls us to this everyday ministry of living, of loving, and of working in ways to reflect the light of God's glory revealed in him alone.—A. Hayden Hollingsworth.

Illustrations

ANGELS WORKING. The Spanish artist, Murillo, pictures some kitchen maids at work. One has a water pitcher, another some meat, a third the vegetables, and a fourth is tending the stove. A common kitchen scene. But look—all the maids are angels! John Newton said, "If two angels were sent from heaven, one to conduct an empire, the other to sweep a street, they would feel no desire to change jobs."

CHRISTIANS IN BUSINESS.   Business and industry are in the world the same as the church. What is the relationship between the church and the world? I am not asking a new question, but I want to put a new kind of slant to it. Do we lose our identity when we leave the sanctuary? Do we become another person? Less concerned with love than with loot? Less concerned about the poor than about the profit? Less concerned with liberation than with license?—Florence Little.

Sermon Suggestions

EVERY MAN'S SERVANT.   Text: I Cor. 9:19 (RSV). What is the test of being every man's servant? (1) The service test was established in Israel. (See Mic. 6:8.) (2) It excludes mere professors of religion from the kingdom. (See Matt. 7:31.) (3) It reveals the quality of love. (See John 21:16.) (4) It will be applied in determining man's final destiny. (See Matt. 25:35-36.)—Roy I. Madsen.

TWELVE ESSENTIAL LESSONS.   (1) The value of time. (2) The need of perseverance. (3) The pleasure of serving. (4) The dignity of simplicity. (5) The true worth of character. (6) The power of kindness. (7) The influence of example. (8) The obligation of duty. (9) The wisdom of economy. (10) The virtue of patience. (11) The nobility of labor. (12) The teachings of him who said, "Learn of me."—*Western Christian Advocate*.

Worship Aids

CALL TO WORSHIP.   "Come unto me, all ye that labor and are heavy laden, and I will give you rest. Take my yoke upon you, and learn of me; for I am meek and lowly in heart: and ye shall find rest unto your souls." Matt. 11:28-29.

INVOCATION.   Almighty and everlasting God, in whom we live and move and have our being, who hast created us for thyself so that we can find rest only in thee: grant unto us purity of heart and strength of purpose so that no selfish passion may hinder us from knowing thy will and no weakness sway us from doing it and that in thy light we may see light clearly and in thy service find perfect freedom.

OFFERTORY SENTENCE.   "Let the beauty of the Lord our God be upon us: and establish thou the work of our hands upon us; yea, the work of our hands establish thou it." Ps. 90:17.

OFFERTORY PRAYER.   God of all good, who hath rewarded our labors, we acknowledge thankfully thy favor and do now dedicate a share of our material gains to the even more satisfying ministries of the spirit.

PRAYER.   Almighty God, in knowledge of whom standeth our life, awaken within us a worthy sense of thy majesty. Create in our hearts true penitence at the remembrance of thy holiness. Keep constantly in our memory thy graciousness toward us in Christ Jesus.

Go with us into the work of this new week. Bestow upon us strength for our burdens, wisdom of our responsibilities, insight to meet the demands of our time. May the things that command our interest enrich our soul.

We pray for the good estate of this nation and of all nations. Let right triumph over wrong, peace over strife, love over hate. Help us, as we have opportunity, to play our part in bringing in the day of brotherhood and ending the night of wrong.—Robert J. McCracken.

EVENING SERVICE

Topic: Why I Believe in the Sunday School

TEXT: Luke 2:52.

I. Because it is the best way yet devised for us from childhood to learn of the life and teachings of Jesus and the mission and work of the church.

II. Because many persons have prayed for it and worked for it, gathering the best teaching Christians and the best materials they can find, using a period each week for in-depth study of God's Word.

III. Because it has given growing minds a sense of Christian fellowship, the radiance of Christian experience, and the blessings of Christian service that changed their lives.

IV. Because it helps the church in teaching the Christian faith so that when people worship and work through the church they know more about why they are doing this and what our faith offers to the modern world.

V. Because of its great history of service in the study of the Word.

VI. Because it so persuasively opened to me the truths, the power, and the revelation of divine love through Jesus Christ.

VII. Because in it and through it I came to have the fellowship of so many Christian friends.

VIII. Because it gave me the opportunity to know the testimonies and the depths of the heart and mind of so many children, young people, and adults who were learning of the love of God, of his Word, and of the workings of the Holy Spirit.

IX. Because it gave me a searching glimpse of the church through history, ministering especially to the weary and heavy-laden, the deprived, and the oppressed.

X. Because it is one of the best ways of learning and applying the eternal truths God has given us and of reaching out into the community in his name.—Richard K. Morton.

SUNDAY: SEPTEMBER TWELFTH

MORNING SERVICE

Topic: A Fourfold Development
TEXT: Luke 2:52.

This one pertinent verse gives us all we know about the years of Jesus' young manhood, the years of twelve through thirty. Yet they reveal a fourfold development: intellectual, physical, social, and religious. Jesus was not just God *and* man nor God *in* man. He was the God-man. If it were necessary for Jesus to have this fourfold development, how much more so for us.

I. Jesus advanced in wisdom and knowledge. He experienced the learning process. He "learned obedience by the things which he suffered" (Heb. 5:8). He probably learned the carpenter's trade under the tutelage of Joseph. How much more important that we learn, that we improve ourselves mentally, that we sharpen the cutting edge of our acumen, that we read and study about the environment in which we are so deeply enmeshed. And especially do we need to delve into God's revealed truth as found in the Word of God.

II. Jesus advanced in stature, growing from the tiny babe laid gently in a manger to the strong and well-developed specimen of manhood who stepped into the Jordan to be baptized by John. How important it is for us to grow and care for our bodies so as to insure the largest and healthiest life possible. Exercise, proper food, and a healthy mental outlook are vitally necessary. Nor should one take within the body—the temple of the Holy Spirit—that which would destroy and take away the normal body function. This would eliminate drugs and alcoholic drinks from the diet of the Christian.

III. Jesus advanced in favor with man. He was no social recluse, for he loved people immensely. In Cana of Galilee he attended a wedding ceremony. Multitudes attended because of his very presence. One crowd was so big that he had to enter into a boat and speak to them a little way from the shore. The development of the social graces is important to us also. There is no place for the social recluse who shuts himself up in a monastery's four walls.

IV. Jesus advanced in favor with God. The spiritual growth is the most important of all; and if this was necessary for Jesus, how much more so for us. (See II Pet. 3:18.) We need to become "spiritual" Christians and not remain "carnal" ones; we need to feed on the meat of the word and not just the milk of the word. (See I Cor. 3:1–3.) We are to become disciples of Christ, remembering that "disciples" mean "learners."—William W. Stevens.

Illustrations

THE CHRISTIAN'S JOY. A girl who knew Principal Rainy, one of Scotland's great scholars, once remarked that she thought he went to heaven every night because he was so happy every day. This godly man of joyful spirits once used a striking metaphor for the Christian's joy. He said: "Joy is the flag that is flown from the castle of the heart when the King is in residence there."—J. Harold Gwynne.

FATE SPINNERS. Nothing we ever do is in strict, scientific literalness ever wiped out. Could the young but realize how soon they will become walking bundles of habits, they would give more heed to their conduct. We are spinning our own fates for good or evil. Every smallest stroke of virtue or of vice leaves its never so little scar. We are imitators and copiers of our past selves.—William James.

Sermon Suggestions

WHAT THE EPISTLES SAY ABOUT CHRIST. (1) Romans: We are justified in Christ. (2) Corinthians: We are dignified in Christ. (3) Galatians: We are sanctified in Christ. (4) Ephesians and Colossians: We are unified in Christ. (5) Thessalonians: We are glorified in Christ. (6) Timothy: We are qualified in Christ.

(7) Titus: We are purified in Christ. (8) Hebrews: We are magnified in Christ. (9) James: We are amplified in Christ. (10) Peter: We are edified in Christ. (11) Jude: We are fortified in Christ. (12) Revelation: We are beautified in Christ.—A. T. Pierson.

IN THE INTEREST OF TIME. Text: Eph. 5:16. (1) Time as substance. (2) Time as opportunity. (3) Time as judgment. (4) Time as eternity. (See John 3:36.)—Max R. Hickerson.

Worship Aids

CALL TO WORSHIP. "Arise, shine; for thy light is come, and the glory of the Lord is risen upon thee. Lift up thine eyes round about and see." Isa. 60:1, 4.

INVOCATION. Lord God Almighty, holy and eternal Father, who dwellest in the high and lofty place, with him also that is of a humble and contrite spirit: we come before thee, beseeching thee to cleanse us by the grace of thy Holy Spirit, that we may give praise to thee, now and forever.

OFFERTORY SENTENCE. "Give, and it shall be given unto you; good measure, pressed down, and shaken together, and running over." Luke 6:38.

OFFERTORY PRAYER. O God, thou giver of all good gifts, in gratitude we bring our gifts on this day of joyous worship. Refine them, we pray thee, in the mint of thy divine purpose and use them to the end that thy kingdom may come and thy will be done on earth as it is in heaven.

PRAYER. O Lord our heavenly Father, from whom cometh every good and perfect gift and under whose loving care we abide always, we bow before thee as a fellowship of kindred minds to thank thee now, our God, with heart and hands and voices.

We praise thee that thou hast surrounded us with thine infinite goodness, that thou hast continually poured forth thy benefits age after age, and that of thy faithfulness there is no end.

For the beauty of the earth and the bounty it produces for our physical need, for the order and constancy of nature which brings us day and night, summer and winter, seedtime and harvest, for all gifts of thy mercy, we are thankful.

For the power of love that binds us together as families and inspires us to establish our homes, to clothe our children, and to provide food for their growth, and for the resources of mind and strength that enable us to do this, we give thee hearty thanks.

For our work that calls forth the noblest within us, for our country founded on thy precepts of liberty and justice, for our schools that lift us above the plain of ignorance, and for the countless organizations whose purposes are for the welfare and happiness of mankind, we express our profound thanks.

Above all, O God, we praise thee for thy Son Jesus Christ who lives within our hearts, for thy Holy Spirit, who renews, comforts, and inspires our souls, for thy Word that reveals truth to our minds, and for thy church whose prophets, saints, martyrs, and ministers have helped us remain steadfast in our faith. For all these channels through which our spiritual needs are met, we raise our voices in humble thanks.

Let the memory of thy goodness fill our hearts with joy and gratitude, and may our lives be an acceptable expression of our thankfulness now and in all days to come.—Donald A. Wenstrom.

EVENING SERVICE

Topic: The Transforming Touch
TEXT: Mark 14:22.

The Christian world remembers the upper room, the low table furnished with cup and loaf, the tender comradeship, and the supper which became a sacrament. All this needs no comment.

I. Consider how whatever Jesus touched was thereafter transformed. He touched wood and tools in the Nazareth carpentry shop and thereby made every workman's tool an instrument of the spirit. He touched a Roman coin and taught the world the proper distribution of loyalties. He touched the sick and healed them. He touched bread and the cup and made them thereafter sacramental.

II. Consider all his unrecorded acts of use and friendship, all the nameless seekers who reached their hands toward his and found therein their help. The secret of it? A divine wisdom and a generosity of power so poured out that even his touch became a gesture of the divine. How much this sad world needs that healing and transforming touch. Jesus wished to share it with all his friends. They can ask from him no more blessed gift.—Gaius Glenn Atkins.

SUNDAY: SEPTEMBER NINETEENTH

MORNING SERVICE

Topic: The Glory of the Ministry
SCRIPTURE: John 20:19–24.

I. It seems certain that the Father sent the Son into the world with *a message to proclaim and a mission to perform.* In like manner Christ sends us into the world. The message is the glad tidings of God's redeeming love in Jesus Christ for all people in all circumstances at all times in all the world. It is God's deed for man's need.

(a) The message is the message of redemption. The message is his; the proclamation must be ours. The Christian ministry must know the difference between the compulsion of having to say something on the one hand and the importance of having something to say on the other hand.

(1) It is the gospel we proclaim. We

sometimes seek new words to express ageless truths, though we always come back to the fact that it is "God's good news" which we proclaim.

(2) The gospel is both real and relevant. It is real if it is biblically based, Christ-centered, and historically verified. It is real if it seeks more to "experience God" than to "explain God." The reality of science is discovered through research and experiment, while the reality of religion comes through revelation and experience. The fruits of the faith are impossible without the roots of the faith. The gospel is relevant when it is allowèd to speak to contemporary man. We do not make the gospel relevant; it is relevant when we discover it is real. Reality precedes relevance; relevance is assured if we give reality a chance to work. The changeless Word of God must be communicated in the changing language of man.

(b) The mission is the mission of reconciliation. (1) In its initial sense reconciliation is a one-way street. Man has alienated himself from God, not God from man. Man has rebelled against God, not God against man. God loves the world; the world does not love God. The minister finds himself unrelentingly in the role of reconciler, attempting by God's grace and through the power of the Holy Spirit to reconcile man to God.

(2) The minister is the reconciler between man and God and also between man and his fellow man. In this second relationship reconciliation becomes a two-way street. The task of the reconciler between man and man is to reconcile each man to God, for when any two persons are close enough to touch the feet of the Christ they are close enough to touch each other.

(3) Reconciliation involves both identification and involvement, identification with man in redemptive love and involvement with man in his needs, his heartache, and his hunger.

(4) Reconciliation demands that we help man see himself as he really is and to see God's love as it really is. The reconciler must listen carefully to man's cry, "O that my eyes were opened," and also to God's pleading in Christ, "Come unto me, all ye that labour and are heavy laden, and I will give you rest."

II. The Father sent the Son into the world with *a passion and a power*. (a) When Jesus looked on the multitudes, either as individuals or en masse, he looked upon them with compassion. Whether as individuals or en masse, they were always persons, and he saw them as persons. Demons trembled before him and begged him to send them away from him, but men possessed with demons knew the full force of his love and his cleansing power. Sin was always his enemy, and with the last drop of his blood he fought and conquered.

(b) Our blessed Lord sends us not only with a passion but also with a power to communicate this redemptive love to others. Without this power we could not do it, and without our consent God's power will not do it.

III. The Father sent the Son into the world with *a commission and a commitment*. The order was from God. It bore the print of his own finger. It was delivered to the Son firsthand, and it comes to us in the same manner.

(a) The commission is a command, and the command is to "make disciples." It is not an elective; it is not one among many delightful alternatives. Of course, we have our freedom of choice, and this freedom makes possible our denial of all he asks us to do, and some of us do rebel in this way. But the commission remains a command, and in the face of a command there are only two alternatives: obedience or disobedience. And I must make my own choice of one of these alternatives.

(b) The commission is his to give, and he gives it. The commitment is ours, and it is up to us to make it. Commitment becomes a response to God's prevenient grace in Christ, to God's divine call to us, to God's divine command. "Whom shall I send, and who will go for us?" is still God's divine announcement to the world. "Here am

I, Lord. Send me." This remains man's response and responsibility.—Kenneth W. Copeland.

Illustrations

EXPRESSING ALIVENESS. Giving is the highest expression of potency. In the very act of giving I experience my strength, my wealth, my power. This experience of heightened vitality and potency fills me with joy. I experience myself as overflowing, spending, alive, hence as joyous. Giving is more joyous than receiving, not because it is deprivation but because in the act of giving lies the expression of my aliveness.—Erich Fromm.

AT THE CENTER. I am a man sent from God to urge people to put Christ in the center of their relationships.—John Wesley.

Sermon Suggestions

GOD'S ETERNAL PURPOSE. Scripture: Eph. 3:1–19. (1) God's eternal purpose made known by revelation. (See v. 3.) (2) God's eternal purpose made known by writings. (See v. 4.) (3) God's eternal purpose made known by preaching. (See vv. 8–9.) (4) God's eternal purpose made known through the church. (See v. 10.) (5) Knowledge of God's eternal purpose should generate confidence. (See v. 13.) —Ard Hoven.

IS THERE ANYTHING RIGHT WITH THE CHURCH? (1) The church has never lost its interest in the individual. (2) The church never allows itself to become localized. (3) The church uses its prosperity for the good of society.—Carl J. Sanders.

Worship Aids

CALL TO WORSHIP. "Delight thyself also in the Lord; and he shall give thee the desires of thine heart. Commit thy way unto the Lord; trust also in him; and he shall bring it to pass." Ps. 37: 4–5.

INVOCATION. Our heavenly Father, who by thy love hast made us, and through thy love has kept us, and in thy love wouldst make us perfect: we humbly confess that we have not loved thee with all our heart and soul and mind and strength and that we have not loved one another as Christ hath loved us. Thy life is within our souls, but our selfishness has hindered thee. We have not lived by faith. We have resisted thy spirit. We have neglected thine inspirations. Forgive what we have been; help us to amend what we are; and in thy spirit direct what we shall be; that thou mayest come into the full glory of thy creation in us and in all men.

OFFERTORY SENTENCE. "If there be first a willing mind, it is accepted according to that which a man hath, and not according to that which he hath not." II Cor. 8:12.

OFFERTORY PRAYER. O God, in whose sight a contrite heart is more than whole burnt offerings: help us with these our gifts to dedicate ourselves, body, soul, and spirit, unto thee, which is our reasonable service.

PRAYER. Spirit of God, we who rejoice in the Christ who died for us would remember that thou hast committed unto us the word of reconciliation. Send us forth as laborers in thy harvest, free from reluctance or shame, to tell others of the Savior. To all who have been at war with themselves and thee, enable us to speak thy word of peace. To dying men, help us to bring thy word of life; to hate-filled men, thy word of love; to despairing men, thy word of hope; to sorrowing men, thy word of comfort; to sinful men, thy word of salvation. Kindle within our hearts fires of compassion for our brothers and sisters who are lost to Christ. May they come to share in his victory and to live in constant rejoicing through his triumph. We ask it in the name of him who faced his cross with faith and who triumphed over death that we might know his victory, even Jesus Christ our Lord.—Marion C. Allen.

EVENING SERVICE

Topic: Encouragement in Prayer
SCRIPTURE: Gen. 18:20–33.

The scripture records the account of Abraham's intercession in behalf of the sparing of the wicked cities of Sodom and Gomorrah.

I. *The subject of his intercession.* He did not pray only for the rescue of Lot and his family from the wicked cities but for the salvation of the cities themselves. He petitioned God to "spare the place" if there could be found fifty righteous people there. He evidenced a tender sympathy and sincere concern for the people living in the wicked cities. He was not one to shut his eyes to the misery of the folk living there and say they deserved it. Naturally he was concerned about his nephew Lot and his family, but his concern went beyond them to the other residents of the cities.

II. *The spirit of his intercession.* (a) Notice *a holy boldness.* "Abraham drew near" (v. 23). This was not only locally but also spiritually. He knew by experience that when one draws near to God he will draw near also. The expression "Abraham drew near" indicated an earnestness of entreaty and faith. This kind of earnestness should be found in the believer's prayer when interceding in behalf of others. (See Heb. 4:16; 10:22.)

(b) Notice in Abraham's prayer the expression of *reverent humility.* No less than three times in his prayer Abraham indicates his own unworthiness. (See vv. 27, 30–32.) Though we are invited to come boldly before the Lord, we must not come into his presence depending upon any merit or righteousness of our own. (See Jas. 4:6.)

(c) Abraham's praying evidenced *fervent importunity.* He asked more of the Lord in each prayer. He implored the Lord to spare the cities if there could be found fifty righteous ones there. Then he asked the Lord to spare the cities if there would be forty-five righteous, then forty, then thirty, then twenty, and finally ten. Here is a picture of persistent demand, incessant insistence, and urgency.

III. *The success of his intercession.* Abraham received from God all that he asked. He ceased asking before God ceased giving. God only ceased giving when Abraham ceased asking.—C. Reuben Anderson.

SUNDAY: SEPTEMBER TWENTY-SIXTH

MORNING SERVICE

Topic: God's Great Design
TEXT: II Tim. 1:9.

What is God's great design which it is so important to see and by which we need to live?

I. If we are to understand God's great design it is necessary that we understand the tremendous words found in the Genesis story of creation: "God created man in his own image." What does this mean?

(a) It does not mean that man is or can be his own God. It is no justifica-

tion for man's self-sufficiency or self-glorification.

(b) It does mean that man is different from the animals. It does mean that man is an embodied soul. It does mean that the only proper life for a human being is "life in God," that is, in harmony with his purposes and spirit. It does mean awareness of and obedience to the higher law. It does mean that no man can really be at peace with himself, or as the psychologist would say, "an integrated personality," until he is at peace with God.

II. If we are to understand God's

great design we must look steadfastly at Christ and come to terms with him, intellectually and spiritually. He is the world's greatest teacher and ours. He is every man's example and the example for each one of us to follow. He is the Savior every sinner needs and each one of us needs. He is the sovereign Lord of all men and of your soul and mine. He is the Christ. He is the embodiment of God's design, the world's hope and our hope. We must come to terms with him.

III. If we are to understand God's great design we must understand discipleship with this Christ. The most complete and adequate response to God is through Christ. He is the way, the truth, and the life.

(a) As people open their lives to God through the revelation of our Lord and Savior, they become united with one another in a unique and special way. Peter, James, and John found themselves united to one another in a great fellowship of witnessing and service. So have all who have accepted Christ down through the centuries and today.

(b) All who come to God through Christ are members of the discipleship, and the discipleship is the Christian church. Every great teacher and leader has his followers, and the greatest ones make such an impression that for centuries there are schools of thought and action which bear their names. The discipleship of Jesus has some of these same characteristics, but it is also unique.

(c) It is unique in that the constraining center of the fellowship is not so much a set of ideas as a person. You remember the words of St. Paul to Timothy, "I know whom I have believed." Notice he did not say and emphasize, "I know what I believe." Paul could have said that, but he chose to speak of and emphasize something different.

(d) Ours is not a religion which is centered only about certain great ideas. It is also a religion which is centered about a person, the greatest and most unique person who ever lived, Jesus Christ. All those who accept Christ as their Lord and Savior and really place upon him their trust and their love find themselves united with one another in a great and unique fellowship. This fellowship, this discipleship, is the church. We must understand this as a very vital part of God's great design.

IV. A fourth aspect of God's great design is the transformation of the whole human family through the faithful and ever-widening witness of the church.

(a) The church of Christian discipleship by its very nature and purpose is not exclusive but inclusive in its love and outreach. It is not a secret society nor an exclusive club. It is a disciplined fellowship of believers and workers, but its doors are wide open to all, regardless of class, race, or nationality. Its underlying faith is that all men are potential sons of God, and its passion is to bring every individual in every part of the world and in every generation to know the fullness of God's love and salvation in Christ. The church is inevitably a great missionary society. It cannot have Christ in a selfish way.

(b) The church reaches also into every area and aspect of human need, both individual and social. The gospel has both its individual and social aspects, and to ignore either one or the other is to imperil the Christian witness. Christ taught us to pray: "Thy kingdom come. Thy will be done in earth, as it is in heaven." No prayer could be more specific and no obligation greater.

(c) As Christians we must pray and work for a better world, a world fashioned according to the intention of God as revealed in the teachings and spirit of Jesus. Because God himself is tremendously in earnest about poor housing conditions, neglect of children, race prejudice, economic and social injustice, and war, so must we as the disciples of Christ be tremendously concerned about them.—Frederick A. Roblee.

Illustration

TWO IMPRESSIONS. After a few days at a hotel, a man was checking out. He had been a difficult guest. As he was turning to go after paying his bill, the desk clerk said, "Sir, you are leaving something behind." "What am I leaving behind?" asked the man. "A bad impression," replied the clerk.

Thomas Cook, one-time principal of Cliff College, England, was a great evangelist and a living exponent of the holy life. He was scheduled to take a weekend appointment in a distant town. The maid in the home in which he was to stay was sent to the butcher's to get the meat for the Sunday dinner. She said to the butcher, "My goodness, you would think with all the fuss they are making at our house that Jesus Christ was coming." A day or two later the maid was again in the shop. "You know what I said about Jesus Christ coming to our house? Well, he came."—J. C. Lowson.

Sermon Suggestions

IS THE GOLDEN RULE ENOUGH? Text: Matt. 7:12. The golden rule is a good beginning, but it is not the whole gospel and is not enough on which to base one's whole life. (1) There is no content in it. (2) There is no grace in it. (3) There is no power in it.—Donald B. Strobe.

THE SEVEN DEADLY VIRTUES. (1) Childishness. (2) Mental timidity. (3) Dullness. (4) Respectability. (5) Sentimentality. (6) Censoriousness. (7) Depression of spirit or false piety.—Dorothy L. Sayers.

Worship Aids

CALL TO WORSHIP. "Bless the Lord, O my soul: and all that is with me, bless his holy name." Ps. 103:1.

INVOCATION. As we begin another day, most gracious Father, make us to know that we never drift out of thy love and care. Faces may change, conditions may alter, but thou art never so near to us as when we need thee most.

OFFERTORY SENTENCE. "Go, and sell that thou hast, and give to the poor, and thou shalt have treasure in heaven: and come and follow me." Matt. 19:21.

OFFERTORY PRAYER. O Lord, who hast given us the privilege of life, help us to magnify eternal values and to show forth by our lives and our tithes the Christ, whom to know aright is life eternal.

PRAYER. Almighty God, our heavenly Father, we thank thee for thy fatherly love. Thou art aware of all that we are and all that we might be. Thou dost know our needs before we express them. Knowing what we may be, thou dost stir us awake in order that we may become what thou hast always intended.

May thy blessing be upon us this day as we gather in this sacred assembly. Here may we put aside the worries and the fretful cares and personal anxieties of our daily life. Here may we remind ourselves of thy wonderful goodness which is our sure help, of thy wonderful love which is our consolation and comfort, or thy promised presence which means that we need never walk alone. May we go from this place fortified in spirit, the better able to confront the anxieties and cares and concerns that are so much a part of every day in our life.

Especially wilt thou so reveal thyself to us that it may be for us a daily challenge to fashion our lives after thy will and to fashion our world after the pattern of thy character. May we be a voice for the things that belong to thy truth, and through our lives may the voiceless decencies of life find expression.—Lowell M. Atkinson.

EVENING SERVICE

Topic: Running a Good Race

TEXT: Heb. 12:1-2 (RSV).

Four things concerning the Christian race are suggested in these verses.

I. *The incentive for running the race:* "since we are surrounded by so great a cloud of witnesses." These included those in the roll call of the faithful in the preceding chapter. For us there are many others including thousands of Christian martyrs through the centuries. Then there are our forefathers, our parents, grandparents, and others. They are in the stands looking down on us as we run our race.

II. *Preparation for the race.* We would lay aside anything that will hinder or handicap us in running the Christian race. This will include "sin which clings so closely" to us or "every sin to which we cling" (NEB).

III. *The perseverance or determination* (TEV) *with which we run the race.* The winner of the race is not always the swiftest. Persistence or determination is as important a factor in running the Christian race as it is for the 440 or the 880. Notice also "the race that is set before us" or "the race for which we are entered" (NEB). Each one has his own distinctive race to run.

IV. *The goal of the race:* "looking to Jesus." Some Grecian races had a piece of statuary at the end of the course. The winner was the one who first reached that statuary. This may provide the background for the statement by the author of Hebrews. Jesus is the goal of the Christian race. We are to fix our eyes on him and measure our lives by his.—T. B. Maston.

SUNDAY: OCTOBER THIRD

MORNING SERVICE

Topic: Belonging to Christ and Our Brother (World Communion Sunday)
SCRIPTURE: Eph. 4:1-6 (NEB).

I. Today is World Communion Sunday, one of those very special days in the life of the Christian church. For many years this unified observance of our Lord's Supper has been part of the Christian calendar. As this day dawns the first communicants are found in the Fiji Islands and New Zealand, the last in the farthest outposts of Alaska. Christians in the Arctic and Antarctica also are involved in this experience. It is interdenominational and international in its scope, a spiritual fellowship transcending all barriers. We become part of a great company, a host of witnesses, confessing the lordship of Christ and the kinship of our neighbor.

(a) We might call it the "Two Loyalties Sunday," the time for affirming again our dual allegiance, which is to gain our allegiance, which is to Christ and to our brother. We belong to him; we belong to each other. Where individuals forget either part of this allegiance, they miss the full meaning of Christianity.

(b) Some people may say, "Lord, Lord," but unless they do among men the deeds he commanded they are not his disciples. Others may embrace mankind and human need, but unless they also confess the sovereignty of Christ they offer their fellows but "half a loaf," a fraction of what they are meant to give. One's Christian commitment yokes him unmistakably to Christ by faith and his neighbor by love.

II. Our relationship with Christ is truly a matter of faith. No one need apologize for that. (a) By faith we say and mean things like these: Christ is lord of life; he is the flesh-and-blood expression of God; he is the Savior or the healer of mankind. These affirmations become translated into our everyday experience in many ways. Christ's lordship signifies the authority we recognize in his teachings, the wisdom we discover in his behavior, the blessings we realize in following him. As the flesh-and-blood expression of God, Christ becomes for us the interpreter of all that is high and holy. He discloses to our human minds the momentous truth that God is love as well as justice and that God is mercy as well as judgment. Our confession that Christ is savior leads us to the heights of personal fulfillment. Whatever we have been that is unworthy, we need not be henceforth. Whatever blemishes there are to our characters, whatever failures we have known, can be healed, forgiven, and left behind. These are testimonies of faith and spiritual experience. These are the understandings we hold as we meet at this communion table.

(b) Christ tells us as much about the nature of God as we need to know or are capable of knowing. His disclosure of God was and is a winsome thing. Like a magnet, Christ drew men to his side. Then he pointed them to God. He called himself "the way," meaning the direct avenue or the primary approach to spiritual reality. "No one comes to the Father, but by me," he said. When by faith we take Christ at his word we embark upon a relationship that is of enduring consequence "not for the years of time alone but for eternity."

(c) "Now you belong to him," wrote the apostle Paul to new converts at Rome. Elsewhere Paul taught, "You are not your own; you were bought with a price." This sense of belonging to another, belonging to Christ, was vividly explained by Martin Luther when he said, "If you knock on my heart and ask, 'Who lives here?' I answer, 'Once upon a time a man named Martin Luther lived here, but he has moved out and Christ now liveth in me.'"

(d) There is a sense in which Christ must dwell in our hearts richly, if we are to lay claim to the title Christian. The symbols shared at our communion table dramatize this desire, for we take into our bodies tokens of Christ's own body. We say by this action that he is a real part of us. Around the world today that kind of witness is being given as congregations take the cup and bread in remembrance of him.

III. As surely as World Communion

Sunday reminds us that we belong to Christ by faith, it tells us also that we belong to each other by love.

(a) How much we belong to each other is becoming clearer all the time. More and more we are recognizing our interdependence as human beings—economically, socially, spiritually. For example, the black man needs the white man, but the reverse is equally true. In a world where black and brown and yellow add up to more than white, it is the sheerest folly which assumes that any one race can "go it alone."

(b) The extension of hands, injured and otherwise, between the peoples of the world—yes, even the peoples of our own community—is one of our urgent needs today. Gestures of forgiveness, love, and reconciliation certainly are implied by World Communion Sunday. These gestures become real as you and I make them a priority concern upon leaving this table today.

(c) Dietrich Bonhoeffer observed that "in normal life we hardly realize how much more we receive than we give . . . it is so easy to overestimate the importance of our own achievements compared with what we owe to the help of others." We belong to each other. We might even go so far as to say that our "center" is outside of ourselves. If it is not, then we qualify for Benjamin Franklin's indictment about the man wrapped up in himself. Such a man, said Franklin, "makes a very small package."

(d) There is one God and Father of all men; he is lord of all. That automatically makes us brothers of all men. We are inescapably related each to the other. Our business is "to preserve the unity" which brotherhood implies and to live by love as the family of God upon the earth. Let this be our expressed intention and desire as we take the bread and cup of communion on this special day.—John H. Townsend.

Illustrations

GIFT OF GRACE. It is easily forgotten

that the fellowship of Christian brethren is a gift of grace, a gift of the kingdom of God that any day may be taken from us, that the time that separates us from utter loneliness may be brief indeed. Therefore, let him who until now has had the privilege of living a common Christian life with other Christians praise God's grace from the bottom of his heart. Let him thank God on his knees and declare: it is grace, nothing but grace, that we are allowed to live in community with Christian brethren.— Dietrich Bonhoeffer.

OF ONE BLOOD.   Asibi, a West African, contracted yellow fever. Because of his illness he was able to supply the specimen of blood by which vaccine for yellow fever was eventually derived. The original strain of virus obtained from a humble man has gone from laboratory to laboratory, offering immunity to millions of people in every land. Through the creative imagination of science, the blood of one man in West Africa has been made to serve people all over the world.—T. Henry Holloway.

Sermon Suggestion

PEACE AND GOOD WILL.   Text: Luke 2:14. (1) Peace depends not upon externalities but upon an inner spirit in the hearts of men. (2) This good will comes from God and is the recognition of our responsibility to his will and the obligation of having his spirit. Only so can we truly glorify God. (3) In the life and teachings of Jesus we learn to glorify God and so create the good will which is the basis of peace.—L. Wendell Fifield, Jr.

Worship Aids

CALL TO WORSHIP.   "The cup of blessing which we bless, is not the communion of the blood of Christ? The bread which we break, is not the communion of the body of Christ? For we being many are one bread, and one body: for we are all partakers of that one bread." I Cor. 10:16–17.

INVOCATION.   Eternal God our Father, who art from everlasting, thou hast made us and not we ourselves. Thou hast set us never far from thee, that we, thy children, may learn the ways of freedom and choose thee with all our hearts. Grant us now thy Holy Spirit, that confident in prayer, we may worship thee with gladness, and become as little children before thee.

OFFERTORY SENTENCE.   "As we have therefore opportunity, let us do good unto all men, especially unto them who are of the household of faith." Gal. 6:10.

OFFERTORY PRAYER.   O thou who art the Father of all, may we live as thy children and brothers of all whom thou hast made to dwell upon the face of the earth that thy kindness may be born in our hearts.

PRAYER.   Almighty God, who from the beginning hath sought, without ceasing, to gather to thyself a chosen race, a royal priesthood, a holy nation, to be thine own people: we praise thee for sending thy Son, Jesus Christ, into thy world to be the firstborn of the new creation, the one in whom all things hold together and the head of thy body, the church.

We praise thee for the church gathered, gathering yet, under the lordship of Christ. For all doxologies, all confessions, all petitions, all proclamations, all tithes and offerings, and all benedictions celebrated by thy people under thy loving scrutiny, we lift to thee our thanksgiving.

We praise thee for the church dispersed, dispersing yet, as ministers of Christ. For all vocations, all avocations, used as vehicles of thy justice and love in the world which thou dost love, we glorify thee.

We rejoice because thou dost create, comprehend, and command diversities of servanthood within the one body of Christ; but we repent of the thoughts, words, and deeds wherein we have allowed these diversities to divide us. Truly thy body, thy church, is wounded by our transgressions, bruised by our iniquities.

Have mercy on us, O God, according to thy steadfast love. According to thy abundant mercy heal our divisions for the sake of thy world in which thou dost place us as thy ministering servants. Prosper all who seek with thee the healing of thy broken body. Cause thy church under the lordship of Christ to be manifest to thy world as the people of one Lord, one faith, one baptism, one God and Father of us all.

EVENING SERVICE

Topic: The Meaning of Reconciliation
SCRIPTURE: II Cor. 5:16—6:2.

Reconciliation is a change of relationship between God and man based on the changed status of man through the redemptive work of Christ. I suggest three aspects of this change.

I. A reconciliation is also a reconciliation of persons between whom there has existed a state of enmity. The Greek denotes an "exchange" to persons, suggests an exchange from enmity to fellowship. Reconciliation is, therefore, God exercising grace toward man who is in enmity because of sin. This changed relationship is possible only because of the changed status of man. God is never said to be reconciled to man but man to God since it is man's sinfulness which creates the enmity.

II. There is also a reconciliation of conditions so that a basis of the enmity relationship is removed and a complete basis of fellowship is established. The Greek word *apokalallasso* denotes a "movement out of" and suggests that since man is redeemed through the righteousness of Christ he is redeemed out of his condition of unrighteousness and thus reconciled to God in the new relationship.

III. There is also the idea of reconciliation arising out of the change in man induced by the action of God.

(a) The Greek word *kalallage* suggests that man is not reconciled merely because his relationship has changed but because God has changed him through Jesus Christ so that he can be reconciled.

(b) Reconciliation arises, therefore, out of God through Christ to man, so that not only may the barriers to fellowship existing in sinful man be removed but the positive basis for fellowship may be established through the righteousness of Christ imputed to man.

(c) When Paul talks about man's being reconciled to God he means a transaction in which God acts. God is not passive in the matter. It is not a transaction in which man does all that is done.—Orvind M. Dangeau in *Baptist and Reflector*.

SUNDAY: OCTOBER TENTH

MORNING SERVICE

Topic: A Theology of Christian Worship
TEXT: John 4:24.

I. *What is worship?* (a) We might better understand what worship is if we look at some of the things it is *not*.

(1) *Worship is not a corporate experience of human feelings alone.* Certainly feelings are involved, but when we try to keep worship on the level of human feelings alone, we achieve little more than humanistic self-examination or mutual autosuggestion and self-help. These have merit and value for human growth, but they do not in any sense meet the Isaiah pattern where God is central.

(2) *Worship is not the rigid structure*

of rutted ritualistic practices participated in by human robots. It is easy for us to make the form most important, the words of ritual sacredly engraved in our procedures. When we make literal use of these words, phrases, prayers, and readings in the particular form we have set up as the only form possible worship, we have made an idol of liturgy and have blocked the true worship of God which puts God at the center of it all.

(3) *Worship cannot be fully defined as unstructured ramblings of the mind.* The psychoanalyst has a contribution to make to the person who needs to dig into his past to retrieve and understand that experience which may well be forcing him into emotional bankruptcy in the present. But worship can never be limited to this kind of self-analysis, else it becomes atheistic in orientation and produces little more than a kind of enjoyment of newly found self-understanding. To be authentic Christian worship, "the worshiper must center his mind upon God, and with alertness and receptivity, enter personally into all the acts of worship in the service" (Georgia Harkness).

(b) Perhaps we can best understand what is meant by worship by culling a few characteristics from a series of definitions provided by many different writers in the field of prayer and worship.

(1) *Worship is the vision of God.* "It takes place when the attention of the whole self is directed to the nature and power of God for his own sake, and when this holy one is honored and celebrated as the center of the universe, the one in all is many, and the center of one's spiritual gravity" (Waldo Beach).

(2) *Worship is man endeavoring to confront God.* "It is man humbly but courageously trying to think God's thoughts after him; it is man trying to get some clear insight into God's will for his life" (Harold A. Bosley).

(3) *Worship is a means of sensing the reality of God.* Its purpose is "to provide special atmosphere in which it is more possible to sense the reality of the living God. It is much easier to feel God's presence and the reality of religious verities in a setting which intensifies our fragile perceptions, increases our spiritual sensitivities." (James A. Pike.)

(4) In essence these various definitions all aim at one idea, and that is the one which Jesus spoke of in the text. He was telling us that worship for Christians must be God-centered, Spirit-filled, and Christ-oriented.

II. *Why we worship.* (a) *We worship because we sense a need for that which worship can bring into our lives of reverence, inspiration, and strength in the spiritual realm.* Writing particularly about the sacraments, Ben Garrison points out that "man's sacramental starting point is his own need."

(b) *We worship because we share the human need for cleansing.* Isaiah in the temple was expressing what every honest person must feel when he finds himself consciously aware of the presence of God. He felt it necessary to confess his own sins and point out his own unworthiness to be in God's presence.

(c) *Worship ministers to our need for wholeness.* None of us is free from the threat to our own personhood, our own self-consciousness as a person among persons in the world. We seek fulfillment of ourselves, and yet so often run away from that fulfillment. The need for man to recover his wholeness has been historically found in Christian theology in the doctrine and experience of forgiveness. Thus Isaiah entered the temple, acknowledged his sin, found the acceptance of God who loved him, and acknowledged his humanity in spite of his sins.

(d) *Worship ministers to our need for a "presence received in Christ."* Isaiah beheld the presence of God and recalled it mystically in the various figures he saw in the temple. In the Christian era we know God's presence as revealed in his Son. Man needs the assurance that he is not alone, that there is a divine dimension which introduces strength beyond his own human limitations, and that there is one whose power is the ultimate power and whose purpose will in the end be fulfilled.

(e) *Worship helps meet our need for community.* We need each other, whether or not we admit it. My life is incomplete without you. God has created us as children in his family. When one is in need, none can be fully satisfied. When one is hungry, none is fully fed. When one is alienated, none is fully in community. Worship offers a path toward the *common-unity* which we can share as persons of wholeness, redeemed by God's love, strengthened and nurtured by our awareness of God's presence.

(f) *Worship helps meet our need for celebration.* We do need to celebrate! In worship we celebrate an Event, or more aptly, *the Event.* In the sacrament of the Lord's Supper, we are celebrating God's coming to us in Christ, and remembering the sacrifice involved by him on our behalf.

(g) *Worship is a duty we owe to God.* "On our side, worship is the first duty we owe to God, the fulfillment of our human greatness, the activity which marks us off from the lower creatures. On God's side, worship is a means of grace, an effective channel whereby he communicates himself to us that we may grow in the knowledge of his love and the understanding of his will." (Leonard Griffith.)

(h) *We worship because it enables us to share in a liturgical reenactment of the drama of human redemption.* We are not onlookers at a stage play where others are the active participants. Here there can be no one offstage for the drama, no seat holders in the loge, no standees in the second balcony. All are a part of the "group of players" who reenact the drama.

(i) *We worship because it is crucial to all of life,* indeed crucial to our very survival as a race. It is difficult sometimes in our day, when so many are indifferent toward the need for worship and some even contemptuous about it, for us to sense how deeply worship infiltrates our lives and living with a quality which we dare not lose as a person and a society of persons.

III. *What worship does.* (a) *Worship should enable us each week to rediscover our identity as persons who are related to God the heavenly Father.* To find ourselves and regain wholeness is to find a renewal of our covenant with God. Thus are we prepared for the daily demands of life in our turbulent world.

(b) *Worship offers us a regular opportunity for the review and renewing of spiritual dynamic.* The invitation to Holy Communion points this up: "Ye that do truly and earnestly repent of your sins and are in love and charity with your neighbors, and intend to lead a new life, following the commandments of God, and walking from henceforth in his holy ways: draw near with faith, and take this holy sacrament to your comfort, and make your humble confession to Almighty God." Here is the opportunity for each of us to go through the Isaiah pattern of worship—awe before God, confession of sin, desire to serve our brothers in God's name, forgiveness of sin, acceptance by the Father, and rededication to the task of Christian service.

(c) *In worship we are enabled to see life in God's perspective* as man has best been able to discover what that perspective is. We need to get away from our workaday world at times to look at where we are and what we are doing there. Worship gives us the chance to view life in the conscious presence of God in a way that we seldom find elsewhere. Worship in the Christian pattern calls us to compare our designs for living with those which God gave Moses on Sinai and those he gave Jesus on the mount from whence came the world's greatest sermon.

(d) *Worship enables life to be more attuned to God through the illumination of life in Christ.* What here may appear to be mixed metaphors actually are correctly found together—to be attuned is to be in harmony. To be in harmony is to have been exposed to the disciplines, the knowledge, and provided the instrument for expressing that harmony. We are illuminated in our minds, find strength to discipline our lives, and emerge to share in providing harmony in the life of God's world and God's people. This affects all of our life resources. For it finds our mind broadened, our emotions stirred, our character developed, and our spirit deepened.—Hoover Rupert.

Illustration

AT WORSHIP. There is nothing more illuminating, more ennobling, than to be one of a company of people who have come together in order to free their spirit from entangling personal bonds, quiet their souls by silence, release their aspiration by music and poetry, concentrate their mind on spoken wisdom, open their heart to all that is good, true, and beautiful, thus to tune themselves to God and to come into touch with Jesus Christ.—Muriel Lester.

Sermon Suggestion

THE SAVING WORK OF CHRIST. He saves with a threefold shepherding. (1) The good shepherd with the cross. (See John 10:11.) (2) The great shepherd with the crook. (See Ps. 23; Heb. 13:20.) (3) The chief shepherd with the crown. (See I Pet. 5:4.)

Worship Aids

CALL TO WORSHIP. "O come, let us sing unto the Lord: let us make a joyful noise to the rock of our salvation. Let us come before his presence with thanksgiving, and make a joyful noise unto him with psalms." Ps. 95:1-2.

INVOCATION. Heavenly Father, we come before thee in trembling because we are conscious of our many sins; yet boldly because we know that thou dost love us. Forgive us our sins, and help us to become more worthy of thy goodness and love. May we gain that strength

from communion with thee which will enable us to walk humbly and righteously before thee and uprightly before the world, manifesting in life's every experience that faith and courage which befit thy children.

OFFERTORY SENTENCE. "Every man shall give as he is able, according to the blessing of the Lord thy God which he hath given thee." Deut. 16:17.

OFFERTORY PRAYER. O Lord Jesus Christ, who hast taught us that to whomsoever much is given, of him shall much be required: grant that we, whose lot is cast in this Christian heritage, may strive more earnestly, by our prayers and tithes, by sympathy and study, to hasten the coming of thy kingdom among all peoples of the earth, that as we have entered into the labors of others, so others may enter into ours, to thy honor and glory.

LITANY. Thou, O Lord, who didst call Matthew from the seat of custom and fishermen from their boats and nets:

Grant us grace to accept thee as our Savior and to follow thee as our Master.

Thou, O Lord, who didst welcome the apostle Peter's confession of faith:

Grant that we may enter into a saving knowledge of thee as the eternal Christ and our Savior.

Thou, O Lord, who didst welcome the inquiry of the Greeks, the faith of the Roman centurion, and the thanks of the grateful Samaritan:

Grant us grace to rise above prejudice for those of different race or creed that our personal relationships may be in harmony with thy love for all mankind.

Thou, O Lord, who didst welcome the support of the disciples who stood by thee in thy trials:

Grant us wisdom to make right decisions at the parting of the ways and courage to pursue the right as thou givest us to see the right.

Thou, O Lord, who didst command

thine apostles James and John to fling away ambition and become as little children.

Deliver us from unseemly ambition and grant us the grace of humility.

Thou, O Lord, who didst declare thyself to the apostle Thomas as the way, the truth, and the life:

Lead us along the path that we should go and bring us to our Father's house in peace.

Thou, O Lord, who didst send forth the seventy disciples through the cities and villages of Galilee to prepare for thy coming:

Use us as ambassadors of good tidings to all whom we meet on life's highway.

Thou, O Lord, who wilt judge men at the last according to their service to the sick and imprisoned, the poor, the hungry, and dispossessed:

Give us grace to serve the needy in thy name, to spend and be spent in the ministry of compassion.—Carl A. Glover.

EVENING SERVICE

Topic: Their Church or Ours? (Laity Sunday)

TEXT: Phil. 1:27.

I. We can learn much about a church member's attitude toward his church by the way he refers to his church in conversation. It is almost always a bad sign when someone speaks of "their" church or "the" church or what "they" are doing down at the church. Usually this means that the speaker, although a member of that church, does not feel himself to be genuinely involved in the work of the church. He feels that he is an "outsider" with no voice in the operation of the affairs of the church while "they" run everything.

II. There are those who speak about "my" church. This possessive pronoun may be used in the good sense as when one identifies himself with his church proudly and lovingly. But it can also be used in a bad sense in which one feels it is his right to be the "foreman" or "boss" and direct the activities of the church as he wants them directed. Sometimes this "bossy" role is assumed by one or more deacons in the church. Sometimes it is the pastor who feels he should operate the church as he does his automobile—by himself. He is the general who gives the orders while the members are the privates who carry them out.

III. The expression "our" church is far better than "their" church or even "my" church. When we say "our" church there is a feeling of unity, a sense of "togetherness," and a feeling of equality as when we talk about the members of our family. Our church is a family. God is our Father and we are all brothers and sisters in Christ. Perhaps if more of us considered the church of which we are members to be "our" church, we would have more love and more harmony than is found in some churches today.—Jack Jones.

SUNDAY: OCTOBER SEVENTEENTH

MORNING SERVICE

Topic: This I Believe

TEXT: II Tim. 1:12.

I. I believe in the Christian way of life because I have seen it work again and again, and I know its redemptive power.

(a) It is the most joyous way. At the heart of the Christian way there is the most radiant personality who ever lived. It is a singing way of poetry. It is a way of sheer beauty. It is a way of goodness overcoming evil.

(b) It is a difficult way, not easy to live. Let no one ever believe that Christian values may come through ease. Perhaps it is good to have a rocking chair, but it is also good to have a walking stick to assist in life's pilgrimage. It is the one way, the straight way, the way of discipline.

(c) It is a way of pilgrimage. The Christian looks at life as a journey. He does not believe that in any stage of his life he can settle down and take his ease in Zion. Thus it means growth. Sometimes there are detours, but we always try to come back to the main track of journeying toward the city of God.

(d) It is a way of great companionship. Think of the ones you meet upon the Christian way. Here are the saints and sages of the Bible. Here's Paul who said, "I know whom I believe." Here are those who through all ages have believed that we are here to make of life a place where God's will shall be done on earth as it is in heaven. Here we meet him who said, "Lo, I am with you alway, even unto the end of the world."

(e) It is a way of handling and dealing with life. It is the way of the Sermon on the Mount, of going the second mile, of returning love for hate, good will for evil, and it is the way of hope and of faith.

(f) The Christian way is centered in the reality of God as a father. Jesus boxed the compass in his belief in God. Sin is being apart from the family of God. Fellowship is belonging to the family of God. Life's fulfillment is doing the will of God. The reason for living is to know God and serve him.

II. I believe in the church of Jesus Christ our Lord. As a scientist would find it difficult to believe in abstract science and must have his laboratory, his tools, and his laws for working, so I have difficulty in understanding abstract Christianity. I believe in Christianity expressed in fellowship and in the life of the church.

(a) I believe in the church and its worship service, using the symbols, the words of faith, the mighty chorus, the organ, the music, the candles, and the cross. I love the service of the church.

(b) I believe in the teaching church and what it can do. We have only touched the fringes of what could be done. We are always hampered by lack of leadership, lack of funds, lack of others who have the vision of what it means to take a group of youngsters and interpret the great eternal truths.

(c) I believe in the baptism, the sacraments, the Bible, the light of truth centered in the life of the church as the way of fellowship in the spirit of Christ.

III. Woven into this belief of the power of the inner spirit is my belief in prayer for my life, my dreams, my hopes, my intentions, my dear ones.

(a) Prayer is an inner cleansing power. It is the joy of thanksgiving. It is the expression of gratitude for life. Prayer is living in communication. Prayer is thinking of the greatness of God who can control and hold the universe so endless and vast, yet so loving that in him we live and move and have our being.

(b) Prayer is service. The real saints of prayer are not so much upon their knees as they are on tiptoe to bring in the new kingdom, to truly be servants in the kingdom of God. My ideal picture of man is the man on tiptoe with arms stretched out to God for new truth, new power, new understanding, a new striving to build the Christlike world.

IV. I believe in love as the greatest thing in the world. Here is the key to life. If you love knowledge you will be a student. If you love truth you will deplore evil and falsehood. If you love your dear ones you will have an inner touchstone to keep you true. If you love your church you worship not as a duty but as a privilege. If you love life you will try to make it Christlike. No wonder Jesus said, "A new commandment I give unto you, that ye love one another" (John 15:12). (See also John 13:35.)—Frank A. Court.

Illustrations

POOR LITTLE HOPE. Our shelves hold many books on the place of faith in science and psychiatry and on the vicissitudes of man's efforts to love and be loved. But when it comes to hope, our shelves are nearly empty, and our scientific journals are silent. *The Encyclopaedia Britannica* devotes many columns to the topic of love and many more to faith. But poor little Hope! She is not even listed!—Karl Menninger in *The Vital Balance*.

CONDUCT AND DOCTRINE. It is worse than useless for Christians to talk about the importance of Christian morality unless they are prepared to take their stand upon the fundamentals of Christian theology.—Dorothy L. Sayers.

Sermon Suggestions

THREE CHEERS. (1) The cheer of forgiveness. (See Matt. 9:2.) (2) The cheer of compansionship. (See Matt. 14:27.) (3) The cheer of victory. (See John 16:33.)—Charles L. Allen.

DESIRE. Text: Ps. 145:16. (1) The desire to be. (2) The desire to belong. (3) The desire to do.—Homer J. R. Elford.

Worship Aids

CALL TO WORSHIP. "The Lord is exalted; for he dwelleth on high: he hath filled Zion with judgment and righteousness. And wisdom and knowledge shall be the stability of thy times, and strength of salvation: the fear of the Lord is his treasure." Isa. 33:5–6.

INVOCATION. Our heavenly Father, we thy humble children invoke thy blessing upon us in this hour of worship. We adore thee, whose nature is compassion, whose presence is joy, whose Word is truth, whose spirit is goodness, whose holiness is beauty, whose will is peace, whose service is perfect freedom, and in knowledge of whom standeth our eternal life. Unto thee be all honor and all glory.

OFFERTORY SENTENCE. "Whatsoever ye would that men should do to you, do ye even so to them: for this is the law and the prophets." Matt. 7:12.

OFFERTORY PRAYER. Almighty God, may we trust more and more in thy kind providence, and may our submission to thy will be revealed in the deep devotion expressed through these gifts we offer in Christ's name.

PRAYER. Our gracious heavenly Father, who sustainest thy creation with wisdom, power, and lovingkindness: we thank thee that thou hast not been unmindful of us. Thy holy loftiness has reached down to us in the loneliness of our erring ways through thy Son Jesus Christ, that we may become conscious of the dignity we have in thee and that we may see the possibilities of our redemption and the renewal of our spirit through thy grace. Thou makest thy loving concern known to us in our weakness, in our sorrows, in our struggles, and in our woes. We are confident in the midst of life's changes that thou hast been our dwelling place in all generations and our refuge in time of trouble. When we doubt thy nearness and ever-present help, O gracious God, forgive our lack of faith and lead us in those ways where, meeting and committing ourselves to thee, we may lose our doubts and conquer our fears. When thou speakest to us through adversity of fortune, through joy or pain, through peace or confusion, may we recognize thy voice and listen. May we heed thy voice that our soul may find peace. When thou seekest to guide us through hitherto unknown and untried ways or even through the familiar paths, O heavenly Father, may we not counter thy wisdom and thy will for us with a proud and rebellious spirit. Teach us from our hearts to say: Thy will be done.—Jesse Jai McNeil.

EVENING SERVICE

Topic: A Debt for All Christians
SCRIPTURE: Rom. 13:8–10.

The main intention of Paul's command is not to give advice on money management but to tell Christians that they have a debt to their fellow men, a debt as binding as the gas bill or mortgage installment or Master Charge balance. Paul's concern is that Christians "owe no one anything *except to love one another.*"

I. For the Christian love is not an optional virtue to be offered when and to whom he pleases, any more than paying his bills is optional. Paul tells believers whom to love, quoting the Lord: "You shall love your neighbor as yourself" (v. 9). And he gives a simple guideline for recognizing what love is not: "Love does no wrong to a neighbor" (v. 10).

II. For Paul love is no tingly feeling of mutual attraction among those who are, at least for a time, highly compatible. Love is a permanent duty to all men, not to be counterfeited by mere profession: "Let love be genuine" (Rom. 12:9). Nor is it incompatible with hatred so long as we "hate what [not who] is evil" (Rom. 12:9). Love is not content to let others take the initiative: "Outdo one another in showing honor" (Rom. 12:10).

III. Love is especially tested in the face of provocation: "Bless those who persecute you; bless and do not curse them" (Rom. 12:14; see also 17–21). Love is not simply to refrain from wronging another, which is hard enough, but to express itself positively: "Contribute to the needs of the saints, practice hospitality" (Rom. 12:13).— *Christianity Today.*

SUNDAY: OCTOBER TWENTY-FOURTH

MORNING SERVICE

Topic: Day of Rest and Gladness
TEXTS: Isa. 58:13; Lev. 23:32.

Modern man doesn't take Sabbath observance seriously. There are no holy days for most Americans. Sunday is the time when we have our big sporting events. It is a time for free relaxation and fun. The world has come of age and all days are secular and the same. Is there something in the Sabbath concept that has value for us?

I. Our scripture speaks of Sabbath as a *delight.* (a) When you read the restraints of the old Jewish Sabbath, you wonder how anyone could be delighted. When I think back to my childhood, my family observed Sunday very rigidly. Those Sundays were not always a delight. I felt suppressed. It was a day to be holy, not human.

(b) Jesus refuted the legalistic reasons for observing the Sabbath, but still the scripture says, "As his custom was on the Sabbath he went to the synagogue." The spiritual disciplines that turned Sabbath observance into a blessing Jesus faithfully followed and fulfilled.

(c) The Sabbath was saying that man should delight in something else besides shopping or commercialism or business. There should be a true delight in realizing he has a soul and in taking time to contemplate on the mysteries of life. Blessed is the man, the scripture seems to say, who look on these opportunities with delight.

II. Sunday should be a time of restoration. The scripture says the Sabbath is for *rest.* The old Hebrew word for Sabbath gets its meaning from a root word which means "stop doing what you are doing."

(a) There is great wisdom in this. We become ill and tired and anxious because we are on a treadmill; we never stop what we are doing. We have no quiet spaces in our week where we can be restored.

(b) Some of those laws on Sunday observance were not made to force people to church. Those laws began in England in the seventh century. Rather than trying to force people to church, they were designed to prevent the enslavement of people by cruel landlords or entrepreneurs.

(c) The Sabbath means stop what you are doing and change the focus of your attention. This is the way of rest. A change in attention means a change in tension. You change the object of your attention, and you discover that the tension in your body or mind is relaxed. You are rested while you are thinking and concentrating on something else.

III. The scriptures speak of the Sabbath as a time of *celebration*. Celebration has many connotations. One is that it is a time to rejoice, to recall the good things of life, and to permit ourselves to praise. Celebration breaks the negative cycle in our lives.

(a) Sunday should be a day of celebration. Not of consuming, not of commercializing. We too often look at life as something to be devoured, used up. We busy our week with taking in more and more things. We need those times of assimilation, of deep understanding, of cherishing the things we confront. So Sunday should be a day of celebration, not consuming alone.

(b) It should be a day to celebrate our faith. Leslie D. Weatherhead was called upon to see an elderly gentleman who was dying and who was very frightened of death. "When," says Weatherhead, "I tried to talk to him as tenderly as I could about God, religion, and the soul, he said very bitterly and brokenly, mumbling as he spoke: 'I have led a very busy life. I have never had time for that sort of thing.' "But," comments Weatherhead, "he had had four thousand Sundays, and Sundays were made expressly for that sort of thing."

(c) So man was not made for the Sabbath, but Sabbath was made for man. Jesus went into the synagogue as was his custom on the Sabbath day. So may we agree that Sunday should be a time of delight, a time of rest, a time of celebration. We're open every Sunday to encourage this in your life and in every man's life.—C. A. McClain, Jr.

Illustrations

TO DELIGHT GOD. The world has a funny idea of religious worship. It does not worship in order to praise God but in order to entertain itself. Religious services have to be made attractive, have to show originality, have to be startling and unexpected. God does not delight in novelty, and if worship is not meant to delight God then why worship?—Dom Hubert van Zeller in *Considerations*.

CELEBRATION. Christian worship is celebration with God. In worship we praise God and give thanks to him for who he is and for what he does; and in worship he continues to reveal who he is and continues to do his work in us for which we praise and give thanks to him. Also Christian worship is celebration with other Christians of all times and places. All Christians are members together of the community of living faith that is the church. In worship we continue to find together new dimensions of the meaning and way of life as members of the community of faith. Christian worship is celebration that relates us to God and to one another, renewing us in the meaning and power of God's victory in Jesus Christ.—*The Celebration of the Gospel*.

Sermon Suggestion

CULTIVATING CHRISTIAN VIRTUES. Scripture: Jas. 5:7–20. (1) Every Christian must be patiently enduring. (See vv. 7–11.) (2) Every Christian must be trustworthy. (See v. 12.) (3) Every Christian should be a person of prayer. (See vv. 13–18.) (4) The true Christian sees his responsibility to his fellow man. (See vv. 19–20.)—James E. Baucom.

Worship Aids

CALL TO WORSHIP. "Sing unto the

Lord, sing psalms unto him. Glory ye in his holy name: let the heart of them rejoice that seek the Lord." Ps. 105:2–3.

INVOCATION. O Lord of light, in this hour of worship in thy house make pure our hearts, and we shall see thee; reveal thyself to us, and we shall love thee. Strengthen our wills, and we shall choose the good from the evil, and day by day manifest in the world the glory and power of thy blessed gospel, which thou hast made known to us through thy Son Jesus Christ.

OFFERTORY SENTENCE. "Every man according as he purposeth in his heart, so let him give; not grudgingly, or of necessity: for God loveth a cheerful giver." II Cor. 9:7.

OFFERTORY PRAYER. Open our eyes that we may see thy goodness, O Father; our hearts that we may be grateful for thy mercies; our lips that we may show forth thy praise; and our hands that we may give these offerings according to thy wish and desire.

PRAYER. O thou eternal God, creator of men and nations, make us into men and nations that fear, honor, love, and serve thee in all ways. When we consider all the ways in which we have dishonored thee and each other, we wonder at thy patience. We wonder that we have been able to tolerate each other. Yet thou hast given us and all thy children the capacities to grow, to develop, to forgive, to forget. We have as many positive qualities as negative, but we fail to nourish the positive.

We acknowledge that we run our lives on flimsy excuses, bad religion, poor relationships, and low purposes. We live from game to game, from meal to meal, from love affair to love affair, from one night of television to the next, and the interims are filled with routine from which we do not know how to escape, and we are afraid to exercise any imagination. Even our pride is so abused that we belittle efforts to lift us up to make us real men, and we refuse to believe that any outside influence is what we need.

O Father, we know that this life has few answers and none are simple. We are afraid of so many things, uneasy around so many people. So many of the things we try to do seem to get out of control and turn out differently from what we wanted. We are disappointed and frustrated, with little prospect except for more of the same.

Put us in touch with reality: teach us individuality and responsibility, independence and mutual affection, when to be aggressive and when patient. Teach us to man our own vessels and not criticize school or church or government for failing to do what we should have done in the first place. Teach us that no institution, not even a congregation, is larger than the vision of its people but that it can be as large as the love and mercy and providence of the Almighty.

Our thoughts and petitions are a jumble as we have come to worship. We are not accustomed to orderly or disciplined thinking; we are not even used to sitting still in serene surroundings. But we ask to be recharged and revitalized today, to be redirected, to be aided in setting our goals, to be given courage where we are weakened with fear. We wait upon thee, thankful, even in our condition, that thy provisions are boundless and fit every situation, and thankful that Jesus Christ came to earth to bring thy will and personality into flower where all could see. At these springs of living water we come to refresh ourselves, believing that we shall not be disappointed.— David V. Pittenger.

EVENING SERVICE

Topic: A Story of Great Faith
SCRIPTURE: Matt. 8:5–13.

I. *The servant's sickness* (v. 6). (a) "Sick of the palsy" is one word in Greek—*paralyitcos,* "paralytic." This is a type of what sin does to humanity; it paralyzes. The sinner is weak, helpless, unable to stand on his feet morally and spiritually and live a godly life. Only the healing power of the Great Physician can give him spiritual life and strength.

(b) The servant was also "grievously tormented"—that is, "suffering great pain" (NASB). Sin brings its torment; it causes deep suffering of body and soul.

II. *The centurion's faith* (vv. 8–9). (a) Moved by compassion, Jesus said, "I will come and heal him." But the centurion remonstrated that he was not worthy to have the Master come under his roof. We must remember that the centurion was an army officer over 100 men and held in high respect. Then he exhibited a remarkable faith: "Just say the word, and my servant will be healed" (v. 8, NASB).

(b) The centurion showed unusual intelligence, as well as faith. He reasoned that since he gave orders to his soldiers and they obeyed, the Master of all things could speak the word and the forces of nature would obey him. Apparently this officer had watched Jesus in Capernaum and listened to his teachings and had decided that he was

indeed the Son of God with divine authority.

III. *The Master's amazement.* (v. 10). (a) When Jesus heard the centurion's words "he marvelled." Only one other time are we told that Jesus marveled, and that was at the unbelief of his own townspeople in Nazareth. (See Mark 6:6.)

(b) Jesus declared that he had not found such great faith on the part of anyone in Israel. Here was a Gentile, a Roman army officer, who probably knew nothing about the true God and the scriptures until he came to Palestine. Yet he had greater faith than the Jews who had attended the synagogue all their lives and listened to the scriptures every Sabbath.

(c) We have a similar situation today. New converts with no Christian background at all often exhibit a purer, simpler faith in God than people who have been brought up in a spiritual church. The new Christians don't know any better than to believe God's Word!— Ralph Earle in *The Preacher's Magazine.*

SUNDAY: OCTOBER THIRTY-FIRST

MORNING SERVICE

Topic: The Question Most Often Asked

Texts: Job 23:3; Matt. 28:19.

The question most often asked is, where can I find God? Job was one of those who asked that question, "Oh, that I knew where I might find him." Is it your question too? It could be, for many know only about God, not God himself. We know him by hearsay. We hear people refer to God. Hardly a day goes by that you do not hear someone say, "God damn." Maybe our parents or church school teachers tried to explain about God. Occasionally we might have prayed, "O God, if there is a God . . ." What each of us desperately needs is a firsthand, personal knowledge

of God. We do not want to take another person's word for God's reality. We want an experience with God. So we ask the question, "Where can I find God?"

I. Let's look at the question as it is expressed in our first text. Why do we raise the question? Why is it a problem for us to find God?

(a) It may be due to the nature of God. (1) We cannot find God because he is so different from us. God is invisible, and this gives us a problem in finding him. When we want to find a thing or a person we look for a concrete, physical object. But God is not physically real and concrete. You cannot see him, hear him, or touch him. No eye can see God, no ear hear him, no hand touch him, and no tongue taste him. How can you know something that is not physically real? How do you get to know a spiritual reality? Jesus said, "Blessed are they who believe but do not see."

(2) God is ubiquitous. That means God is everywhere. He is here and he is there, he is up and down, and he is close and he is afar off. God is everywhere, but this means for many that he is nowhere. If God, all of God, is in one place, how can he be wholly at another place? It is like the experience of giving everybody a job to do, and then nobody does it. It is every Christian's job to witness for Christ and win souls, but just about nobody does it. This makes it tough for us to find God. Though he is supposed to be everywhere, we experience his absence. He is silent to us.

(b) There is the nature of man. This is a factor in the difficulty of knowing and finding God. What is man? Is he good? According to the Bible and our own experience, man is a sinner. God is not like that. God is holy, good, and pure. Man is the very opposite. He is full of hatred, jealousy, and pride. He is by nature sinful and unclean. He sins by thought, word, and deed. How can man in that condition know God? This sin separates him from God. The more we sin the further we go away from God. Sin drives us further and further away from God until we come to such a distance that we no longer can see God, hear him, or sense his presence.

II. The question, how to find God, constitutes a problem for us because of the nature of knowing God. The problem is due to the fact that we think that we can know God just as we know any other subject. Some think that they can use the same scientific methods to get secular knowledge to get to know God. But it just does not work that way. God is not discovered after a period of investigation and experimentation. Man does not come to the truth by his own efforts.

(a) The Bible teaches us that we know God not by human discovery but by God's own self-disclosure called revelation. The common opinion that the Bible is an account of man's search for God is wrong; the Bible is God's search for man. He is the Hound of Heaven described by Francis Thompson in his poem. God pursues man until he finally surrenders.

(b) When blind Bartimaeus cried to Jesus for help, friends said to him: "Take heart. Stand up. He is calling for you." When Jesus came to Mary and Martha at the time of their bereavement, they were told, "The Master is here and calls for you." Some of our hymns express this truth: "God calling yet, shall I not hear?" and "Softly and tenderly Jesus is calling, calling for you and for me."

(c) The truth of the matter is that all our striving and searching for God will not result in knowing or finding God. It is God who must disclose himself to man, for God is too great to be seen with the naked eye. If we are seeking to know God it is because God is already seeking us.

III. So much for the question we ask about finding God. What is the answer? (a) You can find God as God the Father in his creation. What does creation tell us about God?

(1) It tells us that God is the creator of the universe. It does not make sense to say that this marvelous world of nature just happened. Behind the creation there stands a creator. We and the world are not here by chance or by accident. God made us, and he made us and all creation good.

(2) The universe tells us also that God is really great. As the universe is infinite, so God is infinite. He is greater than his creation. It makes us realize how big and great our God is. The universe points to the sovereignty, the majesty, and the power of God. If God is so great and powerful, "Is there anything too hard for God?" Paul once asked, "If God be for us, who can be against us?" If we would put our problem, our disappointment, our tragedy in the hands of God, we need not get upset or worried. God is able to handle our deepest need.

(3) Creation shows us God in terms of the beauty of creation. Just take one flower from your garden and examine it. Look at its perfect color, its marvelous design. This shows us that the Creator is one of beauty, order, purpose, and intelligence. In all of creation we see the footprints of God. We see God the Father—creator, sustainer, preserver, provider of all creation. To be such, God must be a God of infinite wisdom, power, and glory. We cannot help but fall down before him and shout, "How great thou art!"

(b) God can be known and found in God the Son. (1) God the Son is found in the church. God, as Paul said, was in Christ. He is the image of the Father. The fullness of God was pleased to dwell in Jesus. Philip asked Jesus the question, "Show us the Father and we will be satisfied." Jesus replied, "Have I been with you so long and still you do not know me? He who has seen me has seen the Father." In the teachings of Jesus we see the wisdom of God. In the miracles of Jesus we see the power of God. In the cross we see the mercy and love of God. In fact, if you are ever going to find God you will find him at the foot of the cross, because the fullness of God was revealed on the cross. There God bared his heart to mankind.

(2) For some it is true that it is just as hard to find Christ as it is to find God. To find Christ you may go to the church, for the New Testament teaches that the church is the body of Christ. The church is the contemporary Christ in our world. This church belongs to Christ. You worshipers are the people of Christ. Christ speaks to us in his Word as it is read and preached. Christ acts in the sacraments of baptism and the Lord's Supper. In baptism Jesus accepts and cleanses and forgives the sinner. In the Lord's Supper the bread is the body of Christ and the wine is the blood of Christ. To be in the church is to be in Christ. To be in Christ is to be in God.

(c) You can find God the Father in creation, God the Son in the church and God the Spirit can be found in Christians who possess the Spirit.

(1) The Spirit comes into human beings. He is God-in-man. But not every man has God in him by virtue of being a human being. God as Spirit comes into man when man repents, believes and receives the Spirit. Jesus promised the Spirit not to all men but to his disciples. The Spirit came to the disciples gathered on Pentecost and not to the whole world. To find God in men men must be believers in Christ.

(2) Believers in Christ have the Spirit of God in them in terms of love, mercy and forgiveness. When Christians express love and mercy, the recipients of that good will see in those human faces the very face of God. Then and there they have found God.—John R. Brokhoff.

Illustration

RESCUE. Christ offers to men what other religions cannot. Let me illustrate by a man who cannot swim being cast into a lake. What is the best word Confucius has for the man who is sinking? "Profit by your experience." What is the most hopeful message which Buddha has for him? "Struggle." What is the most encouraging teaching of Hinduism for the sinking man? "You may have another opportunity in the next incarnation." What does Mohammed say? "Whether you sink or whether you survive, it is the will of God." And what does Jesus Christ say? "Take my hand."—John R. Mott.

Sermon Suggestions

HOW GOD INVADES HISTORY. (1) He invaded time. (See Gal. 4:4–5.) (2) He invaded the dominion of evil on Calvary. (See Luke 23:34; John 18:37; John 19:10–11.) (3) He invaded death on that first resurrection day. (See John 11:25; Rom. 6:4; I Cor. 6:14.) (4) He invaded life with power on Pentecost. (See John 15:26; 16:13.)—James Z. Nettinga.

WHAT IS FAITH? (1) Faith is the eye by which we look to Jesus. (2) Faith is the hand with which we lay hold of Jesus. (3) Faith is the tongue by which we taste how good the Lord is. (4) Faith is the foot by which we go to Jesus.— George Mueller.

Worship Aids

CALL TO WORSHIP. "O love the Lord, all ye his saints: for the Lord preserveth the faithful. Be of good courage, and he shall strengthen your heart, all ye that hope in the Lord." Ps. 31:23–24.

INVOCATION. O heavenly Father, who hast given us a true faith and a sure hope: help us to live as those who believe and trust in the communion of saints, the forgiveness of sins, and the resurrection to life everlasting; and strengthen this faith and hope in us all the days of our life.

OFFERTORY SENTENCE. "Lay up for ourselves treasures in heaven: for where your treasure is, there will your heart be also." Matt. 6:20–21.

OFFERTORY PRAYER. We pray thee, O God, to give us sight to see the Christ, the insight to choose him, the steadfastness to follow him, and the stewardship of loyalty represented in these gifts offered in his name.

PRAYER FOR ELECTION SUNDAY. Father, we ask for the things you want to give: wisdom, courage, and guidance. We need these as we consider the issues of this election, the candidates, and the future of our country.

We know we cannot choose correctly without your counsel. Give us men courageous in their faith, committed to their endeavors, and continuous in their search for truth and right. Let those leaders appeal to us who will ignite our imaginations and fire our visions. Let those men rise in our esteem who put duty before gain and honesty before honor. Let those men persuade us who put justice above all else. Our nation is too big to be led by little men. It is too wonderful to be guided by terrible men. Its future is too great to be placed in the hands of incapable men.

Show us the men for these days. Show us the true issues. Help us to sift out the honest from the dishonest and determine the servant from the self-seeker. Help us to know the man of compassion from the man cold to human predicament.

We ask these things that our nation might be led to a higher level of living and a deeper commitment of service and good will and that men throughout the world might have peace and a lasting freedom.—C. Neil Strait.

EVENING SERVICE

Topic: Every Man a Priest (Reformation Sunday)

TEXTS: Heb. 4:14–16; I Pet. 2:9–10.

I. What is a priest and who needs one? (a) The word "priest" is not necessarily a pleasant term. It makes us think of some somber, sexless, anemic person, dressed in black, standing at the gate of death to pull us through. Since death is the last enemy, the universal dread, we don't like to think or talk about it.

(b) God is holy and man is sinful. This is universally true. Our sin has broken our communication, our relationship with God. Sin is a barrier between us and our Maker. Man is estranged from God and cannot approach God since sin separates.

(c) Man needs a go-between, a referee, a reconciler. Job longed for what he called a "goel," a redeemer who could make him right with God. That's what a priest is. The Latin for priest is *pontifex,* which literally means a bridge builder. A priest is a "bridge over troubled waters."

(d) Across the centuries man has sought someone to intercede with God for him. He has gone to a wise person, an elder or person of experience; a worthy person, a man of God; a holy person, a priest.

II. The Bible teaches that all believers are priests. (a) In Old Testament times and in the times of Jesus the Jewish high priest entered the holy of holies in the temple only one day in the year. On the Day of Atonement he entered the sacred room and sprinkled blood. This symbolized his request for God's forgiveness on behalf of the people. Behind this priestly ritual was God's instruction to Israel in the wilderness: "You shall be to me a kingdom of priests and a holy nation." God intended that the Jews share their knowledge of him with the nations.

(b) The New Testament teaches that Christ is our high priest. "There is one God and there is one mediator between God and man, the man of Christ Jesus, who gave himself a ransom for all" (I Tim. 2:5). God reaches down in grace that the church may reach inward in faith and reach out in love and service. Christ has shown us the Father. He has opened the way to God for us. Therefore, we can approach God with bold confidence.

(c) Christ is both our high priest and the sacrifice to bring us to God. Therefore we have become "a royal priesthood." Our high priest has made us "kings and priests unto God." Peter wrote that we are "a holy priesthood to offer spiritual sacrifices to God" (I Pet. 2:5). There is no select, elevated priestly caste. The whole church, every Christian, has a priestly function. Every man is a priest for every other man.

III. What does it mean to be a priest? (a) It means you have access to the presence of God. He is your Father. You may approach him in prayer, assured of a hearing. God sometimes seems far away, but he never is.

(b) As a priest you offer sacrifices to God. (1) You first give yourself to God "present your bodies, a living sacrifice of praise to God" (Heb. 13:15). We give God our good works out of gratitude for his grace. While we are not saved by our good works, we are saved for good works. "Do good and share what you have" (Heb. 13:16).

(2) Your witness to the person and work of Christ is also your sacrifice. How shall others hear without a witness? You are the only Bible some people will read. Your life is the only sermon someone will see. Your testimony can be the word used by the Holy Spirit to bring someone to God.

(c) As a priest you, like Jesus, are a man for others. (1) Evangelism is every Christian's task. Who told you about Jesus? You can welcome someone else into the saving presence of God this week.

(2) As a person for others you have a ministry of encouragement. Youth, adults, and the aging go through the dark night of soul crisis and depression. Many are lonely or in crisis, dying for the love you can share. The ministry of intercessory prayer is largely ignored by modern Christians.

(d) As a priest, you are accountable to God for your priestly function. "Each one of you shall give an account of himself to God" (Rom. 14:12). You are a priest before God for yourself and for others.—Alton H. McEachern.

SUNDAY: NOVEMBER SEVENTH

MORNING SERVICE

Topic: The Missionary Perspective
Scripture: Acts 13:1–4.

Here in these few verses is the missionary perspective. The whole panorama of missions is here. The philosophy of missions is here. The unfolding picture of missions is here. It is the biblical perspective of Christian missions.

I. *The church that produces missions.* (a) The church produces missions by cause God has called upon the church by the Holy Spirit to do it. Jesus enunciated it. (See Matt. 28:16–20.)

(b) This producing of missions is furthered as the Lord gives the power with which to do it. (See Acts 2:1–4.)

(c) There is a price, even a monetary one, that is willingly paid by the Spirit-empowered church and Christian. It was demonstrated by the apostolic church in Jerusalem. (See Acts 4:32, 36.)

(d) The final touch in the apostolic church came after Stephen was martyred and persecution lay on the church because of its witness to Christ: "And they that were scattered abroad went everywhere preaching the Word." So it must be today; young people and others must go in all directions and to every place with the gospel.

II. *The climate that creates missions.* (a) In that church at Antioch there were prepared young men. One senses that these were bright young men who were able in various fields of endeavor, professional or otherwise. Barnabas was a deep soul. He was the one who had gone to find Saul in Tarsus and brought him to Antioch. Simeon, called Niger, suggests the presence of the dark-skinned races of Africa already active in that missionary church. Lucius and Manaen had grown up with Herod the Tetrarch. Saul was a brilliant student of theology.

(b) Antioch was a persevering church. In that church they worshiped the Lord and fasted. Here was a church dedicated in glorifying and honoring God in sincere worship and devotion. Their fasting suggests a church which was not praying casually but praying with energy, agony, and aggressiveness.

(c) They were a sacrificial church and were willing to give up anything so that the gospel could be heard.

(d) Do not fail to observe also the prevailing Holy Spirit. It was natural that the Holy Spirit should speak to such a church and select two of its young men for missionary service.

III. *The compulsion that carries missions.* (a) The compulsion is given to those who are commissioned in the church of Jesus Christ by the authority of the Holy Spirit. No other body has been so authorized by God.

(b) Question any missionary organization that has no responsible relevance to the church. Question any missionary body that does not look seriously upon the church as the originating body for the commissioning and support of missionaries and through which it channels its responsibility in God.

(c) It was through the church at Antioch that the missionaries were authorized and to which they returned with their report. The church, in turn, "goes with them" in providing their needs so the gospel is not hindered.

(d) Christian history is the cumulative record from these first missionaries. They went to Seleucia, Cyprus, Asia Minor, Greece, Rome, Spain, city after city around the entire then-known civilized world. Follow them in this day and age. Follow them to Alaska, to Ecuador and Peru, to Africa, China, and the lands around the world. This is the cumulative effect of missions.—Paul P. Fryhling.

Illustrations

BASIS OF HOPE.   When people tell me that my Christian hope is unrealistic, I tell them that the trouble is not with my hope but with their reality. Their reality is too small. They are so petrified by the present that they forget the past and the future. They are so busy looking at the world that they never look up to see God. Of course, in that kind of a world there is no hope. But one of the most important lessons in the whole Bible is that hope is not confined to any one point in space or time. It is tied to a person, Jesus Christ, and it is forever. The real trouble with the world is not that it is running out of physical resources but that it is running out of hope.—Samuel H. Moffett.

SAVING WORD.   We must quit talking as if the church's mission is either to involve itself in action-oriented ministries within the sociopolitical sectors of life or to focus its attention on the individual and his relationship to God and neighbor. The gospel contains the *kerygma* of God's creative, covenantal, redemptive, and consummative activity in history as well as in human lives, in social structures, and in the souls of men. To receive the gospel and then to spread it, as if it contained only the one note and not the other, is to miss the meaning of the gospel itself. If we are to be true to the gospel, hearing it and speaking it, we must recognize that it contains the saving word for the world as well as for us. The world is God's, and we are his, in Christ. Having gained the consciousness of being his, we are free to move out into the world to work with him in reclaiming it for him.—Thor Hall.

Sermon Suggestion

WHEN IS A MAN REALLY FREE? Scripture: Acts 25–26. (1) Freedom from sin. (See Rom. 8:5–6.) (2) Freedom from the law. (See Rom. 5:18; Gal. 5:22.) (3) Freedom from death.—Richard N. Soulen.

Worship Aids

CALL TO WORSHIP. "Whatsoever things are true, whatsoever things are honest, whatsoever things are just, whatsoever things are pure, whatsoever things are lovely, whatsoever things are of good report; if there be any virtue, and if there be any praise, think on these things." Phil. 4:8.

INVOCATION. O Lord God, who hast left unto us thy Holy Word to be a lamp unto our feet and a light unto our path: give unto us all thy Holy Spirit, we humbly pray thee, that out of the same Word we may learn what is thy blessed will, and frame our lives in all holy obedience to the same, to thine honor and glory and the increase of our faith.

OFFERTORY SENTENCE. "If ye then, being evil, know how to give good gifts unto your children: how much more shall your heavenly Father give the Holy Spirit to them that ask him?" Luke 11.13.

OFFERTORY PRAYER. Our Father, forgive our indifference and neglect and help us to hear thy call to partnership with thee in making a new heaven and new earth.

PRAYER. Almighty God, who in raising thy Son from the dead hast made him Lord and Christ, we pray for his increasing lordship over the cultural life of this nation. Pour out his spirit upon our schools and universities. Cleanse our literature of all that is ugly and profane. May the principles of maturity and wholesomeness control our amusements and our channels of communication. May our music and art exalt that which is harmonious and beautiful. To those who shape the thinking of their fellow men give a high sense of responsibility, and to all of us give discernment that we may fill our minds only with that which is pure, lovely, gracious, and of good report. We confess the secularism of our age, the denial of spiritual values, the philosophies that crucify Christ afresh. Yet we rejoice that Christ is glorified, and we beseech thee to strengthen the Christian elements in our culture until that which exalts him shall be supreme, and he shall be Lord of all.—Leonard Griffith.

EVENING SERVICE

Topic: The Way of the Stranger (World Community Day)
SCRIPTURE: Luke 19:1–10.

At times in our life we experience salvation as forgiveness for our guilt; at other times it comes as victory over our sense of defeat or bondage; and yet at other points in life it comes as an end to our alienation. By alienation I do not necessarily mean a hostile estrangement. It can mean to experience oneself as a stranger or an orphan. Loneliness is a chapter in the life story of all of us. Possibly loneliness, which is not the same as aloneness, has become a barrier to a living faith for you. Instead of running from it, let it become a place where you encounter Christ. Two important facts need to be kept in mind as you move through your loneliness.

I. It is a universal experience to know mercy as a stranger. (a) In all of creation it is the particular burden of human beings to know themselves as orphans. Some of the greatest literature in the Bible comes out of the exile of the Jews and Jesus' lonely vigil in the desert.

(b) Aloneness and community are two ends of the same stick. Genuine aloneness prepares us for community, and true community enables aloneness. If we seek community just to escape loneliness we will not find it. There is a gift in aloneness which many of us are rejecting.

II. Jesus was a stranger. (a) He was and still is a stranger to this world. As such he destroys our illusions about community and reminds us that we love our dreams of community more than we love the community he is creating. This stranger understands our need to be a part of others but liberates us from using others.

(b) Isn't it strange that this stranger to the world is the one who binds us strangers to one another? Only when we know ourselves as strangers can we see that community is not something we create but is a gift. As our lives are centered on this stranger we become a part of one another. Community is a precious gift; we do not create by our organizational genius. We probably will not experience it if we think we are above our Master and can escape the experience of being a stranger in this world.—Robert B. Wallace.

SUNDAY: NOVEMBER FOURTEENTH

MORNING SERVICE

Topic: Faithfulness with Possessions (Stewardship Sunday)

SCRIPTURE: Luke 16:1–12, 19–31.

Just as every atom casts its own shadow, so does every man leave his individual record of responsibility before God. Let no person say that he is too small to leave some kind of mark in the universe of substance and use. Labor, as well as the substance received for the use of his abilities, indicates the total of a man's stewardship inventory.

I. *Faithfulness with possessions: a quality of Christian character.* (See Luke 16:10.) The Christian should be just as shrewd as those about him but with the difference that he employs only those methods which are honorable and honest. Jesus maintained that faithfulness in the handling of material resources was just as evident in the administration of small amounts as in large. God judges in principles rather than amounts. If Christians administer small amounts well, they may be judged worthy to handle larger amounts with the same faithfulness.

II. *Faithfulness with possessions: the measure of the Christian trust officer.* (See Luke 16:9.) The true riches are the unseen and eternal possessions to be gained by the faithful person in Christ. (See II Cor. 4:18.) These possessions are to be gained only after the servant of Christ has proved himself to be a wise administrator of earthly possessions. Too few people realize that one of the conditions for gaining eternal life is that of an honest and faithful stewardship of the substance which comes to their hands now.

III. *Faithfulness with possessions: a state of separation from evil.* (See Matt. 6:24.) When the Pharisees, who loved money, heard this statement, they derided Jesus with open insolence. They scoffed at the word of the Christ, for they regarded themselves as the acme of righteousness, and at the same time worshiped at the shrine of their money. Later some of those same Pharisees proved that with their money they would crucify the Son of God. Jesus did not deride the rich of his day, except where wealth was given precedence over righteousness.

IV. *Faithfulness with possessions: a test in moral consistency.* (See Matt. 23:14.) (a) The scribes of Jesus' day loved to adorn themselves with the professional dress of religionists, thus hoping to prove that they were professionally righteous. Whatever their vices, the scribes apparently used their offices as means to advance their own economic interests at the expense of others. In this way unsuspecting people were undoubtedly defrauded in the name of religion.

(b) The Old Testament says some hard things relative to the defrauding of widows. (See Exod. 22:22-24; Deut. 27:19.) If, as some commentators think, the scribes had opportunity to handle widows' estates, they could easily have defrauded their unsuspecting clients. To do so in the name of religion made their crime all the more repulsive.

(c) In our own experience a distinct onus attaches to the person who is regarded as a steward of what God has placed in his hands but in reality is cheating God by his refusal to support properly the work of the kingdom. The covetous man will not enter into eternal life. (See I Cor. 6:10.)

V. *Faithfulness with possessions: a blessed ministry.* (See Luke 21:3.) (a) Motives for giving to the Lord's work may be varied. Motives that represent compulsion and generosity are good, but the highest motive of all is that of sacrifice.

(b) On Tuesday of the final week of our Lord's earthly ministry he was seated with some of his disciples in the temple area calmly inspecting the offerings and those who made them. By this we can assume that Jesus is concerned about what men do in their giving program for God. Apparently the business of watching how much people gave caused some rich worshipers at the temple to deposit large sums in the presence of all so that honor and approbation of men might be received by them. Undoubtedly the poor widow who came by to give her offering must have possessed real courage. Her gift was so small, and people were watching.

(c) When Jesus made the observation that the poor widow had made the greatest gift in that display of spiritual stewardship, he based his analysis on the extent of her sacrifice. Her gift was not limited to the tithe but went far beyond so as to become a genuine sacrifice. Giving to God beyond one's means marks the holy character of the faithful steward.—Ard Hoven in *The Lookout.*

Illustrations

CHRIST'S PATTERN.   Christian stewardship is no more or less than living a Christlike life. For if one follows the pattern set by Christ he cannot but exercise the proper stewardship of all his possessions. He will use with care the natural resources entrusted to him. He will share with others his material possessions. He will use his time and his abilities, his health, his strength, and his intellect in the service of God and man. In short, as one lives a truly Christian life he proves himself a worthy steward of God's bounty.—Thomas S. Buie.

LORD OF OUR MONEY.   Money confronts us personally day in and day out. There are decisions, large and small, to be made about money and its use almost every hour of the day. They may be long-term decisions with consequences for the whole family such as the purchase of a new car, a new house, or how much must be put into daughter Jane's college education. On the other hand, the decision may be simply, "Do I buy this kind of soap powder at 28 cents a pound or that one at 32 cents a pound?"

How can we as Christians, participating in an economy which is extremely complicated, find a guideline for our thinking about money? Our best guideline is to be found in what is perhaps the earliest spoken Christian creed, the *Kurios Ihsous,* "Jesus is Lord" (I Cor. 12:3). Jesus is the Lord of our recreative life, our family life, our love life, our political life, and of our money life in its every dimension.—John R. Crawford in *A Christian and His Money* (Abingdon Press, 1967).

Sermon Suggestions

STEWARDSHIP INVENTORY. (1) Does God come first in my giving? (2) Do I give him what is left over or merely what I don't need? (3) Am I proud of what I am pledging? (4) Would I be ashamed for others to know what I pledge? (5) Do I believe God is proud of my pledge? (6) Do I really make sacrifices for the church? (7) Do I make it difficult for someone to secure my pledge? (8) Does the person who calls on me go away cheerful? (9) Do I set aside in advance what I give? (10) Am I worried about being asked to increase my pledge? (11) Could I increase my pledge? (12) Is my giving planned? (13) Am I trying to do all that I can do? (14) Am I making any effort to tithe my income? (15) If I do not tithe am I trying to give half of a tithe?

THE BANK OF HEAVEN. (1) How to open an account. (See John 3:16, 18.) (2) How to make deposits. (See Matt. 6:1-21.) (3) How to make withdrawals. (See Matt. 7:7; John 14:13.) (4) Banking hours. (See Isa. 55:6.)

Worship Aids

CALL TO WORSHIP. "Blessed is the man that trusteth in the Lord, and whose hope the Lord is." Jer. 17:7.

INVOCATION. O Lord, who hast taught us that the love of money is the root of all evil, teach us to care for what money can buy—not security but opportunity, not withdrawal from the world but a fuller participation within it, not prestige but use. Help us to handle all the goods of life in the same spirit as thy Son, who out of his poverty made many rich.

OFFERTORY SENTENCE. "Upon the first day of the week let every one of you lay by him in store, as God hath prospered him." I Cor. 16:2.

OFFERTORY PRAYER. Our Father, open our eyes, we pray, to the glorious opportunities of sharing with others our blessed experiences of fellowship with one another and with thee.

PRAYER. O thou who alone art good, we seek the healing touch of thy holy presence in our lives. For all of us have sinned and come short of the glory with which thou didst endow us. Humbly believing that we were created in thy image, we are driven to despair by what we see ourselves doing, hear ourselves saying, and know ourselves to be. Humbly believing that thou art the one in whom we live and move and have our being, we nonetheless find ourselves living life as though it were a purely private possession, governed simply by our own desires. Vouchsafe us new and renewed visions of the glory of thy goodness, thy power, and thy love. Grant us eyes to see beyond the sky, clouded as it now is with the darkness of human sin, the silent and majestic wheeling of the universe according to thy will and thy law. Remind us of our slow, silent, sure forces which make growth and creation possible. Keep us ever humbly mindful of the fact that thou art the author and finisher of life.—Harold A. Bosley.

EVENING SERVICE

Topic: The Kind of Disciples Jesus Wants

TEXT: Matt. 15:32.

I. Christ wanted his followers to have vision about God and his kingdom, not to be bound to the view of earth and time. "Blessed are the eyes which see what you see!" (Luke 10:23). And he had earlier said to them when they did not grasp his teaching, "Having eyes, do you not see?" (Mark 8:18).

II. Jesus wanted his disciples to love and live for righteousness. "But seek first his kingdom and his righteousness, and all these things [food, clothing, shelter] shall be yours as well" (Matt. 6:33). The quest of righteousness was far more important to the Master than the pursuit of life, liberty, and happiness or wealth or position or any other temporal value.

III. A third prime quality which Jesus wanted to see in his followers is compassion. Compassion is love ideally expressed, for compassion means being concerned for, caring for others with the pain of love as though the hurts of others were one's own.

IV. Another characteristic which Jesus desires in his disciples is action in witness to and work for the goals of the kingdom of God. He was constantly giving the disciples commissions to accomplish: "Come . . . follow me"; "forgive"; "Let your light so shine"; "Go . . . make disciples of all nations." The current emphasis on the church's going out from the sanctuary into the world is a late realization of what Jesus has wanted his followers to do from the beginning.

V. Courage is a quality without which Christian character is not complete. Living demands courage. But the courage which Christ calls for is far more than braving life. Christ wants in his disciples the stamina to stand for him in the face of the most severe opposition and to endure any required degree of hardship for the sake of his cause. This was one of the great marks of the early disciples who, like Peter and John, did not fear imprisonment and possible death for preaching the gospel of Christ; and like a host of Christians in the first three centuries of church history who had the courage to undergo persecution and death from the state for placing allegiance to Jesus above all.

VI. A characteristic which Christ wants his followers to have is the one with which discipleship begins and ends: commitment to him. It is a commentary on this generation's kind of discipleship that we so often hear the term "committed Christians," as though a Christian needs the added description "committed." One of the qualities Christ most wants in us is steadfast loyalty to him at all times and in all circumstances. As he put it, "No man who puts his hand to the plow and looks back is fit for the kingdom of God." There is no room in discipleship, according to Christ, for reservations, exceptions, deviations, interruptions in loyalty to him.—*The Methodist Christian Advocate.*

SUNDAY: NOVEMBER TWENTY-FIRST

MORNING SERVICE

Topic: Sacrifice of Praise (Thanksgiving Sunday)

TEXT: Heb. 13:15.

To many Americans Thanksgiving as a holiday began with the harvest festival of the Pilgrims. For the Christian this may be included, but sacrifices of thanksgiving date back to Old Testament times. (See Lev. 7:12.)

(1) The traditional purpose of sacrifices in both Judaism and Christianity has been to establish a favorable relationship between God and man. It is true that because Christ became the eternal sacrifice for sin, "there remaineth no more sacrifice for sins" (Heb. 10:26). The idea of sacrifice, however, was and is a New Testament teaching.

(2) Rom. 12:1 charges the believer to present his body a "living sacrifice." (See I Pet. 2:5.) The New Testament believer does have an altar and does have spiritual sacrifices to offer. The material and animal sacrifices of the Old Testament are no longer needed, but "sacrifice of praise" (Heb. 13:15)

can and should be offered unto God continually. What are the sacrifices of praise?

I. "The fruit of our lips giving thanks to his name" (Heb. 13:15) is the first one. (a) An open public acknowledgment of Jesus as the sufficient sacrifice for sins is our primary sacrifice of praise. "Without the camp, bearing his reproach" (Heb. 13:13) may refer to whatever stigma society associates with us as followers of Jesus, but to praise him in a critical, unbelieving society brings added glory to him and enhances our relationship with him. To confess Jesus means to own him, to acknowledge who he is, and to identify with him.

(b) Even though verbalization as a means of praising God is often abused, it is nevertheless desirable. There is an intangible, indefinable therapeutic value in vocal praise. A mutual bond develops between the one praised and the one praising.

(c) Often feelings die and relationships deteriorate from a lack of expression. Vegetable life seems to have a way of justifying its creation, and the animal kingdom appears to have a language of its own by which God is glorified; but what of man? Let the statement "Brutes leave ingratitude to man" be proved false in our lives. May the stones never need to cry out his praises because his highest creation has failed to do so. (See Luke 19:40.)

II. The second sacrifice of praise is made with our possessions. (a) None is so poor but that he has something to share with others. The starving beggar is bound by moral law to share his last morsel with the man who has none. The wounded soldier on the battlefield gladly shares the last bit of water from his canteen with a bleeding comrade who has none. Sharing does not impoverish us but not sharing may.

(b) Sharing our possessions is not compulsory. God wants no unwilling gifts and no offerings given grudgingly. (See II Cor. 9:7.) He is not honored by gifts from those whose houses become larger and more elaborate or by those whose bank accounts are growing day by day if they grumble and complain at the suggestion of sharing. What we do with our possessions—whether we hoard them, waste them, or share them —demonstrates to God not so much our attitude toward things as our attitude toward him. (See Heb. 13:16.)

III. The third sacrifice of praise is the giving of ourselves. (a) In times of material prosperity it is easy to give of our possessions and not of ourselves. It is a mistake to think that a trip to church a few times a year, a contribution to our favorite charity, or an influential endorsement of a good cause sufficiently expresses our praise. God is looking for more than that. God has the right to expect more. We owe him more. To give our possessions and not ourselves is less than acceptable praise.

(b) No amount of prayer or gift-giving fulfills our obligation to praise him. We must share our lives if we would truly praise him. All the traits and powers of personality God has given us, all the potential with which he has endowed us, and all opportunities to which he exposes us become obligations for which he will surely call us into account. In all our attempts to praise him let us not fail in the giving of ourselves. This must be a voluntary act on our part. God never forces us.

IV. Three important observations regarding "sacrifices of praise" are given in Heb. 13:15–16. (a) The sacrifices are *spiritual*. In no way are we encouraged to revert to the Judaistic practice of offering material sacrifices.

(b) The believer, as a priest, offers his sacrifice of *praise* to God *through* and *by* Jesus Christ. In ourselves we have no personal rights to stand before God, but through Jesus we offer the sacrifice of praise.

(c) The sacrifices of praise are to be offered *continually*. Our praises of him should never cease. Today's praise is not sufficient for tomorrow.

V. Sacrificing is not always pleasurable, although the end of sacrifice produces joy and pleasure. The sacrifice of the cross was not joyous for Jesus, yet "for the joy that was set before him [he] endured the cross, despising the shame" (Heb. 12:2.)—Robert S. Thomas in *Church of God Evangel.*

Illustrations

FOR OTHERS. The church is the church only when it exists for others. To make a start it should give away all its property to those in need. The church must share in the secular problems of ordinary human life, not dominating but helping and serving. It must tell men of every calling what it means to live in Christ, to exist for others. It must not underestimate the importance of human example (which has its origin in the humanity of Jesus and is so important in Paul's teaching); it is not abstract argument but example that gives its word emphasis and power.—Dietrich Bonhoeffer.

BELIEVING THE BIBLE. What is the major reason why evangelical Christians believe that the Bible is God's Word written, inspired by his Spirit and authoritative over their lives? It is certainly not that we take a blindfold leap into the darkness and resolve to believe what we strongly suspect is incredible. Nor is it because the universal church consistently taught this for the first eighteen centuries of its life (though it did and this long tradition is not to be lightly set aside). Nor is it because God's Word authenticates itself to us as we read it today—by the majesty of its themes, by the unity of its message, and by the power of its influence (though it does all this and more). No. The overriding reason for accepting the divine inspiration and authority of Scripture is plain loyalty to Jesus.—John Stott.

Sermon Suggestions

MEMORIES THAT BRING GRATITUDE. (1) Thank God for life. (2) Thank God for what you have. (3) Thank God for the world. (4) Thank God for today.—Hugh T. Kerr.

WHAT IS CHARITY? (1) Silence when words would hurt. (2) Patience when neighbors are curt. (3) Deafness when scandal flows. (4) Thoughtfulness for another's woes. (5) Promptness when stern duty calls. (6) Courage when misfortune falls.—*World Christian Digest.*

Worship Aids

CALL TO WORSHIP. "Make a joyful noise unto the Lord, all ye lands. Serve the Lord with gladness: come before his presence with singing. Enter into his gates with thanksgiving, and into his courts with praise: be thankful unto him, and bless his name." Ps. 100:1–2, 4.

INVOCATION. O God our Father, giver of all good things, we are grateful for the Thanksgiving season of the year when we come with gratitude for bountiful harvests filling granary and bin. Give us such a spirit of thankfulness that every day and every season and all thy continuing gifts may be occasions for thanksgiving, and all the year be blessed with an ever-continuing gratitude. As thy mercies are new every morning, so may our praise rise to thee each day and hour.

OFFERTORY SENTENCE. "Thou crownest the year with thy goodness. . . . Samuel took a stone, and set it between Mizpeh and Shen, saying, Hitherto hath the Lord helped us." Ps. 65:11; I Sam. 7:12.

OFFERTORY PRAYER. Our Father, may we who have seen thy providential hand in all the experiences of our lives seek to possess such greatness of mind and spirit that we shall be enabled to offer these gifts with an unselfish joyfulness.

PRAYER. Eternal Spirit, high above yet deep within us all, we gather on this day, dedicated to gratitude, to worship thee. Thanks be to thee for all interior resources of power by which the spirit, even in the midst of this tumultuous world, can nobly live. Thanks to thee for the inward shepherding which can lead us in green pastures and beside still waters, restoring the soul.

For the privilege of the shut door, the quiet hour of tranquillity, and the peace gained in high companionship with thee, for all that the spirit can do with its own solitariness, thanks to thee. In thy sanctuary today, even more deeply, we thank thee for fellowship. With gratitude we lift in thy presence the remembrance of our friends. In our imaginations again we see their faces, in our minds we think their names. For their comfort in the day of trouble, stability in a time of confusion, guidance when we were bewildered, inspiration when we were downcast, gracing our lives with beauty and crowning them with joy, thanks be to thee.

Thanks be to thee for that wider circle of friends from all generations whom we have not seen in the flesh but have met in the spirit. For the interior fellowship of great souls through whom thou hast blessed the world—prophets, apostles, martyrs, creators of beauty, discoverers of truth—who as soon as we are born begin to be our friends and with whom we can walk in an ennobling fellowship, thanks to thee.

Thanks be to thee for the fellowship of our homes. Thou seest how deeply our care for them lies in our hearts and how dear are the faces that our imaginations picture and our spirits love. O God, be merciful as we pray for our families, for the love that sustains them, for the children that go forth from them, and for all the ties of affection and memory and hope that make them beautiful.

Thanks be to thee for the fellowship of the church. Imperfect people, we build imperfect churches, yet our gratitude ascends to thee for the ministry of thy church, which has brought to us so rich a heritage and inspirations that have elevated our common lives to altitudes else impossible. For the great tradition of thy gospel and the corporate testimony of thy saints we thank thee.

We beseech thee for fellowships sadly broken in the earth. Forgive us for sundered nations and divided races and embittered classes. Thou great friend of man, whose dearest wish is the friendship of thy people, beget in us so true a spirit of good will that we may build at last, though it be through sacrifice, a friendly world.

We lift in our petition those who can be helped by no earthly friendship only. So curiously hast thou made us that the soul, though set among many human helpers, is still a lonely traveler on this planet. Temptations are here that must be faced alone and troubles that must be borne alone. For all problems that thy people face in the solitude of their souls we pray to thee. Thou great friend of all the sons of men, let not thy friendship fail us. When most we seem to be alone, people the solitude with the presence of the Unseen Companion, the invisible Friend of our pilgrimage, and make us strong in the spirit of Christ. Grant us a Thanksgiving Day when all that is within us shall praise the Lord.—Harry Emerson Fosdick.

EVENING SERVICE

Topic: How to Read the Bible (Bible Sunday)

TEXT: Luke 24:27.

I. *The Bible should be read in the spirit and practice of prayer.* This is basic. Prayer and Bible readings go hand in hand. Prayer prepares the person, by mellowing his life, to respond to the written Word of God. It sensitizes his inner being to hear the whispers of the Spirit who aided in the preparation of the Bible in the first place.

II. *Various translations and paraphrases should be used.*

III. *The use of a lectionary is important.* This is a list of suggested readings for each day in the year, often for both morning and evening. The lectionary helps in a systematic reading of the most meaningful parts of the Bible and aids in avoiding those parts which have little relevance for our time. But perhaps one of the most important reasons is that it encourages a regular reading of the scriptures rather than a hit-and-miss occasional method.

IV. *The Bible should be read aloud.* We ought to hear the Bible with our ears as well as to read it with our eyes. The moving poetry of the Psalms, the drama of the people of God, the personal witness of the letters, the dialogues with Jesus, the appeals of the sermons, even the judgment of the laws —all become more meaningful when *heard* as well as *seen.* Not the least important reason to hear the Bible is that in this manner it is more easily memorized. Then when we are without a copy of the printed Word, we may still "read" it for ourselves.

V. *We need the aid of commentaries.* It is not completely true that the Bible is its own interpreter. The findings of the scholars are needed to give background material, to help interpret difficult passages, and to relate the ancient message to modern life.

VI. *In small reading groups each person can share insights within the fellowship.* Some books, such as Job and Ruth—or the Psalms, for that matter— may easily be read in dialogue. The records of the Acts of the Apostles are especially suited for group reading. Some of the letters could be read as they were originally intended to be used—directed to the community of faith. This easily precipitates a discussion as to the application for our times.

VII. *There should be an unhurried reading of the Bible.* A "quiet time," particularly in the morning, is most important. A relaxed, receptive mood is needed. Time and again a passage which at first reading seems obscure suddenly will glow with new meaning. There is really no way to explain this except through the ministry of the Holy Spirit.

VIII. *It should be read with pen and pad in hand.* This unhurried reading of the Bible will enable us to write down insights which just "seem to come." These are recorded for meditation and study. In this manner the Bible reader prepares his own "commentary."

IX. *The Bible is a transcript of life in every generation.* It was written out of life itself to reflect the living conditions of the time, but it fits any situation of any time. In this respect it is the most contemporary of books.

X. *It should be read with the inner life completely open to the Holy Spirit.* Completely open, for God to do as he desires with us. Luther urged that the Holy Spirit is the greatest teacher of the Holy Scriptures.—Claude H. Thompson.

SUNDAY: NOVEMBER TWENTY-EIGHTH

MORNING SERVICE

Topic: Three Great Affirmations about Christ (Advent)
SCRIPTURE: John 1:1–14.

I. "The Word was God." Most of us know that when St. John chose the Greek word *logos,* which means "word," he chose a word that had meaning both for Greeks and Jews. It can mean "reason" as well as "word." I heard Dr. Tillich say that it might be called "the universal principle of meaning." Here was a concept current in Greek thinking and familiar to Hellenized Jews. St. John seizes upon it as a general idea of great potency and declares that Jesus is the actualization of it. He is "the universal principle of meaning" come to life, become historic. What all men, ancient and modern, learned and simple, seek for is the meaning and purpose of life. St. John says that Jesus is this. Something like this he surely means by using the word *logos*.

II. "This was the true light which lighteth every man that cometh into the world." The meaning is, "This was the true light coming into the world, the light that lighteth every man."

(a) This says that Jesus is identical with the human conscience. This is the same light, appearing objectively and historically, which shines in every human heart and face. Get down behind all the fakings of conscience which we do in order to escape the real meaning of this for us personally, down behind all the wrongs that other people have done to warp the consciences of their fellows, down to where people really live, and you will find an empty place that Jesus Christ exactly fills. You will find a desire to be better and different and more loving and more like him in them all. They will deny it and fight it and blaspheme about it, but he says this is what people are really longing to be down behind their own pretenses and disclaimers against all faith and religion whatever.

(b) "He came to his own and his own received him not." That doesn't just mean Jews. It means all of us who deny that light and pretend it is not identical with our true inward light. "But as many as received him, to them gave he the right to become the children of God, even to them that believe on his name." Sin has blurred that identical image. What he is saying is that even sin can't wholly destroy it.

(c) What a concept of human nature! This implies that things will never come right till we recognize that conscience within and admit that Jesus Christ is the very picture of it. But as the truth that "the Word was God" takes care of the vast question of the nature of God, so this truth takes care of the vast question of human nature. For it shows us a human nature, not always open to the light and needing to open itself far more widely, but one that finds its answer when it does. It really means that following Christ is, for all of us, the most natural thing we can do. We shall be miserable until we find that his light is also our light.

III. "The world was made through him." We catch this up in the Nicene Creed and say, "By whom all things were made." This involves the Logos in the original creation, which further proves his oneness with the Creator himself. Jesus who appeared in Bethlehem some nineteen centuries ago was there when the morning stars were created. We are continually saying something that lessens the equality of persons of the trinity. This is saying to us that God the Father, creator of heaven and earth, was joined in creation by the Word, who was Jesus. He had part in bringing creation out of chaos at the very beginning.

(a) The very universe was created through him, but also it holds together because of him. It is as if he were saying that the tiny hands that could not reach up to touch the heads of the cattle in Bethlehem's stable are the strong and spiritual sinews that hold up the stars and keep them moving in their orbits. He is not only God, the qualitative center of the universe; he is also the center of its laws and the gigantic management that keeps the whole thing running.

(b) All this does not do so much to magnify Jesus as it does to personalize the universe. If the vast thing we see about us is a "creation," then there must be a creator. And if the creator be the same as the Jesus who lived here among men, we are extraordinarily safe in our universe—almost snug. This world seems a very disobedient and dangerous fragment of it, and we can perhaps destroy the physical part ourselves, and our present civilization, and possibly our planet. The Creator has given us an appalling freedom. But foundationally the whole thing is sound, if this be the truth about it. We have a curious indirect testimony to the fact that we live in a cosmos and not a chaos in the very word "universe."—Samuel M. Shoemaker.

Illustrations

DILEMMA. We have faith in God and we have an involvement in the world, but we have difficulty putting the two together. We sometimes see Christ in the heavens on Sundays, but we don't know how to recognize him in a brother or sister on Monday. We need help in moving from the heavens above to the earth below.

FOR GOD'S USE. Our worship is real only when we hand ourselves over to God for his use in the actual world in which we live. This means giving ourselves to him that he may rule our hearts, cast out our sins, and use us as his messengers and agents wherever sin and misery and distress call for our aid. For ourselves this may mean much discipline; the purifying action of God will search us when he takes us at our word and makes us instruments of his kingdom.—Olive Wyon.

Sermon Suggestions

BEHOLD THE ONE WHO COMES! Scripture: Isa. 55:6–13. (1) He rules the world which is his by creation, preservation, and salvation. (2) He feeds with the bread of life. (3) He gathers his flock into a fellowship of interdependence. (4) He carries those who fall through folly or fatigue until they may walk again. (5) He gently leads through valleys and vales with the tender assurance that he has overcome all evil.

HIS COMING. (1) The meaning of his coming. (See Rev. 11:15.) (2) The time of his coming. (See Mark 13:32.) (3) The manner of his coming. (See Matt. 25:37.) (4) The preparation of his coming. (See Luke 17:20–21.) (5) Has he ever gone? (See Matt. 28:20.)

Worship Aids

CALL TO WORSHIP. "O Zion, that bringeth good tidings, get thee up into the high mountain; O Jerusalem, that bringeth good tidings, lift up thy voice with strength; lift it up, be not afraid; say onto the cities of Judah, Behold your God!" Isa. 40:9.

INVOCATION. Our Father, help us during this special season to remember the many ways thou hast pointed out to us the coming of our Lord Jesus Christ. May we be ever mindful that thou wilt not let us sit in darkness, but if we are receptive we will see the light of thy many signs in the prophets, in the lives of our neighbors, and in the eyes of our family.

OFFERTORY SENTENCE. "I will freely sacrifice unto thee: I will praise thy name, O Lord; for it is good." Ps. 54:6.

OFFERTORY PRAYER. Our Father, help us to love thee so well that we shall have all thy kingdom interests and all thy children at heart.

PRAYER. Our precious Savior, we thank thee for the gift of thyself. We praise thee for the countless opportunities to serve in thy name. Make us responsive to thy call and eager to do thy will, whatever the cost. Discipline us that we may become strong and courageous, tenderhearted and forgiving, compassionate and sacrificial. Help us wholly to abandon ourselves to thee. Guide us in all life's plans and purposes. Increase, dear Lord, our faith. We would not be fainthearted but ever pressing on to advance thy cause throughout the world. Use us to bear fruit for thee. May we realize the value of time and the need of doing today what thou hast for us to do. May every talent which thou hast given us be wisely invested so as to hasten the coming of thy kingdom.—W. Marshall Craig.

EVENING SERVICE

Topic: The God Who Never Gives Up
SCRIPTURE: Luke 15:1–24.

I. In three parables Jesus speaks of several kinds of lostness. (a) People get lost as sheep get lost, not through intentional wickedness but through foolishness.

(1) Sheep wander from the fold, become preoccupied with things directly in front of them, and rarely look up to see where they are going.

(2) People tend to forget the bitter lessons of the past and to stumble blindly into new follies.

(b) People get lost as coins get lost, that is, through no fault of their own but through the carelessness of others.

(1) The coin was lost because it was out of circulation, rendering no useful service, making no contribution.

(2) There are people who are lost because of the force of circumstances, who are born with two strikes against them, who are more sinned against than sinning.

(c) People get lost as the two sons got lost, that is, through pride and rebellion.

(1) One son was lost because he was out of fellowship with his father and ran away and wasted his life.

(2) The other son was lost because he was out of sympathy with his father and did not share his father's goals nor his father's concern for his lost brother.

II. In these parables Jesus speaks about God and his attitude toward lost people.

(a) God seeks. God is an activist, involved in his world. Our human experiences, if we interpret them rightly, are God's quest for us. We are told that the one new element in Jesus' teachings is that of the "seeking God," but that is the most important element.

(b) God places infinite value on a single human soul. How often the word "one" appears in these parables! God is not impressed by big figures, by quantity. One is enough for his love, and every person is precious.

(c) God never gives up. (1) Theologians call this "prevenient grace," meaning that God is always running ahead of us, trying to catch us at unsuspected moments, drawing us to himself. When a person "finds God" he usually experiences the strange sensation that it was God who actually found him.

(2) Jesus again and again uses the word "until." The shepherd searched until he found the sheep, and the woman searched until she found the coin. Does "until" mean that God never gives up on any human soul and that he continues the search for man?—Donald B. Strobe.

SUNDAY: DECEMBER FIFTH

MORNING SERVICE

Topic: Global Vision (Advent)
SCRIPTURE: Gen. 12:1–3.

The whole Bible reveals a missionary God, who creates a missionary church and entrusts it with a missionary task.

I. *The God of the Old Testament is a missionary God.* (a) Many people would say that the God of the Old Testament is the God of Israel, who chose this one nation to be his people, redeemed them from Egypt, and entered into a covenant with them. This is true, but it is only part of the truth. The Old Testament begins not with the redemption of Israel but with the creation of the world. It declares that Jehovah, the God of Israel, is not a petty tribal godling like Chemosh, god of the Moabites, or Milcom, god of the Ammonites, but the creator of the universe and of all mankind.

(b) The call of Abraham in Gen. 12 does not undermine this fact; it establishes it. Abraham's call is a classic example of divine election. God chose one man and one family, singling them out from other men and other families. But election is not the same as elitism. If God blessed one family, it was in order through them to bless all the families of the earth. The tragedy of the Old Testament story is that Israel, blind to her worldwide vocation, degraded the doctrine of election to one of favoritism.

So the prophets kept recalling Israel to her mission and promised that the Messiah, although a Jew, would be a light to lighten the nations.

II. *The Christ of the gospels is a missionary Christ.* (a) It is true that twice Jesus said that his ministry was restricted to "the lost sheep of the house of Israel." But this was a temporary, historical restriction, related to his earthly ministry. He added that through his death, resurrection, ascension, gift of the Spirit, and commission of the church, the good news would be published to all nations.

(b) Even Matthew, the most Jewish of the four gospels, begins with the visit of the magi to the infant Christ, foreshadowing the Gentiles who would worship Jesus; ends with the great commission of the risen Lord, sending the church to make disciples of all nations; and includes Jesus' saying that "many will come from the east and from the west [that is, from the nations] and sit at table with Abraham, Isaac and Jacob in the kingdom of God."

III. *The Holy Spirit of the Acts is a missionary Spirit.* (a) Before the ascension the apostles asked Jesus if now he was going to restore the kingdom to Israel. Jesus contradicted their narrow nationalism. The Holy Spirit would come upon them, he said, and give them power: not political or military power to liberate Israel from the colonial yoke of Rome but spiritual power to be his witnesses both in Palestine and far beyond the borders of Palestine to the ends of the earth.

(b) So Pentecost was a missionary event, and the rest of Acts is an unfolding of that beginning. We watch enthralled as the missionary spirit drives the church out in mission—first to the Jews in and around Jerusalem, then to the Samaritan, the halfway house between Jews and Gentiles, and then to the Gentiles, now through the apostle Peter, who wins Cornelius, the first Gentile convert, and next through the apostle Paul in his three missionary journeys in which the gospel reached Asia Minor and Europe and as a prisoner in Rome, the capital of the world.

IV. *The church of the epistles is a missionary church.* (a) The twenty-seven letters of the New Testament, even those addressed to individuals, are intended for the church. They set forth Christ's purpose for his church and are concerned with its edification, its growth into maturity.

(b) One of the many facets of the church's life, which recurs constantly in these letters, is that Christ has reconciled us not only to the Father but also to each other, across the barriers of sex, culture, and race. Gentiles and Jews are equally the children of Abraham by faith and heirs of God's promised blessing. So this little first-century church of Jesus was the beginning of that great worldwide community which he would build and bring to completion.

V. *The consummation of the Revelation is a missionary consummation.* (a) The vision of God's redeemed people in Rev. 7, gathered round his throne, is of "a great multitude which no man can number." I derive great comfort from this text. Some scriptures appear to suggest the redeemed people of God will be a small minority, but this verse says that they will be such a great crowd as to be countless.

(b) So the church's missionary task will not be fruitless. It will result in a huge international ingathering. Only then will God's promise to Abraham be fulfilled, that his seed would be as numerous as the stars in the sky, the dust of the earth, and the sand on the seashore. Moreover, this countless multitude will be drawn "from every nation, tribe, people, and language." It will be an innumerable, international community.

(c) So the religion of the Bible is a missionary religion. So-called "missions" are not a regrettable lapse in tolerance and decency, the hobby of a few eccentric enthusiasts. On the contrary, missions are the outcome of mission, and mission lies in the very nature of God himself and of the church which he is building. A church without mission is not a church. The church is mission. Mission is the global concern of the global people of a global God.—John Stott.

Illustrations

TWO LANGUAGES. The Christian is bilingual; he must learn to live, think, and speak in two completely different languages—the language of the Bible and the language of modern man. Any attempt to short-circuit this difficulty —to be either wholly biblical or wholly relevant—does violence to a Christian's vocation. One must live in both worlds at once.—Henry E. Horn in *The Christian in Modern Style*.

RATIO. If the whole world were a village of 1,000 people, sixty would be Americans; all others would represent the rest of the world; 303 would be white; 330 Christian; 500 would be unable to read or write; and 800 would be constantly hungry and sickly. The sixty Americans would have one half the total income and a life expectancy almost twice as long as the others. Of the sixty Americans, the lowest income group among them would be better off than the average of the remaining 940 villagers.—*A. D.*

Sermon Suggestions

THE GOD OF CHRISTMAS. (1) God acts. (See Gal. 4:4.) (2) God speaks. (See II Pet. 1:20–21.) (3) God loves us. (See John 3:16.) (4) God identifies with us. (Matt. 1:23.)—Bernie Wiebe.

THE REVOLT OF SIMPLICITY. Text: Luke 2:12. How better could we prepare for a deeper Christmas than by trying to cut through to the real essentials of life? (1) Everyone needs a self to respect. (2) Everyone needs a work to do. (3) Everyone needs a love to share. (4) Everyone needs God to whom we give our trust.—Gene E. Bartlett.

Worship Aids

CALL TO WORSHIP. "And we declare unto you glad tidings, how that the promise which was made unto the fathers, God hath fulfilled the same unto us their children." Acts 13:32–33.

INVOCATION. We turn our minds unto thee, O God, that thou wilt give us deeper insight into the meanings of the birth of thy Son, our Lord. We turn our hearts unto thee that thy love may flow through them. We turn our wills unto thee that thou mayst guide us in all that we do and in all that we say.

OFFERTORY SENTENCE. "Prepare ye the way of the Lord, make straight in the desert a highway for our God." Isa. 40:3.

OFFERTORY PRAYER. May we find it to be a joyful experience, O Lord, to offer these gifts in the name of Jesus. Grant unto us the wisdom of the men of old who found a token in a star, worshiped the child as a newborn king, and made offerings at his feet.

PRAYER. Our Father God, who didst so love the world as to send thine only begotten Son to save us from our sins, we rejoice before thee in the memories and inspirations of Advent. We thank thee for this holy season with its gladness and melody, its wholesome conspiracies of kindness, its contagion of good cheer, its summons to give and to forgive. Help us to remember that there was "no room in the inn" for the Christ Child so that we may not share the ancient guilt but may make ever larger room in our hearts for the Lord Jesus, who went about doing good and who continues to lead his true followers into every ministry of helpfulness. Yea, in every service to mankind may we feel the loving heartthrobs of him who was born a babe in Bethlehem's manger; in every agency of mercy, of sympathy, of friendship, may we feel that the heart and hands of Jesus are busy still; and may it be our high privilege to help in creating the radiant Christmas music, which is the merry laughter of little children who are dear to our living, loving Lord. And so may we help to spread through all the earth the wondrous Christmas light, especially among those little ones who are in the darkness of heartache and hunger and neglect.—Paul Seibert Leinbach.

EVENING SERVICE

Topic: Little David

TEXT: II Sam. 3:36 (RSV).

The human hunger for identity is such that it demands someone with whom to identify. In the stories of David we have no portrait of a distant, celestial figure but of a very real human being. But that human being demonstrated such divine qualities that his coming son was considered the Son of God. What did David have? How did he exhibit it?

I. David was a giant killer. (a) All of us have giants of whom we are scared to death, and if someone with whom we can identify can kill our giants then we can kill them and we can overcome our fears. Most people could identify with David because he was the youngest son, the baby of Jesse's family, left out in the field to take care of the sheep while all the rest were brought in to meet Samuel, the prophet of Israel. Most people feel inferior, so the inferior aspect of David's condition appeals. But Samuel wanted David because he who had anointed Saul, the first king of Israel, had regretted his action and felt impelled to follow the guidance of God in anointing David, the future king, even as a boy, thus indicating that the lad was a chosen one of God.

(b) Though David was a youngster, he was strong in genius and capable. When sent down with food for his brothers in the armies of Saul facing the Philistines, he already had slain the lion and the bear for protection of his sheep. He was also noted as a great singer, one with poetry in his soul who had been asked to sing before the king when Saul was in his black moods. When Goliath, the giant of the Philistines, challenged anyone in the camp of the Israelites, everyone was scared except David. He rejected the armor of Saul and was armed only with his slingshot. In passing over the brook he picked up five smooth stones. The first one went right into the forehead of Goliath.

II. David had a profound loyalty which in turn evoked loyalty from others. Time and again David demonstrated his loyalty.

(a) Saul had taken 3,000 men into the wilderness to pursue David who with a few followers was hiding in a cave into which Saul went for a few moments. There David was close enough to have killed the king. Instead he sliced off an end of his garment to show that he could have killed Saul but chose not to. Saul when confronted wept, went home, but still hated David. David eventually had to flee for safety to the land of the Philistines but not without defending Israel, even though rejected. He always refused to fight with the Philistines against Saul. Try to be loyal and help the mad man responsible for your being fired. Help the company that let you go. That's loyalty. At another time, while Saul surrounded by his army lay asleep at night, David and one of his men took Saul's spear and watering jug. Across the next valley David shouted asking Saul's general, Abner, how come he failed to protect Saul when Saul could easily have fallen into the hand of David.

(b) Even after Saul had been killed in battle, David maintained his loyalty, first to the one surviving son of Saul who was king of the northern tribes of Israel while David had taken over Judah in the south, and later on to Saul's general Abner who had been murdered by David's general Joash. Though Abner had been the tool of Saul to destroy David, David wept at his funeral and sang the song: "Should

Abner as a fool die? Your hands were not bound. Your feet were not fettered. As one hauled before the wicked you have fallen." All the people wept, trying to persuade David to eat when he was fasting in lament for Abner. But David swore, saying, "God do so to me and more also if I taste bread or anything else until the sun goes down." Then came that famous passage: "And all the people took notice and it pleased them as everything that the king did pleased all the people."

(c) In a day of vengeance, filled with hate, David healed the hates of his people, indeed even of his enemies, by being loyal, by showing forgiveness and patience and love. Not abstract was David's love but his was exact so that everyone, even his enemies, could understand his loyalty for even Abner was praiseworthy.

III. David became one with whom all could identify in his human weakness, the trouble he knew. (a) Well-known is the time when he saw the beautiful Bathsheba bathing. David sent messengers and took her, though she was the wife of his general Uriah. Since Bathsheba was with David's child, directions were sent that Uriah should be put in the forefront of the battle and abandoned. So Uriah died and Bathsheba became the wife of David. Nathan the prophet came, wagged his finger at David, and told of an evil man who stole his poor neighbor's lamb. David was angry at the man, vowing to avenge him. Nathan said to David, "You are the man." Nathan told him that the Lord as punishment would raise up evil out of his own household. Indeed, Absalom, David's most beloved son, stirred up rebellion against his father until he died a tragic death.

(b) David had many troubles, some of his own making but many more due to the harshness and sin of others. David, always repentant, always sought to do the will of his Lord God until he was gathered unto his fathers.—Ensworth Reisner.

SUNDAY: DECEMBER TWELFTH

MORNING SERVICE

Topic: God's Unspeakable Gift (Advent)

Text: II Cor. 9:15.

I. *God's gift is an unmerited gift.* (a) The Bible says that God's love is not activated by our goodness but by our need, not by our spiritual depth but by our spiritual depravity. His action in history to redeem sinful man was not initiated by our loveliness but by his love.

(b) The Bible says that God showed his love toward us in that while we were yet sinners he sent Jesus to die for our sins. There is not a person whom God does not love and desire to save.

(c) Thanks be to God for his unspeakable gift, for it comes to us when we do not deserve it, before we could ever possibly hope to earn it, and it opens up to us the possibility of new life.

II. *God's gift is an unprejudiced gift.* (a) The qualifications for accepting that love are the same for every person. As one man has said it, "The ground is wondrously level at the foot of the cross."

(b) Regardless of the outward form which your decision takes and regardless of the obstacles that stand in the way, this gift makes the same demand on every person and that demand is to come and follow after Jesus Christ with your life. That's the only way you can become his disciple.

(c) Thanks be to God for his unspeakable gift, for it is not ferreted out according to our social standing or our worldly success or our prestigious pedigree, but it comes to every one of us, regardless of who we are, with the same challenge to commitment and the same offer of eternal life.

III. *God's gift is an unparalleled gift.* The gift of salvation in Jesus Christ has no counterpart or equal in history.

(a) No other religion has a risen savior. Jesus Christ left nothing behind but an empty tomb and a glorious chorus of angels and disciples singing to the world: "He is not here. He is risen. Come see the place where he lay."

(b) No other religion has a perfect Lord: Into the lives of all the great religious leaders of the world sin came. Imperfections were noted. But no imperfection—no blemish—was ever detected in Jesus. No other person in history has been able to make the claim of perfection and back it up with his life. That does set Jesus apart.

(c) No other religion has a loving God who seeks man. In every other religion it is not God who seeks man but man who seeks God. The Bible pictures a God who diligently searches for man, a God who comes finally to man in the form of Jesus Christ to confront man personally with his love. The God of Christianity, climaxed by the revelation in Jesus Christ, is a God who seeks man in love.

(d) No other religion provides a living personality who helps meet the needs of day-by-day living. Christianity offers a living personality who cares enough to come to the nitty-gritty struggles of life and lift men out of the pit into which they have fallen.

IV. *God's gift is an untapped gift.* We have not tapped the power of God which is available to us through Jesus Christ. The power that comes when the atom is split—that is an awesome power. The power that lifts the giant capsule into space—that is a fantastic power. The power that is channeled into the engines of our cars that speed along the highway—that is enormous power. But the greatest power in all the world is the power of God released in the lives of individual men, for that power can literally move mountains, melt human hearts, and determine the destiny of our world. And that power is available to us.

V. *God's gift is an uncontainable gift.* When a person is really right with God and in touch with this unspeakable gift, he will not be able to hold it in.

(a) This says something to us as individuals. If you are a true disciple you will be a witness. If you can't give your faith away you'd better give it up—or get your battery recharged. We spontaneously share with other people the exciting happenings of our lives—a new job, a new car, a new baby. And if we are excited enough about Jesus Christ we will find ways to share him.

(b) This says something to us as a church. If we can't share our Savior with the world, if we are not excited enough about Jesus Christ to visit and witness to the people and bring them to the Lord, then we need to draw closer to him because the New Testament tells us that the major purpose for the church is to share Christ with the world and to be a light for a world of darkness.

VI. *God's gift is an unending gift.* God's gift is not for this world only but for the next world as well. It is not only good for life but also for death.—Brian L. Harbour.

Illustrations

THE CHRISTMAS SPIRIT.   Christmas comes again to glorify human life and to lift it into the realm of the hallowed. It bridges social separations in humanity, releases the world's frozen assets of kindness, stirs men to tender recollection of their fellows, and spreads the spirit of him whose birth it celebrates throughout the world. It is in this spirit that we wish your Christmas to be "merry."—Henry Sloane Coffin.

HEAVEN INVADING EARTH.   Each year as the season of Christ's birth returns a great wave of love rolls across the world, and the hearts of men and women become tender and compassionate. They begin to see in the face of every fellow creature the features of a brother. Once again heaven is invading our earth, and for a little time it becomes possible for us to dream of, to hope for, and to believe in universal peace. At least once a year the babe of Bethlehem comes into his own. This earth is never more like heaven than at Christmastime.—John Sutherland Bonnell.

Sermon Suggestions

CHRIST'S APPEARING.   Scripture: I Cor. 15:1–11. (1) His appearance is personal: "to me." (2) His appearance is special: "even to me." (3) His appearance is conclusive: "in the end."—Samuel G. Warr.

GIFTS THAT LAST.   (1) Give the peace of Christmas. (2) Give tender kindness. (3) Give inner stillness. (4) Give appreciation for common things. (5) Give the Christmas faith.—Roy L. Felder.

Worship Aids

CALL TO WORSHIP.   "Lo, the star, which they saw in the east, went before them, till it came and stood over where the young child was. When they saw the star, they rejoiced with exceeding great joy." Matt. 2:9–10.

INVOCATION.   Almighty God, who in thy providence hath made all ages a preparation for the kingdom of thy Son: we beseech thee to make ready our hearts for the brightness of thy glory and the fullness of thy blessing.

OFFERTORY SENTENCE.   "And they came, every one whose heart stirred him up, and every one whom his spirit made willing, and they brought the Lord's offering to the work of the tabernacle of the congregation, and for all his service." Exod. 35:21.

OFFERTORY PRAYER.   Our Lord Jesus Christ, whose birthday has become a season of benevolence and giving, bless these our gifts which we offer in thankfulness for thyself, God's unspeakably precious gift.

PRAYER.   Eternal God, who in great love didst come to thy world in Jesus Christ, we lift up thankful hearts to thee for thy gift.

We thank thee for the new look into ourselves which his coming inspired. No longer do we feel alone in a foreign land. Rather do we realize our sonship to thee, confident that underneath us are thine everlasting arms.

We thank thee for the new look he has given us about life. No longer do we feel that life is meaningless but that beyond it and in it are thy kingdom purposes.

We lift up our hearts for the new insight he has brought concerning thee. No longer need we cringe before thee as a slave before his master. We now call upon thee as heavenly Father, whom to know aright is life at its fullest.

We are grateful for every joy at this holy season—the significance of home; homes united after long separation; the blessings of loving and the knowledge of being loved; these and all other blessings, remembered by us or forgotten.

We remember in tender concern all whose joy at this season has been shadowed by sorrow—the passing of a loved one, some crushing illness, some suffering whose cause we do not know. O thou in whom we are held steady, send thy comfort and strength. Upon each of us, no matter what our need, send thy Spirit. In thy will is our peace and in thy companionship our strength.—Warren Arthur Nyberg.

EVENING SERVICE

Topic: What's in a Name?
SCRIPTURE: Acts 4:5–12.

In the Bible, names are very important. (1) So far as the Old Testament is concerned, nothing exists that has no name. To have a name is to have an existence, and to have an existence is to have a name. Moreover, one's name is to be equated with the essence of one's personality.

(2) The dynamic is much the same in the New Testament. Here again one's name in some way is the bearer of one's uniqueness. This is revealed on the very first page of the New Testament when an angel says this to Joseph about the impending birth of Mary's son: "She will bear a son; and you shall give him the name Jesus, for he will save his people from their sins." The fact that Jesus is a savior is directly tied to his name, which means savior.

(3) We also see in the New Testament the idea of acting in the name of Jesus Christ. As we invite you to partake of the bread and the cup during communion each month, we often preface our invitation to you by saying, "Ministering to you in the name of Christ Jesus, we give you this bread and this cup." This means acting in Christ's behalf and with his authority. What is happening here is very much akin to what happens when we grant our lawyer the authority to act in our behalf before a court of law. He is acting for us, with our consent.

(4) Against this backdrop, I wish to talk about three senses of a name.

I. The first is rather superficial in terms of its rewards but can be deadly with respect to its demands: that sense of name we sometimes associate with "the family name."

(a) It's sometimes said that every man wants a son so that the family name will be continued. To carry on the family name means to engage in those kinds of pursuits and be in those locales that will insure that the family name remains before the public eye.

(b) The "family name" syndrome is superficial because more often than not it does not meet the deeper needs of the person who is asked to "carry the name" (the person wants to put his own unique stamp on the name and not carry someone else's) and it is often

deadly because it insidiously undermines the spiritual health of both the person who is asked to "carry the name" and the person who is asking that the name be "carried." When we get caught up in the "family name" syndrome we are doing little else than weaving "nets to catch the wind."

II. The second sense of name is tied to the idea of "making a name" for oneself. We often say of a person, "He's making quite a name for himself."

(a) There is certainly nothing intrinsically harmful about making a name for oneself. It is often a sign of the trust that people place in us. A doctor who has made a good name for himself is a doctor who has done an effective piece of work in the lives of many people. But there is a difference between making a goal out of making a name and finding a growing reputation to be a byproduct of vocational conscientiousness. By their own confession this is what was plaguing the men at the tower of Babel and the reason that God confounded their language: "Come," they said, "let us build ourselves a city and a tower with its top in the heavens, and make a name for ourselves."

(b) "Making a name" smacks of selfishness and is narcissistic. People are quick to sniff the smells of opportunism. And I think it axiomatic that the minute we begin to try to structure our own fame we are in fact beginning to structure our own doom. This is because the best kind of fame is that which comes to us not because we have sought it but because in our relationships with people they sense something of the genuineness and humanity that is so universally sought and in gladness tell others about it.

III. The third sense has to do with our spiritual availability to other people and their availability to us and indeed the availability of God to us all.

(a) When I link names to availability I am suggesting that when I repeat a person's name and when he hears mine, there is summoned to each of our consciousnesses a very distinct image. A person becomes available to me and I to him—I am able to begin to enter his world and know him and he is able to enter my world and know me—when we exchange our names.

(b) This truth also sheds light on our conscious moments with God. We don't pray blindly; we don't pray to something or someone who is "out there"; we don't pray to hear our own voices. We pray to God and say, "Our Father, who art in heaven." The eternal has a name and a place. "Our help is in the name of the Lord, maker of heaven and earth." And to know that our help "is in the name of the Lord" is to realize that when we earnestly seek God and call upon him by name, he is listening to us and feeling with us. And what's more, God knows the names of his children. For what the gospel tells us about God's Son it is also telling us about God: "He calls his own sheep by name, and leads them out."—Robert A. Noblett.

SUNDAY: DECEMBER NINETEENTH

MORNING SERVICE

Topic: Joy to the World (Christmas)
Scripture: Ps. 98.

When Isaac Watts wrote this hymn more than 250 years ago, his mood and his words were a reflection of Ps. 98. The psalm begins "O sing to the Lord a new song, for he has done marvelous things!" and continues "Make a joyful noise to the Lord, all the earth; break forth into joyous song!" That is vigorous language, not timid, not demure, one might even say not dignified! Don't sing softly; let yourself go and make a joyful noise. Don't restrain yourself; break forth into joyous song.

I. "The Lord is come." This is the bright discovery, the good news, the exhilarating liberation, the marvelous salvation. The Lord, the almighty God, he who to our faithless spirits and to a faithless generation still seems so often far away, unapproachable, unconcerned about either the delights or the burdens of our life—he is come and his name is Emmanuel, God with us.

(a) What then is the right word for us and for our times? It is none of the supposedly wise modern words endlessly repeated in novels and plays and philosophical essays. It is not "anxiety to the world." It is not "despair to the world." It is not "woe to the world." It is not "doom to the world." The right word for us and for our times is "joy to the world."

(b) These glad tidings are sung to the world. They embrace all the earth, and if there are sentient beings on any other planet in the grand reaches of space, the good news is for them also. "Let earth [the whole wide world] receive her king; let every heart prepare him room."

(c) The good news is for "every heart" —it overleaps distance, boundaries, segregation, discrimination, all superiorities. We can't cage it as our property and deny its joy to others; we can't fence it, no matter how perversely we try.

II. "Let every heart prepare him room, and heaven and nature sing." Does it surprise us that both psalmist and poet address their invitation not only to us but also to the natural world above us and about us? If we are surprised, the surprise mounts with the second stanza of the carol: "Let men their songs employ; while fields and floods, rocks, hills, and plains, repeat the sounding joy."

(a) Does it seem strange that God's presence in the world, his power, his grace, his love, have meaning for his whole creation and not for us human beings only? This religious insight belongs to our faith, and it is very old in the long tradition to which we are heirs. The psalmists sing it again and again in poetry of vivid imagery and great beauty.

(b) Isaac Watts had no need to search for such words when he wrote this carol. He found them readily in Ps. 98. But Ps. 96:11-13 would have spoken to him in equally strong cadences.

(c) In this carol we and the whole creation are urged to shout for joy in celebration of the coming of the Lord. From beginning to end it is a hymn of triumphant, almost tumultuous jubilee. But it is not without a sober note. "Let earth receive her King" appears early in the first stanza. "Joy to the earth! the Savior reigns" opens the second stanza. These words, "King" and "Savior," bring a note of soberness into our Christmas gaiety. That is because we are part of a world which has little use for kings and their disciplines, a world which in its self-sufficiency sees little need for saviors.

(d) The spirit of our world—often very cold, very cruel, very haughty—is not altogether alien to us. We are tempted by it. Sometimes we are overwhelmed by it, and the coldness and the cruelty and the haughtiness enter us and rule us and shape us, to our embarrassment and shame.

(e) If we truly receive the King of the world we acknowledge his sovereignty over men and nations and commit ourselves to obedience to him. If we sincerely welcome him as Savior we are bound to confess our sins and to yield to his redemption.

III. In the third stanza the sober note and the glad note unite in deep and glorious harmony. It is true the singing words say the Lord who comes and stays with his people is a just God, a righteous God, but he is also full of grace, and he pours out upon the world gifts of truth and wonder that no nation, no man, deserves.

(a) Why does he come to stay with us? Not because we have done justly and loved righteousness and walked humbly before him but because he has loved us, loves us now, and will continue to love us with a gracious love beyond our measuring. Therefore let the heavens be glad and let the earth rejoice.

(b) In the liturgy of the churches we use a simple invitation and response that always moves me. The pastor says, "Lift up your hearts," and the congregation answers, "We lift them up unto the Lord." In this carol psalmist and poet say to us, in effect, "Lift up your hearts," and we respond with grateful voices, "We lift them up unto the Lord."—Fred D. Wentzel.

Illustrations

RESPONSE TO A PRAYER.   In England a small boy went to the nativity scene in front of a church. He removed the small doll from it and took it for a ride in his new wagon. Then he returned it. As he was leaving, the pastor stopped him and asked the reason for his action. The little boy immediately told the pastor that he had prayed for a wagon for Christmas. So when he got it, he wanted to give Jesus the first ride in it. —Vera Mae Ernst.

CHRISTMAS DAWN.   The custom in some of the churches in the West Indies is to hold a special service at 5 o'clock on Christmas morning. Always a very large congregation is there in spite of the early hour. One of the remarkable features of that early morning service is that darkness still prevails, and the church lights are all bright. It seems more like an evening service. Toward the end of the hour's service, heralding the great day of rejoicing and peace in commemoration of Christ's birth, the dawn breaks suddenly. In a matter of minutes the darkness disappears, giving place to the glorious light of the morning. The sun shines in all its tropical brightness and warmth.—Harry Edwards.

Sermon Suggestions

FOUR FACTS OF CHRISTMAS.   (1) The babe who is the center of the Christmas drama is Jesus Christ, an individual known by that name at a particular point in history and as real and strikingly individualistic as any other person that ever lived. (See John 1:14.) (2) Christmas stands for the truth that the link between history and eternity is so strong that the person who became incarnate as Jesus of Nazareth and the Son of God are one and the same. (3) Christmas introduces us to the prophetic office of Jesus Christ. He came among men to reveal God to man and to reveal man to himself. (See John 1:18; Col. 1:15.) (4) Christmas stands for the beginning of that self-identification that carries through to Calvary and beyond. (See Phil. 2:5–8.)—John Wick Bowman.

CHRISTMAS PARADOX. (1) A sanctuary in a stable. (2) Majesty in a manger. (3) Vastness and nearness. (4) The uniqueness of a child.—Charles L. Seasholes.

Worship Aids

CALL TO WORSHIP. "Behold, I bring you good tidings of great joy, which shall be to all people. For unto you is born this day in the city of David a Savior, which is Christ the Lord. Glory to God in the highest, and on earth peace, good will toward men." Luke 2:10–11, 14.

INVOCATION. Hushed be our hearts, O God, by the mystery and the wonder of the birth of the Christ Child. Make us truly wise with the wisdom of a little child that once again the highest truth may be born afresh in our hearts. Let not our souls be busy inns that have no room for thy Son, but this day throw wide the doors of our lives to welcome our holy guest.

OFFERTORY SENTENCE. "When they were come into the house, they saw the young child with Mary his mother, and fell down, and worshiped him. And they presented unto him gifts; gold, and frankincense, and myrrh." Matt. 2:11.

OFFERTORY PRAYER. O God, who didst give to us the gift of thy Son, stir us with such love toward thee that we may gladly share whatever thou hast entrusted to us for the relief of the world's sorrow and the coming of thy kingdom.

PRAYER. Eternal God, who on that bright and radiant night long ago sent thy Son to be our king, we sing praises to thee and bless thy holy name. We who live in a world of crowns and thrones are humbled by his lowly birth. We had not thought that creation's story could be told from a manger. Yet Christ is here, crowned with a star and surrounded by heavenly choirs singing peace on earth, good will to men. Christ is here bearing kindness and mercy that put our threatenings and slaughter to shame. Thou hast sent thy dayspring from on high to visit us.

Thou, who didst come in Christ to bring peace on earth, bring peace to our troubled souls. We so often lose our faith and wander in darkness when we may follow thee and live in the light. Teach us that the darkness may pass away in the glory that surrounds us. Teach us that the tribulations and sufferings of this present time are not worthy to be compared with the glory that shall be revealed to us.

Bring peace to our world, sore burdened with war and rumors of war, oppression and inhumanity of man toward man. Darkness covers the earth. When shall the darkness fade and the light appear? We need him who is called Wonderful, Counsellor, Mighty God, Everlasting Father, Prince of peace. We would have our Savior come to us anew, teaching us humility and charity, peace and good will.

We worship in thy church, surrounded by symbols of thy royal birth. We seek in this heavenly setting the true direction of our lives. Thou, who art our Father, fill us with the knowledge of Christ and surround us with thy beauteous heavenly light.—Albert Buckner Coe.

EVENING SERVICE

Topic: What Is Christmas?

TEXT: Matt. 4:16.

I. Christmas is a day for remembering. I am glad there is one day when we cannot help remembering. I do not know how it is with you, but on Christmas morning I am no longer a man in middle life with cares, responsibilities, and children. I am a boy again in the old house.

II. Christmas is a day for hoping. This is what Joseph and Mary did, I suppose, on the first Christmas. The little thing in the manger was not much yet. Only a baby, sleeping the day away, or blinking now and then at the lights, or looking wonderingly into the big eyes of the oxen. But they looked at him and hoped he would grow great and strong, hoped he would be good and gentle, hoped he would be a prophet like Elijah, a deliverer, a messiah, hoped all the things that parents ever hope.

III. Christmas is a time for giving. We complain that people overdo this side of it until it becomes a burden. It need not be. The real joy of Christmas is to exercise your ingenuity and to buy the greatest amount of happiness for the least possible money. Give so that you can give a little afterward, also, if you want to and can keep it up as long as you live.

IV. Christmas is for receiving. How little you earn of what you live by! You pay your bills with your salary or your profits. But you live on the love of your wife, the affection of your children, the good nature of your friends, the great fund of humankindness that is daily poured into your heart. All this is just given to you.

V. Christmas is the day for opening up again those roads that lead out from the world of duty and labor and responsibility and into the world of fancy, of imagination of the ideal. We cannot believe in Santa Claus always. But above us grown folks also there hovers a world of light and beauty and blessing, a world of imagination, of dreams, of ideals, of things that may be but are not. We cannot live in this ideal world all the time. But once in a while we can get a glimpse of it.—Carl S. Patton.

SUNDAY: DECEMBER TWENTY-SIXTH

MORNING SERVICE

Topic: What Will We Leave Behind? (New Year Sunday)

SCRIPTURE: Deut. 6:1–15; Luke 19:11–27.

God will be asking each one of us when our lives are complete: "What have you left behind? I have given you many resources," he will say. "How many do you return to me to be given again to those who follow you?"

I. The wonderful gift of the universe is one of those resources. (a) God made it all, looked at it, saw it was good, and loved it. After the flood, when Noah was so worried about the future, he promised Noah he would never destroy it. "But," says Dan Thrapp, "Noah made no such promise on the part of man to the Almighty." It takes no special knowledge or insight to know today that man is well on his way to such destruction.

(b) While most observers give us some time to become more responsible in the work of our world, some reputable scientists frighten us by saying we may have only thirty to fifty years before our planet can no longer support human life.

(c) It doesn't need to be that way. God in his wisdom has written renewal into his creation, and air and water, land and forests, sky and sea can be clean and bright again if we are willing to work with his plan instead of against it. It depends on whether we care more about pleasure and comfort and selfish freedom now or what we leave behind.

II. The oneness of mankind is another

resource which God has given us, another of the pounds entrusted to man.

(a) The scripture makes clear God's intention regarding man's relationship to man. All men have come from that common stock in God's creative plan. "All the nations of the earth shall be blessed in him," God says of Abraham, and Paul reiterates this great truth when he says, "He has made of one blood all nations." Yet again from the beginning man has set about the destruction of that resource. When Cain slew Abel and left the family to become from that time on the "enemy," he symbolized what has happened to man through the ages. The nationalism, racism, and classism of today are the result of our selfish use of the resource of the community of man.

(b) Though none of us is directly responsible for any of these divisions, we will be held responsible for the part we have as one member of our society. We will be held responsible for the kind of judgments we make, as we consider those who antagonize us so much. Were they divisive and uninformed, or were they judgments of grace, as with Jesus who said, "Father, forgive them, for they know not what they do"? We will be held responsible for the actions we take, for the programs and candidates we support, for such support does influence events, and the results are part of what we leave behind.

(c) We will be asked whether we really cared about those persons we do not know—cannot see or touch—and whether we have been able to love our enemies. For it is our caring that leads to judgments of grace and actions to correct the evils which divide men.

III. The heavenly Father has provided us the resource of ourselves. (a) "Who are you, what are you, what kind of person do you leave behind in the memory of all who knew you?" might be the question the Lord will put. If we are to please him with our answer we must look now at the temptations we all face to be less than our best.

(b) From the beginning each man has sought to make himself God and to exploit other men for his own benefit. We see that happening in the earliest experience of man as Eve sought to use Adam to share her guilt for eating the forbidden fruit, and Adam in turn sought to justify his disobedience by blaming Eve. We see it in Jacob's trickery with his brother Esau to gain the family birthright, Abraham as he sold his wife Sarah for his own safety, David as he sent Uriah to his death to protect his reputation and to make it possible to take Bathsheba as his wife, James and John who sought to use Jesus to gain a preferable place in the presence of God, and Paul who sought the lives of Christians to strengthen his place in the Jewish hierarchy and his own sense of righteousness.

(c) Reuel Howe says God intended man to love persons and use things, but our temptation and often our action is to love things and use persons. He says that implicit in our need to save ourselves is the corresponding need to sacrifice the other. Thus we become our own God, isolated and withdrawn from our brother and the real God, our heavenly Father.

(d) Such a person is just the opposite of what God intended. We are called to be open and accepting, loving and forgiving, understanding and serving. To become that kind of person is to be a good steward of the resource of ourselves and to leave behind for others memories and influence that will strengthen God's kingdom.

IV. The greatest resource is the resource of God himself. (a) "What kind of God have you left behind?" may seem like an impossible question, since God is the alpha and the omega, the beginning and the end, the unchangeable factor in the universe. It is a question which we will face, or though God may not change in reality, the God man knows is changing and changeable.

(b) The God of the psalmist, pleased with him who takes the Edomites' "little ones and dashes them against the rock," is the same God of whom Jesus said, "It is not the will of my Father who is in heaven that one of these little ones should perish." Yet men, even those inspired to share with us through the scriptures themselves, certainly understood him differently, and so it is today.

(c) It is said by those who take such surveys that the average man on the street thinks to be a Christian is to live by the golden rule or to obey the ten commandments. That means that he believes that God is a God of rules, whom we can please by being good, by being righteous. His God is one who sets up rules and who rewards and punishes people according to how well they follow them.

(d) God may be known as a God of no demands at all. For some today he is something to be contacted, enjoyed, absorbed for the excitement of an inner experience but never to be understood or defined, and so abstract as to render irrelevant words like obedience, discipleship, or service. He can be discovered by "turning on with drugs" or by the manipulation of group dynamics, enjoyed and disregarded as soon as the experience is over.

(e) The God of Jesus is a God of grace and beauty, as well as strength and justice, and we know it is so because we know Jesus. Jesus said, "I and the Father are one" and "He who has seen me has seen the Father." Through him we know a God who loves sinner and saint alike, who sits comfortably in the presence of poor and rich, who walks and serves immovably for the cause of justice and peace but whose love is unlimited even for those who hate him and seek to kill him, who calls men to service in response to his love and goodness rather than in fear of punishment or desire for reward.—Albert H. Babcock.

Illustrations

TRUST. As I enter this new day God himself goes with me. His love, his care, his guidance, his protection surround me. They surround me as the silent sunlight surrounds a tree. If I encounter a difficult task I can trust God to give me, through the processes operating within my body, the physical strength I must have. If I encounter a hard problem I can trust God to give me, through the operations of my mind, the wisdom I need. If I must endure hardship, endure it because there is no honorable way of escape from it, I can trust God to give me the strength, the patience, the inward quietness which my difficult situation demands. I need never be afraid. I need never feel confused, bewildered, inadequate. Whatever happens, God's love and care encompass me. Secure within them I can face life, and any situation which life may create, undismayed.—James Gordon Gilkey.

DAILY CHALLENGE. A friend was given an elaborate scroll commending him for his humanitarian efforts to help the mentally retarded. When I visited him I asked why he didn't have it displayed in his living room since it was definitely something to be proud of. He led me to his bedroom and there, nearly hidden at the top of his bureau, was the scroll. In answer to my "how come?" my friend said: "Each morning when I fix my tie I see that scroll and I remind myself that that award was for yesterday. Then I ask myself: 'What can I do today?' "—Norman Vincent Peale.

Sermon Suggestions

A RACE TO BE RUN! Text: Phil. 3:13–14. (1) Recognize that a good beginning does not guarantee victory. (2) Pick up momentum by forgetting past successes about which you boast and past failures over which you brood. (3) Keep an unbroken stride by seeking to know and do God's will.—Wallace E. Fisher.

THE PAST IS PROLOGUE. (1) Don't worship the past; build on it. (2) Don't condemn the present; live in it. (3) Don't fear the future; believe in it.—Hoover Rupert.

Worship Aids

CALL TO WORSHIP. "Ho, every one that thirstest, come ye to the waters. Incline your ear, and come unto me: hear, and your soul shall live; and I will make an everlasting covenant with you, even the sure mercies of David." Isa. 55:1, 3.

INVOCATION. Almighty God, our eternal Father, with whom a thousand years are as one day and one day as a thousand years: we children of brief time draw near to thee as we stand within the doorway of another year. Teach us so to number our days that we shall apply our hearts unto wisdom. Teach us to walk this year in trustful fellowship with thee, our God.

OFFERTORY SENTENCE. "Verily, verily, I say unto you, he that believeth on me, the works that I do shall he do also; and greater works than these shall he do. And whatsoever ye shall ask in my name, that will I do, that the Father may be glorified in the Son." John 14:12–13.

OFFERTORY PRAYER. Our Father, take us with all of our failures and develop us after thine own heart. Give us more of the mind of the Master, more of his spirit of compassion, and more of his sacrificial and loving heart.

PRAYER. O God, whose redeeming purpose continues steadfast through the years, we praise thee for thy goodness and thy love. Sustain and guide us, we beseech thee, in the days that lie before us.

Overrule in all lands, we pray thee, the sin and folly that bring strife and hatred upon the world. Raise up in every nation men and women who shall be wise in establishing those just and generous relations among men on which alone secure peace can be built.

Give to all Christian people humility and grace to see thy hand in new and strange situations, courage to undertake hard tasks, patience in the endurance of hardship and failure, and never-failing confidence and hope in thee.

These things and all else needful for us in the unknown year we ask in faith. —Anna V. Rice.

EVENING SERVICE

Topic: We Are a Pilgrim People (Watch Night)

TEXT: Ps. 33:12.

I. The church repeatedly prays for herself under the title of "pilgrim church on earth." The church was born in the past; she works in the present; her final destiny is in God's future. The people of God are forever being reminded that we are a pilgrim people. Like Abraham, we travel through this life knowing that this world is not our final destiny. We look forward to a city whose designer and maker is God.

II. Our world judges success in life by credit card standing. The gospel, however, says that life means much more than money received and money spent. Christ says that the lilies of the field are more beautiful than the wealthy Solomon. The rich man who gathers great harvests into his barns and who gives no thoughts to the kingdom of God is a foolish rich man. The things of this world are not the things that we can take from this world.

III. Christ tells us to be careful about the things that we value most in life. We must be careful where our treasure lies. In an age that is embarrassed to talk about the soul of man, we must be on guard for our soul's salvation. In a world that is ashamed to pray, we must be religiously loyal and faithful. We are a pilgrim people. Our treasure should not be reckoned in credit cards. Our treasure must be the kingdom of God. The psalm says, "Happy the people the Lord has chosen." Happy the people who have chosen the Lord.—*Dimension.*

SECTION XII. A Little Treasury of Illustrations

LEARNING ABOUT CHRISTIANITY. Trying to impress on her pupils the need for more missionaries, the Sunday school teacher told of a villager who broke his arm and had it set at a crude jungle hospital. And there he learned the first rudiments of the meaning of Christianity. "Soon," she went on, "he returned to his village. Now tell me, how could he learn more about the Christian religion?" One eager little boy raised his hand. "He could break his other arm."—Betty Gorsuch.

MISUNDERSTANDING. In Charles Schulz's comic strip, Lucy shouts at Linus, "You blockhead!" and Linus counters, "What did you call me . . . a dumbbell?" Lucy replies, "I didn't say 'dumbbell' . . . I said 'blockhead.' " Walking away, Linus says, "Oh, I thought you said 'dumbbell.' " Contemplating by herself with her chin in her hands and her elbows resting on the top of a wall, Lucy says, "That's what causes so much trouble between people today . . . there's no real understanding!"

COVERED. A couple came out of a store carrying a thirty-gallon trash can. They approached their little sports car and spent some time trying to figure out how to get the trash can in. Finally the wife climbed into the passenger seat and her husband put the can over her head and shoulders and drove off! A lot of people psychologically go through life like that.—C. A. McClain, Jr.

DIRECTIONS. A blind man, tapping a white cane along a busy city sidewalk, stopped near a group of people and asked directions to the museum. "Museum?" asked one man. "Why, yes, you take the next corner to your left." "No," objected another man. "You take the second corner on your right." "You are both wrong," stated a young woman. "If you keep straight ahead for about three blocks you will run directly into it." The other woman in the group simply murmured, "I haven't the faintest idea." At that moment a policeman appeared. "Sorry, but you people will have to move along. You're blocking the entrance to the museum."—Ada F. Hamer.

HANDLE WITH CARE. Former representative William J. Scherle of Iowa says the employees at the Des Moines post office found a large package that had broken open and spilled its contents. When they examined the contents they found a supply of pamphlets from the United States Postal Service which explained how to wrap parcels to insure undamaged delivery.

PUSHERS AND PULLERS. John Steinbeck's play entitled *The Short Reign of Pippin IV* includes a remarkable exchange between the king and an old man. The king in disguise visits the French town of Gambais. He notices, as he nears a castle, that a statue of the Greek god Pan has been removed from its pedestal and thrown into the moat. Pippin asks the old man who seems concerned about rescuing the statue, "How did he get into the moat?" "Oh, someone pushed him in. They always do, sometimes two or three times a year." "But why?" asks the king. "Who knows?" comes the reply. "There's people that push things in the moat. Pretty hard work, too. There's just people that push things in the moat."

The king, watching the old man's efforts to do something about the situation, goes on to ask, "Are you the owner here?" "No," the man says, "I'm not. I live hereabouts." "Then why do you pull [the statue] out?" That question puzzles the oldtimer, and he searches for an answer. "Why, I don't know. I guess there's people that pull things out— that's what they do. I guess that's how things get done."—John H. Townsend.

TOMORROW. As Tommy's mother tucked him into bed she asked, "Did you put your toys away?" "All but my teddy bear," he replied. "Why did you not put him away?" "Because he was a bad boy," replied Tommy. "He has to be punished by staying in the corner all night. I'll forgive him tomorrow— if I don't forget."—A. E. Purviance.

THE DEVIL'S BEATITUDES. Blessed are they who are too tired and busy to assemble with the church on Sunday, for they are my best workers.

Blessed are they who are bored with the minister's mannerisms and mistakes, for they get nothing out of the sermon.

Blessed is the church member who expects to be invited to his own church; he is important to me.

Blessed are they who do not meet with the church on Sunday, for they cause the world to say, "The church is failing."

Blessed are they who are easily offended, for they get angry and quit.

Blessed are they who do not give to carry on God's work and mission, for they are my helpers.

Blessed is he who professes to love God but hates his brother, for he will be with me forever.

Blessed are the trouble-makers, for they shall be called the children of the devil.

Blessed is he who has no time to pray, for he shall be easy prey for me.— Quoted by David A. MacLennan.

HAPPY ENDING. A little boy was petting his beagle dog. His mother said, "That dog has a sad countenance." "Yea, a very sad face," replied the boy, adding, as he looked at the tail wagging, "Mommy, it has a happy ending."

MAJORING IN MINORS. While the troops of Mahomet II surrounded Constantinople in 1495 and it had to be decided if the Balkans would be under Christian or Mohammedan domination for centuries, a local church council in the besieged city discussed the following problems: What color were the eyes of the holy virgin? What sex have the angels? What happens when a fly falls into sanctified water—is the fly sanctified or is the water polluted?—John K. Wilson.

QUESTIONS AND ANSWERS. Once I heard a man say: "I spent twenty years trying to come to terms with my doubts. Then one day it dawned on me that I had better come to terms with my faith. Now I have passed from the agony of questions I cannot answer into the agony of answers I cannot escape. And it's a great relief."—David Roberts.

NO MONOPOLY. We should never have anything which is too precious, too nice, or too beautiful to share with others because such things are never given to anyone but for the purpose of sharing. One would hardly refuse his neighbor the right to see a beautiful sunset because he wanted it all for himself. One would hardly refuse another a drink from the Amazon or Mississippi on the basis that he wanted all the water for himself. The things in life which are most real and most valuable cannot be bought or sold, nor can they be denied to another on the basis that someone has a monopoly on them.—Charles H. Ashcraft in *Arkansas Baptist Newsletter*.

COMMITMENT TO WHAT.   Bishop Charles Gore of the Church of England several years ago caused an audience to smile quite audibly in the midst of a very serious address. In a deep, sepulchral voice he told an audience how all his life he had been profoundly convinced that—and then he forgot what he had been profoundly convinced about and had to peer down ignominiously at his notes! The Christian ought to have profound convictions about God and the true way of life. How about our convictions? Can we speak them without looking them up in a book?—Halford E. Luccock.

GOD'S SUPREME EFFORT.   Jesus Christ is God's supreme effort to save us from ourselves, from the evil of undisciplined and insubordinate passion and pride; from the evil of ignorant and brutal ways; from callous indifference to the needs and rights of our brothers; and from the horror of their inexorable vengeance. Christ is God addressing us about all that really matters in life.— Harold A. Bosley.

WHOSE CHURCH?   An old man was standing on the corner when the stranger stopped for the traffic light and leaned out of the window of his automobile and called to him, "What kind of churches are these on these four corners?" The old man replied: "This church here is Mr. Smith's church. That one over there is Mr. Brown's church. The one across the street is Mr. Jones' church. That other church I don't know for sure, but I think folks call it Jesus' church."— H. Eugene Peacock.

TEMPER AND TALENT.   When Leonardo da Vinci was working on his painting "The Last Supper," he became angry with a certain man. Losing his temper he lashed the other fellow with bitter words and threats. Returning to his canvas he attempted to work on the face of Jesus but was unable to do so. He was so upset he could not compose himself for the painstaking work. Finally he put down his tools and sought out the man and asked his forgiveness. The man accepted his apology, and Leonardo was able to return to his workshop and finish painting the face of Jesus.

ADDED PILLARS.   The famed English architect, Sir Christopher Wren, designed a large church dome so unique that he became the object of jealous criticism among his colleagues. During the construction they created such a stir that authorities demanded Wren add two huge supporting pillars to keep the dome from collapsing. Wren bitterly objected, insisting on the strength of his structure and the wisdom of his design. Nevertheless opposition prevailed and the pillars were added.

Fifty years passed and the dome needed repainting. When workers began they discovered the two added pillars did not even touch the roof. They were short by two feet each.

Wren had confidence in his work. The authorities during his lifetime saw the pillars and assumed they reached the roof, so the controversy died. They felt secure although the pillars were freestanding and supported nothing.— Charles R. Hembree.

EXPERIENCE.   "Captain," a passenger said on a Mississippi steamboat in the old days, "I suppose you know every sandbank in the river." "No, I don't," replied the captain. "It would be a waste of time." "What! A waste of time?" exclaimed the passenger. "If you don't know where the sandbanks are how can you pilot the boat?" "Yes, a waste of time," the captain repeated. "Why should I go kicking about among the sandbanks. I know where the deep waters are." A whole Christian philosophy of life was in that reply.—Robert J. McCracken.

LEARNING TO LOVE. There are many who want me to tell them of secret ways of becoming perfect, and I can only tell them that the whole secret is a hearty love of God, and the only way of attaining that love is by loving. You learn to speak by speaking, to run by running, to work by working, and just so you learn to love God and man by loving. Begin as a mere apprentice and the very power of love will lead you on to become a master of the art.—St. Francis of Sales.

THE WARM AND KIND METHOD. A man was walking in the countryside with his grandson when they came across a small land turtle. The boy picked up his find, examined it, and tried to pry open the shell with a stick. The turtle promptly pulled in its head. "That will never get you anywhere," the grandfather remarked. "Let me show you." They returned to the house, and the man put the turtle on the warm hearth. A few minutes later the turtle stuck out its head and feet and started crawling toward the boy. "Never try to force a fellow into anything" was the grandfather's observation. "Just warm him up with a little kindness, and he'll probably respond."—The Christophers.

INDIVIDUAL UNIQUENESS. We are called to be engaged, to meet and to share, to go forth into all the world to discover that the thing we have in common with the rest of humanity is our individual uniqueness; that black eyes can share faith and love with blue eyes, that red skin and yellow skin and black skin and white skin can worship God and serve God together, and that the most practical opportunity is to serve God by serving and sharing with one another.—John Maury Allin.

GIVING TO MISSIONS. Little Betsy had just been given a quarter to invest in an ice cream cone. "Why don't you give your quarter to missions, Betsy?" asked the minister, who happened to be visiting in the home at the time. "Well, sir,

I thought about that," she replied, "but then I thought it would be better to buy the ice cream cone and give the ice cream man something to give to missions."—John W. Wade.

ATMOSPHERE ELEVATED. D. L. Moody once sat next to young Woodrow Wilson in a barbershop. The evangelist made a deep impression upon him. Wilson later wrote, "I left that barbershop as I might have left a place of worship because the whole atmosphere of the place was elevated by the man in the next chair."—Albert Burnside.

MEN AND WOMEN TOGETHER. In word and by example the church undervalues women and exalts men—thus flying in the face of a theology that preaches acceptance by God, uniqueness in creation, and oneness in the Christ we are called to serve. I firmly believe that anything that denies full humanity to anyone is essentially non-, or better, anti-Christian. If we take our theology seriously let us affirm it together. We are one in Christ without distinction. Without rank. I am optimistic. Together we can do it. We can share our lives together—instead of feeding on each other. We can learn to become fully human together, balancing, supporting, leading, and following. We can do it. With love, faith, and a bit of humor.—Marjorie Heller Adler.

MIND SET. The spiritually minded person differs from the materially minded person not in that he deals with different things but in that he deals with the same things differently.—William Temple.

A LOVELY TRAIT. Half the time people are dying for somebody to pay a little attention to them. But fear of being conspicuous or rejected—these are the locks behind which we quake, lonely, bored. What a lovely trait is cordiality—that giving of love which makes everyone, friend or stranger, feel welcomed, wanted. Shyness is actually a form of selfishness!—Marjorie Holmes in *Love and Laughter*.

SUBSTITUTION. A clergyman in Philadelphia was once supposed to have substituted a hideous electric chair on top of the altar in place of the beautiful gold cross. This was the scene that greeted the parishioners on Easter morning, and they of course were furious. But why? Certainly an electric chair is the most fitting translation of what the cross meant in Jesus' day. It was an instrument of execution. In fact one could argue that the electric chair is more humane, quicker, more antiseptic, and less offensive than a cross as an instrument of execution. I won't pursue the details of the comparison any further, but if you consider it a moment I'm sure you'll agree that in a sense the congregation had no reason to object. But of course they did. In fact I believe the clergyman happened to leave shortly after this incident.—C. Fitzsimmons Allison.

HELP NEEDED. To be gentle in an age of violence, to be obedient in a time of reckless violation, to be honest in a day when extravagance and propaganda pay more than the truth, to love in a world full of hate, to hope in a world that is so grim and dark, to hold fast to that which is good in a world where it is hard even to hold on to what you have —you need all the help you can get.— Theodore P. Ferris.

MAYBE. Not a victory gained, not a deed of faithfulness or courage is done, except upon a maybe; not a service, not a sally of generosity, not a scientific exploration or experiment or textbook that may not be a mistake. It is only by risking our persons from one hour to another that we live at all. And often enough our faith beforehand in an uncertified result is the only thing that makes that result come true.—William James.

THE SHAPE OF THE CROSS. An Anglican priest once showed me a cross with a bend in it. He had taken it from around his neck and given it to a dying woman who was afraid. "When the fear comes," he said, "take this cross and hold it tightly in your hand because this is the sign of a love that will not let you go." She held it so tightly that she bent it. He became the priest with the crumpled cross. The cross had in part assumed the shape of the woman's hand. It is only a pretty symbol until it does.— D. Bruce Johnson.

INDEX OF CONTRIBUTORS

SERMON TITLE INDEX

(Children's stories and sermons are identified CS;

sermon suggestions SS)

SCRIPTURAL INDEX

INDEX KEYED TO THE AMERICAN BICENTENNIAL

INDEX OF PRAYERS

INDEX OF MATERIALS USEFUL AS CHILDREN'S STORIES
AND SERMONS

INDEX OF MATERIALS USEFUL FOR SMALL GROUPS

INDEX OF SPECIAL DAYS AND OCCASIONS

TOPICAL INDEX